BRITISH RAILWAYS

LOCOMOTIVES & COACHING STOCK 2012

The Complete Guide to all Locomotives & Coaching Stock which operate on the National Rail network and Eurotunnel

Robert Pritchard & Peter Hall

PLATFORM 5

Published by Platform 5 Publishing Ltd.,
3 Wyvern House, Sark Road, Sheffield S2 4HG, England.

Printed in England by Information Press, Eynsham, Oxford.

ISBN 978 1 902336 92 3

CONTENTS

Peter Fox 1942–2011 4
Provision of Information 5
Acknowledgements 5
Britain's Railway System 6

SECTION 1 – LOCOMOTIVES

Introduction 13
General Information 15
1.1. Diesel Locomotives 18
1.2. Electro-Diesel & Electric Locomotives 56
1.3. Eurotunnel Locomotives 81
1.4. Former BR main line locos in industrial service 84
1.5. Locomotives awaiting disposal 87
1.6. Locomotives exported for use abroad 88

SECTION 2 – LOCO-HAULED COACHING STOCK

Introduction 93
The development of BR Standard Coaches 98
2.1. BR Number Series Stock 100
2.2. High Speed Train Trailer Cars 132
2.3 HST set formations 162
2.4. Saloons 166
2.5. Pullman Car Company Series 169
2.6. Locomotive Support Coaches 172
2.7. 99xxx Range Number Conversion Table 174
2.8. Set formations 174
2.9. Service Stock 176
2.10 Coaching Stock Awaiting Disposal 184

SECTION 3 – DIESEL MULTIPLE UNITS

Introduction 186
General Information 187
3.1. Diesel Mechanical & Diesel Hydraulic Units 189
3.1.1. First Generation Units 189
3.1.2. Parry People Movers 190
3.1.3. Second Generation Units 190
3.2. Diesel-Electric DMUs 242
3.3. Service DMUs 248
3.4. DMUs Awaiting Disposal 249

SECTION 4 – ELECTRIC MULTIPLE UNITS

Introduction . . . 250
General Information . . . 251
4.1. 25 kV AC 50 Hz Overhead & Dual-Voltage Units . . . 253
4.2. 750 V DC Third Rail Units . . . 302
4.3. Eurostar Units . . . 340
4.4. Internal Use EMUs . . . 342
4.5. EMUs Awaiting Disposal . . . 342

SECTION 5 – ON-TRACK MACHINES

5. On-Track Machines . . . 343

SECTION 6 – UK Light Rail & Metro Systems

6.1. Blackpool & Fleetwood Tramway . . . 354
6.2. Docklands Light Railway . . . 357
6.3. Edinburgh Tramway . . . 358
6.4. Glasgow Subway . . . 359
6.5. Greater Manchester Metrolink . . . 360
6.6. London Tramlink . . . 362
6.7. Nottingham Express Transit . . . 363
6.8. Midland Metro . . . 364
6.9. Sheffield Supertram . . . 365
6.10. Tyne & Wear Metro . . . 365

SECTION 7 – CODES

7.1. Livery Codes . . . 368
7.2. Owner Codes . . . 371
7.3. Locomotive Pool Codes . . . 373
7.4. Operator Codes . . . 376
7.5. Allocation & Location Codes . . . 377
7.6. Abbreviations . . . 382
7.7. Builders . . . 383

COVER PHOTOGRAPHS

Front Cover: In Northern Belle livery, 47790 "Galloway Princess" crosses Eskmeals Viaduct, on the Cumbrian Coast line just south of Ravenglass, hauling the luxury train back from Ravenglass to Newcastle on 10 September 2011 (47832 is on the rear).
Phil Chilton

Rear Cover: Grand Central's 43484 "PETER FOX 1942–2011 PLATFORM 5" and 43480 pass Sleaford with the 14.58 London King's Cross–Sunderland (diverted via the Joint Line) on 22 October 2011.
Inset: A close up of the nameplate. **Robert Pritchard (2)**

PETER FOX 1942–2011

This is the first edition of British Railways Locomotives & Coaching Stock to be compiled since the untimely death of Peter Fox in February 2011. Peter was the founder of Platform 5 Publishing and had been the lead author of every edition of this book since it was first published in 1985.

Peter and his then partner Neil Webster began publishing their Platform 5 Pocket Books in the late 1970s, a time when railway enthusiasm was entering a period of renaissance. Since the end of steam on British Railways in August 1968, many railway enthusiasts had drifted away from the railway, unable to maintain their interest in the diesels and electrics now in charge of the network. But by the late 1970s a new generation of enthusiasts had appeared who were keen to know more than ever about the locomotive fleet.

Although many locomotives were almost identical in appearance to other members of their class, the type of work they could undertake was determined by their detail differences, particularly their braking and train heating facilities. Peter soon realised this information was essential to the enthusiasts of the day and that the rolling stock handbooks being produced at the time simply didn't cater well for that demand. Peter and Neil decided to produce their own book and "Motive Power Pocket Book" was born, the first edition appearing in early 1978.

In the intervening 34 years much has changed on Britain's railways and this book is a far cry from that first publication, but throughout his time in charge Peter always strove to embrace the changes and incorporate the level of information demanded by both enthusiasts and latterly the railway industry. To ensure the utmost accuracy he devised and wrote his own computer programs to produce the books, at a time when personal computer usage was in its infancy.

Many users of this book will already be very familiar with Peter's work as his books have provided an invaluable introduction to the railway for thousands of today's enthusiasts. It will be impossible to replace Peter but we at Platform 5 aim to continue his legacy by maintaining and building upon the high standards that he set.

In May 2011 Grand Central Railway Company honoured Peter by naming one of its HST power cars – 43484 – "PETER FOX 1942–2011 – PLATFORM 5" on Platform 5 at Sheffield station.

PROVISION OF INFORMATION

This book has been compiled with care to be as accurate as possible, but in some cases information is not officially available and the publisher cannot be held responsible for any errors or omissions. We would like to thank the companies and individuals which have been co-operative in supplying information to us. The authors of this book will be pleased to receive notification of any inaccuracies readers may find in the series, and also any additional information to supplement our records and thus enhance future editions. Please send comments to:

Robert Pritchard, Platform 5 Publishing Ltd, 3Wyvern House, Sark Road, Sheffield, S24HG, England.

Tel: 0114 255 2625 **Fax:** 0114 255 2471
e-mail: robert@platform5.com.

This book is updated to January 2012.

ACKNOWLEDGEMENTS

The author would like to thank all Train Operating Companies, Freight Companies, Rolling Stock Leasing Companies and spot-hire companies that have helped with the compilation of this book. Special mention should also be made to the Rolling Stock Library for its assistance.

Thanks are also due to those who sent reports of changes observed during 2011 for the **Today's Railways UK** magazine "Stock Changes" column and for corrections given to the 2012 "pocket book" series.

BRITAIN'S RAILWAY SYSTEM

INFRASTRUCTURE & OPERATION

Britain's national railway infrastructure is owned by a "not for dividend" company, Network Rail (NR). Many stations and maintenance depots are leased to and operated by Train Operating Companies (TOCs), but some larger stations remain under Network Rail control. The only exception is the infrastructure on the Isle of Wight, which is nationally owned and is leased to South West Trains.

Trains are operated by TOCs over Network Rail, regulated by access agreements between the parties involved. In general, TOCs are responsible for the provision and maintenance of the locomotives, rolling stock and staff necessary for the direct operation of services, whilst NR is responsible for the provision and maintenance of the infrastructure and also for staff to regulate the operation of services.

DOMESTIC PASSENGER TRAIN OPERATORS

The large majority of passenger trains are operated by the TOCs on fixed-term franchises. Franchise expiry dates are shown in the list of franchisees below:

Franchise	*Franchisee*	*Trading Name*
Chiltern Railways	Deutsche Bahn (Arriva) (until 31 December 2021)	**Chiltern Railways**

Chiltern Railways operates a frequent service between London Marylebone, Banbury and Birmingham Snow Hill, with some peak services extending to Kidderminster. There are also regular services from Marylebone to Stratford-upon-Avon and to Aylesbury Vale Parkway via Amersham (along the London Underground Metropolitan Line). The fleet consists of DMUs of Classes 121 (used on the Princes Risborough–Aylesbury route), 165, 168 and 172 plus a number of loco-hauled rakes used on some of the Birmingham trains, worked by Class 67s.

Cross-Country[1]	Deutsche Bahn (Arriva) (until 11 November 2013)	**CrossCountry**

CrossCountry operates a network of long-distance services between Scotland and North-East England, also Manchester to the South West of England, Reading, Southampton, Bournemouth and Guildford, centred on Birmingham New Street. These trains are mainly formed of diesel Class 220/221 Voyagers, supplemented by a small number of HSTs on the NE–SW route. Inter-urban services also operate between Birmingham, Leicester and Stansted Airport and Nottingham, Birmingham and Cardiff. These use Class 170 DMUs.

East Midlands[2]	Stagecoach Group plc (until 11 November 2013)	**East Midlands Trains**

EMT operates a mix of long distance high speed services on the Midland Main Line (MML), from London St Pancras to Sheffield (Leeds at peak times and some extensions to York/Scarborough) and Nottingham, and local and regional services ranging from the Norwich–Liverpool route to Nottingham–Skegness, Nottingham–Mansfield/Worksop, Nottingham–Matlock and Derby–Crewe. It also operates local services in Lincolnshire. Trains on the MML are worked by a fleet of Class 222 DMUs and ten HSTs, whilst the local and regional fleet consists of DMU Classes 153, 156 and 158.

Greater Western[3] First Group plc (until 31 March 2013) **First Great Western**

First Great Western operates long distance trains from London Paddington to South Wales, the West Country and Worcester and Hereford. In addition there are frequent trains along the Thames Valley corridor to Newbury and Oxford, plus local and regional trains throughout the South-West including the Cornish, Devon and Thames Valley branches, the Reading–Gatwick North Downs line and Cardiff–Portsmouth Harbour and Bristol–Weymouth regional routes. A fleet of 53 HSTs is used on the long distance trains, with DMUs of Classes 165 and 166 (and 180 from summer 2012) on the Thames Valley and North Downs work, and Classes 143, 150, 153 and 158 on local and regional trains in the South West. A small fleet of four Class 57s are maintained to work the overnight Sleeper service between London and Penzance.

Greater Anglia[4] National Express Group plc (until 4 February 2012) **National Express East Anglia** (**Abellio Greater Anglia** from Feb 2012)

NXEA operates main line trains between London Liverpool Street, Ipswich and Norwich and local trains across Norfolk, Suffolk and parts of Cambridgeshire. It also runs local and commuter services into Liverpool Street from the Great Eastern (including Southend, Braintree and Clacton) and West Anglia (including Cambridge and Stansted Airport) routes. It operates a very varied fleet of Class 90s with loco-hauled Mark 3 sets, DMUs of Classes 153, 156 and 170 and EMUs of Classes 315, 317, 321, 360 and 379.

Integrated Kent Govia Ltd (Go-Ahead/Keolis) (until 31 March 2014) **Southeastern**

Southeastern operates all services in the South-East London suburbs, the whole of Kent and part of Sussex, which are primarily commuter services to/from London. It also operates domestic high speed trains on HS1 from St Pancras to Ashford, Ramsgate, Dover and Faversham with additional peak services on other routes. EMUs of Classes 375, 376, 465 and 466 are used, along with Class 395s on the High Speed trains.

InterCity East Coast[5] **East Coast**

East Coast operates frequent long distance trains on the East Coast Main Line between London King's Cross, Leeds, York, Newcastle and Edinburgh, with less frequent services to Bradford, Harrogate, Skipton, Hull, Lincoln, Glasgow, Aberdeen and Inverness. A mixed fleet of Class 91s and 30 Mark 4 sets, and 14 HST sets, are used on these trains.

InterCity West Coast Virgin Rail Group Ltd. (until 8 December 2012) **Virgin Trains**

Virgin Trains operates long distance services along the West Coast Main Line from London Euston to Birmingham/Wolverhampton, Manchester, Liverpool and Glasgow using Class 390 Pendolino EMUs. It also operates Class 221 Voyagers between London and Chester/Holyhead, and also between Birmingham and Glasgow/Edinburgh. One rake of Mark 3 loco-hauled stock is also retained and is used on an ad-hoc basis, with just one booked Euston–Crewe via Birmingham working each week.

London Rail[6] MTR/Deutsche Bahn (until 31 March 2014) **London Overground**

London Overground operates services on the Richmond–Stratford North London Line and the Willesden Jn–Clapham Jn West London Line, plus the new East London Line from Highbury & Islington to New Cross and New Cross Gate, with extensions to Crystal Palace and West Croydon. It also runs services from London Euston to Watford Junction. All these use new Class 378 EMUs. Class 172 DMUs are used on the Gospel Oak–Barking route.

LTS Rail National Express Group plc (until 26 May 2013) **c2c**

c2c operates an intensive, principally commuter, service from London Fenchurch Street to Southend and Shoeburyness. The fleet consists entirely of Class 357 EMUs.

Merseyrail Electrics[7] Serco/Abellio (until 19 July 2028) **Merseyrail**

Merseyrail operates services between Liverpool and Southport, Ormskirk, Kirby, Hunts Cross, New Brighton, West Kirby, Chester and Ellesmere Port, all worked by EMUs of Classes 507 and 508.

Northern Rail[8] Serco/Abellio (until 1 April 2014) **Northern**

Northern operates a range of inter-urban, commuter and rural services throughout the North of England, including those around the cities of Leeds, Manchester, Sheffield, Liverpool and Newcastle. The network extends from Chathill in the north to Nottingham in the south, and Cleethorpes in the east to St Bees in the west. Longer distance services include Leeds–Carlisle, Middlesbrough–Carlisle, Leeds–Nottingham and York–Blackpool North. The operator uses a large fleet of DMUs of Classes 142, 144, 150, 153, 155, 156 and 158 and EMUs of Classes 321, 322, 323 and 333.

ScotRail First Group plc (until 8 November 2014) **ScotRail**

ScotRail provides almost all passenger services within Scotland and also trains from Glasgow to Carlisle via Dumfries, some of which extend to Newcastle (jointly operated with Northern). The company also operates the overnight Caledonian Sleeper services between London and Glasgow, Edinburgh, Inverness, Aberdeen and Fort William. In addition to the Sleeper loco-hauled stock (hauled by Class 67s and 90s hired from DB Schenker), the company operates a large fleet of DMUs of Classes 156, 158 and 170 and EMU Classes 314, 318, 320, 334 and 380. Two loco-hauled rakes are also used on Fife Circle commuter trains, hauled by Class 67s.

South Central[9] Govia Ltd (Go-Ahead/Keolis) (until 25 July 2015) **Southern**

Southern operates predominantly commuter services between London, Surrey and Sussex, as well as services along the South Coast between Southampton, Brighton, Hastings and Ashford, and also the cross-London service from South Croydon to Milton Keynes. It also operates metro services in South London, and Gatwick Express, which is a premium non-stop service between London Victoria and Gatwick Airport. Class 171 DMUs are used on Brighton–Ashford and London Bridge–Uckfield services, whilst all other services are in the hands of EMUs of Classes 313, 377, 442, 455 and 456 (and occasional 460 if required).

South Western[10] Stagecoach Group plc (until 3 February 2014) **South West Trains**

South West Trains operates trains from London Waterloo to destinations across the South and South West including Woking, Basingstoke, Southampton, Portsmouth, Salisbury, Exeter, Reading and Weymouth. It also runs services between Ryde and Shanklin on the Isle of Wight, using former London Underground 1938 stock (Class 483). The rest of the fleet comprises of DMUs Classes 158 and 159 and EMUs Classes 444, 450, 455 and 458.

Thameslink/Great Northern[11] First Group plc (until September 2013) **First Capital Connect**

First Capital Connect operates trains on the Thameslink route between Bedford and Brighton via central London and the Sutton and Wimbledon loop. A joint service with Southeastern is also operated to Sevenoaks, Orpington and Ashford. FCC also runs services on the Great Northern route between London King's Cross and Moorgate to Welwyn Garden City, Hertford North, Peterborough, Cambridge and Kings Lynn. The fleet consists of EMU Classes 319 and 377 for Thameslink route services and Classes 313, 317, 321 and 365 for Great Northern route services.

Trans-Pennine Express[12] First Group/Keolis (until 1 April 2014) **TransPennine Express**

TransPennine Express operates predominantly long distance inter-urban services linking major cities across the North of England, along with Edinburgh and Glasgow in Scotland. The main services are Manchester Airport/Manchester Piccadilly–Newcastle/Middlesbrough/Hull plus Liverpool–Scarborough along the North Trans-Pennine route via Huddersfield, Leeds and York, and Manchester Airport–Cleethorpes along the South Trans-Pennine route via Sheffield. It also operates Manchester Airport–Blackpool/Barrow/Windermere/Edinburgh/Glasgow. The fleet consists of DMU Classes 170 (mainly used on the Hull route) and 185.

Wales & Borders Deutsche Bahn (Arriva) (until 6 December 2018) **Arriva Trains Wales**

Arriva Trains Wales operates a mix of long distance, regional and local services throughout Wales, including the Valley Lines network of lines around Cardiff, and also through services to the English border counties and to Manchester and Birmingham. The fleet consists of DMUs of Classes 121 (used on the Cardiff Bay branch), 142, 143, 150, 158 and 175 and one loco-hauled rake used on the Cardiff–Holyhead route (this is hauled by Class 57s at the time of writing but was due to change to Class 67s in spring 2012).

West Midlands[13] Govia Ltd (Go-Ahead/Keolis) (until 11 November 2013) **London Midland**

London Midland operates long distance/regional services from London Euston to Northampton and Birmingham/Crewe and also between Birmingham and Liverpool as well as local and regional services around Birmingham, including to Stratford-upon-Avon, Worcester, Redditch and Shrewsbury. It also operates the Bedford–Bletchley and Watford Jn–St Albans Abbey branches. The fleet consists of DMU Classes 150, 153, 170 and 172 and EMU Classes 321, 323 and 350.

Notes on franchise end dates:

[1] Awarded for six years to 2013 with an extension for a further two years and five months to 31 March 2016 if performance targets are met.

[2] Awarded for six years to 2013 with an extension for a further one year and five months to 31 March 2015 if performance targets are met.

[3] May be extended for four weeks to 28 April 2013 due to engineering works at Reading over the Easter 2013 period.

[4] A new short-term Greater Anglia franchise is due to commence on 5 February 2012, operated by Abellio, and will run until July 2014 when a new 15-year franchise is due to start.

[5] Currently run on an interim basis by DfT management company Directly Operated Railways (trading as East Coast). This arrangement is due to continue until December 2013.

[6] The London Rail Concession is different from other rail franchises, as fares and service levels are set by Transport for London instead of the DfT.

[7] Under the control of Merseytravel PTE instead of the DfT. Franchise reviewed every five years to fit in with the Merseyside Local Transport Plan.

[8] Franchise extended in 2011 to end between April 2014 and March 2015 to align with the end of the Trans-Pennine Express franchise.

[9] Upon termination of the Southern franchise in July 2015 it is to be combined with the Thameslink/Great Northern franchise.

[10] Awarded for seven years to 2014 with an extension for a further three years to 3 February 2017 if performance targets are met.

[11] Awarded for six years to 2012 with an extension for up to a further three years to 31 March 2015 if performance targets were met. This was cut by 18 months in 2011 so the franchise would finish in September 2013. The new franchise will be combined with Southern from July 2015.

[12] Originally awarded for eight years to 2012 with a possible extension for five years to 31 January 2017. The end date was revised in 2011 to be aligned with the end of the Northern franchise – the present contract will finish between April 2014 and March 2015.

[13] Awarded for six years to 2013 with an extension for a further two years to 19 September 2015 if performance targets are met.

All new franchises officially start at 02.00 on the first day, although the last dates shown above are the last full day of operation.

Where termination dates are dependent on performance targets being met, the earliest possible termination date is given. However, with Merseyrail the end date is based on the maximum franchise length.

The following operators run non-franchised services only:

Operator	*Trading Name*	*Route*
BAA	Heathrow Express	London Paddington–Heathrow Airport
First Hull Trains	First Hull Trains	London King's Cross–Hull
Grand Central	Grand Central	London King's Cross–Sunderland/ Bradford Interchange
North Yorkshire Moors Railway Enterprises	North Yorkshire Moors Railway	Pickering–Grosmont–Whitby/ Battersby
West Coast Railway Company	West Coast Railway Company	Birmingham–Stratford-upon-Avon* Fort William–Mallaig* York–Leeds–York–Scarborough*

* Special summer-dated services only.

INTERNATIONAL PASSENGER OPERATIONS

Eurostar (UK) operates passenger services between the UK and mainland Europe, jointly with the national operators of France (SNCF) and Belgium (SNCB/NMBS). Eurostar (UK) is a subsidiary of London & Continental Railways, which is jointly owned by National Express Group and British Airways.

In addition, a service for the conveyance of accompanied road vehicles through the Channel Tunnel is provided by the tunnel operating company, Eurotunnel.

FREIGHT TRAIN OPERATIONS

The following operators operate freight services or empty passenger stock workings under "Open Access" arrangements:

Colas Rail: In addition to its On-Track Machines and infrastructure activities, Colas Rail operates a number of freight flows, principally steel traffic to Boston using its Class 47s and coal from Wolsingham (on the Weardale Railway) to Scunthorpe and Ratcliffe plus timber from Carlisle, Ribblehead and Teignbridge to Chirk using its Class 66s.

DB Schenker Rail (UK): Still the biggest freight operator in the country, DBS (formerly EWS before being bought by DB) has seen some of its core traffic lost to competitors in recent years. It is still the largest provider of infrastructure trains to Network Rail and operates coal, steel, intermodal and aggregate trains nationwide. The core fleet is Class 66s. Of the original 250 ordered around 180 are still used in the UK, with the remainder having moved to DB's French and Polish operations, although some of the French locos do return to the UK at times of high demand such as during the autumn. A small number of Class 60s are also used on the heavier trains, although more are currently being overhauled to cover for more 66s due to be exported to Poland.

DBS's six Class 59/2s are used alongside the Mendip Rail 59/0s and 59/1s on stone traffic from the Mendip quarries and around the South-East. DBS's fleet of Class 67s are used on passenger or standby duties for Chiltern

Railways, ScotRail and East Coast (and Arriva Trains Wales from March 2012) plus charter trains and a small number of freight duties. Class 90s are hired to ScotRail for use on the Sleeper services and also to National Express East Anglia but see little use on freight, whilst the fleet of Class 92s are mainly used on intermodal duties, including, from 2011, a limited number of overnight trains on High Speed 1.

DBS also operates a number of both steam and diesel charter trains.

Devon & Cornwall Railway (a subsidiary of British American Railway Services): Although it has a freight license, so far D&CR has mainly only operated light locomotive movements plus a small number of trial freight services and empty stock moves using Class 31s and 56s.

Direct Rail Services: DRS has built on its original nuclear flask traffic to operate a number of different services. The main flows are intermodal (mostly Anglo-Scottish) plus the provision of crews and locos to Network Rail for autumn Railhead Treatment Trains. Its Class 47s are also used on charter work. DRS has the most varied fleet of locomotives of all the operators, with Class 20s, 37s, 47s, 57s and 66s. At the start of 2012 it placed an order for 15 new Vossloh "Eurolight" locomotives.

Freightliner: Freightliner has two divisions: Intermodal operates container trains from the main Ports at Southampton, Felixstowe, Tilbury and Thamesport to major cities including London, Manchester, Leeds and Birmingham. The Heavy Haul division covers the movement of coal, cement, infrastructure and aggregates nationwide. Most services are worked by Class 66s, with new Class 70s used on some of the longer intermodal trains and some Heavy Haul flows, principally coal. A small fleet of Class 86 and 90 electrics are used on intermodal trains on the Great Eastern and West Coast Main Lines, the Class 86s mainly being used in pairs on the WCML between Crewe and Coatbridge.

GB Railfreight: GBRf, formerly owned by First Group and now by Eurotunnel, operates a mixture of traffic types, mainly using Class 66s together with a small fleet of Class 73s used on infrastructure duties in the South-East. A growing fleet of Class 92s are also used on some intermodal flows to/from Dollands Moor. Traffic types include coal, intermodal, biomass and gypsum as well as infrastructure services for Network Rail and London Underground.

West Coast Railway Company: WCRC has a freight license but doesn't operate any freight as such – only empty stock movements. Its fleet of 47s, supplemented by a smaller number of 33s, 37s and 57s, are used on charter work nationwide, including the prestigious Royal Scotsman.

MAINTENANCE OF LOCOMOTIVES

Depot allocation codes for all locomotives are shown in this book (apart from shunters where the actual location of each is shown). It should be noted that today much locomotive maintenance is undertaken away from these depots. This may be undertaken at fuelling points, berthing sidings or similar, or by mobile maintenance teams. Therefore locomotives in particular may not return to their "home" depots (for example Toton for most DB Schenker locomotives) as often as in the past.

1. LOCOMOTIVES

INTRODUCTION

SCOPE

This section contains details of all locomotives which can run on Britain's national railway network, plus those of Eurotunnel. Locomotives which are owned by, for example, DB Schenker and Freightliner which have been withdrawn from service and awaiting disposal are listed in the main part of the book. Locos which are awaiting disposal at scrapyards are listed in the "Locomotives Awaiting Disposal" section.

Only preserved locomotives which are currently used on the National Rail network are included. Others, which may still be Network Rail registered but not at present certified for use, are not included, but will be found in the Platform 5 book, "Preserved Locomotives and Multiple Units".

LOCO CLASSES

Loco classes are listed in numerical order of class. Principal details and dimensions are quoted for each class in metric and/or imperial units as considered appropriate bearing in mind common UK usage.

Builders: These are shown in class headings. Abbreviations used are found in section 7.6.

All dimensions and weights are quoted for locomotives in an "as new" condition with all necessary supplies (eg oil, water and sand) on board. Dimensions are quoted in the order length x width. Lengths quoted are over buffers or couplers as appropriate. All widths quoted are maxima. Where two different wheel diameter dimensions are shown, the first refers to powered wheels and the second refers to non-powered wheels. All weights are shown as metric tonnes (t = tonnes).

NUMERICAL LISTINGS

Locomotives are listed in numerical order. Where numbers actually carried are different from those officially allocated, these are noted in class headings where appropriate. Where locomotives have been recently renumbered, the most immediate previous number is shown in parentheses. Each locomotive entry is laid out as in the following example:

RSL No.	*Detail*	*Livery*	*Owner*	*Pool*	*Allocn.*	*Name*
57302	d	**VT**	P	IWCA	MA	VIRGIL TRACY

Detail Differences. Only detail differences which currently affect the areas and types of train which locomotives may work are shown. All other detail differences are excluded. Where such differences occur within a class or part class, they are shown in the "Detail" column alongside the individual locomotive number.

Standard abbreviations used for the locomotives section are:

a	Train air brake equipment only.
b	Drophead buckeye couplers.
c	Scharfenberg couplers.
d	Fitted with retractable Dellner couplers.
e	European Railway Traffic Management System (ERTMS signalling equipment fitted.
k	Fitted with Swinghead Automatic "buckeye" combination couplers.
p	Train air, vacuum and electro-pneumatic brakes.
r	Radio Electric Token Block signalling equipment fitted.
s	Slow Speed Control equipment.
v	Train vacuum brake only.
x	Train air and vacuum brakes ("Dual brakes").
+	Additional fuel tank capacity.
§	Sandite laying equipment.

In all cases use of the above abbreviations indicates the equipment indicated is normally operable. Meaning of non-standard abbreviations and symbols is detailed in individual class headings.

Codes: Codes are used to denote the livery, owner, pool and depot of each locomotive. Details of these will be found in section 7 of this book.
(S) denotes that the locomotive is currently stored.

Names: Only names carried with official sanction are listed. Names are shown in UPPER/lower case characters as actually shown on the name carried on the locomotive.

GENERAL INFORMATION

CLASSIFICATION AND NUMBERING

All locomotives are classified and allocated numbers by the Rolling Stock Library under the TOPS numbering system, introduced in 1972. This comprises a two-digit class number followed by a three-digit serial number. Where the actual number carried by a locomotive differs from the allocated number, or where an additional number is carried to the allocated number, this is shown by a note in the class heading.

For diesel locomotives, class numbers offer an indication of engine horsepower as shown in the table below.

Class No. Range	*Engine h.p.*
01–14	0–799
15–20	800–1000
21–31	1001–1499
32–39	1500–1999
40–54, 57	2000–2999
55–56, 58–70	3000+

For electric locomotives class numbers are allocated in ascending numerical order under the following scheme:

Class 71–80	direct current and DC/diesel dual system locomotives.
Class 81 onwards	alternating current and AC/DC dual system locos.

Numbers in the 89xxx series are allocated by the Rolling Stock Library to locomotives which have been de-registered but subsequently re-registered for use on the Network Rail network and whose original number has already been re-used. 89xxx numbers are normally only carried inside locomotive cabs and are not carried externally in normal circumstances.

WHEEL ARRANGEMENT

For main line locomotives the number of driven axles on a bogie or frame is denoted by a letter (A = 1, B = 2, C = 3 etc.) and the number of non-powered axles is denoted by a number. The use of the letter "o" after a letter indicates each axle is individually powered, whilst the "+" symbol indicates bogies are inter-coupled.

For shunting locomotives, the Whyte notation is used. In this notation the number of leading wheels are given, followed by the number of driving wheels and then the trailing wheels.

HAULAGE CAPABILITY OF DIESEL LOCOMOTIVES

The haulage capability of a diesel locomotive depends upon three basic factors:

1. Adhesive weight. The greater the weight on the driving wheels, the greater the adhesion and more tractive power can be applied before wheelslip occurs.

2. The characteristics of its transmission. To start a train the locomotive has to exert a pull at standstill. A direct drive diesel engine cannot do this, hence the need for transmission. This may be mechanical, hydraulic or electric. The present British Standard for locomotives is electric transmission. Here the diesel engine drives a generator or alternator and the current produced is fed to the traction motors. The force produced by each driven wheel depends on the current in its traction motor. In other words, the larger the current, the harder it pulls. As the locomotive speed increases, the current in the traction motor falls, hence the *Maximum Tractive Effort* is the maximum force at its wheels the locomotive can exert at a standstill. The electrical equipment cannot take such high currents for long without overheating. Hence the *Continuous Tractive Effort* is quoted which represents the current which the equipment can take continuously.

3. The power of its engine. Not all power reaches the rail, as electrical machines are approximately 90% efficient. As the electrical energy passes through two such machines (the generator or alternator and the traction motors), the *Power at Rail* is approximately 81% (90% of 90%) of the engine power, less a further amount used for auxiliary equipment such as radiator fans, traction motor blowers, air compressors, battery charging, cab heating, Electric Train Supply (ETS) etc. The power of the locomotive is proportional to the tractive effort times the speed. Hence when on full power there is a speed corresponding to the continuous tractive effort.

HAULAGE CAPABILITY OF ELECTRIC LOCOMOTIVES

Unlike a diesel locomotive, an electric locomotive does not develop its power on board and its performance is determined only by two factors, namely its weight and the characteristics of its electrical equipment. Whereas a diesel locomotive tends to be a constant power machine, the power of an electric locomotive varies considerably. Up to a certain speed it can produce virtually a constant tractive effort. Hence power rises with speed according to the formula given in section three above, until a maximum speed is reached at which tractive effort falls, such that the power also falls. Hence the power at the speed corresponding to the maximum tractive effort is lower than the maximum speed.

BRAKE FORCE

The brake force is a measure of the braking power of a locomotive. This is shown on the locomotive data panels so operating staff can ensure sufficient brake power is available on freight trains.

ELECTRIC TRAIN SUPPLY (ETS)

A number of locomotives are equipped to provide a supply of electricity to the train being hauled to power auxiliaries such as heating, cooling fans, air conditioning and kitchen equipment. ETS is provided from the locomotive by means of a separate alternator (except Class 33 locos, which have a DC generator). The ETS index of a locomotive is a measure of the electrical power available for train supply.

Similarly, most loco-hauled coaches also have an ETS index, which in this case is a measure of the power required to operate equipment mounted in the coach. The sum of the ETS indices of all the hauled vehicles in a train must not exceed the ETS index of the locomotive.

ETS is commonly (but incorrectly) known as ETH (Electric Train Heating), which is a throwback to the days before loco-hauled coaches were equipped with electrically powered auxiliary equipment other than for train heating.

ROUTE AVAILABILITY (RA)

This is a measure of a railway vehicle's axle load. The higher the axle load of a vehicle, the higher the RA number on a scale from 1 to 10. Each Network Rail route has a RA number and in general no vehicle with a higher RA number may travel on that route without special clearance.

MULTIPLE & PUSH-PULL WORKING

Multiple working between vehicles (ie two or more powered vehicles being driven from one cab) is facilitated by jumper cables connecting the vehicles. However, not all types are compatible with each other, and a number of different systems are in use, each system being incompatible with any other.

Association of American Railroads (AAR) System: Classes 59, 66, and 67.
Blue Star Coupling Code: Classes 20, 25, 31, 33, 37 40 and 73.
DRS System: Classes 20/3, 37 and 47.
Green Circle Coupling Code: Class 47 (not all equipped).
Orange Square Coupling Code: Class 50.
Red Diamond Coupling Code: Classes 56 and 58.
SR System: Classes 33/1, 73 and various electric multiple units.
Within Own Class only: Classes 43 and 60.

Many locomotives use a time-division multiplex (TDM) system for push-pull and multiple working which utilises the existing RCH jumper cables fitted to coaching stock vehicles. Previously these cables had only been used to control train lighting and public address systems.

Class 47 locos 47701–717 were equipped with an older non-standard TDM system.

1.1. DIESEL LOCOMOTIVES

CLASS 08 BR/ENGLISH ELECTRIC 0-6-0

Built: 1955–62 by BR at Crewe, Darlington, Derby Locomotive, Doncaster or Horwich Works.
Engine: English Electric 6KT of 298 kW (400 hp) at 680 rpm.
Main Generator: English Electric 801.
Traction Motors: Two English Electric 506.
Maximum Tractive Effort: 156 kN (35000 lbf).
Continuous Tractive Effort: 49 kN (11100 lbf) at 8.8 mph.
Power At Rail: 194 kW (260 hp).
Train Brakes: Air & vacuum.
Brake Force: 19 t.
Dimensions: 8.92 x 2.59 m.
Weight: 49.6–50.4 t.
Wheel Diameter: 1372 mm.
Design Speed: 20 mph.
Maximum Speed: 15 mph.
Fuel Capacity: 3037 litres.
RA: 5.
Train Supply: Not equipped.
Multiple Working: m Equipped for multiple working. All others not equipped.

Notes: † – Fitted with remote control equipment.

For shunting locomotives, instead of the two-letter depot code, actual locations at the time of writing are given.

Class 08s that don't have Network Rail engineering acceptance are considered to be "in industrial service" and can be found in section 1.4 of this book.

08850 has acceptance for use between Battersby and Whitby only, for rescue purposes.

Non-standard liveries/numbering:

08308 All over ScotRail "Caledonian Sleeper" purple.
08480 Yellow with a red bodyside band. Carries number "TOTON No 1".
08616 Carries number 3783.
08696 Carries no number.
08701 Carries number "Tyne 100".
08721 As **B**, but with a black roof & "Express parcels" branding with red & yellow stripe.
08824 Carries number "IEMD01".

Originally numbered in series D3000–D4192.

Class 08/0. Standard Design.

08077		**FL**	P	DHLT	LH Group, Barton-under-Needwood (S)
08308	a	**0**	RL	MRSO	Inverness Depot
08405	a†	**E**	DB	WSSK	Doncaster Yards
08410	a	**GL**	FW	EFSH	Plymouth Laira Depot
08428	a	**E**	DB	WSSK	Bescot Yards
08451		**GB**	AM	ATZZ	Manchester Longsight Depot (S)
08454		**K**	AM	ATLO	Wembley Depot
08472	a	**WA**	WA	RFSH	Edinburgh Craigentinny Depot

08480	a	**O**	DB	WNYX	Toton Depot (S)
08483	a	**GL**	FW	EFSH	Old Oak Common HST Depot
08495	†	**E**	DB	WSSK	Eastleigh Yards
08500		**E**	DB	WNTS	Doncaster Depot (S)
08525		**ST**	EM	EMSL	Leeds Neville Hill Depot
08530		**FL**	P	DFLS	LH Group, Barton-under-Needwood (S)
08531	a	**FL**	P	DFLS	Trafford Park FLT
08567		**E**	DB	WSSK	Mossend Yards
08571	a	**WA**	WA	HBSH	Bounds Green Depot
08575		**FL**	P	DHLT	Southampton Maritime FLT (S)
08578	†	**E**	DB	WNYX	Toton Depot (S)
08580		**E**	DB	WNTS	Bescot Depot (S)
08585		**FL**	P	DFLS	Trafford Park FLT
08593		**E**	DB	WNTS	Toton Yards (S)
08596	a†	**WA**	WA	RFSH	Bounds Green Depot
08605		**E**	DB	WNYX	Toton Depot (S)
08611		**V**	AM	ATLO	Manchester Longsight Depot
08615		**WA**	WA	RFSH	Edinburgh Craigentinny Depot
08616		**LM**	LM	EJLO	Birmingham Tyseley Depot
08617		**K**	AM	ATLO	Wembley Depot
08623		**E**	DB	WSSK	Hams Hall Distribution Park, Coleshill
08624		**FL**	P	DFLS	Southampton Maritime FLT
08630		**E**	DB	WNYX	Toton Yards (S)
08632	†	**E**	DB	WNYX	Toton Depot (S)
08633		**E**	DB	WSSK	Hoo Junction Yards
08641		**FB**	FW	EFSH	Plymouth Laira Depot
08644		**GL**	FW	EFSH	Penzance Long Rock Depot
08645		**FB**	FW	EFSH	Plymouth Laira Depot
08653		**E**	DB	WNYX	Toton Yards (S)
08663	a	**GL**	FW	EFSH	Bristol St Philip's Marsh Depot
08669	a	**WA**	WA	RFSH	Wabtec, Doncaster Works
08676		**E**	DB	WSSK	Doncaster Yards
08690		**ST**	EM	EMSL	Leeds Neville Hill Depot
08691		**FL**	FL	DFLS	Tilbury FLT
08696	a	**G**	AM	ATLO	Manchester Longsight Depot
08701	a	**RX**	DB	WNTS	Toton Yards (S)
08703	a	**E**	DB	WNYX	Crewe International (S)
08706	†	**E**	DB	WSSK	Mountsorrel Stone Terminal
08709		**E**	DB	WNTS	Bescot Depot (S)
08711	k	**RX**	DB	WSSI	Immingham Depot
08714		**E**	DB	WSXX	Axiom Rail, Stoke-on-Trent Works (S)
08721		**O**	AM	ATLO	Liverpool Edge Hill Depot
08724		**WA**	WA	HBSH	Leeds Neville Hill Depot
08735	†	**E**	DB	WSSK	Eastleigh Yards
08737	a	**E**	DB	WSSK	Westbury Yards
08738	m	**ECR**	DB	WNYX	Toton Yards (S)
08742	†	**RX**	DB	WNYX	Toton Depot (S)
08745		**FE**	P	DHLT	Southampton Maritime FLT (S)
08752	†	**E**	DB	WSSI	Margam Yards
08757		**RG**	DB	WSSK	Didcot Yards
08782	a†	**CU**	DB	WSSK	Fowey Docks

08784	†	**E**	DB	WNYX	Toton Depot (S)
08785	a	**FL**	P	DFLS	Felixstowe FLT
08788		**K**	RL	MRSO	Inverness Depot
08790		**B**	AM	ATLO	Wolverhampton Oxley Depot
08795		**GL**	FW	EFSH	Swansea Landore Depot
08799	a	**E**	DB	WNYX	Toton Yards (S)
08802	†	**E**	DB	WSSK	Mossend Yards
08804	†	**E**	DB	WNYX	Doncaster Depot (S)
08805		**B**	LM	EJLO	Birmingham Soho Depot
08822		**GL**	FW	EFSH	Bristol St Philip's Marsh Depot
08824	ak	**K**	DB	WSXX	Crewe International Depot (S)
08836		**FB**	FW	EFSH	Old Oak Common HST Depot
08847		**CD**	RL	MRSO	Norwich Crown Point Depot
08850		**B**	NY	MBDL	Grosmont Depot
08853	a	**WA**	WA	RFSH	Wabtec, Doncaster Works
08865		**E**	DB	WSSK	Crewe International Depot
08871		**CD**	RL	MRSO	Hanson Traction/Cemex UK, Washwood Heath
08873		**RX**	HU	DFLS	Southampton Maritime FLT
08874		**SL**	RL	MRSO	Norwich Crown Point Depot
08877		**DG**	DB	WSXX	Wigan Springs Branch Depot (S)
08879		**E**	DB	WSSK	Warrington Yards
08886	†	**E**	DB	WSSK	Hinksey Yard
08887	a	**VP**	AM	ATZZ	Manchester Longsight Depot (S)
08888	†	**E**	DB	WSSI	Scunthorpe Yards
08891		**FL**	P	DHLT	LH Group, Barton-under-Needwood (S)
08899		**MA**	EM	EMSL	Derby Etches Park Depot
08904		**E**	DB	WNYX	Toton Depot (S)
08907		**E**	DB	WSSK	Carlisle Yards
08908		**ST**	EM	EMSL	Leeds Neville Hill Depot
08922		**DG**	DB	WNYX	Toton Depot (S)
08925		**B**	GB	GBWM	Cardiff Tidal Steelworks
08934	a	**VP**	GB	GBWM	Cardiff Tidal Steelworks
08939	m	**ECR**	DB	WNYX	Toton Yards (S)
08948	c	**EP**	EU	GPSS	Temple Mills Depot
08950		**ST**	EM	EMSL	Leeds Neville Hill Depot

Class 08/9. Reduced height cab. Converted 1985–87 by BR at Landore.

08993		**E**	DB	WNYX	Doncaster Depot (S)
08994	a	**E**	DB	WNYX	Toton Depot (S)
08995	a	**E**	DB	WSSK	Hoo Junction Yards

CLASS 09 BR/ENGLISH ELECTRIC 0-6-0

Built: 1959–62 by BR at Darlington or Horwich Works.
Engine: English Electric 6KT of 298 kW (400 hp) at 680 rpm.
Main Generator: English Electric 801.
Traction Motors: English Electric 506.
Maximum Tractive Effort: 111 kN (25000 lbf).
Continuous Tractive Effort: 39 kN (8800 lbf) at 11.6 mph.
Power At Rail: 201 kW (269 hp).
Brake Force: 19 t.
Weight: 49 t.
Design Speed: 27 mph.
Fuel Capacity: 3037 litres.
Train Supply: Not equipped.
Train Brakes: Air & vacuum.
Dimensions: 8.92 x 2.59 m.
Wheel Diameter: 1372 mm.
Maximum Speed: 27 mph.
RA: 5.
Multiple Working: Not equipped.

Class 09/0 were originally numbered D3665–D3671, D3719–D3721, D4099–D4114.

Class 09/0. Built as Class 09.

09002	**G**	GB	GBWM	Trafford Park FLT
09006	**E**	DB	WNTS	Doncaster Depot (S)
09009	**G**	GB	GBWM	Trafford Park FLT
09026 a	**G**	SN	HWSU	Brighton Lovers Walk Depot

Class 09/1. Converted from Class 08. 110 V electrical equipment.
Converted: 1992–1993 by RFS Industries, Kilnhurst.

09106 (08759)	**E**	DB	WSSK	Dagenham Yards

Class 09/2. Converted from Class 08. 90 V electrical equipment.
Converted: 1992 by RFS Industries, Kilnhurst.

09201 (08421) ak	**DG**	DB	WSSI	Knottingley Depot

Class 08/09 names:

08483	DUSTY Driver David Miller
08495	NOEL KIRTON OBE
08525	DUNCAN BEDFORD
08585	Vicky
08611	M.A. Smith
08616	TYSELEY 100
08630	BOB BROWN
08645	Mike Baggott
08669	Bob Machin
08690	DAVID THIRKHILL
08691	Terri
08696	LONGSIGHT TMD
08721	DOWNHILL C.S.
08782	CASTLETON WORKS
08790	STARLET
08799	FRED
08805	CONCORDE
08874	Catherine
08908	IVAN STEPHENSON
08950	DAVID LIGHTFOOT
09026	Cedric Wares

CLASS 20 ENGLISH ELECTRIC Bo-Bo

Built: 1957–68 by English Electric at Vulcan Foundry, Newton-le-Willows or by Robert Stephenson & Hawthorns at Darlington.
Engine: English Electric 8SVT Mk II of 746 kW (1000 hp) at 850 rpm.
Main Generator: English Electric 819/3C.
Traction Motors: English Electric 526/5D or 526/8D.
Maximum Tractive Effort: 187 kN (42000 lbf).
Continuous Tractive Effort: 111 kN (25000 lbf) at 11 mph.
Power At Rail: 574 kW (770 hp).
Brake Force: 35 t.
Weight: 73.4–73.5 t.
Design Speed: 75 mph.
Fuel Capacity: 1727 litres.
Train Supply: Not equipped.
Train Brakes: Air & vacuum.
Dimensions: 14.25 x 2.67 m.
Wheel Diameter: 1092 mm.
Maximum Speed: 75 mph.
RA: 5.
Multiple Working: Blue Star.

Originally numbered in series D8007–D8190, D8315–D8325.

Non-standard livery/numbering:

20088 RFS grey (carries No. 2017).
20906 Carries no number.

Class 20/0. Standard Design.

20016	**B**	HN	HNRS	LM (S)
20057	**B**	HN	HNRS	LM (S)
20081	**B**	HN	HNRS	LM (S)
20088	**0**	HN	HNRS	LM (S)
20092	**U**	HN	HNRS	LM (S)
20096	**B**	HN	HNRL	BH
20107	**B**	HN	HNRL	BH (S)
20142	**B**	20	MBDL	SK
20189	**G**	20	MOLO	SK
20227	**FO**	2L	MOLO	SK

Class 20/3. Direct Rail Services refurbished locos. Details as Class 20/0 except:

Refurbished: 1995–96 by Brush Traction at Loughborough (20301–305) or 1997–98 by RFS(E) at Doncaster (20306–315). Disc indicators or headcode panels removed.
Train Brakes: Air.
Weight: 73 t (+ 76 t).
Brake Force: 35 t (+ 31 t).
Multiple Working: DRS system.
Maximum Speed: 60 mph (+ 75 mph).
Fuel Capacity: 2909 (+ 4909) litres.
RA: 5 (+ 6).

Note: t Fitted with tripcocks for working over London Underground tracks between Harrow-on-the-Hill and Amersham.

20301	(20047)	rt	**DR**	DR	GBEE	KM	Max Joule 1958–1999
20302	(20084)	rt	**DR**	DR	GBEE	KM	
20303	(20127)	r	**DR**	DR	XHNC	KM	
20304	(20120)	rt	**DR**	DR	GBEE	KM	
20305	(20095)	rt	**DR**	DR	GBEE	KM	Gresty Bridge
20306	(20131)	r+	**DR**	DR	XHSS	BH (S)	

20307	(20128) r+	**DR**	DR	XHSS	KM (S)
20308	(20187) r+	**DS**	DR	XHNC	KM
20309	(20075) r+	**DS**	DR	XHNC	KM
20310	(20190) r+	**DR**	DR	XHSS	KM (S)
20311	(20102) r+	**DR**	HN	HNRL	BH (S)
20312	(20042) r+	**DS**	DR	XHSS	KM (S)
20313	(20194) r+	**DR**	DR	XHSS	KM (S)
20314	(20117) r+	**DS**	HN	HNRL	BH (S)
20315	(20104) r+	**DR**	DR	XHSS	CR (S)

Class 20/9. Harry Needle Railroad Company (former Hunslet-Barclay/ DRS) locos. Details as Class 20/0 except:

Refurbished: 1989 by Hunslet-Barclay at Kilmarnock.
Train Brakes: Air. **Fuel Capacity:** 1727 (+ 4727) litres.
RA: 5 (+ 6).

20901	(20101)	**F**	HN	HNRL	BH
20903	(20083) +	**DR**	HN	HNRS	BO (S)
20904	(20041)	**DR**	HN	HNRS	BO (S)
20905	(20225) +	**F**	HN	HNRL	BH
20906	(20219)	**DR**	HN	HNRS	BH (S)

CLASS 25 BR/BEYER PEACOCK/SULZER Bo-Bo

Built: 1965 by Beyer Peacock at Gorton.
Engine: Sulzer 6LDA28-B of 930 kW (1250 hp) at 750 rpm.
Main Generator: AEI RTB15656. **Traction Motors:** AEI 253AY.
Maximum Tractive Effort: 200 kN (45000 lbf).
Continuous Tractive Effort: 93 kN (20800 lbf) at 17.1 mph.
Power At Rail: 708 kW (949 hp). **Train Brakes:** Air & vacuum.
Brake Force: 38 t. **Dimensions:** 15.39 x 2.73 m.
Weight: 71.5 t. **Wheel Diameter:** 1143 mm.
Design Speed: 90 mph. **Maximum Speed:** 60 mph.
Fuel Capacity: 2270 litres. **RA:** 5.
Train Supply: Not equipped. **Multiple Working:** Blue Star.

Original number is D7628, which the loco currently carries.

Note: Only certified for use on Network Rail metals between Whitby and Battersby, as an extension of North Yorkshire Moors Railway services.

25278	**GG**	NY	MBDL	NY	SYBILLA

CLASS 31 BRUSH/ENGLISH ELECTRIC A1A-A1A

Built: 1958–62 by Brush Traction at Loughborough.
Engine: English Electric 12SVT of 1100 kW (1470 hp) at 850 rpm.
Main Generator: Brush TG160-48. **Traction Motors:** Brush TM73-68.
Maximum Tractive Effort: 160 kN (35900 lbf).
Continuous Tractive Effort: 83 kN (18700 lbf) at 23.5 mph.
Power At Rail: 872 kW (1170 hp). **Train Brakes:** Air & vacuum.
Brake Force: 49 t. **Dimensions:** 17.30 x 2.67 m.
Weight: 106.7–111 t. **Wheel Diameter:** 1092/1003 mm.

Design Speed: 90 mph. **Maximum Speed:** 90 mph.
Fuel Capacity: 2409 litres. **RA:** 5 or 6.
Train Supply: Not equipped. **Multiple Working:** Blue Star.

Originally numbered D5520–D5699, D5800–D5862 (not in order).

Non-standard numbering:

31190 Also carries number D5613.

Class 31/1. Standard Design. RA: 5.

31105		**Y**	NR	QADD	ZA	
31106	a	**B**	RE	RVLO	ZA	
31128		**B**	NS	NRLO	BH	CHARYBDIS
31190		**G**	BA	HTLX	WH	
31233	a	**Y**	NR	QADD	ZA	
31285		**Y**	NR	QADD	ZA	

Class 31/4. Electric Train Supply equipment. RA: 6.
Train Supply: Electric, index 66.

31422	**IC**	RE	RVLO	ZA (S)	
31452	**DC**	BA	RVLO	ZA	
31454	**IC**	BA	HTLX	WH	
31459	**K**	RE	RVLO	ZA	CERBERUS
31465	**Y**	NR	QADD	ZA	
31468	**FR**	BA	RVLO	WO (S)	HYDRA

Class 31/6. ETS through wiring and controls. RA: 5.

31601	(31186)	**DC**	BA	HTLX	WH	
31602	(31191)	**Y**	RE	RVLO	ZA	DRIVER DAVE GREEN

CLASS 33 BRCW/SULZER Bo-Bo

Built: 1960–62 by the Birmingham Railway Carriage & Wagon Company at Smethwick.
Engine: Sulzer 8LDA28 of 1160 kW (1550 hp) at 750 rpm.
Main Generator: Crompton Parkinson CG391B1.
Traction Motors: Crompton Parkinson C171C2.
Maximum Tractive Effort: 200 kN (45000 lbf).
Continuous Tractive Effort: 116 kN (26000 lbf) at 17.5 mph.
Power At Rail: 906 kW (1215 hp). **Train Brakes:** Air & vacuum.
Brake Force: 35 t. **Dimensions:** 15.47 x 2.82 (2.64 m 33/2).
Weight: 76-78 t. **Wheel Diameter:** 1092 mm.
Design Speed: 85 mph. **Maximum Speed:** 85 mph.
Fuel Capacity: 3410 litres. **RA:** 6.
Train Supply: Electric, index 48 (750 V DC only).
Multiple Working: Blue Star.

Originally numbered in series D6500–D6597 but not in order.

Non-standard numbering:

33012 Carries number D6515.

Class 33/0. Standard Design.

33012	**G**	71	MBDL	Swanage Rly	
33025	**WC**	WC	MBDL	CS	Glen Falloch
33029	**WC**	WC	MBDL	CS	Glen Loy
33030	**DR**	WC	MBDL	CS (S)	

Class 33/2. Built to former Loading Gauge of Tonbridge–Battle Line.
Equipped with slow speed control.

33207	**WC**	WC	MBDL	CS	Jim Martin

CLASS 37 ENGLISH ELECTRIC Co-Co

Built: 1960–66 by English Electric at Vulcan Foundry, Newton-le-Willows or by Robert Stephenson & Hawthorns at Darlington.
Engine: English Electric 12CSVT of 1300 kW (1750 hp) at 850 rpm.
Main Generator: English Electric 822/10G.
Traction Motors: English Electric 538/A.
Maximum Tractive Effort: 245 kN (55500 lbf).
Continuous Tractive Effort: 156 kN (35000 lbf) at 13.6 mph.
Power At Rail: 932 kW (1250 hp).
Train Brakes: Air & vacuum.
Brake Force: 50 t.
Dimensions: 18.75 x 2.74 m.
Weight: 102.8–108.4 t.
Wheel Diameter: 1092 mm.
Design Speed: 90 mph.
Maximum Speed: 80 mph.
Fuel Capacity: 4046 (+ 7683) litres.
RA: 5 (§ 6).
Train Supply: Not equipped.
Multiple Working: Blue Star († DRS system).

Originally numbered D6600–D6608, D6700–D6999 (not in order).

Note: Class 37s exported for use abroad are listed in section 1.6 of this book.

Non-standard liveries/numbering:

37402 Light grey lower bodyside & dark grey upper bodyside.
37411 Also carries number D6990.

Class 37/0. Standard Design. Details as above.

37038	a†	**DR**	DR	XHNC	KM	
37059	ar+†	**DS**	DR	XHNC	KM	
37069	ar+†	**DS**	DR	XHNC	KM	
37087	a+	**DR**	DR	XHNC	KM	Keighley & Worth Valley Railway 40th Anniversary 1968–2008
37165	a+	**CE**	WC	MBDL	CS (S)	
37194	a+	**DS**	DR	XHNC	KM	
37197	a+	**DS**	DR	XHHP	BH (S)	
37198	+	**Y**	NR	MBDL	GCR	
37214		**WC**	WC	MBDL	CS (S)	Loch Laidon
37218	ar+†	**DS**	DR	XHNC	KM	
37229	a+	**DS**	DR	XHNC	KM	Jonty Jarvis 8-12-1998 to 18-3-2005
37259	ar†	**DS**	DR	XHSS	BH (S)	
37261	a+	**DS**	DR	XHNC	KM	

Class 37/4. Refurbished with electric train supply equipment. Main generator replaced by alternator. Regeared (CP7) bogies. Details as Class 37/0 except:
Main Alternator: Brush BA1005A. **Power At Rail**: 935 kW (1254 hp).
Traction Motors: English Electric 538/5A.
Maximum Tractive Effort: 256 kN (57440 lbf).
Continuous Tractive Effort: 184 kN (41250 lbf) at 11.4 mph.
Weight: 107 t. **Design Speed**: 80 mph.
Fuel Capacity: 7683 litres.
Train Supply: Electric, index 30.

37401	ar	**E**	DR	XHHP	KM (S)	
37402	a	**0**	DR	WNSO	TO (S)	
37405	ar	**E**	DR	WNSO	TO (S)	
37406	ar	**E**	DR	XHHP	KM (S)	
37409	ar†	**DS**	DR	XHAC	KM	Lord Hinton
37410	ar	**E**	DR	XHHP	KM (S)	
37411	ar	**G**	DR	XHHP	KM (S)	
37412	a	**F**	DR	XHHP	BH (S)	
37415		**E**	HN	HNRS	LM (S)	
37416	ar	**GS**	DR	XHHP	KM (S)	
37417	ar	**E**	DR	XHHP	KM (S)	
37419	ar	**DS**	DR	XHHP	BH (S)	
37422	ar	**E**	DR	XHHP	KM (S)	
37423	ar†	**DS**	DR	XHAC	KM	Spirit of the Lakes
37425	ar	**DS**	DR	XHHP	BH (S)	
37426	a	**E**	DR	XHHP	KM (S)	
37427	ar	**E**	DR	XHHP	KM (S)	
37428		**GS**	HN	HNRS	LM (S)	

Class 37/5. Refurbished without train supply equipment. Main generator replaced by alternator. Regeared (CP7) bogies. Details as Class 37/4 except:
Maximum Tractive Effort: 248 kN (55590 lbf).
Weight: 106.1–110.0 t.

37503	r§	**E**	HN	HNRS	BH (S)
37510	ar	**DS**	DR	XHNC	KM
37516	s	**WC**	WC	MBDL	CS
37517	as	**LH**	WC	MBDL	CS (S)
37521	r§	**E**	HN	HNRS	BH (S)

Class 37/6. Originally refurbished for Nightstar services. Main generator replaced by alternator. UIC jumpers. Details as Class 37/5 except:
Maximum Speed: 90 mph. **Train Brake**: Air.
Train Supply: Not equipped, but electric through wired.
Multiple Working: DRS system.

37601	a	**DS**	DR	XHNC	KM	Class 37-'Fifty'
37602	ar	**DS**	DR	XHNC	KM	
37603	a	**DS**	DR	XHNC	KM	
37604	a	**DS**	DR	XHNC	KM	
37605	ar	**DR**	DR	XHSS	ZA (S)	
37606	a	**DS**	DR	XHNC	KM	
37607	ar	**DR**	DR	XHNC	KM	

37608	ar	**DS**	DR	XHNC	KM	
37609	a	**DR**	DR	XHSS	CR (S)	
37610	ar	**DS**	DR	XHNC	KM	T.S.(Ted) Cassady 14.5.61–6.4.08
37611	a	**DS**	DR	XHNC	KM	
37612	a	**DS**	DR	XHNC	KM	

Class 37/5 continued.

37667	ast	**DS**	DR	XHNC	KM	
37668	s	**E**	WC	MBDL	CS (S)	
37669	r	**E**	WC	MBDL	CS (S)	
37670	r	**DB**	HN	HNRS	EMR, Kingsbury	
37676	a	**WC**	WC	MBDL	CS	Loch Rannoch
37682	ar	**DS**	DR	XHNC	KM	
37683	a	**DS**	DR	XHHP	CQ (S)	
37685	a	**WC**	WC	MBDL	CS	Loch Arkaig
37688	art	**DS**	DR	XHNC	KM	Kingmoor TMD
37696	as	**F**	HN	HNRS	LM (S)	

Class 37/7. Refurbished locos. Main generator replaced by alternator. Regeared (CP7) bogies. Ballast weights added. Details as Class 37/5 except:
Main Alternator: GEC G564AZ (37796–803) Brush BA1005A (others).
Maximum Tractive Effort: 276 kN (62000 lbf).
Weight: 120 t. **RA**: 7.

37706		**WC**	WC	MBDL	CS
37710		**LH**	WC	MBDL	CS (S)
37712	a	**WC**	WC	MBDL	CS (S)

Class 97/3. Class 37s refurbished for Network Rail for use on the Cambrian Lines pilot ERTMS signalling project. Details as Class 37/0.

97301	(37100)		**Y**	NR	QETS	ZA	
97302	(37170)	e	**Y**	NR	QETS	ZA	
97303	(37178)	e	**Y**	NR	QETS	ZA	
97304	(37217)	e	**Y**	NR	QETS	ZA	John Tiley

CLASS 40 ENGLISH ELECTRIC 1Co-Co1

Built: 1958–62 by English Electric at Vulcan Foundry, Newton-le-Willows.
Engine: English Electric 16SVT Mk2 of 1490 kW (2000 hp) at 850 rpm.
Main Generator: English Electric 822/4C.
Traction Motors: English Electric 526/5D or EE526/7D.
Maximum Tractive Effort: 231 kN (52000 lbf).
Continuous Tractive Effort: 137 kN (30900 lbf) at 18.8 mph.
Power At Rail: 1160 kW (1550 hp). **Train Brakes**: Air & vacuum.
Brake Force: 51 t. **Dimensions**: 21.18 x 2.78 m.
Weight: 132 t. **Wheel Diameter**: 914/1143 mm.
Design Speed: 90 mph. **Maximum Speed**: 90 mph.
Fuel Capacity: 3250 litres. **RA**: 6.
Train Supply: Steam. **Multiple Working**: Blue Star.

Originally numbered D345.

40145	**BL**	40	ELRD	BQ	East Lancashire Railway

CLASS 43 BREL/PAXMAN Bo-Bo

Built: 1975–82 by BREL at Crewe Works.
Engine: MTU 16V4000R41R of 1680kW (2250 hp) at 1500 rpm.
(* Paxman 12VP185 of 1565 kW (2100 hp) at 1500 rpm.)
Main Alternator: Brush BA1001B.
Traction Motors: Brush TMH68–46 or GEC G417AZ, frame mounted.
Maximum Tractive Effort: 80 kN (17980 lbf).
Continuous Tractive Effort: 46 kN (10340 lbf) at 64.5 mph.
Power At Rail: 1320 kW (1770 hp). **Train Brakes:** Air.
Brake Force: 35 t. **Dimensions:** 17.79 x 2.74 m.
Weight: 70.25 t. **Wheel Diameter:** 1020 mm.
Design Speed: 125 mph. **Maximum Speed:** 125 mph.
Fuel Capacity: 4500 litres. **RA:** 5.
Train Supply: Three-phase electric.
Multiple Working: Within class, jumpers at non-driving end only.

Notes: † Buffer fitted.

43013, 43014 & 43062 are fitted with measuring apparatus & front-end cameras.

43002	**FB**	A	EFPC	LA	
43003	**FB**	A	EFPC	LA	ISAMBARD KINGDOM BRUNEL
43004	**FB**	A	EFPC	LA	First for the future/ First ar gyfer y dyfodol
43005	**FB**	A	EFPC	LA	
43009	**FB**	A	EFPC	LA	First transforming travel
43010	**FB**	A	EFPC	LA	
43012	**FB**	A	EFPC	LA	
43013 †	**Y**	P	QCAR	EC	
43014 †	**Y**	P	QCAR	EC	
43015	**FB**	A	EFPC	LA	
43016	**FB**	A	EFPC	LA	
43017	**FB**	A	EFPC	LA	
43018	**FB**	A	EFPC	LA	
43020	**FB**	A	EFPC	LA	MTU Power. Passion. Partnership
43021	**FB**	A	EFPC	LA	David Austin – Cartoonist
43022	**FB**	A	EFPC	LA	
43023	**FB**	A	EFPC	LA	
43024	**FB**	A	EFPC	LA	Great Western Society 1961–2011 Didcot Railway Centre
43025	**FB**	A	EFPC	LA	IRO The Institution of Railway Operators 2000–2010 TEN YEARS PROMOTING OPERATIONAL EXCELLENCE
43026	**FB**	A	EFPC	LA	
43027	**FB**	A	EFPC	LA	Glorious Devon
43028	**FB**	A	EFPC	LA	
43029	**FB**	A	EFPC	LA	
43030	**FB**	A	EFPC	LA	Christian Lewis Trust
43031	**FB**	A	EFPC	LA	
43032	**FB**	A	EFPC	LA	

43033		**FB**	A	EFPC	LA	Driver Brian Cooper 15 June 1947–5 October 1999
43034		**FB**	A	EFPC	LA	TravelWatch SouthWest
43035		**FB**	A	EFPC	LA	
43036		**FB**	A	EFPC	LA	
43037		**FB**	A	EFPC	LA	PENYDARREN
43040		**FB**	A	EFPC	LA	Bristol St. Philip's Marsh
43041		**FB**	A	EFPC	OO	Meningitis Trust Support for Life
43042		**FB**	A	EFPC	OO	
43043	*	**ST**	P	EMPC	NL	
43044	*	**ST**	P	EMPC	NL	
43045	*	**ST**	P	EMPC	NL	
43046	*	**ST**	P	EMPC	NL	
43047	*	**ST**	P	EMPC	NL	
43048	*	**ST**	P	EMPC	NL	T.C.B. Miller MBE
43049	*	**ST**	P	EMPC	NL	Neville Hill
43050	*	**ST**	P	EMPC	NL	
43052	*	**ST**	P	EMPC	NL	
43053		**FB**	P	EFPC	LE	University of Worcester
43054	*	**ST**	P	EMPC	NL	
43055	*	**ST**	P	EMPC	NL	
43056		**FB**	P	EFPC	LE	The Royal British Legion
43058	*	**ST**	P	EMPC	NL	
43059	*	**ST**	P	EMPC	NL	
43060	*	**ST**	P	EMPC	NL	
43061	*	**ST**	P	EMPC	NL	
43062		**Y**	P	QCAR	EC	John Armitt
43063		**FB**	P	EFPC	OO	
43064	*	**ST**	P	EMPC	NL	
43066	*	**ST**	P	EMPC	NL	
43069		**FB**	P	EFPC	OO	
43070		**FB**	P	EFPC	OO	The Corps of Royal Electrical and Mechanical Engineers
43071		**FB**	P	EFPC	OO	
43073	*	**ST**	P	EMPC	NL	
43075	*	**ST**	P	EMPC	NL	
43076	*	**ST**	P	EMPC	NL	IN SUPPORT OF HELP for HEROES
43078		**FB**	P	EFPC	OO	
43079		**FB**	P	EFPC	OO	
43081	*	**ST**	P	EMPC	NL	
43082	*	**ST**	P	EMPC	NL	RAILWAY children – THE VOICE FOR STREET CHILDREN WORLDWIDE
43083	*	**ST**	P	EMPC	NL	
43086		**FB**	P	EFPC	OO	
43087		**FB**	P	EFPC	OO	11 Explosive Ordnance Disposal Regiment Royal Logistic Corps
43088		**FB**	P	EFPC	OO	
43089	*	**ST**	P	EMPC	NL	
43091		**FB**	P	EFPC	OO	
43092		**FB**	FG	EFPC	OO	
43093		**FB**	FG	EFPC	OO	

43094	**FB**	FG	EFPC	OO	
43097	**FB**	FG	EFPC	OO	Environment Agency
43098	**FB**	FG	EFPC	OO	
43122	**FB**	FG	EFPC	OO	
43124	**FB**	A	EFPC	LE	
43125	**FB**	A	EFPC	LE	
43126	**FB**	A	EFPC	LE	
43127	**FB**	A	EFPC	LE	Sir Peter Parker 1924–2002 Cotswold Line 150
43128	**FB**	A	EFPC	LE	
43129	**FB**	A	EFPC	LE	
43130	**FB**	A	EFPC	LE	
43131	**FB**	A	EFPC	LE	
43132	**FB**	A	EFPC	LE	We Save the Children – Will You?
43133	**FB**	A	EFPC	LE	
43134	**FB**	A	EFPC	LE	
43135	**FB**	A	EFPC	LE	
43136	**FB**	A	EFPC	LE	
43137	**FB**	A	EFPC	LE	Newton Abbot 150
43138	**FB**	A	EFPC	LE	
43139	**FB**	A	EFPC	LE	Driver Stan Martin 25 June 1950 – 6 November 2004
43140	**FB**	A	EFPC	LE	
43141	**FB**	A	EFPC	LE	
43142	**FB**	A	EFPC	LE	Reading Panel Signal Box 1965–2010
43143	**FB**	A	EFPC	LE	Stroud 700
43144	**FB**	A	EFPC	LE	
43145	**FB**	A	EFPC	LE	
43146	**FB**	A	EFPC	LE	
43147	**FB**	A	EFPC	LE	
43148	**FB**	A	EFPC	LE	
43149	**FB**	A	EFPC	LE	University of Plymouth
43150	**FB**	A	EFPC	LE	
43151	**FB**	A	EFPC	LE	
43152	**FB**	A	EFPC	LE	
43153	**FB**	FG	EFPC	OO	
43154	**FB**	FG	EFPC	OO	
43155	**FB**	FG	EFPC	OO	
43156	**FB**	P	EFPC	OO	Dartington International Summer School
43158	**FB**	FG	EFPC	OO	
43159	**FB**	P	EFPC	OO	
43160	**FB**	P	EFPC	OO	Sir Moir Lockhead OBE
43161	**FB**	P	EFPC	OO	
43162	**FB**	P	EFPC	OO	
43163	**FB**	A	EFPC	OO	Exeter Panel Signal Box 21st Anniversary 2009
43164	**FB**	A	EFPC	OO	
43165	**FB**	A	EFPC	OO	Prince Michael of Kent
43168	**FB**	A	EFPC	OO	
43169	**FB**	A	EFPC	OO	THE NATIONAL TRUST
43170	**FB**	A	EFPC	OO	

43171	**FB**	A	EFPC	OO	
43172	**FB**	A	EFPC	OO	
43174	**FB**	A	EFPC	OO	
43175	**FB**	A	EFPC	OO	GWR 175TH ANNIVERSARY
43176	**FB**	A	EFPC	OO	
43177	**FB**	A	EFPC	OO	
43179	**FB**	A	EFPC	OO	Pride of Laira
43180	**FB**	P	EFPC	OO	
43181	**FB**	A	EFPC	OO	
43182	**FB**	A	EFPC	OO	
43183	**FB**	A	EFPC	OO	
43185	**FB**	A	EFPC	OO	Great Western
43186	**FB**	A	EFPC	OO	
43187	**FB**	A	EFPC	OO	
43188	**FB**	A	EFPC	OO	
43189	**FB**	A	EFPC	OO	RAILWAY HERITAGE TRUST
43190	**FB**	A	EFPC	OO	
43191	**FB**	A	EFPC	OO	
43192	**FB**	A	EFPC	OO	
43193	**FB**	P	EFPC	OO	
43194	**FB**	FG	EFPC	OO	
43195	**FB**	P	EFPC	OO	
43196	**FB**	P	EFPC	OO	
43197	**FB**	P	EFPC	OO	
43198	**FB**	FG	EFPC	OO	Oxfordshire 2007

Class 43/2. Rebuilt East Coast, CrossCountry and Grand Central power cars. Power cars have been renumbered by adding 200 to their original number or 400 to their original number (Grand Central) except 43123 which became 43423.

43206	(43006)	**NX**	A	IECP	EC	
43207	(43007)	**XC**	A	EHPC	EC	
43208	(43008)	**NX**	A	IECP	EC	Lincolnshire Echo
43238	(43038)	**NX**	A	IECP	EC	
43239	(43039)	**NX**	A	IECP	EC	
43251	(43051)	**NX**	P	IECP	EC	
43257	(43057)	**NX**	P	IECP	EC	
43272	(43072)	**EC**	P	IECP	EC	
43274	(43074)	**EC**	P	IECP	EC	
43277	(43077)	**NX**	P	IECP	EC	
43285	(43085)	**XC**	P	EHPC	EC	
43290	(43090)	**EC**	P	IECP	EC	mtu fascination of power
43295	(43095)	**NX**	A	IECP	EC	
43296	(43096)	**EC**	A	IECP	EC	
43299	(43099)	**NX**	P	IECP	EC	
43300	(43100)	**EC**	P	IECP	EC	Craigentinny
43301	(43101)	**XC**	P	EHPC	EC	
43302	(43102)	**EC**	P	IECP	EC	
43303	(43103)	**XC**	P	EHPC	EC	
43304	(43104)	**XC**	A	EHPC	EC	
43305	(43105)	**NX**	A	IECP	EC	
43306	(43106)	**NX**	A	IECP	EC	

43307 (43107)	**NX**	A	IECP	EC	
43308 (43108)	**EC**	A	IECP	EC	
43309 (43109)	**NX**	A	IECP	EC	
43310 (43110)	**NX**	A	IECP	EC	
43311 (43111)	**EC**	A	IECP	EC	
43312 (43112)	**NX**	A	IECP	EC	
43313 (43113)	**NX**	A	IECP	EC	
43314 (43114)	**EC**	A	IECP	EC	
43315 (43115)	**EC**	A	IECP	EC	
43316 (43116)	**NX**	A	IECP	EC	
43317 (43117)	**NX**	A	IECP	EC	
43318 (43118)	**NX**	A	IECP	EC	
43319 (43119)	**NX**	A	IECP	EC	
43320 (43120)	**NX**	A	IECP	EC	
43321 (43121)	**XC**	P	EHPC	EC	
43357 (43157)	**XC**	P	EHPC	EC	
43366 (43166)	**XC**	A	EHPC	EC	
43367 (43167)	**NX**	A	IECP	EC	DELTIC 50 1955–2005
43378 (43178)	**XC**	A	EHPC	EC	
43384 (43184)	**XC**	A	EHPC	EC	
43423 (43123) †	**GC**	A	GCHP	HT	'VALENTA' 1972–2010
43465 (43065) †	**GC**	A	GCHP	HT	
43467 (43067) †	**GC**	A	GCHP	HT	
43468 (43068) †	**GC**	A	GCHP	HT	
43480 (43080) †	**GC**	A	GCHP	HT	
43484 (43084) †	**GC**	A	GCHP	HT	PETER FOX 1942–2011 PLATFORM 5

CLASS 47 BR/BRUSH/SULZER Co-Co

Built: 1963–67 by Brush Traction, at Loughborough or by BR at Crewe Works.
Engine: Sulzer 12LDA28C of 1920 kW (2580 hp) at 750 rpm.
Main Generator: Brush TG160-60 Mk4 or TM172-50 Mk1.
Traction Motors: Brush TM64-68 Mk1 or Mk1A.
Maximum Tractive Effort: 267 kN (60000 lbf).
Continuous Tractive Effort: 133 kN (30000 lbf) at 26 mph.
Power At Rail: 1550 kW (2080 hp). **Train Brakes**: Air.
Brake Force: 61 t. **Dimensions**: 19.38 x 2.79 m.
Weight: 111.5–120.6 t. **Wheel Diameter**: 1143 mm.
Design Speed: 95 mph.
Maximum Speed: 95 mph (* 75 mph).
Fuel Capacity: 3273 (+ 5887). **RA**: 6 or 7.
Train Supply: Not equipped.
Multiple Working: m Green Circle (operational locos only).

Originally numbered in series D1100–D1111, D1500–D1999 but not in order.

Non-standard liveries/numbering:

47270 Also carries number D1971.
47773 Also carries number D1755.
47812 Also carries number D1916.

47815 Also carries number D1748.
47829 "Police" livery of white with a broad red band outlined in yellow.
47853 "XP64 blue" with red cabside panels. Also carries number D1733.

Class 47/0 (Dual-braked locos) or Class 47/2 (Air-braked locos). Standard Design. Details as above.

47194	a+	**F**	WC	MBDL	CS (S)	
47236	+	**FE**	WC	MBDL	CS (S)	
47237	x+	**WC**	WC	MBDL	CS	
47245	x+m	**WC**	WC	MBDL	CS	
47270	a+	**B**	PO	MBDL	CS	SWIFT

Class 47/3 (Dual-braked locos) or Class 47/2 (Air-braked locos).
Details as Class 47/0 except: **Weight**: 113.7 t.

47355	am+	**WC**	WC	MBDL	CS (S)	
47368	x	**F**	WC	MBDL	CS (S)	
47375	+m	**B**	NS	NRLO	BO	

Class 47/4. Electric Train Supply equipment.
Details as Class 47/0 except:

Weight: 120.4–125.1 t.
Fuel Capacity: 3273 (+ 5537) litres.
Train Supply: Electric. ETH 66.
RA: 7.

47492	x	**RX**	WC	MBDL	CS (S)	
47500	x	**WC**	WC	MBDL	CS	
47501	xm+	**DS**	DR	XHAC	KM	Craftsman
47526	x	**BL**	WC	MBDL	CS (S)	
47580	x	**BL**	47	MBDL	TM	County of Essex

Class 47/7. Previously fitted with an older form of TDM.

Details as Class 47/4 except:
Weight: 118.7 t.
Fuel Capacity: 5887 litres.
Maximum Speed: 100 mph.

47709	xm	**DS**	DR	XHHP	ZG (S)	
47712	xm	**DS**	DR	XHSS	CR (S)	Pride of Carlisle

Class 47/7. Former Railnet dedicated locos. All have twin fuel tanks.

47727	m	**CS**	CS	COLO	WH	Rebecca
47739	m	**CS**	CS	COLO	WH	Robin of Templecombe
47746		**RX**	WC	MBDL	CS (S)	
47747		**E**	DR	XHHP	CD (S)	
47749	m	**CS**	CS	COLO	WH	Demelza
47760	x	**WC**	WC	MBDL	CS	
47768		**RX**	WC	MBDL	CS (S)	
47769		**V**	RV	RTLO	CD (S)	Resolve
47772	x	**RX**	WC	MBDL	CS (S)	
47773	x	**GG**	70	MBDL	TM	
47776	x	**RX**	WC	MBDL	CS (S)	
47786		**WC**	WC	MBDL	CS	Roy Castle OBE
47787		**WC**	WC	MBDL	CS	Windsor Castle
47790	m	**VN**	DR	XHAC	KM	Galloway Princess

47791		**DS**	DR	XHHP	BH (S)	

Class 47/4 continued. RA6. Most fitted with extended-range fuel tanks (+).

47798		**RP**	NM	MBDL	YK	Prince William
47802	+m	**DS**	DR	XHAC	KM	Pride of Cumbria
47804		**WC**	WC	MBDL	CS	
47805	+m	**DS**	DR	XHHP	BH (S)	
47810	+m	**DS**	DR	XHAC	KM	Peter Bath MBE 1927–2006
47811	+	**GL**	FL	DFLH	BA	
47812	+m	**GG**	RV	RTLO	CP	
47813	+m	**CD**	DR	XHHP	ZG (S)	
47815	+m	**GG**	RV	RTLO	CP	GREAT WESTERN
47816	+	**GL**	FL	DFLH	BA (S)	
47818	+	**DS**	DR	XHAC	KM	
47826	+	**WC**	WC	MBDL	CS	
47828	+m	**DS**	DR	XHAC	KM	
47829	+	**0**	HN	HNRS	LM (S)	
47830	+	**GL**	FL	DFLH	BH (S)	
47832	+m	**VN**	DR	XHAC	KM	Solway Princess
47839	+m	**RV**	DR	XHHP	CR (S)	
47841	+	**DS**	DR	XHAC	KM	
47843	+m	**RV**	RV	RTLO	CP	VULCAN
47847	+m	**BL**	RV	RTLO	EH (S)	
47848	+m	**RV**	RV	RTLO	CP	TITAN STAR
47851	+	**WC**	WC	MBDL	CS	
47853	+m	**0**	DR	XHHP	ZG (S)	
47854	+	**WC**	WC	MBDL	CS	

CLASS 50 ENGLISH ELECTRIC Co-Co

Built: 1967–68 by English Electric at Vulcan Foundry, Newton-le-Willows.
Engine: English Electric 16CVST of 2010 kW (2700 hp) at 850 rpm.
Main Generator: English Electric 840/4B.
Traction Motors: English Electric 538/5A.
Maximum Tractive Effort: 216 kN (48500 lbf).
Continuous Tractive Effort: 147 kN (33000 lbf) at 23.5 mph.
Power At Rail: 1540 kW (2070 hp).
Brake Force: 59 t.
Weight: 116.9 t.
Design Speed: 105 mph.
Fuel Capacity: 4796 litres.
Train Supply: Electric, index 61.
Train Brakes: Air & vacuum.
Dimensions: 20.88 x 2.78 m.
Wheel Diameter: 1092 mm.
Maximum Speed: 90 mph.
RA: 6.
Multiple Working: Orange Square.

Originally numbered D444 & D449.

50044	**B**	50	CFOL	CF	Exeter
50049	**BL**	50	CFOL	CF	Defiance

CLASS 52 BR/MAYBACH C-C

Built: 1961–64 by BR at Swindon Works.
Engine: Two Maybach MD655 of 1007 kW (1350 hp) at 1500 rpm.
Transmission: Hydraulic. Voith L630rV.
Maximum Tractive Effort: 297 kN (66700 lbf).
Continuous Tractive Effort: 201 kN (45200 lbf) at 14.5 mph.
Power At Rail: 1490 kW (2000 hp). **Train Brakes**: Air & vacuum.
Brake Force: 83 t. **Dimensions**: 20.7 m x 2.78 m.
Weight: 110 t. **Wheel Diameter**: 1092 mm.
Design Speed: 90 mph. **Maximum Speed**: 90 mph.
Fuel Capacity: 3900 litres. **RA**: 6.
Train Supply: Steam. **Multiple Working**: Not equipped.

Never allocated a number in the 1972 number series.

Registered on TOPS as No. 89416.

D1015 **M** DT MBDL TM WESTERN CHAMPION

CLASS 55 ENGLISH ELECTRIC Co-Co

Built: 1961 by English Electric at Vulcan Foundry, Newton-le-Willows.
Engine: Two Napier-Deltic D18-25 of 1230 kW (1650 hp) each at 1500 rpm.
Main Generators: Two English Electric 829/1A.
Traction Motors: English Electric 538/A.
Maximum Tractive Effort: 222 kN (50000 lbf).
Continuous Tractive Effort: 136 kN (30500 lbf) at 32.5 mph.
Power At Rail: 1969 kW (2640 hp). **Train Brakes**: Air & vacuum.
Brake Force: 51 t. **Dimensions**: 21.18 x 2.68 m.
Weight: 100 t. **Wheel Diameter**: 1092 mm.
Design Speed: 105 mph. **Maximum Speed**: 100 mph.
Fuel Capacity: 3755 litres. **RA**: 5.
Train Supply: Electric, index 66. **Multiple Working**: Not equipped.

Originally numbered D9000.

Registered on TOPS as No. 89500.

55022 **B** MW ELRD BQ ROYAL SCOTS GREY

CLASS 56 BRUSH/BR/RUSTON Co-Co

Built: 1976–84 by Electroputere at Craiova, Romania (as sub contractors for Brush) or BREL at Doncaster or Crewe Works.
Engine: Ruston Paxman 16RK3CT of 2460 kW (3250 hp) at 900 rpm.
Main Alternator: Brush BA1101A.
Traction Motors: Brush TM73-62.
Maximum Tractive Effort: 275 kN (61800 lbf).
Continuous Tractive Effort: 240 kN (53950 lbf) at 16.8 mph.
Power At Rail: 1790 kW (2400 hp). **Train Brakes**: Air.
Brake Force: 60 t. **Dimensions**: 19.36 x 2.79 m.
Weight: 126 t. **Wheel Diameter**: 1143 mm.

Design Speed: 80 mph.
Fuel Capacity: 5228 litres.
Train Supply: Not equipped.
Maximum Speed: 80 mph.
RA: 7.
Multiple Working: Red Diamond.

Note: All equipped with Slow Speed Control.

Non-standard liveries:

56311 Light grey with yellow cabsides.
56312 Purple with yellow cabsides & green lining.

56006	**B**	X	WNSO	BH (S)	
56007	**FER**	PO	WNSO	CE (S)	
56018	**FER**	PO	WNSO	WT (S)	
56031	**FER**	X	WNSO	CD (S)	
56032	**FER**	X	WNSO	CD (S)	
56037	**E**	X	WNSO	CD (S)	
56038	**FER**	X	WNSO	CD (S)	
56049	**FER**	X	WNSO	CD (S)	
56051	**FER**	X	WNSO	CD (S)	
56058	**FER**	X	WNSO	CD (S)	
56060	**FER**	X	WNSO	CD (S)	
56065	**FER**	X	WNSO	CD (S)	
56069	**FER**	X	WNSO	CD (S)	
56074	**FER**	X	WNSO	CD (S)	
56077	**LH**	X	WNSO	CD (S)	
56078	**FER**	X	WNSO	CD (S)	
56081	**FER**	X	WNSO	CD (S)	
56087	**FER**	X	WNSO	CD (S)	
56090	**FER**	X	WNSO	CD (S)	
56091	**FER**	BA	WNSO	BS (S)	
56094	**FER**	X	WNSO	CD (S)	
56096	**FER**	X	WNSO	CD (S)	
56101	**BL**	EP		BH (S)	Frank Hornby
56103	**FER**	BA	WNSO	CD (S)	
56104	**FER**	X	WNSO	CD (S)	
56105	**FER**	X	WNSO	CD (S)	
56106	**FER**	X	WNSO	CD (S)	
56113	**FER**	X	WNSO	CD (S)	
56114	**E**	BA	MBDL	WH (S)	
56115	**FER**	EP	WNSO	BS (S)	
56117	**FER**	EP	WNSO	BS (S)	
56128	**F**	BA	MBDL	WF (S)	

56301	(56045)	**FA**	56	MBDL	BO	
56302	(56124)	**FA**	ED	MBDL	BO	
56303	(56125)	**DC**	BA	HTLX	WH	
56311	(56057)	**0**	BA	HTLX	WF	
56312	(56003)	**0**	BA	HTLX	WF	ARTEMIS

CLASS 57 BRUSH/GM Co-Co

Built: 1964–65 by Brush Traction at Loughborough or BR at Crewe Works as Class 47. Rebuilt 1997–2004 by Brush Traction at Loughborough.
Engine: General Motors 12 645 E3 of 1860 kW (2500 hp) at 904 rpm.
Main Alternator: Brush BA1101D.
Traction Motors: Brush TM64-68 Mark 1 or Mark 1a.
Maximum Tractive Effort: 244.5 kN (55000 lbf).
Continuous Tractive Effort: 140 kN (31500 lbf) at ?? mph.
Power at Rail: 1507 kW (2025 hp).
Train Brakes: Air.
Brake Force: 80 t.
Dimensions: 19.38 x 2.79 m.
Weight: 120.6 t.
Wheel Diameter: 1143 mm.
Design Speed: 75 mph.
Maximum Speed: 75 mph.
Fuel Capacity: 5550 litres.
RA: 6
Train Supply: Not equipped.
Multiple Working: † DRS system.

Class 57/0. No Train Supply Equipment. Rebuilt 1998–2000.

57001	(47356)		**WC**	WC	MBDL	CS	
57002	(47322)	†	**DS**	P	XHCK	KM	
57003	(47317)	†	**DS**	P	XHCK	KM	
57004	(47347)	†	**DS**	DR	XHCK	KM	
57005	(47350)		**AZ**	WC	MBDL	CS (S)	
57006	(47187)		**AZ**	WC	MBDL	CS (S)	
57007	(47332)	†	**DS**	P	XHCK	KM	
57008	(47060)	†	**DS**	P	XHCK	KM	Telford International Railfreight Park June 2009
57009	(47079)	†	**DS**	P	XHCK	KM	
57010	(47231)	†	**DS**	P	XHSS	CR (S)	
57011	(47329)	†	**DS**	P	XHCK	KM	
57012	(47204)	†	**DS**	P	XHSS	KM (S)	

Class 57/3. Electric Train Supply Equipment. Virgin Trains locos. Rebuilt 2002–04. Details as Class 57/0 except:

Engine: General Motors 12645F3B of 2050 kW (2750 hp) at 954 rpm.
Main Alternator: Brush BA1101F (recovered from a Class 56) or Brush BA1101G.
Fuel Capacity: 5887 litres.
Train Supply: Electric, index 100.
Design Speed: 95 mph.
Maximum Speed: 95 mph.
Brake Force: 60 t.
Weight: 117 t.

Note: 57313–316 are on sub-lease to Arriva Trains Wales and are used on the Holyhead–Cardiff loco-hauled service.

Non-standard livery: 57313 & 57316 All over blue.

57301	(47845)	d	**Y**	NR	QADD	HQ	
57302	(47827)	d	**VT**	P	IWCA	MA	VIRGIL TRACY
57303	(47705)	d	**Y**	NR	QADD	HQ	
57304	(47807)	d	**VT**	P	IWCA	MA	GORDON TRACY
57305	(47822)	d	**Y**	NR	QADD	HQ	
57306	(47814)	d	**Y**	NR	QADD	HQ	
57307	(47225)	d	**VT**	P	IWCA	MA	LADY PENELOPE
57308	(47846)	d	**VT**	P	IWCA	MA	TIN TIN

57309 (47806) d	**VT**	P	IWCA	MA	BRAINS
57310 (47831) d	**VT**	NR	QADD	HQ	
57311 (47817) d	**VT**	P	IWCA	MA	PARKER
57312 (47330) d	**Y**	NR	QADD	HQ	
57313 (47371) d	**0**	P	IWCA	MA	
57314 (47372) d	**AB**	P	IWCA	MA	
57315 (47234) d	**AB**	P	IWCA	MA	
57316 (47290) d	**0**	P	IWCA	MA	

Class 57/6. Electric Train Supply Equipment. Prototype ETS loco. Rebuilt 2001. Details as Class 57/0 except:

Main Alternator: Brush BA1101E.
Train Supply: Electric, index 95.
Design Speed: 95 mph.
Brake Force: 60 t.
Fuel Capacity: 3273 litres.
Weight: 113t.
Maximum Speed: 95 mph.

57601 (47825)	**WC**	WC	MBDL	CS

Class 57/6. Electric Train Supply Equipment. First Great Western locos. Rebuilt 2004. Details as Class 57/3.

57602 (47337)	**FB**	P	EFOO	OO	Restormel Castle
57603 (47349)	**FB**	P	EFOO	OO	Tintagel Castle
57604 (47209)	**GW**	P	EFOO	OO	PENDENNIS CASTLE
57605 (47206)	**FB**	P	EFOO	OO	Totnes Castle

CLASS 58 BREL/RUSTON Co-Co

Built: 1983–87 by BREL at Doncaster Works.
Engine: Ruston Paxman 12RK3ACT of 2460 kW (3300 hp) at 1000 rpm.
Main Alternator: Brush BA1101B.
Traction Motors: Brush TM73-62.
Maximum Tractive Effort: 275 kN (61800 lbf).
Continuous Tractive Effort: 240 kN (53950 lbf) at 17.4 mph.
Power At Rail: 1780 kW (2387 hp).
Train Brakes: Air.
Brake Force: 60 t.
Dimensions: 19.13 x 2.72 m.
Weight: 130 t.
Wheel Diameter: 1120 mm.
Design Speed: 80 mph.
Maximum Speed: 80 mph.
Fuel Capacity: 4214 litres.
RA: 7.
Train Supply: Not equipped.
Multiple Working: Red Diamond.

Notes: All equipped with Slow Speed Control.

Class 58s exported for use abroad are listed in section 1.6 of this book.

58002	**ML**	DB	WNTS	EH (S)
58008	**ML**	DB	WNTS	EH (S)
58012	**F**	DB	WNTS	TO (S)
58017	**F**	DB	WNTS	EH (S)
58022	**F**	DB	WNTS	CD (S)
58023	**ML**	DB	WNTS	TO (S)
58037	**E**	DB	WNTS	EH (S)
58048	**E**	DB	WNTS	CE (S)

CLASS 59 GENERAL MOTORS Co-Co

Built: 1985 (59001/002/004) or 1989 (59005) by General Motors, La Grange, Illinois, USA or 1990 (59101–104), 1994 (59201) and 1995 (59202–206) by General Motors, London, Ontario, Canada.
Engine: General Motors 16-645E3C two stroke of 2460 kW (3300 hp) at 904 rpm.
Main Alternator: General Motors AR11 MLD-D14A.
Traction Motors: General Motors D77B.
Maximum Tractive Effort: 506 kN (113 550 lbf).
Continuous Tractive Effort: 291 kN (65 300 lbf) at 14.3 mph.
Power At Rail: 1889 kW (2533 hp).
Brake Force: 69 t.
Weight: 121 t.
Design Speed: 60 (* 75) mph.
Fuel Capacity: 4546 litres.
Train Supply: Not equipped.
Train Brakes: Air.
Dimensions: 21.35 x 2.65 m.
Wheel Diameter: 1067 mm.
Maximum Speed: 60 (* 75) mph.
RA: 7.
Multiple Working: AAR System.

Class 59/0. Owned by Aggregate Industries.

59001	**AI**	AI	XYPO	MD	YEOMAN ENDEAVOUR
59002	**FY**	AI	XYPO	MD	ALAN J DAY
59004	**FY**	AI	XYPO	MD	PAUL A HAMMOND
59005	**AI**	AI	XYPO	MD	KENNETH J PAINTER

Class 59/1. Owned by Hanson Quarry Products.

59101	**HA**	HA	XYPA	MD	Village of Whatley
59102	**HA**	HA	XYPA	MD	Village of Chantry
59103	**HA**	HA	XYPA	MD	Village of Mells
59104	**HA**	HA	XYPA	MD	Village of Great Elm

Class 59/2. Owned by DB Schenker.

59201 *	**E**	DB	WDAK	MD	Vale of York
59202 *	**E**	DB	WNTR	MD	Vale of White Horse
59203 *	**E**	DB	WDAK	MD	Vale of Pickering
59204 *	**E**	DB	WDAK	MD	Vale of Glamorgan
59205 *b	**E**	DB	WDAK	MD	L Keith McNair
59206 *b	**DB**	DB	WDAK	MD	John F. Yeoman Rail Pioneer

CLASS 60 BRUSH/MIRRLEES Co-Co

Built: 1989–93 by Brush Traction at Loughborough.
Engine: Mirrlees 8MB275T of 2310 kW (3100 hp) at 1000 rpm.
Main Alternator: Brush BA1006A.
Traction Motors: Brush TM2161A.
Maximum Tractive Effort: 500 kN (106500 lbf).
Continuous Tractive Effort: 336 kN (71570 lbf) at 17.4 mph.
Power At Rail: 1800 kW (2415 hp).
Brake Force: 74 (+ 62) t.
Weight: 129 (+ 131) t.
Design Speed: 62 mph.
Train Brakes: Air.
Dimensions: 21.34 x 2.64 m.
Wheel Diameter: 1118 mm.
Maximum Speed: 60 mph.

Fuel Capacity: 4546 (+ 5225) litres. **RA**: 8.
Train Supply: Not equipped. **Multiple Working**: Within class.

Important note, DB Schenker Fleet Management Unit: As all operational Class 60s are effectively treated as "common user" by DB Schenker, and allocated to operational pools depending on which duties they are on at the time, all operational locos are shown in the WFMU Fleet Management pool here. Details of the other individual pools can be found in the codes section of this book.

Notes: All equipped with Slow Speed Control.

* Refurbished DB Schenker locos.

60034, 60064, 60066, 60072, 60073, 60077, 60082, 60084 and 60090 carry their names on one side only.

60500 originally carried the number 60016.

Advertising/promotional liveries:

60040 Territorial Army Centenary (maroon).
60074 Teenage Cancer Trust (light blue).
60099 Tata Steel (silver).

60001		**E**	DB	WNTS	TO (S)	The Railway Observer
60002	+	**E**	DB	WNTS	CD (S)	High Peak
60003	+	**E**	DB	WNWX	TO (S)	FREIGHT TRANSPORT ASSOCIATION
60004	+	**E**	DB	WNTS	TO (S)	
60005	+	**E**	DB	WNTS	TO (S)	
60006		**CU**	DB	WNTS	TO (S)	
60007	+*	**DB**	DB	WFMU	TO	The Spirit of Tom Kendell
60008		**E**	DB	WNTS	TO (S)	Sir William McAlpine
60009	+	**E**	DB	WNTS	TO (S)	
60010	+	**E**	DB	WNWX	TO (S)	
60011		**DB**	DB	WFMU	TO	
60012	+	**E**	DB	WNWX	TO (S)	
60013		**EG**	DB	WNTS	TO (S)	Robert Boyle
60014		**EG**	DB	WNTS	TO (S)	
60015	+	**EG**	DB	WNWX	TO (S)	Bow Fell
60017	+	**E**	DB	WNWX	TO (S)	Shotton Works Centenary Year 1996
60018		**E**	DB	WNTS	TO (S)	
60019		**E**	DB	WNWX	TO (S)	PATHFINDER TOURS 30 YEARS OF RAILTOURING 1973–2003
60020	+	**E**	DB	WNTS	TO (S)	
60021	+	**E**	DB	WNWX	TO (S)	
60022	+	**E**	DB	WNTS	TO (S)	
60023	+	**E**	DB	WNTS	TO (S)	
60024		**E**	DB	WFMU	TO	
60025	+	**E**	DB	WNTS	TO (S)	
60026	+	**E**	DB	WNTS	TO (S)	
60027	+	**E**	DB	WNTS	TO (S)	
60028	+	**EG**	DB	WNTS	CD (S)	John Flamsteed
60029		**E**	DB	WNTS	CD (S)	Clitheroe Castle
60030	+	**E**	DB	WNTS	TO (S)	

60031		**E**	DB	WNTS	TO (S)	
60032		**F**	DB	WNWX	TO (S)	
60033	+	**CU**	DB	WNWX	TO (S)	Tees Steel Express
60034		**EG**	DB	WNTS	TO (S)	Carnedd Llewelyn
60035		**E**	DB	WNTS	TO (S)	
60036		**E**	DB	WNTS	TO (S)	GEFCO
60037	+	**E**	DB	WNWX	TO (S)	
60038	+	**E**	DB	WNTS	CD (S)	AvestaPolarit
60039		**E**	DB	WNTS	CE (S)	
60040		**AL**	DB	WNWX	TO (S)	The Territorial Army Centenary
60041	+	**E**	DB	WNTS	TO (S)	
60042		**E**	DB	WNTS	TO (S)	
60043		**E**	DB	WNTS	CD (S)	
60044		**ML**	DB	WNTS	TO (S)	
60045		**E**	DB	WFMU	TO	The Permanent Way Institution
60046	+	**EG**	DB	WNTS	CD (S)	William Wilberforce
60047		**E**	DB	WNTS	CD (S)	
60048		**E**	DB	WNTS	TO (S)	
60049		**E**	DB	WFMU	TO	
60050		**E**	DB	WNWX	TO (S)	
60051	+	**E**	DB	WNTS	TO (S)	
60052	+	**E**	DB	WNTS	TO (S)	Glofa Twr – The last deep mine in Wales – Tower Colliery
60053		**E**	DB	WNTS	TO (S)	
60054	+*	**DB**	DB	WFMU	TO	
60055	+	**EG**	DB	WNTS	CD (S)	Thomas Barnardo
60056	+	**EG**	DB	WNTS	CD (S)	William Beveridge
60057		**EG**	DB	WNWX	TO (S)	Adam Smith
60058	+	**E**	DB	WNTS	TO (S)	
60059	+	**LH**	DB	WNWX	TO (S)	
60060		**EG**	DB	WNWX	TO (S)	
60061		**F**	DB	WNTS	TO (S)	
60062		**E**	DB	WNTS	TO (S)	
60063		**EG**	DB	WNWX	TO (S)	
60064	+	**EG**	DB	WNWX	TO (S)	Back Tor
60065		**E**	DB	WFMU	TO	Spirit of JAGUAR
60066		**EG**	DB	WNTS	TO (S)	John Logie Baird
60067		**EG**	DB	WNWX	TO (S)	
60068		**EG**	DB	WNTS	TO (S)	
60069		**E**	DB	WNWX	TO (S)	Slioch
60070	+	**F**	DB	WNTS	TO (S)	John Loudon McAdam
60071	+	**E**	DB	WFMU	TO	Ribblehead Viaduct
60072		**EG**	DB	WNWX	TO (S)	Cairn Toul
60073		**EG**	DB	WNTS	TO (S)	Cairn Gorm
60074	*	**AL**	DB	WFMU	TO	Teenage Spirit
60075		**E**	DB	WNTS	TO (S)	
60076		**EG**	DB	WNTS	CD (S)	
60077	+	**EG**	DB	WNWX	TO (S)	Canisp
60078		**ML**	DB	WNTS	TO (S)	
60079		**EG**	DB	WNWX	TO (S)	
60080	+	**E**	DB	WNTS	TO (S)	

60081 +	**GW**	DB	WNTS	TO (S)	
60082	**EG**	DB	WNTS	CD (S)	Mam Tor
60083	**E**	DB	WNTS	TO (S)	
60084	**EG**	DB	WNTS	TO (S)	Cross Fell
60085	**E**	DB	WNWX	TO (S)	MINI Pride of Oxford
60086	**EG**	DB	WNWX	TO (S)	
60087	**E**	DB	WNWX	TO (S)	
60088	**F**	DB	WNWX	TO (S)	
60089 +	**E**	DB	WNTS	TO (S)	
60090 +	**EG**	DB	WNTS	TO (S)	Quinag
60091 +*	**DB**	DB	WFMU	TO	
60092 +	**EG**	DB	WNWX	CD (S)	Reginald Munns
60093	**E**	DB	WNTS	TO (S)	
60094	**E**	DB	WNTS	TO (S)	Rugby Flyer
60095	**EG**	DB	WNTS	CD (S)	
60096 +	**E**	DB	WNTS	TO (S)	
60097 +	**E**	DB	WNTS	TO (S)	
60098 +	**E**	DB	WNTS	TO (S)	
60099	**AL**	DB	WFMU	TO	
60100	**E**	DB	WNTS	TO (S)	
60500	**E**	DB	WNTS	TO (S)	

CLASS 66 GENERAL MOTORS/EMD Co-Co

Built: 1998–2008 by General Motors/EMD, London, Ontario, Canada (Model JT42CWR (low emission locos Model JT42CWRM)).
Engine: General Motors 12N-710G3B-EC two stroke of 2385 kW (3200 hp) at 904 rpm.
Main Alternator: General Motors AR8/CA6.
Traction Motors: General Motors D43TR.
Maximum Tractive Effort: 409 kN (92000 lbf).
Continuous Tractive Effort: 260 kN (58390 lbf) at 15.9 mph.
Power At Rail: 1850 kW (2480 hp).
Train Brakes: Air.
Brake Force: 68 t.
Dimensions: 21.35 x 2.64 m.
Weight: 127 t.
Wheel Diameter: 1120 mm.
Design Speed: 87.5 mph.
Maximum Speed: 75 mph (* 60 mph).
Fuel Capacity: 6550 litres.
RA: 7.
Train Supply: Not equipped.
Multiple Working: AAR System.

Important note, DB Schenker Fleet Management Unit: As all DB Schenker Class 66s are effectively now treated as "common user" by DB Schenker, and allocated to operational pools depending on which duties they are on at the time, all operational locos are shown in the WFMU Fleet Management pool here. Details of the other individual pools can be found in the codes section of this book.

Notes: All equipped with Slow Speed Control.

Class 66s previously used in the UK but now in use abroad are listed in section 1.6 of this book. Some of the 60 DBS 66s moved to France return to Great Britain from time to time, those here at the time of writing are: 66010/071/218/249.

Advertising livery: 66048 Stobart Rail (two tone blue & white).

Class 66 delivery dates. The Class 66 design evolved over a 10-year period with over 400 delivered. For clarity the delivery dates (by year) for each batch of locos is as follows:

66001–66250	EWS (now DB Schenker). 1998–2000 (some now in use in France or Poland)
66301–66305	Fastline. 2008. Now used by DRS.
66401–66410	DRS. 2003. Now in use with GB Railfreight or Colas Rail and renumbered 66733–737 and 66742–746.
66411–66420	DRS. 2006. Now leased by Freightliner (some being exported to Poland).
66421–66430	DRS. 2007
66431–66434	DRS. 2008
66501–66505	Freightliner. 1999
66506–66520	Freightliner. 2000
66521–66525	Freightliner. 2000 (66521 since scrapped).
66526–66531	Freightliner. 2001
66532–66537	Freightliner. 2001
66538–66543	Freightliner. 2001
66544–66553	Freightliner. 2001
66554	Freightliner. 2002*
66555–66566	Freightliner. 2002
66567–66574	Freightliner. 2003. 66573–574 now used by Colas Rail and renumbered 66846–847.
66575–66577	Freightliner. 2004. Now used by Colas Rail and renumbered 66848–850.
66578–66581	Freightliner. 2005. Now used by GBRf and renumbered 66738–741.
66582–66594	Freightliner. 2007 (66582/583/584/586 exported to Poland).
66595–66599	Freightliner. 2008
66601–66606	Freightliner. 2000
66607–66612	Freightliner. 2002 (66607/609/611/612 exported to Poland)
66613–66618	Freightliner. 2003
66619–66622	Freightliner. 2005
66623–66625	Freightliner. 2007 (66624/625 exported to Poland).
66701–66707	GB Railfreight. 2001
66708–66712	GB Railfreight. 2002
66713–66717	GB Railfreight. 2003
66718–66722	GB Railfreight. 2006
66723–66727	GB Railfreight. 2006
66728–66732	GB Railfreight. 2008
66951–66952	Freightliner. 2004
66953–66957	Freightliner. 2008

* Replacement for 66521, written off in the Great Heck accident in 2001.

Class 66/0. DB Schenker-operated locos.

Notes: All fitted with Swinghead Automatic "Buckeye" Combination Couplers except 66001 and 66002.

† Fitted with additional lights and drawgear for Lickey banking duties.

* Locos originally modified for use in France and returned to Britain. Maximum speed 60 mph.

t Fitted with tripcocks for working over London Underground tracks between Harrow-on-the-Hill and Amersham.

66001 t	**E**	A	WFMU	TO	
66002	**E**	A	WFMU	TO	Lafarge Quorn
66003	**E**	A	WFMU	TO	
66004	**E**	A	WFMU	TO	
66005	**E**	A	WFMU	TO	
66006	**E**	A	WFMU	TO	
66007	**E**	A	WFMU	TO	
66008	**E**	A	WFMU	TO	
66009	**E**	A	WFMU	TO	
66010 *	**E**	A	WBES	TO	
66011	**E**	A	WFMU	TO	
66012	**E**	A	WFMU	TO	
66013	**E**	A	WNTR	TO	
66014	**E**	A	WFMU	TO	
66015	**E**	A	WFMU	TO	
66016	**E**	A	WFMU	TO	
66017 t	**E**	A	WFMU	TO	
66018	**E**	A	WFMU	TO	
66019 t	**E**	A	WFMU	TO	
66020	**E**	A	WFMU	TO	
66021	**E**	A	WFMU	TO	
66023	**E**	A	WFMU	TO	
66024	**E**	A	WFMU	TO	
66025	**E**	A	WFMU	TO	
66027	**E**	A	WFMU	TO	
66030	**E**	A	WFMU	TO	
66031	**E**	A	WFMU	TO	
66034	**E**	A	WFMU	TO	
66035	**E**	A	WFMU	TO	
66037	**E**	A	WFMU	TO	
66039	**E**	A	WFMU	TO	
66040	**E**	A	WNTR	TO	
66041	**E**	A	WFMU	TO	
66043	**E**	A	WFMU	TO	
66044	**E**	A	WFMU	TO	
66046	**E**	A	WFMU	TO	
66047	**E**	A	WFMU	TO	
66048	**AL**	A	WNTS	TO (S)	James the Engine
66050	**E**	A	WFMU	TO	EWS Energy
66051	**E**	A	WFMU	TO	
66053	**E**	A	WFMU	TO	
66054	**E**	A	WFMU	TO	
66055 †	**E**	A	WNTR	TO	
66056 †	**E**	A	WFMU	TO	
66057 †	**E**	A	WFMU	TO	
66058 †	**E**	A	WFMU	TO	

66059	†	**E**	A	WFMU	TO	
66060		**E**	A	WFMU	TO	
66061		**E**	A	WFMU	TO	
66063		**E**	A	WFMU	TO	
66065		**E**	A	WFMU	TO	
66066		**E**	A	WFMU	TO	
66067		**E**	A	WFMU	TO	
66068		**E**	A	WFMU	TO	
66069		**E**	A	WFMU	TO	
66070		**E**	A	WFMU	TO	
66071	*	**E**	A	WBES	TO	
66074		**E**	A	WFMU	TO	
66075		**E**	A	WFMU	TO	
66076		**E**	A	WFMU	TO	
66077		**E**	A	WFMU	TO	Benjamin Gimbert G.C.
66078		**E**	A	WFMU	TO	
66079		**E**	A	WFMU	TO	James Nightall G.C.
66080		**E**	A	WFMU	TO	
66081		**E**	A	WNTR	TO	
66082		**E**	A	WFMU	TO	
66083		**E**	A	WNTR	TO	
66084		**E**	A	WFMU	TO	
66085		**E**	A	WFMU	TO	
66086		**E**	A	WFMU	TO	
66087		**E**	A	WFMU	TO	
66088		**E**	A	WFMU	TO	
66089		**E**	A	WFMU	TO	
66090		**E**	A	WFMU	TO	
66091		**E**	A	WFMU	TO	
66092		**E**	A	WFMU	TO	
66093		**E**	A	WFMU	TO	
66094		**E**	A	WFMU	TO	
66095		**E**	A	WFMU	TO	
66096		**E**	A	WFMU	TO	
66097		**DB**	A	WFMU	TO	
66098		**E**	A	WFMU	TO	
66099	r	**E**	A	WFMU	TO	
66100	r	**E**	A	WFMU	TO	
66101	r	**DB**	A	WNTR	TO	
66102	r	**E**	A	WFMU	TO	
66103	r	**E**	A	WFMU	TO	
66104	r	**E**	A	WFMU	TO	
66105	r	**E**	A	WFMU	TO	
66106	r	**E**	A	WFMU	TO	
66107	r	**E**	A	WFMU	TO	
66108	r	**E**	A	WFMU	TO	
66109		**E**	A	WFMU	TO	
66110	r	**E**	A	WFMU	TO	
66111	r	**E**	A	WFMU	TO	
66112	r	**E**	A	WFMU	TO	
66113	r	**E**	A	WFMU	TO	

66114 r	**E**	A	WFMU	TO	
66115	**E**	A	WFMU	TO	
66116	**E**	A	WFMU	TO	
66117	**E**	A	WFMU	TO	
66118	**E**	A	WFMU	TO	
66119	**E**	A	WFMU	TO	
66120	**E**	A	WFMU	TO	
66121	**E**	A	WFMU	TO	
66122	**E**	A	WFMU	TO	
66124	**E**	A	WFMU	TO	
66125	**E**	A	WFMU	TO	
66126	**E**	A	WFMU	TO	
66127	**E**	A	WFMU	TO	
66128	**E**	A	WFMU	TO	
66129	**E**	A	WFMU	TO	
66130	**E**	A	WFMU	TO	
66131	**E**	A	WFMU	TO	
66132	**E**	A	WFMU	TO	
66133	**E**	A	WFMU	TO	
66134	**E**	A	WFMU	TO	
66135	**E**	A	WFMU	TO	
66136	**E**	A	WFMU	TO	
66137	**E**	A	WFMU	TO	
66138	**E**	A	WFMU	TO	
66139	**E**	A	WFMU	TO	
66140	**E**	A	WFMU	TO	
66141	**E**	A	WFMU	TO	
66142	**E**	A	WFMU	TO	
66143	**E**	A	WFMU	TO	
66144	**E**	A	WFMU	TO	
66145	**E**	A	WFMU	TO	
66147	**E**	A	WFMU	TO	
66148	**E**	A	WFMU	TO	
66149	**E**	A	WFMU	TO	
66150	**E**	A	WFMU	TO	
66151	**E**	A	WFMU	TO	
66152	**DB**	A	WFMU	TO	Derek Holmes Railway Operator
66154	**E**	A	WFMU	TO	
66155	**E**	A	WFMU	TO	
66156	**E**	A	WFMU	TO	
66158	**E**	A	WFMU	TO	
66160	**E**	A	WFMU	TO	
66161	**E**	A	WFMU	TO	
66162	**E**	A	WFMU	TO	
66164	**E**	A	WFMU	TO	
66165	**E**	A	WFMU	TO	
66167	**E**	A	WFMU	TO	
66168	**E**	A	WFMU	TO	
66169	**E**	A	WFMU	TO	
66170	**E**	A	WFMU	TO	
66171	**E**	A	WFMU	TO	

66172		**E**	A	WNTR	TO	PAUL MELLENEY
66174		**E**	A	WFMU	TO	
66175		**E**	A	WNTR	TO	
66176		**E**	A	WFMU	TO	
66177		**E**	A	WFMU	TO	
66181		**E**	A	WFMU	TO	
66182		**E**	A	WFMU	TO	
66183		**E**	A	WFMU	TO	
66184		**E**	A	WFMU	TO	
66185		**E**	A	WFMU	TO	
66186		**E**	A	WFMU	TO	
66187		**E**	A	WFMU	TO	
66188		**E**	A	WFMU	TO	
66192		**E**	A	WFMU	TO	
66193		**E**	A	WFMU	TO	
66194		**E**	A	WFMU	TO	
66197		**E**	A	WFMU	TO	
66198		**E**	A	WFMU	TO	
66199		**E**	A	WFMU	TO	
66200		**E**	A	WFMU	TO	RAILWAY HERITAGE COMMITTEE
66201		**E**	A	WFMU	TO	
66204		**E**	A	WFMU	TO	
66206		**E**	A	WFMU	TO	
66207		**E**	A	WFMU	TO	
66213		**E**	A	WFMU	TO	
66218	*	**E**	A	WBEI	TO	
66221		**E**	A	WFMU	TO	
66230		**E**	A	WFMU	TO	
66232		**E**	A	WFMU	TO	
66238		**E**	A	WFMU	TO	
66249	*	**E**	A	WBEI	TO	
66250		**E**	A	WFMU	TO	

Class 66/3. Former Fastline-operated loco now operated by DRS. Low emission. Details as Class 66/0 except:

Engine: EMD 12N-710G3B-U2 two stroke of 2420 kW (3245 hp) at 904 rpm.
Traction Motors: General Motors D43TRC.
Fuel Capacity: 5150 litres.

66301	**DS**	BN	XHIM	KM
66302	**DS**	BN	XHIM	KM
66303	**DS**	BN	XHIM	KM
66304	**DS**	BN	XHIM	KM
66305	**DS**	BN	XHIM	KM

66412–434. Low emission. Lloyds Banking Group-owned. Details as Class 66/0 except:

Engine: EMD 12N-710G3B-U2 two stroke of 2420 kW (3245 hp) at 904 rpm.
Traction Motors: General Motors D43TRC.
Fuel Capacity: 5150 litres.

Non-standard liveries: 66412 All over black with a red solebar stripe (formerly Malcolm Rail).
66414 Two tone blue & white (formerly Stobart Rail).

Advertising livery: 66434 Malcolm Rail (blue).

66412	**0**	LY	DHLT	LD (S)
66413	**DS**	LY	DFHG	LD
66414	**0**	LY	DFTZ	LD
66415	**DS**	LY	DFTZ	LD
66416	**DS**	LY	DFTZ	LD
66417	**DS**	LY	DFEP	LD (S)
66418	**DS**	LY	DFTZ	LD
66419	**DS**	LY	DFTZ	LD
66420	**DS**	LY	DFTZ	LD
66421	**DS**	LY	XHIM	KM
66422	**DS**	LY	XHIM	KM
66423	**DS**	LY	XHIM	KM
66424	**DS**	LY	XHIM	KM
66425	**DS**	LY	XHIM	KM
66426	**DS**	LY	XHIM	KM
66427	**DS**	LY	XHIM	KM
66428	**DS**	LY	XHIM	KM
66429	**DS**	LY	XHIM	KM
66430	**DS**	LY	XHIM	KM
66431	**DS**	LY	XHIM	KM
66432	**DS**	LY	XHIM	KM
66433	**DS**	LY	XHIM	KM
66434	**AL**	LY	XHIM	KM

Class 66/5. Freightliner-operated locos. Details as Class 66/0.

Advertising livery: 66522 Shanks Waste (one half of loco Freightliner green and one half Shanks' Waste light green).

66501	**FL**	P	DFGM	LD	Japan 2001
66502	**FL**	P	DFGM	LD	Basford Hall Centenary 2001
66503	**FL**	P	DFGM	LD	The RAILWAY MAGAZINE
66504	**FL**	P	DFGM	LD	
66505	**FL**	P	DFGM	LD	
66506	**FL**	E	DFHH	LD	Crewe Regeneration
66507	**FL**	E	DFHH	LD	
66508	**FL**	E	DFRT	LD	
66509	**FL**	E	DFHH	LD	
66510	**FL**	E	DFRT	LD	
66511	**FL**	E	DFRT	LD	
66512	**FL**	E	DFHH	LD	

66513	**FL**	E	DFHH	LD	
66514	**FL**	E	DFRT	LD	
66515	**FL**	E	DFRT	LD	
66516	**FL**	E	DFGM	LD	
66517	**FL**	E	DFGM	LD	
66518	**FL**	E	DFHH	LD	
66519	**FL**	E	DFHH	LD	
66520	**FL**	E	DFRT	LD	
66522	**AL**	E	DFRT	LD	
66523	**FL**	E	DFRT	LD	
66524	**FL**	E	DFHH	LD	
66525	**FL**	E	DFHH	LD	
66526	**FL**	P	DFHH	LD	Driver Steve Dunn (George)
66527	**FL**	P	DFRT	LD	Don Raider
66528	**FL**	P	DFHH	LD	
66529	**FL**	P	DFHH	LD	
66530	**FL**	P	DFHH	LD	
66531	**FL**	P	DFHH	LD	
66532	**FL**	P	DFGM	LD	P&O Nedlloyd Atlas
66533	**FL**	P	DFGM	LD	Hanjin Express/Senator Express
66534	**FL**	P	DFGM	LD	OOCL Express
66535	**FL**	P	DFGM	LD	
66536	**FL**	P	DFGM	LD	
66537	**FL**	P	DFGM	LD	
66538	**FL**	E	DFIM	LD	
66539	**FL**	E	DFIM	LD	
66540	**FL**	E	DFIM	LD	Ruby
66541	**FL**	E	DFIM	LD	
66542	**FL**	E	DFIM	LD	
66543	**FL**	E	DFIM	LD	
66544	**FL**	P	DFHG	LD	
66545	**FL**	P	DFHG	LD	
66546	**FL**	P	DFHG	LD	
66547	**FL**	P	DFHG	LD	
66548	**FL**	P	DFHG	LD	
66549	**FL**	P	DFHG	LD	
66550	**FL**	P	DFHG	LD	
66551	**FL**	P	DFHG	LD	
66552	**FL**	P	DFHG	LD	Maltby Raider
66553	**FL**	P	DFHG	LD	
66554	**FL**	E	DFHG	LD	
66555	**FL**	E	DFHG	LD	
66556	**FL**	E	DFIM	LD	
66557	**FL**	E	DFHG	LD	
66558	**FL**	E	DFIM	LD	
66559	**FL**	E	DFHG	LD	
66560	**FL**	E	DFHG	LD	
66561	**FL**	E	DFHG	LD	
66562	**FL**	E	DFIM	LD	
66563	**FL**	E	DFIM	LD	
66564	**FL**	E	DFIM	LD	

66565	**FL**	E	DFIM	LD	
66566	**FL**	E	DFIM	LD	
66567	**FL**	E	DFIM	LD	
66568	**FL**	E	DFIM	LD	
66569	**FL**	E	DFIM	LD	
66570	**FL**	E	DFIM	LD	
66571	**FL**	E	DFIM	LD	
66572	**FL**	E	DFIM	LD	

Class 66/5. Freightliner-operated low emission locos. Details as Class 66/0 except:

Engine: EMD 12N-710G3B-U2 two stroke of 2420 kW (3245 hp) at 904 rpm.
Traction Motors: General Motors D43TRC.
Fuel Capacity: 5150 litres.

66585	**FL**	LY	DFHG	LD	The Drax Flyer
66587	**FL**	LY	DFIN	LD	
66588	**FL**	LY	DFIN	LD	
66589	**FL**	LY	DFIN	LD	
66590	**FL**	LY	DFIN	LD	
66591	**FL**	LY	DFIN	LD	
66592	**FL**	LY	DFIN	LD	Johnson Stevens Agencies
66593	**FL**	LY	DFIN	LD	3MG MERSEY MULTIMODAL GATEWAY
66594	**FL**	LY	DFIN	LD	NYK Spirit of Kyoto
66595	**FL**	BN	DFHG	LD	
66596	**FL**	BN	DFHG	LD	
66597	**FL**	BN	DFHG	LD	Viridor
66598	**FL**	BN	DFHG	LD	
66599	**FL**	BN	DFHG	LD	

Class 66/6. Freightliner-operated locomotives with modified gear ratios. Details as Class 66/0 except:

Maximum Tractive Effort: 467 kN (105080 lbf).
Continuous Tractive Effort: 296 kN (66630 lbf) at 14.0 mph.
Design Speed: 65 mph. **Maximum Speed**: 65 mph.

66601	**FL**	P	DFHH	LD	The Hope Valley
66602	**FL**	P	DFHH	LD	
66603	**FL**	P	DFHH	LD	
66604	**FL**	P	DFHH	LD	
66605	**FL**	P	DFHH	LD	
66606	**FL**	P	DFHH	LD	
66607	**FL**	P	DFHG	LD	
66610	**FL**	P	DFHG	LD	
66613	**FL**	E	DFHG	LD	
66614	**FL**	E	DFHG	LD	
66615	**FL**	E	DFHG	LD	
66616	**FL**	E	DFHG	LD	
66617	**FL**	E	DFHG	LD	
66618	**FL**	E	DFHG	LD	Railways Illustrated Annual Photographic Awards Alan Barnes
66619	**FL**	E	DFHG	LD	Derek W. Johnson MBE
66620	**FL**	E	DFHG	LD	

66621	**FL**	E	DFHG	LD	
66622	**FL**	E	DFHG	LD	

Class 66/6. Freightliner-operated low emission loco with modified gear ratios.
Fuel Capacity: 5150 litres.

Advertising livery: 66623 Bardon Aggregates (blue).

66623	**AL**	LY	DFHG	LD	Bill Bolsover

Class 66/7. GB Railfreight-operated locos. Details as Class 66/0.

Non-standard/Advertising liveries:

66705 **GB** livery but with the addition of "Union Jack" bodyside vinyls.
66709 Black & orange with MEDITE branding.
66720 Day and night (various colours, different on each side).

66701	**GB**	E	GBCM	PG	
66702	**GB**	E	GBCM	PG	Blue Lightning
66703	**GB**	E	GBCM	PG	Doncaster PSB 1981–2002
66704	**GB**	E	GBCM	PG	Colchester Power Signalbox
66705	**GB**	E	GBCM	PG	Golden Jubilee
66706	**GB**	E	GBCM	PG	Nene Valley
66707	**GB**	E	GBCM	PG	Sir Sam Fay GREAT CENTRAL RAILWAY
66708	**GB**	E	GBCM	PG	Jayne
66709	**AL**	E	GBCM	PG	Joseph Arnold Davies
66710	**GB**	E	GBCM	PG	Phil Packer BRIT
66711	**GB**	E	GBCM	PG	
66712	**GB**	E	GBCM	PG	Peterborough Power Signalbox
66713	**GB**	E	GBCM	PG	Forest City
66714	**GB**	E	GBCM	PG	Cromer Lifeboat
66715	**GB**	E	GBCM	PG	VALOUR – IN MEMORY OF ALL RAILWAY EMPLOYEES WHO GAVE THEIR LIVES FOR THEIR COUNTRY
66716	**GB**	E	GBCM	PG	LOCOMOTIVE & CARRIAGE INSTITUTION CENTENARY 1911–2011
66717	**GB**	E	GBCM	PG	Good Old Boy

66718–746. Low emission. GB Railfreight locos. 66733–737 renumbered from former DRS locos 66401–405. 66738–741 renumbered from former Freightliner locos 66578–581. 66742–746 renumbered from former DRS/ Colas Rail locos 66406–410/841–845).

All details as Class 66/0 except 66718–732 as below:

Engine: EMD 12N-710G3B-U2 two stroke of 2420 kW (3245 hp) at 904 rpm.
Traction Motors: General Motors D43TRC.
Fuel Capacity: 5546 litres (66718–722) or 5150 litres (66723–732).

66718	**MT**	E	GBCM	PG	Gwyneth Dunwoody
66719	**MT**	E	GBCM	PG	METRO-LAND
66720	**0**	E	GBCM	PG	
66721	**MT**	E	GBCM	PG	Harry Beck
66722	**MT**	E	GBCM	PG	Sir Edward Watkin
66723	**FS**	E	GBSD	PG	Chinook

66724	**FS**	E	GBSD	PG	Drax Power Station
66725	**FS**	E	GBSD	PG	SUNDERLAND
66726	**FS**	E	GBSD	PG	SHEFFIELD WEDNESDAY
66727	**FS**	E	GBSD	PG	Andrew Scott CBE
66728	**GB**	P	GBCM	PG	Institution of Railway Operators
66729	**GB**	P	GBCM	PG	DERBY COUNTY
66730	**GB**	P	GBCM	PG	Whitemoor
66731	**GB**	P	GBCM	PG	interhub GB
66732	**GB**	P	GBCM	PG	GBRf The First Decade 1999–2009 John Smith – MD

66733	(66401) r	**GB**	P	GBFM	PG	
66734	(66402) r	**GB**	P	GBFM	PG	
66735	(66403) r	**GB**	P	GBFM	PG	
66736	(66404) r	**GB**	P	GBFM	PG	WOLVERHAMPTON WANDERERS
66737	(66405) r	**GB**	P	GBFM	PG	Lesia
66738	(66578)	**FL**	GB	GBRT	PG	
66739	(66579)	**FL**	GB	GBRT	PG	
66740	(66580)	**FL**	GB	GBRT	PG	
66741	(66581)	**FL**	GB	GBRT	PG	
66742	(66406, 66841)	**CS**	GB	GBHL	PG	
66743	(66407, 66842)	**CS**	GB	GBHL	PG	
66744	(66408, 66843)	**CS**	GB	GBHL	PG	
66745	(66409, 66844)	**CS**	GB	GBHL	PG	
66746	(66410, 66845)	**CS**	GB	GBHL	PG	

Class 66/8. Colas Rail locos. Renumbered from former Freightliner locos 66573–577. Details as Class 66/0.

66846	(66573)	**CS**	CS	COLO	RU	
66847	(66574)	**CS**	CS	COLO	RU	
66848	(66575)	**CS**	CS	COLO	RU	
66849	(66576)	**CS**	CS	COLO	RU	Wylam Dilly
66850	(66577)	**CS**	CS	COLO	RU	

Class 66/9. Freightliner locos. Low emission "demonstrator" locos. Details as Class 66/0 except:

Engine: EMD 12N-710G3B-U2 two stroke of 2420 kW (3245 hp) at 904 rpm.
Traction Motors: General Motors D43TRC.
Fuel Capacity: 5905/5150 litres.

66951	**FL**	E	DFHG	LD
66952	**FL**	E	DFHG	LD

Class 66/9. Freightliner-operated low emission locos. Owing to the 665xx number range being full further orders of 66/5s are to be numbered from 66953 onwards. Details as Class 66/5 (low emission):

66953	**FL**	BN	DFHG	LD	
66954	**FL**	BN	DFIN	LD	
66955	**FL**	BN	DFIN	LD	
66956	**FL**	BN	DFIN	LD	
66957	**FL**	BN	DFHG	LD	Stephenson Locomotive Society 1909–2009

CLASS 67 ALSTOM/GENERAL MOTORS EMD Bo-Bo

Built: 1999–2000 by Alstom at Valencia, Spain, as sub-contractors for General Motors (General Motors model JT42 HW-HS).
Engine: GM 12N-710G3B-EC two stroke of 2385 kW (3200 hp) at 904 rpm.
Main Alternator: General Motors AR9A/HEP7/CA6C.
Traction Motors: General Motors D43FM.
Maximum Tractive Effort: 141 kN (31770 lbf).
Continuous Tractive Effort: 90 kN (20200 lbf) at 46.5 mph.
Power At Rail: 1860 kW.
Brake Force: 78 t.
Weight: 90 t.
Design Speed: 125 mph.
Fuel Capacity: 4927 litres.
Train Supply: Electric, index 66.
Train Brakes: Air.
Dimensions: 19.74 x 2.72 m.
Wheel Diameter: 965 mm.
Maximum Speed: 125 mph.
RA: 8.
Multiple Working: AAR System.

Notes: All equipped with Slow Speed Control and Swinghead Automatic "Buckeye" Combination Couplers.

67004, 67007, 67009 and 67011 are fitted with cast iron brake blocks for working the Fort William Sleeper. **Maximum Speed**: 80 mph.

67004 and 67027 carry their names on one side only.

Non-standard livery: 67029 All over silver with EWS logos.

67001	**AB**	A	WATN	CE	
67002	**AB**	A	WATN	CE	
67003	**AB**	A	WATN	CE	
67004 r	**E**	A	WABN	CE	Post Haste
67005	**RZ**	A	WAAN	CE	Queen's Messenger
67006	**RZ**	A	WAAN	CE	Royal Sovereign
67007 r	**E**	A	WABN	CE	
67008	**E**	A	WAAN	CE	
67009 r	**E**	A	WABN	CE	
67010	**WS**	A	WNWX	CE (S)	
67011 r	**E**	A	WABN	CE	
67012	**WS**	A	WAWN	CE	A Shropshire Lad
67013	**WS**	A	WAWN	CE	Dyfrbont Pontcysyllte
67014	**WS**	A	WAWN	CE	Thomas Telford
67015	**WS**	A	WAWN	CE	David J. Lloyd
67016	**E**	A	WAAN	CE	
67017	**E**	A	WAAN	CE	Arrow
67018	**DB**	A	WAAN	CE	Keith Heller
67019	**E**	A	WAAN	CE	
67020	**E**	A	WAAN	CE	
67021	**E**	A	WAAN	CE	
67022	**E**	A	WAAN	CE	
67023	**E**	A	WNWX	CE (S)	
67024	**E**	A	WAAN	CE	
67025	**E**	A	WAAN	CE	Western Star
67026	**E**	A	WAAN	CE	
67027	**E**	A	WAAN	CE	Rising Star

67028	**E**	A	WAAN	CE	
67029	**0**	A	WAAN	CE	Royal Diamond
67030 r	**E**	A	WABN	CE	

CLASS 70 GENERAL ELECTRIC Co-Co

New GE "PowerHaul" locos currently being delivered to Freightliner. The first six locos arrived in late 2009. An option exists for a further ten locos. 70012 was badly damaged whilst being unloaded in 2011 and was returned to Pennsylvania.

Built: 2009–11 by General Electric, Erie, Pennsylvania, USA.
Engine: General Electric PowerHaul P616LDA1 of 2848 kW (3820 hp) at 1500 rpm.
Main Alternator: General Electric GTA series.
Traction Motors: AC-GE 5GEB30.
Maximum Tractive Effort: 544 kN (122 000 lbf).
Continuous Tractive Effort: 427 kN (96 000 lbf) at ?? m.p.h.
Power At Rail:
Brake Force: 96.7 t.
Weight: 129 t.
Design Speed: 75 mph.
Fuel Capacity: 6000 litres.
Train Supply: Not equipped.
Train Brakes: Air.
Dimensions: 21.71 x 2.64 m.
Wheel Diameter: 1066 mm.
Maximum Speed: 75 mph.
RA: 7.
Multiple Working: AAR System.

70001	**FH**	LY	DFGI	LD	PowerHaul
70002	**FH**	LY	DFGH	LD	
70003	**FH**	LY	DFGH	LD	
70004	**FH**	LY	DFGH	LD	The Coal Industry Society
70005	**FH**	LY	DFGH	LD	
70006	**FH**	LY	DFGH	LD	
70007	**FH**	LY	DFGI	LD	
70008	**FH**	LY	DFGI	LD	
70009	**FH**	LY	DFGI	LD	
70010	**FH**	LY	DFGH	LD	
70011	**FH**	LY	DFGH	LD	
70013	**FH**	LY	DFGH	LD	
70014	**FH**	LY	DFGH	LD	
70015	**FH**	LY	DFGH	LD	
70016	**FH**	LY	DFGH	LD	
70017	**FH**	LY			
70018	**FH**	LY			
70019	**FH**	LY			
70020	**FH**	LY			

1.2. ELECTRO-DIESEL & ELECTRIC LOCOMOTIVES

CLASS 73 BR/ENGLISH ELECTRIC Bo-Bo

Electro-diesel locomotives which can operate either from a DC supply or using power from a diesel engine.

Built: 1965–67 by English Electric Co. at Vulcan Foundry, Newton-le-Willows.
Engine: English Electric 4SRKT of 447 kW (600 hp) at 850 rpm.
Main Generator: English Electric 824/5D.
Electric Supply System: 750 V DC from third rail.
Traction Motors: English Electric 546/1B.
Maximum Tractive Effort (Electric): 179 kN (40000 lbf).
Maximum Tractive Effort (Diesel): 160 kN (36000 lbf).
Continuous Rating (Electric): 1060 kW (1420 hp) giving a tractive effort of 35kN (7800 lbf) at 68 mph.
Continuous Tractive Effort (Diesel): 60 kN (13600 lbf) at 11.5 mph.
Maximum Rail Power (Electric): 2350 kW (3150 hp) at 42 mph.
Train Brakes: Air, vacuum & electro-pneumatic († Air & electro-pneumatic).
Brake Force: 31 t.
Weight: 77 t.
Design Speed: 90 mph.
Fuel Capacity: 1409 litres.
Dimensions: 16.36 x 2.64 m.
Wheel Diameter: 1016 mm.
Maximum Speed: 90 mph.
RA: 6.
Train Supply: Electric, index 66 (on electric power only).
Multiple Working: SR 27-way System & Blue Star.

Formerly numbered E6001–E6020/E6022–E6026/E6028–E6049 (not in order).

Note: Locomotives numbered in the 732xx series are classed as 73/2 and were originally dedicated to Gatwick Express services.

Non-standard liveries: 73107 Two-tone grey.
73139 Weardale Railway Brown & cream.

73104	**IC**	RE	RVLO	ZA (S)	
73107	**0**	20	MBED	SE	Redhill 1844–1994
73109	**SD**	TT	MBED	SL	Battle of Britain 50th Anniversary
73119	**B**	GB	GBED	SE	
73133	**TT**	TT	MBED	SU	
73136	**TT**	TT	MBED	SU	Perseverance
73138	**Y**	NR	QADD	ZA	
73139	**0**	RE	RVLO	ZA	
73141	**FS**	GB	GBED	SE	Charlotte
73201 †	**B**	20	MBED	SE	Broadlands
73202 †	**GV**	P	IVGA	SL	Dave Berry
73204 †	**GB**	GB	GBED	SE	Janice
73205 †	**IC**	GB	GBED	SE	Jeanette
73206 †	**GB**	GB	GBED	SE	Lisa
73207 †	**BL**	GB	GBED	SE	

73208 †	**B**	GB	GBED	SE	Kirsten
73209 †	**GB**	GB	GBZZ	LB (S)	Alison
73211 †	**GX**	RE	RVLO	ZA (S)	
73212 †	**FS**	GB	GBED	SE	
73213 †	**FS**	GB	GBED	SE	
73235 †	**SD**	P	HYWD	WD	

CLASS 86 BR/ENGLISH ELECTRIC Bo-Bo

Built: 1965–66 by English Electric Co at Vulcan Foundry, Newton-le-Willows or by BR at Doncaster Works.
Electric Supply System: 25 kV AC 50 Hz overhead.
Train Brakes: Air. **Brake Force**: 40 t.
Dimensions: 17.83 x 2.65 m. **Weight**: 83–86.8 t.
RA: 6. **Multiple Working**: TDM system.
Train Supply: Electric, index 66.

Formerly numbered E3101–E3200 (not in order).

Class 86/1. Class 87-type bogies & motors.

Details as above except:
Traction Motors: GEC 412AZ frame mounted.
Maximum Tractive Effort: 258 kN (58000 lbf).
Continuous Rating: 3730 kW (5000 hp) giving a tractive effort of 95 kN (21300 lbf) at 87 mph.
Maximum Rail Power: 5860 kW (7860 hp) at 50.8 mph.
Wheel Diameter: 1150 mm. **Weight**: 86.8 t.
Design Speed: 110 m.p.h. **Maximum Speed**: 110 mph.

86101	**B**	EL	ACAC	WN	Sir William A Stanier FRS

Class 86/2. Standard design rebuilt with resilient wheels & Flexicoil suspension.

Traction Motors: AEI 282BZ axle hung.
Maximum Tractive Effort: 207 kN (46500 lbf).
Continuous Rating: 3010 kW (4040 hp) giving a tractive effort of 85 kN (19200 lbf) at 77.5 mph.
Maximum Rail Power: 4550 kW (6100 hp.) at 49.5 mph.
Wheel Diameter: 1156 mm. **Weight**: 85–86.2 t.
Design Speed: 125 mph. **Maximum Speed**: 100 mph.

Non-standard livery/numbering: 86233 & 86259 BR "Electric blue" livery. 86233 Also carries number E3172.

86213	**IC**	EL	ACXX	WB (S)	Lancashire Witch
86215	**AR**	EP	EPXS	LM (S)	
86217	**AR**	EP	EPXX	LM (S)	
86228	**IC**	EP	EPXS	LM (S)	
86229	**V**	EP	EPXX	LM (S)	
86231	**V**	E	SAXL	LM (S)	
86233	**0**	EP	EPXX	LM (S)	
86234	**AR**	E	SAXL	LM (S)	

86235	**AR**	EP	EPXS	LM (S)	
86242	**AR**	EP	EPXX	LM (S)	
86246	**AR**	EP	EPXS	LM (S)	
86247	**EX**	EP	EPXS	LM (S)	
86251	**V**	EP	EPXX	LM (S)	
86259	**0**	PP	MBEL	TM	Les Ross

Class 86/4.

Traction Motors: AEI 282AZ axle hung.
Maximum Tractive Effort: 258 kN (58000 lbf).
Continuous Rating: 2680 kW (3600 hp) giving a tractive effort of 89kN (20000lbf) at 67 mph.
Maximum Rail Power: 4400 kW (5900 hp) at 38 mph.
Wheel Diameter: 1156 mm. **Weight:** 83–83.9 t.
Design Speed: 100 mph. **Maximum Speed:** 100 mph.

86401	**N**	EL	ACXX	CP (S)	Northampton Town
86424	**Y**	EL	ACXX	CP (S)	

Class 86/5. Regeared locomotive operated by Freightliner.

Details as Class 86/4 except:

Continuous Rating: 2680 kW (3600 hp) giving a tractive effort of 117kN (26300lbf) at 67 mph.
Maximum Speed: 75 mph. **Train Supply:** Electric, isolated.

86501 (86608) **FL** FL DFGC CP

Class 86/6. Freightliner-operated locomotives.

Details as Class 86/4 except:

Maximum Speed: 75 mph. **Train Supply:** Electric, isolated.

86604	**FL**	FL	DFNC	CP
86605	**FL**	FL	DFNC	CP
86607	**FL**	FL	DFNC	CP
86609	**FL**	FL	DFNC	CP
86610	**FL**	FL	DFNC	CP
86612	**FL**	P	DFNC	CP
86613	**FL**	P	DFNC	CP
86614	**FL**	P	DFNC	CP
86621	**FL**	P	DHLT	CP (S)
86622	**FH**	P	DFNC	CP
86627	**FL**	P	DFNC	CP
86628	**FL**	P	DFNC	CP
86632	**FL**	P	DFNC	CP
86633	**FF**	P	DHLT	CP (S)
86635	**FL**	P	DHLT	CP (S)
86637	**FH**	P	DFNC	CP
86638	**FL**	P	DFNC	CP
86639	**FL**	P	DFNC	CP

Class 86/7. Europhoenix-owned locomotives. Refurbished Class 86/2s for the UK spot-hire market. Details as Class 86/2 unless stated.

Maximum Speed: 110 mph. **Weight:** 85 t.
Train Supply: Electric, index 74.

86701 (86205)	**EL**	EP	ETLO	WN	Orion
86702 (86260)	**EL**	EP	ETLO	WN	Cassiopeia

Class 86/9. Network Rail-owned locomotives. Rebuilt from Class 86/2s for use as Mobile Load Bank test locos to test Overhead Line Equipment, initially on the WCML. No. 1 end Traction Motors isolated. Can still move under own power.

Maximum Speed: 60 mph. **Train Supply:** Electric, isolated.

86901 (86253)	**Y**	NR	QACL	CP	CHIEF ENGINEER
86902 (86210)	**Y**	NR	QACL	CP	RAIL VEHICLE ENGINEERING

CLASS 87 BREL/GEC Bo-Bo

Built: 1973–75 by BREL at Crewe Works.
Electric Supply System: 25 kV AC 50 Hz overhead.
Traction Motors: GEC G412AZ frame mounted.
Maximum Tractive Effort: 258 kN (58000 lbf).
Continuous Rating: 3730 kW (5000 hp) giving a tractive effort of 95 kN (21300 lbf) at 87 mph.
Maximum Rail Power: 5860 kW (7860 hp) at 50.8 mph.
Train Brakes: Air.
Brake Force: 40 t.
Dimensions: 17.83 x 2.65 m.
Weight: 83.3 t.
Wheel Diameter: 1150 mm.
Design Speed: 110 mph.
Maximum Speed: 110 mph.
Train Supply: Electric, index 95.
RA: 6.
Multiple Working: TDM system.

87002	**B**	EL	ACAC	WN	Royal Sovereign
87009	**V**	EP	EPXS	LM (S)	
87017	**EX**	EP	EPXS	LM	Iron Duke
87023	**EX**	EP	EPXS	LM	Velocity
87025	**V**	X	SBXL	LM (S)	

CLASS 90 GEC Bo-Bo

Built: 1987–90 by BREL at Crewe Works (as sub contractors for GEC).
Electric Supply System: 25 kV AC 50 Hz overhead.
Traction Motors: GEC G412CY frame mounted.
Maximum Tractive Effort: 258 kN (58000 lbf).
Continuous Rating: 3730 kW (5000 hp) giving a tractive effort of 95 kN (21300 lbf) at 87 mph.
Maximum Rail Power: 5860 kW (7860 hp) at 68.3 mph.
Train Brakes: Air.
Brake Force: 40 t.
Dimensions: 18.80 x 2.74 m.
Weight: 84.5 t.
Wheel Diameter: 1150 mm.
Design Speed: 110 mph.
Maximum Speed: 110 mph.
Train Supply: Electric, index 95.
RA: 7.
Multiple Working: TDM system.

Non-standard livery: 90036 As **FE** but with a yellow roof. EWS stickers.

90001	b	**1**	P	IANA	NC	
90002	b	**1**	P	IANA	NC	
90003	b	**NX**	P	IANA	NC	Rædwald of East Anglia
90004	b	**1**	P	IANA	NC	Eastern Daily Press 1870–2010 SERVING NORFOLK FOR 140 YEARS
90005	b	**1**	P	IANA	NC	Vice-Admiral Lord Nelson
90006	b	**1**	P	IANA	NC	Modern Railways Magazine/ Roger Ford
90007	b	**1**	P	IANA	NC	Sir John Betjeman
90008	b	**NX**	P	IANA	NC	The East Anglian
90009	b	**1**	P	IANA	NC	
90010	b	**1**	P	IANA	NC	BRESSINGHAM STEAM & GARDENS
90011	b	**1**	P	IANA	NC	Let's Go East of England
90012	b	**1**	P	IANA	NC	Royal Anglian Regiment
90013	b	**1**	P	IANA	NC	The Evening Star PRIDE OF IPSWICH 1885–2010 125 YEARS OF SERVING SUFFOLK
90014	b	**1**	P	IANA	NC	Norfolk and Norwich Festival
90015	b	**NX**	P	IANA	NC	Colchester Castle
90016		**FL**	P	DFLC	CP	
90017	b	**E**	DB	WNTS	CE (S)	
90018	b	**E**	DB	WEFE	CE	
90019	b	**FS**	DB	WEFE	CE	
90020	b	**E**	DB	WEFE	CE	Collingwood
90021		**FS**	DB	WEFE	CE	
90022		**EG**	DB	WNTS	CE (S)	Freightconnection
90023		**E**	DB	WNTS	CE (S)	
90024		**FS**	DB	WEGE	CE	
90025		**F**	DB	WNTS	CE (S)	
90026		**E**	DB	WEFE	CE	
90027		**F**	DB	WNTS	CE (S)	Allerton T&RS Depot
90028		**E**	DB	WEFE	CE	
90029		**E**	DB	WNTR	CE	The Institution of Civil Engineers
90030		**E**	DB	WNTS	CE (S)	Crewe Locomotive Works
90031		**E**	DB	WNTS	CE (S)	The Railway Children Partnership Working For Street Children Worldwide
90032		**E**	DB	WNTS	CE (S)	
90033		**FE**	DB	WNTS	CE (S)	
90034		**E**	DB	WNTS	CE (S)	
90035		**E**	DB	WEFE	CE	
90036		**0**	DB	WEFE	CE	
90037		**E**	DB	WNTS	CE (S)	Spirit of Dagenham
90038		**FE**	DB	WNTS	CE (S)	
90039		**E**	DB	WEFE	CE	
90040		**E**	DB	WNTS	CE (S)	The Railway Mission
90041		**FL**	P	DFLC	CP	
90042		**FF**	P	DFLC	CP	
90043		**FF**	P	DFLC	CP	Freightliner Coatbridge
90044		**FF**	P	DFLC	CP	

90045	**FH**	P	DFLC	CP
90046	**FL**	P	DFLC	CP
90047	**FF**	P	DFLC	CP
90048	**FF**	P	DFLC	CP
90049	**FH**	P	DFLC	CP
90050	**FF**	DB	WNTS	CE (S)

CLASS 91 GEC Bo-Bo

Built: 1988–91 by BREL at Crewe Works (as sub contractors for GEC).
Electric Supply System: 25 kV AC 50 Hz overhead.
Traction Motors: GEC G426AZ.
Maximum Tractive Effort: 190 kN (43 000 lbf).
Continuous Rating: 4540 kW (6090 hp) giving a tractive effort of 170kN at 96mph.
Maximum Rail Power: 4700 kW (6300 hp) at ?? mph.
Train Brakes: Air.
Brake Force: 45 t.
Weight: 84 t.
Design Speed: 140 mph.
Train Supply: Electric, index 95.
Multiple Working: TDM system.
Dimensions: 19.41 x 2.74 m.
Wheel Diameter: 1000 mm.
Maximum Speed: 125 mph.
RA: 7.

Note: Locos originally numbered in the 910xx series, but renumbered upon completion of overhauls at Bombardier, Doncaster by the addition of 100 to their original number. The exception to this rule was 91023 which was renumbered 91132.

Advertising livery: 91101 Flying Scotsman (purple).

91101	**AL**	E	IECA	BN	
91102	**EC**	E	IECA	BN	City of York
91103	**EC**	E	IECA	BN	
91104	**GN**	E	IECA	BN	
91105	**EC**	E	IECA	BN	
91106	**EC**	E	IECA	BN	
91107	**EC**	E	IECA	BN	
91108	**EC**	E	IECA	BN	
91109	**EC**	E	IECA	BN	Sir Bobby Robson
91110	**EC**	E	IECA	BN	
91111	**NX**	E	IECA	BN	
91112	**GN**	E	IECA	BN	
91113	**GN**	E	IECA	BN	
91114	**GN**	E	IECA	BN	
91115	**GN**	E	IECA	BN	
91116	**EC**	E	IECA	BN	
91117	**EC**	E	IECA	BN	WEST RIDING LIMITED
91118	**GN**	E	IECA	BN	
91119	**GN**	E	IECA	BN	
91120	**EC**	E	IECA	BN	
91121	**GN**	E	IECA	BN	
91122	**EC**	E	IECA	BN	
91124	**GN**	E	IECA	BN	

91125	**GN**	E	IECA	BN
91126	**GN**	E	IECA	BN
91127	**EC**	E	IECA	BN
91128	**EC**	E	IECA	BN
91129	**GN**	E	IECA	BN
91130	**EC**	E	IECA	BN
91131	**GN**	E	IECA	BN
91132	**EC**	E	IECA	BN

CLASS 92 BRUSH Co-Co

Built: 1993–96 by Brush Traction at Loughborough.
Electric Supply System: 25 kV AC 50 Hz overhead or 750 V DC third rail.
Traction Motors: Asea Brown Boveri design. Model 6FRA 7059B (Asynchronous 3-phase induction motors).
Maximum Tractive Effort: 400 kN (90 000 lbf).
Continuous Rating: 5040 kW (6760 hp) on AC, 4000 kW (5360 hp) on DC.
Maximum Rail Power:
Train Brakes: Air.
Brake Force: 63 t.
Dimensions: 21.34 x 2.67 m.
Weight: 126 t.
Wheel Diameter: 1070 mm.
Design Speed: 140 km/h (87 mph).
Maximum Speed: 145 km/h (90 mph).
Train Supply: Electric, index 108 (AC), 70 (DC).
RA: 7.

Advertising livery: 92017 Stobart Rail (two tone blue & white).

92001	**E**	LY	WTAE	CE	Victor Hugo
92002	**EG**	LY	WNWX	CE (S)	H.G. Wells
92003	**EG**	LY	WTAE	CE	Beethoven
92004	**EG**	LY	WNWX	CE (S)	Jane Austen
92005	**EG**	LY	WNTR	CE	Mozart
92006	**EP**	ET	PTXX	CO (S)	Louis Armand
92007	**EG**	LY	WNTR	CE	Schubert
92008	**EG**	LY	WNWX	CE (S)	Jules Verne
92009	**DB**	LY	WTHE	CE	Marco Polo
92010	**EP**	ET	PTXX	CO	Molière
92011	**EG**	LY	WNWX	CE (S)	Handel
92012	**EG**	LY	WTAE	CE	Thomas Hardy
92013	**EG**	LY	WNWX	CE (S)	Puccini
92014	**EP**	ET	PTXX	CO (S)	Emile Zola
92015	**DB**	LY	WTAE	CE	
92016	**DB**	LY	WTHE	CE	
92017	**AL**	LY	WTAE	CE	Bart the Engine
92018	**EP**	ET	PTXX	CO (S)	Stendhal
92019	**EG**	LY	WTAE	CE	Wagner
92020	**EP**	ET	PTXX	CO (S)	Milton
92021	**EP**	ET	PTXX	CO (S)	Purcell
92022	**EG**	LY	WNTR	CE	Charles Dickens
92023	**EP**	ET	PTXX	CO (S)	Ravel
92024	**EG**	LY	WNWX	CE (S)	J.S. Bach
92025	**EG**	LY	WNWX	CE (S)	Oscar Wilde
92026	**EG**	LY	WNTR	CE	Britten

92027	**EG**	LY	WNWX	CE (S)	George Eliot
92028	**EP**	ET	GBET	CO	Saint Saëns
92029	**EG**	LY	WNWX	CE (S)	Dante
92030	**EG**	LY	WNTR	CE	Ashford
92031	**DB**	LY	WNTR	CE	
92032	**GB**	ET	GBET	CO	
92033	**EP**	ET	PTXX	CO (S)	Berlioz
92034	**EG**	LY	WTAE	CE	Kipling
92035	**EP**	LY	WNWX	CE (S)	Mendelssohn
92036	**EG**	LY	WTAE	CE	Bertolt Brecht
92037	**EG**	LY	WTAE	CE	Sullivan
92038	**EP**	ET	GBET	CO	Voltaire
92039	**EG**	LY	WNWX	CE (S)	Johann Strauss
92040	**EP**	ET	PTXX	CO (S)	Goethe
92041	**EG**	LY	WTAE	CE	Vaughan Williams
92042	**DB**	LY	WTHE	CE	
92043	**EP**	ET	GBET	CO	Debussy
92044	**EP**	ET	GBET	CO	Couperin
92045	**EP**	ET	PTXX	LB (S)	Chaucer
92046	**EP**	ET	PTXX	LB (S)	Sweelinck

▲ One of three Class 08s based at Bombardier's Derby Litchurch Lane Works, 004 (08602) is seen on site on 13/10/10. **Robert Pritchard**

▼ 08649 "Wolverton" is used at Railcare's Wolverton Works site where it is seen on 03/05/11. **Mark Beal**

▲ DRS still uses a number of Class 20s on nuclear flask traffic. On 06/07/11 20308 and 20309 cross Snargate Crossing on the Dungeness branch with 6M95 16.35 Dungeness–Willesden. **Nigel Gibbs**

▼ British American Railway Services-liveried 31601 is pictured working a Bounds Green–Cambridge–Selhurst test train at Shepreth Branch Junction on 18/01/11. **Nigel Gibbs**

▲ DRS-liveried 37688 "Kingmoor TMD" and 37510 pass Ferrybridge 6Z50 09.25 Stockton–Sheerness loaded scrap on 03/02/11 **Oliver Turner**

▲ BR Green-liveried 33012 returned to the main line in 2011. On 15/09/11 it passes Slitting Mill Crossing (north of Chesterfield) with 0Z34 10.25 Barrow Hill–Grosmont hauling 73136, 20096 and 20107 to a diesel gala at the NYMR. **Ben Wheeler**

▼ Grand Central-liveried HST 43465 and 43468 pass Marston, near Grantham, with the 16.48 London King's Cross–Sunderland on 02/08/11. **Paul Biggs**

▲ CrossCountry HST 43366 and 43301 passes Syston South Junction with the 08.10 Leeds–Plymouth (diverted via Leicester) on 03/07/11. **Paul Biggs**

▼ Colas Rail-liveried 47727 "Rebecca" passes Attenborough with 6Z56 06.04 Washwood Heath–Boston Docks empty steel on 27/06/11. **Mick Tindall**

▲ DRS-liveried 47818 stands at Holyhead with a VSOE Northern Belle charter to Crewe on 19/06/11. **Jamie Squibbs**

▼ In all over grey livery with DCR brandings, British American Railway Services 56311 stands at Grimsby Docks prior to departure with a scrap train for Cardiff Tidal on 11/07/11. **Richard Tuplin**

▲ BR Blue-liveried 50044 "Exeter" returned to the main line in 2011. On 04/09/11 it leaves Llandudno Junction with the 12.00 Holyhead–Llanrwst leg of a two day PTG railtour.
Phil Chilton

▲ WCRC maroon-liveried 57001 hauls the Royal Scotsman luxury train west at Bo'ness Junction heading for Spean Bridge on 20/05/11. **Ian Lothian**

▼ Aggregate Industries-liveried 59001 "YEOMAN ENDEAVOUR" and Foster Yeoman-liveried 59002 "ALAN J DAY" make for an unusual sight at the head of 6W33 23.00 Westerleigh Jn–Westbury ballast train at Bathampton on 25/07/11. **Dave Gommersall**

▲ Tata Steel-liveried 60099 passes Ashley with 6F05 15.19 Tunstead–Oakleigh loaded stone on 02/05/11. **Cliff Beeton**

▼ Carrying the new look GB Railfreight livery, 66728 "Institution of Railway Operators" passes Welney Road, near Manea, with 6Z85 12.10 Bow–Tyne Dock loaded spoil. **Nigel Gibbs**

▲ DRS-liveried 66302 and 66420 top-and-tail Mark 2A Escort Coaches 9419 and 9428 at St Bees on 24/06/11 working a 5Z20 09.02 Carlisle–Sellafield special. **Steven J Allen**

▲ Freightliner-liveried 66515 passes Kincardine with 6G05 09.29 Ravenstruther–Longannet loaded coal train on 15/09/11. **Ian Lothian**

▼ Royal Train-liveried 67006 "Royal Sovereign" passes Alsager with an empty stock working from Crewe to Stoke prior to working a football special on 17/04/11. **Cliff Beeton**

▲ Freightliner-liveried 70008 passes Roade, south of Northampton, with 4L97 04.59 Trafford Park–Felixstowe intermodal on 30/07/11. **John Turner**

▲ Network Rail yellow-liveried 73138 is pictured working a Dollands Moor–Derby test train (with 31285 on the rear) at Cossington on the Midland Main Line on 04/06/11.
Ben Wheeler

▼ BR Blue-liveried 87002 "Royal Sovereign" and 86101 "Sir William A Stanier FRS" see limited use on main line charters. On 24/07/11 they are seen leaving Claypole loop at Stubton with a Doncaster–Acton Lane empty stock working.
Lindsay Atkinson

▲ National Express-liveried 90015 "Colchester Castle" passes Bentley with the 15.00 Norwich–London Liverpool Street on 08/04/09. **Antony Guppy**

▼ 91101 carries a special promotional livery for the Flying Scotsman – the 05.40 departure from Edinburgh which is booked to take 4 hours to London. On 13/09/11 it arrives at Doncaster with the 06.15 London King's Cross–Newcastle. **Paul Abell**

▲ EWS-liveried 90028 passes Old Linslade, near Leighton Buzzard, with 1M16 20.46 Inverness–London Euston ScotRail Highland Sleeper on 30/07/11.
Nigel Gibbs

▲ DB Schenker-liveried 92009 "Marco Polo" is seen at Botany Bay on the East Coast Main Line with 4E32 11.52 Dollands Moor–Scunthorpe empty steel on 01/09/11. The electric loco will take the train to Doncaster. **Andrew Wills**

▼ One of the rebuilt Eurotunnel 9/7 locos, 9712 (formerly 9102) is seen about to enter the French portal of the Channel Tunnel with a lorry shuttle on 01/12/10. **Robert Pritchard**

1.3. EUROTUNNEL LOCOMOTIVES

DIESEL LOCOMOTIVES

0001–0007 MaK Bo-Bo

Built: 1991–92 by MaK at Kiel, Germany (Model DE1004).
Engine: MTU 12V 396 TC13 of 940 kW (1260 hp) at 1800 rpm.
Main Alternator: ABB.
Traction Motors: ABB.
Maximum Tractive Effort: 305 kN (68600 lbf).
Continuous Tractive Effort: 140 kN (31500 lbf) at 20 mph.
Power At Rail: 750 kW (1012 h.p.).
Dimensions: 14.40 x ?? m.
Brake Force: 120 kN.
Wheel Diameter: 1000 mm.
Weight: 82 t.
Maximum Speed: 100 km/h.
Design Speed: 120 km/h.
Train Brakes: Air.
Fuel Capacity: 3500 litres.
Multiple Working: Within class.
Train Supply: Not equipped.
Signalling System: TVM430 cab signalling.

Note: Registered on TOPS as 21901–907.

0001	**GY**	ET	CO
0002	**GY**	ET	CO
0003	**GY**	ET	CO
0004	**GY**	ET	CO
0005	**GY**	ET	CO

The following two locos were rebuilt from NS 6400 Class 6456 and 6457 (built 1991) and added to the Eurotunnel fleet in 2011.

0006	**GY**	ET	CO
0007	**GY**	ET	CO

0031–0042 HUNSLET/SCHÖMA 0-4-0

Built: 1989–90 by Hunslet Engine Company at Leeds as 900 mm gauge.
Rebuilt: 1993–94 by Schöma in Germany to 1435 mm. gauge.
Engine: Deutz of 270 kW (200 hp) at ???? rpm.
Transmission: Mechanical.
Maximum Tractive Effort:
Cont. Tractive Effort:
Power At Rail:
Brake Force:
Dimensions:
Weight:
Wheel Diameter:
Design Speed: 50 km/h.
Maximum Speed: 50 km/h.
Fuel Capacity:
Train Brakes: Air.
Train Supply: Not equipped.
Multiple Working: Not equipped.

Note: * Rebuilt with inspection platforms to check overhead catenary.

0031	**GY**	ET	CO	FRANCES
0032	**GY**	ET	CO	ELISABETH
0033	**GY**	ET	CO	SILKE

0034		**GY**	ET	CO	AMANDA
0035		**GY**	ET	CO	MARY
0036		**GY**	ET	CO	LAURENCE
0037		**GY**	ET	CO	LYDIE
0038		**GY**	ET	CO	JENNY
0039	*	**GY**	ET	CO	PACITA
0040		**GY**	ET	CO	JILL
0041	*	**GY**	ET	CO	KIM
0042		**GY**	ET	CO	NICOLE

ELECTRIC LOCOMOTIVES

9005–9838 BRUSH/ABB Bo-Bo-Bo

Built: 1993–2002 by Brush Traction at Loughborough.
Supply System: 25 kV AC 50 Hz overhead.
Traction Motors: Asea Brown Boveri design. Asynchronous 3-phase motors. Model 6FHA 7059 (as built). Model 6FHA 7059C (7000 kW rated locos).
Maximum Tractive Effort: 400kN (90 000 lbf).
Continuous Rating: Class 9/0 and 9/1: 5760 kW (7725 hp). Class 9/7 and 9/8: 7000 kW (9387 hp).
Maximum Rail Power:
Brake Force: 50 t.
Weight: 136 t.
Design Speed: 100 mph.
Train Supply: Electric.
Multiple Working: TDM system.
Dimensions: 22.01 x 2.97 x 4.20 m.
Wheel Diameter: 1250 mm.
Maximum Speed: 100 mph.
Train Brakes: Air.

Class 9/0 Original build locos. Built 1993–94.

9005	**EB**	ET	CO	JESSYE NORMAN
9007	**EB**	ET	CO	DAME JOAN SUTHERLAND
9011	**EB**	ET	CO	JOSÉ VAN DAM
9013	**EB**	ET	CO	MARIA CALLAS
9015	**EB**	ET	CO	LÖTSCHBERG 1913
9018	**EB**	ET	CO	WILHELMENIA FERNANDEZ
9022	**EB**	ET	CO	DAME JANET BAKER
9024	**EB**	ET	CO	GOTTHARD 1882
9026	**EB**	ET	CO	FURKATUNNEL 1982
9029	**EB**	ET	CO	THOMAS ALLEN
9033	**EB**	ET	CO	MONTSERRAT CABALLE
9036	**EB**	ET	CO	ALAIN FONDARY
9037	**EB**	ET	CO	GABRIEL BACQUIER

Class 9/1. Freight Shuttle dedicated locos. Built 1998–2001. These locos are being refurbished and renumbered in the 9/7 series.

9105	**EB**	ET	CO
9109	**EB**	ET	CO
9110	**EB**	ET	CO

Class 9/7. Increased power freight shuttle locos. Built 2001–02 (9711–9723 built 1998–2001).

9701		**EB**	ET	CO
9702		**EB**	ET	CO
9703		**EB**	ET	CO
9704		**EB**	ET	CO
9705		**EB**	ET	CO
9706		**EB**	ET	CO
9707		**EB**	ET	CO
9711	(9101)	**EB**	ET	CO
9712	(9102)	**EB**	ET	CO
9713	(9103)	**EB**	ET	CO
9714	(9104)	**EB**	ET	CO
9715	(9105)			
9716	(9106)	**EB**	ET	CO
9717	(9107)	**EB**	ET	CO
9718	(9108)	**EB**	ET	CO
9719	(9109)			
9720	(9110)			
9721	(9111)	**EB**	ET	CO
9722	(9112)	**EB**	ET	CO
9723	(9113)	**EB**	ET	CO

Class 9/8 Locos rebuilt from Class 9/0 by adding 800 to the loco number. Uprated to 7000 kW.

9801	**EB**	ET	CO	LESLEY GARRETT
9802	**EB**	ET	CO	STUART BURROWS
9803	**EB**	ET	CO	BENJAMIN LUXON
9804	**EB**	ET	CO	VICTORIA DE LOS ANGELES
9806	**EB**	ET	CO	REGINE CRESPIN
9808	**EB**	ET	CO	ELISABETH SODERSTROM
9809	**EB**	ET	CO	FRANÇOISE POLLET
9810	**EB**	ET	CO	JEAN-PHILIPPE COURTIS
9812	**EB**	ET	CO	LUCIANO PAVAROTTI
9814	**EB**	ET	LB (S)	LUCIA POPP
9816	**EB**	ET	CO	WILLARD WHITE
9817	**EB**	ET	CO (S)	JOSÉ CARRERAS
9819	**EB**	ET	CO	MARIA EWING
9820	**EB**	ET	CO	NICOLAI GHIAROV
9821	**EB**	ET	CO	TERESA BERGANZA
9823	**EB**	ET	CO	DAME ELISABETH LEGGE-SCHWARZKOPF
9825	**EB**	ET	CO	
9827	**EB**	ET	CO	BARBARA HENDRICKS
9828	**EB**	ET	CO	DAME KIRI TE KANAWA
9831	**EB**	ET	CO	
9832	**EB**	ET	CO	RENATA TEBALDI
9834	**EB**	ET	CO	MIRELLA FRENI
9835	**EB**	ET	CO	NICOLAI GEDDA
9838	**EB**	ET	CO	HILDEGARD BEHRENS
9840	**EB**	ET	CO	

1.4. FORMER BR MAIN LINE LOCOS IN INDUSTRIAL SERVICE

Former British Rail main line locomotives considered to be in "industrial use" are listed here. These locomotives do not currently have Network Rail engineering acceptance for operation on the national railway network.

Number	*Other no./name*	*Location*
Class 11		
12088		Butterwell Disposal Point, Ashington
Class 03		
03112	D2112	Victoria Group, Port of Boston, Boston
03179	CLIVE	First Capital Connect, Hornsey Depot, London
03196	JOYCE/GLYNIS	West Coast Railway Company, Carnforth
D2381		West Coast Railway Company, Carnforth
Class 07		
07001		Barrow Hill Roundhouse, Chesterfield
D2991	07007	Knights Rail Services, Eastleigh Works
07013		Barrow Hill Roundhouse, Chesterfield
Class 08		
08202	CHUFFER	The Potter Group, Queen Adelaide, Ely
08331		Hanson Traction/Cemex UK, Washwood Heath, Birmingham
08375	21	PD Ports, Teesport, Grangetown, Middlesbrough
08389		Nemesis Rail, Burton-upon-Trent, Staffordshire
08393		LH Group Services, Barton-under-Needwood
08401		Whitemoor Yard, March, Cambridgeshire
08411		Colne Valley Railway, Halstead, Essex
08417		RVEL, RTC Business Park, Derby
08418		West Coast Railway Company, Carnforth
08423	H011 14	PD Ports, Teesport, Grangetown, Middlesbrough
08441		Felixstowe Dock & Railway Company, Felixstowe
08442	RICHARD J. WENHAM EASTLEIGH DEPOT	LNWR, Eastleigh Depot, Hampshire
08445		Daventry International Railfreight Terminal, Crick
08447		John G Russell (Transport), Hillington, Glasgow
08460		Colne Valley Railway, Halstead, Essex
08484	CAPTAIN NATHANIEL DARELL	Felixstowe Dock & Railway Company, Felixstowe
08485		West Coast Railway Company, Carnforth
08492		Barrow Hill Roundhouse, Chesterfield
08499		Pullman Rail, Canton Depot, Cardiff
08502	Lybert Dickinson	Northern, Heaton Depot, Newcastle
08503		Railway Support Services, Rye Farm, Wishaw, Sutton Coldfield
08507		Victoria Group, Port of Boston, Boston

08511		Felixstowe Dock & Railway Company, Felixstowe
08516	RORY	LNWR, Barton Hill Depot, Bristol
08523		Weardale Railway, Wolsingham, County Durham
08527		Flixborough Wharf, Flixborough, Scunthorpe
08536		RVEL, RTC Business Park, Derby
08568	St. Rollox	Railcare, Springburn Depot, Glasgow
08573		Bombardier Transportation, Ilford Works, London
08588	17	Weardale Railway, Wolsingham, County Durham
08598	H016 HERCULES	The Potter Group, Queen Adelaide, Ely
08600		AV Dawson, Ayrton Rail Terminal, Middlesbrough
08602	004 BOMBER	Bombardier Transportation, Derby Works
08613	H064	Celtic Energy, Onllwyn Coal & Distribution Centre, West Glamorgan
08622	H028 19	Hanson Cement, Ketton Cement Works, Stamford
08629	Bradwell	Railcare, Wolverton Works, Milton Keynes
08643		Bardon Aggregates, Merehead Stone Terminal
08648	OLD GEOFF 20	PD Ports, Teesport, Grangetown, Middlesbrough
08649	Wolverton	Railcare, Wolverton Works, Milton Keynes
08650	ISLE OF GRAIN	Bardon Aggregates, Isle of Grain, Kent
08652		Hanson Aggregates, Whatley Quarry, near Frome
08670		Colne Valley Railway, Halstead, Essex
08678	ARTILA	West Coast Railway Company, Carnforth
08682	D3849 Lionheart	Bombardier Transportation, Derby Works
08683		Colne Valley Railway, Halstead, Essex
08685		Barrow Hill Roundhouse, Chesterfield
08697		RVEL, RTC Business Park, Derby
08699		Tata Steel, Shotton Works, Deeside, Flintshire
08704	D3871	Victoria Group, Port of Boston, Boston
08730	The Caley	Railcare, Springburn Depot, Glasgow
08743	Bryan Turner	LH Group Services, Barton-under-Needwood
08750		Hanson Cement, Ketton Cement Works, Stamford
08754		Wabtec Rail, Doncaster Works
08756		Tata Steel, Shotton Works, Deeside, Flintshire
08762		Hanson Traction/Cemex UK, Washwood Heath, Birmingham
08764		Maritime Transport, Tilbury Railport, Tilbury
08765		Nemesis Rail, Burton-upon-Trent, Staffordshire
08774	ARTHUR VERNON DAWSON	AV Dawson, Ayrton Rail Terminal, Middlesbrough
08786		Barrow Hill Roundhouse, Chesterfield
08787	08296	Hanson Aggregates, Machen Quarry, nr Newport
08807		AV Dawson, Ayrton Rail Terminal, Middlesbrough
08809		Hanson Traction/Cemex UK, Washwood Heath, Birmingham
08810		LNWR, Eastleigh Depot, Hampshire
08818	MOLLY	Flixborough Wharf, Flixborough, Scunthorpe
08823	LIBBIE	Thamesteel, Sheerness Steelworks, Isle of Sheppy
08834		Bombardier Transportation, Old Dalby Test Centre, Asfordby
08846	003	Bombardier Transportation, Derby Works
08868		LNWR, Crewe Carriage Depot
08870	H024	Weardale Railway, Wolsingham, County Durham
08881		Gloucestershire Warwickshire Railway
08885	H042 18	PD Ports, Teesport, Grangetown, Middlesbrough

08892		Nemesis Rail, Burton-upon-Trent, Staffordshire
08903	JOHN W. ANTILL	SembCorp Utilities Teesside, Wilton, Middlesbrough
08905		Lafarge Cement, Blue Circle Cement Works, Hope, Derbyshire
08912		AV Dawson, Ayrton Rail Terminal, Middlesbrough
08913		Daventry International Railfreight Terminal, Crick
08918		Nemesis Rail, Burton-upon-Trent, Staffordshire
08924		Barrow Hill Roundhouse, Chesterfield
08933		Knights Rail Services, Eastleigh Works
08936		Tata Steel, Shotton Works, Deeside, Flintshire
08937	BLUEBELL MEL	Bardon Aggregates, Meldon Quarry, Okehampton
08943		Bombardier Transportation, Central Rivers Depot, Barton-under-Needwood
08947		Bardon Aggregates, Merehead Stone Terminal
08954		Nemesis Rail, Burton-upon-Trent, Staffordshire
08956		Bombardier Transportation, Old Dalby Test Centre, Asfordby

Class 09

09007		London Overground, Willesden Depot, London
09012	Dick Hardy	Barrow Hill Roundhouse, Chesterfield
09014		Boden Rail Engineering, Washwood Heath, Birmingham
09018		Bombardier Transportation, Old Dalby Test Centre, Asfordby
09019		Barrow Hill Roundhouse, Chesterfield
09022		Boden Rail Engineering, Washwood Heath, Birmingham
09204		LNWR, Tyne Yard Depot, Lamesley, Tyne & Wear

Class 14

D9504		Kent & East Sussex Railway
D9529		Nene Valley Railway

Class 20

20056	81	Tata Steel, Appleby-Frodingham Works, Scunthorpe
20066	82	Tata Steel, Appleby-Frodingham Works, Scunthorpe
20118		Lafarge Cement, Blue Circle Cement Works, Hope, Derbyshire
20168	SIR GEORGE EARLE	Lafarge Cement, Blue Circle Cement Works, Hope, Derbyshire

Class 47

47714		Bombardier Transportation, Old Dalby Test Centre, Asfordby

Class 56

56009	56201	Brush Traction, Loughborough Works

1.5. LOCOMOTIVES AWAITING DISPOSAL

Locomotives that are still extant but at scrapyards are listed here.

Class 08

08646	**F**	European Metal Recycling, Kingsbury
08662	**E**	TJ Thomson, Stockton
08664	**E**	European Metal Recycling, Kingsbury
08665	**E**	European Metal Recycling, Kingsbury
08783	**E**	European Metal Recycling, Kingsbury
08798	**E**	European Metal Recycling, Kingsbury
08842	**E**	European Metal Recycling, Kingsbury
08844	**E**	European Metal Recycling, Kingsbury
08854	**E**	European Metal Recycling, Kingsbury
08866	**E**	European Metal Recycling, Kingsbury
08872	**E**	European Metal Recycling, Attercliffe
08921	**E**	European Metal Recycling, Kingsbury
08953	**DG**	European Metal Recycling, Attercliffe

Class 09

09020	**E**	European Metal Recycling, Kingsbury
09023	**E**	European Metal Recycling, Kingsbury
09107	**E**	European Metal Recycling, Kingsbury
09205	**DG**	TJ Thomson, Stockton

Class 20

20032	**B**	European Metal Recycling, Hartlepool
20072	**B**	European Metal Recycling, Hartlepool

Class 37

37893	**E**	Ron Hull Junior, Rotherham

Class 56

56022	**F**	European Metal Recycling, Kingsbury
56046	**CE**	European Metal Recycling, Kingsbury
56073	**F**	European Metal Recycling, Kingsbury
56112	**LH**	European Metal Recycling, Kingsbury
56133	**F**	European Metal Recycling, Kingsbury

1.6. LOCOMOTIVES EXPORTED FOR USE ABROAD

This section details former BR (plus privatisation era) diesel and electric locomotives that have been exported from the UK for use in industrial locations or by a main line operator abroad. Not included are locos that are "preserved" abroad, which are included in our "Preserved Locomotives" publication. Generally locos are included here if they are expected to remain abroad for more than one year.

Number	*Other no./name*	*Location*
Class 04		
D2289		Lonato SpA, Lonato Steelworks, Lonato, Brescia, Italy
Class 37		
37703	L25	DB Schenker, Perpignan, France (stored)
37714	L26	DB Schenker, Perpignan, France (stored)
37716	L23	DB Schenker, Perpignan, France (stored)
37718	L22	DB Schenker, Perpignan, France (stored)
37799	L27	Continental Rail, Spain (sold for scrap)
37800	L33	DB Schenker, Perpignan, France (stored)
37801	L29	Continental Rail, Spain (sold for scrap)
37883	L28	Continental Rail, Spain (sold for scrap)
37884	L34	DB Schenker, Perpignan, France (stored)
Class 58		
58001		Axiom Rail, Alizay, France (stored)
58004		Axiom Rail, Alizay, France (stored)
58005		Axiom Rail, Alizay, France (stored)
58006		Axiom Rail, Alizay, France (stored)
58007		Axiom Rail, Alizay, France (stored)
58009		Axiom Rail, Alizay, France (stored)
58010		Axiom Rail, Alizay, France (stored)
58011		Axiom Rail, Alizay, France (stored)
58013		Axiom Rail, Alizay, France (stored)
58015	L54	Transfesa, Spain
58018		Axiom Rail, Alizay, France (stored)
58020	L43	Transfesa, Spain
58021		Axiom Rail, Alizay, France (stored)
58024	L42	Transfesa, Spain
58025	L41	Continental Rail, Spain (stored)
58026		Axiom Rail, Alizay, France (stored)
58027	L52	Continental Rail, Spain (stored)
58029	L44	Transfesa, Spain
58030	L46	Transfesa, Spain
58031	L45	Transfesa, Spain
58032		Axiom Rail, Alizay, France (stored)
58033		Axiom Rail, Alizay, France (stored)

58034		Axiom Rail, Alizay, France (stored)
58035		Axiom Rail, Alizay, France (stored)
58036		Axiom Rail, Alizay, France (stored)
58038		Axiom Rail, Alizay, France (stored)
58039		Axiom Rail, Alizay, France (stored)
58040		Axiom Rail, Alizay, France (stored)
58041	L36	Transfesa, Spain
58042		Axiom Rail, Alizay, France (stored)
58043	L37	Transfesa, Spain
58044		Axiom Rail, Alizay, France (stored)
58046		Axiom Rail, Alizay, France (stored)
58047	L51	Transfesa, Spain
58049		Axiom Rail, Alizay, France (stored)
58050	L53	Continental Rail, Spain (stored)

Class 59

59003	YEOMAN HIGHLANDER	
	259 003-2	Heavy Haul Power International, Germany

Class 66

66022	Euro Cargo Rail, France
66026	Euro Cargo Rail, France
66028	Euro Cargo Rail, France
66029	Euro Cargo Rail, France
66032	Euro Cargo Rail, France
66033	Euro Cargo Rail, France
66036	Euro Cargo Rail, France
66038	Euro Cargo Rail, France
66042	Euro Cargo Rail, France
66045	Euro Cargo Rail, France
66049	Euro Cargo Rail, France
66052	Euro Cargo Rail, France
66062	Euro Cargo Rail, France
66064	Euro Cargo Rail, France
66072	Euro Cargo Rail, France
66073	Euro Cargo Rail, France
66123	Euro Cargo Rail, France
66146	DB Schenker Rail Polska, Poland
66153	DB Schenker Rail Polska, Poland
66159	DB Schenker Rail Polska, Poland
66157	DB Schenker Rail Polska, Poland
66163	DB Schenker Rail Polska, Poland
66166	DB Schenker Rail Polska, Poland
66173	DB Schenker Rail Polska, Poland
66178	DB Schenker Rail Polska, Poland
66179	Euro Cargo Rail, France
66180	DB Schenker Rail Polska, Poland
66189	DB Schenker Rail Polska, Poland
66190	Euro Cargo Rail, France
66191	Euro Cargo Rail, France
66195	Euro Cargo Rail, France

66196		DB Schenker Rail Polska, Poland
66202		Euro Cargo Rail, France
66203		Euro Cargo Rail, France
66205		Euro Cargo Rail, France
66208		Euro Cargo Rail, France
66209		Euro Cargo Rail, France
66210		Euro Cargo Rail, France
66211		Euro Cargo Rail, France
66212		Euro Cargo Rail, France
66214		Euro Cargo Rail, France
66215		Euro Cargo Rail, France
66216		Euro Cargo Rail, France
66217		Euro Cargo Rail, France
66219		Euro Cargo Rail, France
66220		DB Schenker Rail Polska, Poland
66222		Euro Cargo Rail, France
66223		Euro Cargo Rail, France
66224		Euro Cargo Rail, France
66225		Euro Cargo Rail, France
66226		Euro Cargo Rail, France
66227		DB Schenker Rail Polska, Poland
66228		Euro Cargo Rail, France
66229		Euro Cargo Rail, France
66231		Euro Cargo Rail, France
66233		Euro Cargo Rail, France
66234		Euro Cargo Rail, France
66235		Euro Cargo Rail, France
66236		Euro Cargo Rail, France
66237		DB Schenker Rail Polska, Poland
66239		Euro Cargo Rail, France
66240		Euro Cargo Rail, France
66241		Euro Cargo Rail, France
66242		Euro Cargo Rail, France
66243		Euro Cargo Rail, France
66244		Euro Cargo Rail, France
66245		Euro Cargo Rail, France
66246		Euro Cargo Rail, France
66247		Euro Cargo Rail, France
66248		DB Schenker Rail Polska, Poland
66411	66012	Freightliner, Poland
66582	66009	Freightliner, Poland
66583	66010	Freightliner, Poland
66584	66011	Freightliner, Poland
66586	66008	Freightliner, Poland
66608	66603	Freightliner, Poland
66609	66604	Freightliner, Poland
66611	66605	Freightliner, Poland
66612	66606	Freightliner, Poland
66624	66602	Freightliner, Poland
66625	66601	Freightliner, Poland

Class 86

86218	0450 004-1	FLOYD, Hungary
86232	0450 003-3	FLOYD, Hungary
86248	0450 001-7	FLOYD, Hungary
86250	0450 002-5	FLOYD, Hungary

Class 87

87003	87003-0	BZK, Bulgaria
87004	87004-8 Britannia	BZK, Bulgaria
87006	87006-3	BZK, Bulgaria
87007	87007-1	BZK, Bulgaria
87008	87008-9	BZK, Bulgaria (stored)
87010	87010-5	BZK, Bulgaria
87012	87012-1	BZK, Bulgaria
87013	87013-9	BZK, Bulgaria
87014	87014-7	BZK, Bulgaria (stored)
87019	87019-6	BZK, Bulgaria
87020	87020-4	BZK, Bulgaria
87022	87022-0	BZK, Bulgaria
87026	87026-1	BZK, Bulgaria
87028	87028-7	BZK, Bulgaria
87029	87029-5	BZK, Bulgaria
87033	87033-7	BZK, Bulgaria
87034	87034-5	BZK, Bulgaria

The Allocation History of BR Diesel Multiple Units
PART I
Allocations
Storage Points
Namings
Preservation
Exports
Disposals
compiled by
Roger
Harris
Departmentals
GWR Railcars
Railbuses
HST Stock
Blue Pullmans
Prototypes

2. LOCO-HAULED COACHING STOCK

INTRODUCTION

NUMBERING SYSTEMS

Seven different numbering systems were in use on British Rail. These were the British Rail series, the four pre-nationalisation companies' series', the Pullman Car Company's series and the UIC (International Union of Railways) series. BR number series coaches and former Pullman Car Company series are listed separately. There is also a separate listing of "Saloon" type vehicles which are registered to run on the national railway system, Locomotive Support Coaches and Service Stock. Please note the Mark 2 Pullman vehicles were ordered after the Pullman Car Company had been nationalised and are therefore numbered in the British Rail series.

Also listed separately are the British Rail and Pullman Car Company number series coaches used on North Yorkshire Moors Railway services on the national railway system. This is due to their very restricted sphere of operation.

The BR number series grouped vehicles of a particular type together in chronological order. Major modifications affecting type of accommodation resulted in renumbering into a more appropriate or new number series. Since privatisation such renumbering has not always taken place resulting in renumbering which has been more haphazard and greater variations within numbering groups.

LAYOUT OF INFORMATION

Coaches are listed in numerical order of painted number in batches according to type.

Each coach entry is laid out as in the following example (previous number(s) column may be omitted where not applicable):

No.	*Prev. No.*	*Notes*	*Livery*	*Owner*	*Operator*	*Depot/Location*
42346	(41053)	*h	**FD**	A	GW	OO

Notes:

The owner is the responsible custodian of the coach and this may not always be the owner by law.

The operator is the organisation which facilitates the use of the coach and may not be the actual train operating company which runs the train.

The depot is the facility primarily responsible for the coaches maintenance. Light maintenance and heavy overhauls may be carried out elsewhere.

The location is where coaches not in use are currently being kept/stored.

DETAILED INFORMATION & CODES

Under each type heading, the following details are shown:

- "Mark" of coach (see below).
- Descriptive text.
- Number of first class seats, standard class seats, lavatory compartments and wheelchair spaces shown as F/S nT nW respectively.
- Bogie type (see below).
- Additional features.
- ETH Index.
- Weight: All weights are shown as metric tonnes (t = tonnes).

BOGIE TYPES

BR Mark 1 (BR1). Double bolster leaf spring bogie. Generally 90 mph, but Mark 1 bogies may be permitted to run at 100 mph with special maintenance. Weight: 6.1 t.

BR Mark 2 (BR2). Single bolster leaf-spring bogie used on certain types of non-passenger stock and suburban stock (all now withdrawn). Weight: 5.3 t.

COMMONWEALTH (C). Heavy, cast steel coil spring bogie. 100 mph. Weight: 6.75 t.

B4. Coil spring fabricated bogie. Generally 100 mph, but B4 bogies may be permitted to run at 110 mph with special maintenance. Weight: 5.2 t.

B5. Heavy duty version of B4. 100 mph. Weight: 5.3 t.

B5 (SR). A bogie originally used on Southern Region EMUs, similar in design to B5. Now also used on locomotive-hauled coaches. 100 mph.

BT10. A fabricated bogie designed for 125 mph. Air suspension.

T4. A 125 mph bogie designed by BREL (now Bombardier Transportation).

BT41. Fitted to Mark 4 vehicles, designed by SIG in Switzerland. At present limited to 125 mph, but designed for 140 mph.

BRAKES

Air braking is now standard on British main line trains. Vehicles with other equipment are denoted:

b Air braked, through vacuum pipe.
v Vacuum braked.
x Dual braked (air and vacuum).

HEATING & VENTILATION

Electric heating and ventilation is now standard on British main-line trains. Certain coaches for use on charter services may also have steam heating facilities, or be steam heated only.

PUBLIC ADDRESS

It is assumed all coaches are now fitted with public address equipment, although certain stored vehicles may not have this feature. In addition, it is assumed all vehicles with a conductor's compartment have public address transmission facilities, as have catering vehicles.

COOKING EQUIPMENT

It is assumed that Mark 1 catering vehicles have gas powered cooking equipment, whilst Mark 2, 3 and 4 catering vehicles have electric powered cooking equipment unless stated otherwise.

ADDITIONAL FEATURE CODES

d	Secondary door locking.
dg	Driver–Guard communication equipment.
f	Facelifted or fluorescent lighting.
h	"High density" seating
k	Composition brake blocks (instead of cast iron).
n	Day/night lighting.
pg	Public address transmission and driver-guard communication.
pt	Public address transmission facility.
q	Catering staff to shore telephone.
w	Wheelchair space.
★	Blue star multiple working cables fitted.

NOTES ON ETH INDICES

The sum of ETH indices in a train must not be more than the ETH index of the locomotive. The normal voltage on British trains is 1000 V. Suffix "X" denotes 600 amp wiring instead of 400 amp. Trains whose ETH index is higher than 66 must be formed completely of 600 amp wired stock. Class 33 and 73 locomotives cannot provide a suitable electric train supply for Mark 2D, Mark 2E, Mark 2F, Mark 3, Mark 3A, Mark 3B or Mark 4 coaches. Class 55 locomotives provide an e.t.s. directly from one of their traction generators into the train line. Consequently voltage fluctuations can result in motor-alternator flashover. Thus these locomotives are not suitable for use with Mark 2D, Mark 2E, Mark 2F, Mark 3, Mark 3A, Mark 3B or Mark 4 coaches unless modified motor-alternators are fitted. Such motor alternators were fitted to Mark 2D and 2F coaches used on the East Coast main line, but few remain fitted.

BUILD DETAILS

Lot Numbers
Vehicles ordered under the auspices of BR were allocated a lot (batch) number when ordered and these are quoted in class headings and sub-headings.

Builders
These are shown for each lot. Abbreviations used are shown in Section 7.6.

Information on sub-contracting works which built parts of vehicles eg the underframes etc. is not shown.
In addition to the above, certain vintage Pullman cars were built or rebuilt at the following works:

Metropolitan Carriage & Wagon Company, Birmingham
Midland Carriage & Wagon Company, Birmingham
Pullman Car Company, Preston Park, Brighton
Conversions have also been carried out at the Railway Technical Centre, Derby, LNWR, Crewe and Blakes Fabrications, Edinburgh.

VEHICLE NUMBERS

Where a coach has been renumbered, the former number is shown in parentheses. If a coach has been renumbered more than once, the original number is shown first in parentheses, followed by the most recent previous number.

THE DEVELOPMENT OF BR STANDARD COACHES

Mark 1

The standard BR coach built from 1951 to 1963 was the Mark 1. This type features a separate underframe and body. The underframe is normally 64 ft 6 in long, but certain vehicles were built on shorter (57 ft) frames. Tungsten lighting was standard and until 1961, BR Mark 1 bogies were generally provided. In 1959 Lot No. 30525 (Open Standard) appeared with fluorescent lighting and melamine interior panels, and from 1961 onwards Commonwealth bogies were fitted in an attempt to improve the quality of ride which became very poor when the tyre profiles on the wheels of the BR1 bogies became worn. Later batches of Open Standard and Open Brake Standard retained the features of Lot No. 30525, but compartment vehicles – whilst utilising melamine panelling in Standard Class – still retained tungsten lighting. Wooden interior finish was retained in First Class vehicles where the only change was to fluorescent lighting in open vehicles (except Lot No. 30648, which had tungsten lighting). In later years many Mark 1 coaches had BR 1 bogies replaced by B4.

XP64

In 1964, a new prototype train was introduced. Known as "XP64", it featured new seat designs, pressure heating & ventilation, aluminium compartment doors and corridor partitions, foot pedal operated toilets and B4 bogies. The vehicles were built on standard Mark 1 underframes. Folding exterior doors were fitted, but these proved troublesome and were later replaced with hinged doors. All XP64 coaches have been withdrawn, but some have been preserved.

Mark 2

The prototype Mark 2 vehicle (W 13252) was produced in 1963. This was a Corridor First of semi-integral construction and had pressure heating & ventilation, tungsten lighting, and was mounted on B4 bogies. This vehicle has now been preserved at the Mid Norfolk Railway. The production build was similar, but wider windows were used. The Open Standard vehicles used a new seat design similar to that in the XP64 and fluorescent lighting was provided. Interior finish reverted to wood. Mark 2 vehicles were built from 1964–66.

Mark 2A–2C

The Mark 2A design, built 1967–68, incorporated the remainder of the features first used in the XP64 coaches, ie foot pedal operated toilets (except Open Brake Standard), new First Class seat design, aluminium compartment doors and partitions together with fluorescent lighting in first class compartments. Folding gangway doors (lime green coloured) were used instead of the traditional one-piece variety.

Mark 2B coaches had wide wrap around doors at vehicle ends, no centre doors and a slightly longer body. In Standard Class there was one toilet at each end instead of two at one end as previously. The folding gangway doors were red.

Mark 2C coaches had a lowered ceiling with twin strips of fluorescent lighting and ducting for air conditioning, but air conditioning was never fitted.

Mark 2D–2F

These vehicles were fitted with air conditioning. They had no opening toplights in saloon windows, which were shallower than previous ones.

Mark 2E vehicles had smaller toilets with luggage racks opposite. The folding gangway doors were fawn coloured.

Mark 2F vehicles had a modified air conditioning system, plastic interior panels and InterCity 70 type seats.

Mark 3

The Mark 3 design has BT10 bogies, is 75 ft (23 m) long and is of fully integral construction with InterCity 70 type seats. Gangway doors were yellow (red in Kitchen Buffet First) when new, although these were changed on refurbishment. Loco-hauled coaches are classified Mark 3A, Mark 3 being reserved for HST trailers. A new batch of Open First and Open Brake First, classified Mark 3B, was built in 1985 with Advanced Passenger Train-style seating and revised lighting. These are now in use on First Great Western sleeping car trains, but the seats have been replaced with former HST First Class seats. The last vehicles in the Mark 3 series were the driving brake vans ("Driving Van Trailers") built for West Coast Main Line services.

A number of Mark 3 vehicles have recently been converted for use as HST trailers with Grand Central, CrossCountry and First Great Western.

Mark 4

The Mark 4 design was built by Metro-Cammell for use on the East Coast Main Line after electrification and featured a body profile suitable for tilting trains, although tilt is not fitted, and is not intended to be. This design is suitable for 140 mph running, although is restricted to 125 mph because the signalling system on the route is not suitable for the higher speed. The bogies for these coaches were built by SIG in Switzerland and are designated BT41. Power operated sliding plug exterior doors are standard. All Mark 4s were rebuilt with completely new interiors in 2003–05 for GNER and referred to as "Mallard" stock. These rakes generally run in fixed formations and are now operated by East Coast.

2.1. BR NUMBER SERIES COACHING STOCK

KITCHEN FIRST

Mark 1. Spent most of its life as a Royal Train vehicle and was numbered 2907 for a time. Built with Commonwealth bogies, but B5 bogies substituted. 24/–. ETH 2.

Lot No. 30633 Swindon 1961. 41 t.

325	**VN**	OE	*NB*	CP	DUART

PULLMAN KITCHEN

Mark 2. Pressure Ventilated. Built with First Class seating but this has been replaced with a servery area. 2T. B5 bogies. ETH 6.

Lot No. 30755 Derby 1966. 40 t.

504	**PC**	WC	*WC*	CS	ULLSWATER
506	**PC**	WC	*WC*	CS	WINDERMERE

PULLMAN OPEN FIRST

Mark 2. Pressure Ventilated. 36/– 2T. B4 bogies. ETH 5.

Non-standard livery: 546 Maroon & beige.

Lot No. 30754 Derby 1966. 35 t.

546	**0**	WC		CS	CITY OF MANCHESTER
548	**PC**	WC	*WC*	CS	GRASMERE
549	**PC**	WC	*WC*	CS	BASSENTHWAITE
550	**PC**	WC	*WC*	CS	RYDAL WATER
551	**PC**	WC	*WC*	CS	BUTTERMERE
552	**PC**	WC	*WC*	CS	ENNERDALE WATER
553	**PC**	WC	*WC*	CS	CRUMMOCK WATER

PULLMAN OPEN BRAKE FIRST

Mark 2. Pressure Ventilated. 30/– 2T. B4 bogies. ETH 4.

Lot No. 30753 Derby 1966. 35 t.

586	**PC**	WC	*WC*	CS	DERWENTWATER

BUFFET FIRST

Mark 2F. Air conditioned. Converted 1988–89/91 at BREL, Derby from Mark 2F Open Firsts. 1200/01/03/11/20/21/50/52 have Stones equipment, others have Temperature Ltd. 25/– 1T 1W (except 1253 which is 26/– 1T). B4 bogies. d. ETH 6X.

1200/03/11/20/52. Lot No. 30845 Derby 1973. 33 t.
1201/07/10/12/13/21/50/54/58. Lot No. 30859 Derby 1973–74. 33 t.
1253. Lot No. 30873 Derby 1974–75. 33 t.

1200	(3287, 6459)	**RV**	RV	*RV*	EH	AMBER
1201	(3361, 6445)	**CH**	RV	*VT*	TM	
1203	(3291)	**IC**	RV	*RV*	EH	
1207	(3328, 6422)	**V**	OE		ZG	
1210	(3405, 6462)	**FS**	E	*SR*	IS	
1211	(3305)	**IC**	RA		BO	
1212	(3427, 6453)	**V**	RV	*RV*	EH	
1213	(3419)	**G**	DM		MQ	
1220	(3315, 6432)	**FS**	E	*SR*	IS	
1221	(3371)	**IC**	OE		ZG	
1250	(3372)	**V**	RV		EH	
1252	(3280)	**V**	CG		LM	
1253	(3432)	**V**	CG		KT	
1254	(3391)	**BG**	DR		BH	
1258	(3322)	**V**	WC		CS	

KITCHEN WITH BAR

Mark 1. Built with no seats but three Pullman-style seats now fitted in bar area. B5 bogies. ETH 1.

Lot No. 30624 Cravens 1960–61. 41 t.

1566	**VN**	OE	*NB*	CP

KITCHEN BUFFET UNCLASSIFIED

Mark 1. Built with 23 loose chairs. All remaining vehicles refurbished with 23 fixed polypropylene chairs and fluorescent lighting. ETH 2 (* 2X). 1683/91/92/99 were further refurbished with 21 chairs, wheelchair space and carpets.

s Modified for use as servery vehicle with some or all seating removed.
t Modified with 11 chairs with a food preparation area replacing part of the former seating area.

1651–99. Lot No. 30628 Pressed Steel 1960–61. Commonwealth bogies. 39 t.
1730. Lot No. 30512 BRCW 1960–61. B5 bogies. 37 t.

Non-standard liveries: 1683 and 1699 Oxford Blue.
1679 and 1680 British racing green & cream lined out in gold.

1651	t	**CC**	RV		EH
1657	s	**DR**	RV		ZG
1658	t	**BG**	DB		FA
1659	s	**PC**	RA	*ST*	CS
1671	x*t	**CH**	RV	*RV*	EH
1679	t	**0**	DB		EH
1680	*t	**0**	DB		EH
1683		**0**	RV	*RV*	EH
1691	t	**CC**	RV	*RV*	EH
1692	t	**CH**	RV	*RV*	EH
1696	t	**G**	DB		FA
1699	t	**0**	RV	*RV*	EH
1730	x	**M**	BK	*BK*	BT

BUFFET STANDARD

Mark 2F. Air conditioned. Temperature Ltd. equipment. InterCity 70 seats. Converted 1974 from Mark 2F Open Standard 5970 as a prototype self-service buffet for APT-P. Sold to Northern Ireland Railways 1983, regauged to 5'3" and numbered 546. Since withdrawn, repatriated to Great Britain and converted back to standard gauge. –/24. B5 bogies. ETH 12X.

Lot No. 30860 Derby 1973–74. 33 t.

1800	**PC**	WC	*WC*	CS	TINTAGEL

BUFFET STANDARD

Mark 1. –/44 2T. These vehicles are basically an open standard with two full window spaces removed to accommodate a buffet counter, and four seats removed to allow for a stock cupboard. All remaining vehicles now have fluorescent lighting. Commonwealth bogies. ETH 3.

1813–32. Lot No. 30520 Wolverton 1960. 38 t.
1840–42. Lot No. 30507 Wolverton 1960. 37 t.
1859–63. Lot No. 30670 Wolverton 1961–62. 38 t.
1882. Lot No. 30702 Wolverton 1962. 38 t.

Notes:

1842 is refurbished and fitted with a microwave oven.
1861 has had its toilets replaced with store cupboards.

1813	x	**M**	RV	*RV*	EH
1832	x	**CC**	RV	*RV*	EH
1840	v	**G**	WC	*WC*	CS
1842		**CH**	RV	*RV*	EH
1859	x	**M**	BK	*BK*	BT
1860	x	**M**	WC	*WC*	CS
1861	x	**M**	WC	*WC*	CS
1863	x	**CH**	RV	*RV*	EH
1882	x	**M**	WC	*WC*	CS

KITCHEN BUFFET UNCLASSIFIED

Mark 1. These vehicles were built as Unclassified Restaurants. They were rebuilt with buffet counters and 23 fixed polypropylene chairs, then further refurbished by fitting fluorescent lighting. ETH 2X.

s Modified for use as servery vehicle with seating removed.

1953. Lot No. 30575 Swindon 1960. B4/B5 bogies. 36.5 t.
1961. Lot No. 30632 Swindon 1961. Commonwealth bogies. 39 t.

1953	s	**VN**	OE	*NB*	CP
1961	x	**G**	WC	*WC*	CS

CHARTER TRAIN STAFF COACHES

Mark 1. Converted from Corridor Brake Composites in 1988. Commonwealth bogies. ETH 2.

Lot No. 30732 Derby 1964. 37 t.

2833	(21270)	**M**	WC	*WC*	CS
2834	(21267)	**M**	RV		EH

HM THE QUEEN'S SALOON

Mark 3. Converted from an Open First built 1972. Consists of a lounge, bedroom and bathroom for HM The Queen, and a combined bedroom and bathroom for the Queen's dresser. One entrance vestibule has double doors. Air conditioned. BT10 bogies. ETH 9X.

Lot No. 30886 Wolverton 1977. 36 t.

2903	(11001)	**RP**	NR	*RP*	ZN

HRH THE DUKE OF EDINBURGH'S SALOON

Mark 3. Converted from an Open Standard built 1972. Consists of a combined lounge/dining room, a bedroom and a shower room for the Duke, a kitchen and a valet's bedroom and bathroom. Air conditioned. BT10 bogies. ETH 15X.

Lot No. 30887 Wolverton 1977. 36 t.

2904	(12001)	**RP**	NR	*RP*	ZN

ROYAL HOUSEHOLD SLEEPING CAR

Mark 3A. Built to similar specification as Sleeping Cars 10647–729. 12 sleeping compartments for use of Royal Household with a fixed lower berth and a hinged upper berth. 2T plus shower room. Air conditioned. BT10 bogies. ETH 11X.

Lot No. 31002 Derby/Wolverton 1985. 44 t.

2915		**RP**	NR	*RP*	ZN

HRH THE PRINCE OF WALES'S DINING CAR

Mark 3. Converted from HST TRUK built 1976. Large kitchen retained, but dining area modified for Royal use seating up to 14 at central table(s). Air conditioned. BT10 bogies. ETH 13X.

Lot No. 31059 Wolverton 1988. 43 t.

2916	(40512)	**RP**	NR	*RP*	ZN

ROYAL KITCHEN/HOUSEHOLD DINING CAR

Mark 3. Converted from HST TRUK built 1977. Large kitchen retained and dining area slightly modified with seating for 22 Royal Household members. Air conditioned. BT10 bogies. ETH 13X.

Lot No. 31084 Wolverton 1990. 43 t.

2917	(40514)	**RP**	NR	*RP*	ZN

ROYAL HOUSEHOLD CARS

Mark 3. Converted from HST TRUKs built 1976/77. Air conditioned. BT10 bogies. ETH 10X.

Lot Nos. 31083 (* 31085) Wolverton 1989. 41.05 t.

2918	(40515)	**RP**	NR		ZN
2919	(40518) *	**RP**	NR		ZN

ROYAL HOUSEHOLD COUCHETTES

Mark 2B. Converted from Corridor Brake First built 1969. Consists of luggage accommodation, guard's compartment, workshop area, 350 kW diesel generator and staff sleeping accommodation. B5 bogies. ETH 2X.

Lot No. 31044 Wolverton 1986. 48 t.

2920	(14109, 17109)	**RP**	NR	*RP*	ZN

Mark 2B. Converted from Corridor Brake First built 1969. Consists of luggage accommodation, kitchen, brake control equipment and staff accommodation. B5 bogies. ETH 7X.

Lot No. 31086 Wolverton 1990. 41.5 t.

2921	(14107, 17107)	**RP**	NR	*RP*	ZN

HRH THE PRINCE OF WALES'S SLEEPING CAR

Mark 3B. BT10 bogies. Air conditioned. ETH 7X.

Lot No. 31035 Derby/Wolverton 1987.

2922	**RP**	NR	*RP*	ZN

ROYAL SALOON

Mark 3B. BT10 bogies. Air conditioned. ETH 6X.

Lot No. 31036 Derby/Wolverton 1987.

2923	**RP**	NR	*RP*	ZN

OPEN FIRST

Mark 1. 42/– 2T. ETH 3. Many now fitted with table lamps.

3058–69. Lot No. 30169 Doncaster 1955. B4 bogies. 33 t (* 35 t).
3093. Lot No. 30472 BRCW 1959. B4 bogies. 33 t.
3096–3100. Lot No. 30576 BRCW 1959. B4 bogies. 33 t.

3058 was numbered DB 975313, 3068 was numbered DB 975606 and 3093 was numbered DB 977594 for a time when in departmental service for BR.

3058	*x	**M**	WC	*WC*	CS	FLORENCE
3066		**CC**	RV	*RV*	EH	
3068		**CC**	RV	*RV*	EH	
3069		**CC**	RV	*RV*	EH	
3093	x	**M**	WC	*WC*	CS	PAULA
3096	x	**M**	BK	*BK*	BT	
3097		**CC**	RV	*RV*	EH	
3098	x	**CH**	RV	*RV*	EH	
3100	x	**CH**	RV	*RV*	EH	

Later design with fluorescent lighting, aluminium window frames and Commonwealth bogies.

3105–28. Lot No. 30697 Swindon 1962–63. 36 t.
3130–50. Lot No. 30717 Swindon 1963. 36 t.

3128/36/41/43/44/46/47/48 were renumbered 1058/60/63/65/66/68/69/70 when reclassified Restaurant Open First, then 3600/05/08/09/02/06/04/10 when declassified to Open Standard, but have since regained their original numbers. 3136 was numbered DB 977970 for a time when in use with Serco Railtest as a Brake Force Runner.

Note: 3105 has had its luggage racks removed and has tungsten lighting.

3105	x	**M**	WC	*WC*	CS
3106	x	**M**	WC	*WC*	CS
3107	x	**CH**	RV	*RV*	EH
3110	x	**CH**	RV	*RV*	EH
3112	x	**CH**	RV	*RV*	EH
3113	x	**M**	WC	*WC*	CS
3114		**G**	RV		EH
3115	x	**M**	BK	*BK*	BT
3117	x	**M**	WC	*WC*	CS
3119		**CC**	RV	*RV*	EH
3120		**CC**	RV	*RV*	EH
3121		**CH**	RV	*RV*	EH
3122	x	**CH**	RV	*RV*	EH
3123		**CC**	RV	*RV*	EH
3124		**G**	RV		EH
3125	x	**CH**	JH	*VT*	TM
3127		**G**	RV		EH
3128	x	**M**	WC	*WC*	CS
3130	v	**M**	WC	*WC*	CS
3131	x	**M**	RV		EH
3132	x	**M**	RV		EH
3133	x	**M**	RV		EH
3136		**M**	WC	*WC*	CS
3140	x	**CH**	RV	*RV*	EH
3141		**M**	RV	*RV*	EH
3143		**M**	WC	*WC*	CS
3144	x	**M**	RV	*RV*	EH
3146		**M**	RV	*RV*	EH
3147		**CH**	RV	*RV*	EH
3148		**M**	JH	*WC*	CS
3149		**CC**	RV	*RV*	EH
3150		**M**	BK	*BK*	BT

Names:

3105	JULIA
3106	ALEXANDRA
3113	JESSICA
3117	CHRISTINA
3128	VICTORIA
3130	PAMELA
3136	DIANA
3143	PATRICIA

OPEN FIRST

Mark 2D. Air conditioned. Stones equipment. 42/– 2T. B4 bogies. ETH 5.

† Interior modified to Pullman Car standards with new seating, new panelling, tungsten lighting and table lights for the "Northern Belle".

Lot No. 30821 Derby 1971–72. 34 t.

3174	†	**VN**	OE	*NB*	CP	GLAMIS
3182	†	**VN**	OE	*NB*	CP	WARWICK
3188		**PC**	RA	*ST*	CS	SOVEREIGN

OPEN FIRST

Mark 2E. Air conditioned. Stones equipment. 42/– 2T (p 36/– 2T). B4 bogies. ETH 5.

r Refurbished with new seats.
† Interior modified to Pullman Car standards with new seating, new panelling, tungsten lighting and table lights for the "Northern Belle".

3255 was numbered 3525 for a time when fitted with a pantry.

Lot No. 30843 Derby 1972–73. 32.5 t. († 35.8 t).

3223		**RV**	RA		BO	DIAMOND
3231	p	**PC**	RA	*ST*	CS	APOLLO
3232	dr	**BG**	OE		BH	
3240		**RV**	RA		BO	SAPPHIRE
3241	dr	**FP**	CG		LM	
3247	†	**VN**	OE	*NB*	CP	CHATSWORTH
3255	dr	**M**	DB		FA	
3267	†	**VN**	OE	*NB*	CP	BELVOIR
3269	dr	**M**	DB		EH	
3273	†	**VN**	OE	*NB*	CP	ALNWICK
3275	†	**VN**	OE	*NB*	CP	HARLECH

OPEN FIRST

Mark 2F. Air conditioned. 3277–3318/58–79 have Stones equipment, others have Temperature Ltd. 42/– 2T. All now refurbished with power-operated vestibule doors, new panels and new seat trim. B4 bogies. d. ETH 5X.

3277–3318. Lot No. 30845 Derby 1973. 33.5 t.
3325–3426. Lot No. 30859 Derby 1973–74. 33.5 t.
3431–38. Lot No. 30873 Derby 1974–75. 33.5 t.

r Further refurbished with table lamps and modified seats with burgundy seat trim.
u Fitted with power supply for Mark 1 Kitchen Buffet Unclassified.

3277		**AR**	RV	*RV*	EH
3279	u	**M**	DB	*SR*	TO
3292		**M**	DB	*SR*	TO
3295		**AR**	RV	*RV*	EH
3303		**AR**	DB		CE
3304	r	**V**	RV	*RV*	EH

3309		**IC**	VT		TM
3312		**IC**	RA		LM
3313	r	**M**	WC	*WC*	CS
3314	r	**V**	RV	*RV*	EH
3318		**M**	DB	*SR*	TO
3325	r	**V**	RV	*RV*	EH
3326	r	**M**	WC	*WC*	CS
3330	r	**RV**	RV	*RV*	EH
3331		**M**	DB	*SR*	TO
3333	r	**V**	RV	*RV*	EH
3334		**AR**	RV	*RV*	EH
3336	u	**AR**	RV		CD
3338	u	**M**	DB		EH
3340	r	**V**	RV	*RV*	EH
3344	r	**V**	RV	*RV*	EH
3345	r	**V**	RV	*RV*	EH
3348	r	**RV**	RV	*RV*	EH
3350	r	**M**	WC	*WC*	CS
3351		**CH**	VT	*VT*	TM
3352	r	**M**	WC	*WC*	CS
3353	r	**G**	DM		MQ
3354	r	**V**	DM		YJ
3356	r	**RV**	RV	*RV*	EH
3358		**M**	DB	*SR*	TO
3359	r	**M**	WC	*WC*	CS
3360	r	**M**	WC	*WC*	CS
3362	r	**M**	WC	*WC*	CS
3364	r	**RV**	RV	*RV*	EH
3366	r	**BG**	DR		BH
3368		**M**	DB		FA
3374		**BG**	DR		BH
3375		**M**	DB		EH
3379	u	**AR**	RV	*RV*	EH
3384	r	**RV**	RV	*RV*	EH
3386	r	**V**	RV	*RV*	EH
3387	r	**V**	DM		MQ
3388		**M**	DB		EH
3390	r	**RV**	RV	*RV*	EH
3392	r	**M**	WC	*WC*	CS
3395	r	**M**	WC	*WC*	CS
3397	r	**RV**	RV	*RV*	EH
3399	u	**M**	DB		EH
3400		**M**	DB	*SR*	TO
3402	r	**V**	DM		YJ
3408	r	**M**	WC		CS
3411	r	**V**	DM		MQ
3414		**M**	DB		EH
3416		**IC**	VT		TM
3417		**AR**	RV	*RV*	EH
3424		**M**	DB	*SR*	TO
3425	r	**V**	DM		YJ
3426	r	**RV**	RV	*RV*	EH
3431	r	**M**	WC	*WC*	CS
3438	r	**V**	E		LM

Names:

3330	BRUNEL
3348	GAINSBOROUGH
3356	TENNYSON
3364	SHAKESPEARE
3384	DICKENS
3390	CONSTABLE
3397	WORDSWORTH
3426	ELGAR

OPEN STANDARD

Mark 1. This coach has narrower seats than later vehicles. Built with BR Mark 1 bogies. –/64 2T. ETH 4.

Lot No. 30079 York 1953. Commonwealth bogies. 36 t.

3766	x	**M**	WC	*WC*	CS

OPEN STANDARD

Mark 1. These vehicles are a development of the above with fluorescent lighting and modified design of seat headrest. Built with BR Mark 1 bogies. –/64 2T. ETH 4.

4831–36. Lot No. 30506 Wolverton 1959. Commonwealth bogies. 33 t.
4856. Lot No. 30525 Wolverton 1959–60. B4 bogies. 33 t.

4831	x	**M**	BK	*BK*	BT
4832	x	**CC**	BK	*BK*	BT
4836	x	**M**	BK	*BK*	BT
4856	x	**M**	BK	*BK*	BT

OPEN STANDARD

Mark 1. Later vehicles built with Commonwealth bogies. –/64 2T. ETH 4.

4902–12. Lot No. 30646 Wolverton 1961. BR Mark 1 bogies substituted by the SR. All now re-rebogied. B4 34 t, C 36 t.
4927–5044. Lot No. 30690 Wolverton 1961–62. Aluminium window frames. 37 t.

4902	x B4	**CH**	RV	*RV*	EH
4905	x C	**M**	WC	*WC*	CS
4912	x C	**M**	WC	*WC*	CS
4927	x	**CH**	RV	*RV*	EH
4931	v	**M**	WC	*WC*	CS
4940	x	**M**	WC	*WC*	CS
4946	x	**M**	RV		MI
4949	x	**CH**	RV	*RV*	EH
4951	x	**M**	WC	*WC*	CS
4954	v	**M**	WC	*WC*	CS
4959		**CH**	RV	*RV*	EH
4960	x	**M**	WC	*WC*	CS
4973	x	**M**	WC	*WC*	CS
4984	x	**M**	WC	*WC*	CS
4986		**G**	RV		EH
4991		**CH**	RV	*RV*	EH
4994	x	**M**	WC	*WC*	CS
4996	x	**M**	RV		CD
4998		**M**	RV		ZA
5007		**G**	RV		EH
5008	x	**M**	RV		CD
5009	x	**CH**	RV	*RV*	EH
5023		**G**	RV		EH
5027		**G**	RV		EH
5028	x	**CC**	BK	*BK*	BT
5032	x	**M**	WC	*WC*	CS
5033	x	**M**	WC	*WC*	CS
5035	x	**M**	WC	*WC*	CS
5040	x	**CH**	RV	*RV*	EH
5044	x	**M**	WC	*WC*	CS

OPEN STANDARD

Mark 2. Pressure ventilated. –/64 2T. B4 bogies. ETH 4.

Lot No. 30751 Derby 1965–67. 32 t.

5148	v	**RR**	VT		TM
5157	v	**CH**	VT	*VT*	TM
5171	v	**G**	WC	*WC*	CS
5177	v	**CH**	VT	*VT*	TM
5179	v	**RR**	VT		TM
5183	v	**RR**	VT		TM
5186	v	**RR**	VT		TM
5191	v	**CH**	VT	*VT*	TM
5193	v	**LN**	VT		TM
5194	v	**RR**	VT		TM
5198	v	**CH**	VT	*VT*	TM
5200	v	**G**	WC	*WC*	CS
5212	v	**LN**	VT		TM
5216	v	**G**	WC	*WC*	CS
5221	v	**RR**	VT		TM
5222	v	**M**	WC	*WC*	CS

Names:

5193 CLAN MACLEOD
5212 CAPERKAILZIE

OPEN STANDARD

Mark 2. Pressure ventilated. –/48 2T. B4 bogies. ETH 4.

Lot No. 30752 Derby 1966. 32 t.

5229		**M**	WC	*WC*	CS
5236	v	**G**	WC	*WC*	CS
5237	v	**G**	WC	*WC*	CS
5239		**M**	WC	*WC*	CS
5249	v	**G**	WC	*WC*	CS

OPEN STANDARD

Mark 2A. Pressure ventilated. –/64 2T (w –/62 2T). B4 bogies. ETH 4.

5276–5341. Lot No. 30776 Derby 1967–68. 32 t.
5350–5419. Lot No. 30787 Derby 1968. 32 t.

f Facelifted vehicles.

5276	f	**RV**	RV	*RV*	EH
5278		**M**	WC	*WC*	CS
5292	f	**CC**	RV	*RV*	EH
5322	f	**RV**	RV	*RV*	EH
5331		**M**	DB		FA
5341	f	**CC**	RV	*RV*	EH
5350		**CH**	RV	*RV*	EH
5366	f	**CH**	RV	*RV*	EH
5386	w	**M**	DB		FA
5412	w	**M**	BK	*BK*	BT
5419	w	**M**	WC	*WC*	CS

OPEN STANDARD

Mark 2B. Pressure ventilated. –/62 2T. B4 bogies. d. ETH 4.

Lot No. 30791 Derby 1969. 32 t.

5453	**M**	WC	*WC*	CS
5463	**M**	WC	*WC*	CS
5478	**M**	WC	*WC*	CS
5487	**M**	WC	*WC*	CS
5491	**M**	WC	*WC*	CS

OPEN STANDARD

Mark 2C. Pressure ventilated. –/62 2T. B4 bogies. d. ETH 4.

Lot No. 30795 Derby 1969–70. 32 t.

5569	**M**	WC	*WC*	CS

OPEN STANDARD

Mark 2D. Air conditioned. Stones equipment. Refurbished with new seats and end luggage stacks. –/58 2T. B4 bogies. d. ETH 5.

Lot No. 30822 Derby 1971. 33 t.

5631	**M**	DB	*SR*	TO
5632	**M**	DB	*SR*	TO
5657	**M**	DB	*SR*	TO
5669	**M**	WC	*WC*	CS
5679	**FP**	E		KT
5700	**FP**	AV		HT
5710	**FP**	AV		HT
5737	**FP**	WC		CS
5740	**FP**	WC		CS

OPEN STANDARD

Mark 2E. Air conditioned. Stones equipment. –/64 2T (w –/62 2T 1W). B4 bogies. d. ETH 5.

5745–97. Lot No. 30837 Derby 1972. 33.5 t.
5810–5906. Lot No. 30844 Derby 1972–73. 33.5 t.

r Refurbished with new interior panelling.
s Refurbished with new interior panelling, modified design of seat headrest and centre luggage stack. –/60 2T (w –/58 2T 1W).
t Refurbished with new interior panelling and new seats.

5745	s	**V**	WC		CS
5748	r pt	**IC**	RV		EH
5769	r	**IC**	RV	*RV*	EH
5787	s	**V**	CG		LM
5788	r	**IC**	E		KT
5789	r pt	**IC**	E		LM
5792	r	**IC**	RV	*RV*	EH
5793	wspt	**V**	E		KT
5797	r★	**IC**	RA		LM
5810	s	**BG**	DR		TO
5815	ws	**V**	CG		LM
5821	r pt	**V**	E		KT
5853	t	**AV**	AV		CF
5866	r pt★	**IC**	CG		WN
5869	t	**AV**	AV		LM
5876	s pt	**V**	CG		LM
5888	wr	**IC**	WC		CS
5900	wspt	**V**	WC		CS
5901	s	**BG**	DR		BH
5903	s	**V**	WC		CS
5906	wspt★	**IC**	CG		BH

OPEN STANDARD

Mark 2F. Air conditioned. Temperature Ltd. equipment. InterCity 70 seats. All were refurbished in the 1980s with power-operated vestibule doors, new panels and seat trim. –/64 2T. (w –/62 2T 1W) B4 bogies. d. ETH 5X.

5910–58. Lot No. 30846 Derby 1973. 33 t.
5959–6170. Lot No. 30860 Derby 1973–74. 33 t.
6173–83. Lot No. 30874 Derby 1974–75. 33 t.

* Early Mark 2 style seats. These vehicles have undergone a second refurbishment with carpets and new seat trim.

q Fitted with two wheelchair spaces. –/60 2T 2W.
s Fitted with centre luggage stack. –/60 2T.
t Fitted with centre luggage stack and wheelchair space. –/58 2T 1W.

5910	q	**V**	RV	*RV*	EH
5912	s	**V**	RA		KT
5913	s	**AV**	AV		LM
5919	s pt	**BG**	DR		BH
5920		**V**	DM		YJ
5921		**AR**	RV		EH
5922		**M**	DB		EH
5924		**M**	DB		EH
5925	s pt★	**IC**	CG		LM
5928		**CH**	VT	*VT*	TM
5929		**AR**	RV	*DR*	EH
5930	t	**V**	E		KT
5936		**AR**	E		LM
5937		**V**	RV	*RV*	EH
5945		**V**	RV	*RV*	EH
5946		**V**	RV	*RV*	EH
5948	q	**V**	WC		CS
5950		**AR**	RV		EH
5952		**V**	RV	*RV*	EH
5954		**M**	DB	*SR*	TO
5955		**V**	RV	*RV*	EH
5958	s★	**IC**	CG		BH
5959	n	**M**	DB		EH
5960	s	**V**	E		KT
5961	s pt	**V**	RV	*RV*	EH
5962	s pt	**V**	E		KT
5964		**AR**	RV	*RV*	EH
5965	t	**AB**	AV	*AW*	CF
5971	s	**BG**	DR		TO
5976	t	**AB**	AV	*AW*	CF
5983	s	**V**	WC		CS
5985		**AR**	RV	*RV*	EH
5987		**V**	RV	*RV*	EH
5991	s	**V**	RA		KT
5995	s	**BG**	DR		TO
5997		**V**	RV	*RV*	EH
5998		**AR**	RV	*RV*	EH
6000	t	**M**	WC	*WC*	CS
6001	q	**BG**	DR		TO
6002		**V**	DM		YJ
6006		**AR**	RV	*DR*	EH
6008	s	**BG**	DR		BH
6013	s	**AV**	AV		LM
6022	s	**M**	WC	*WC*	CS
6024	s	**V**	RV	*RV*	EH
6027	q	**V**	RV	*RV*	EH
6035	t★	**AV**	AV		LM
6036	*	**M**	DB		EH
6041	s	**M**	WC		CS
6042		**AR**	RV	*DR*	EH
6045	w	**V**	CG		KT
6046	s	**BG**	DR		BH
6049		**V**	E		KT
6051		**V**	RV	*RV*	EH
6052	tw	**IC**	E		KT
6054		**V**	RV	*RV*	EH
6059	s	**V**	E		KT
6064	s	**BG**	DR		BH
6065		**V**	DM		KT
6066	s★	**AV**	AV		CF
6067	s pt	**V**	RV	*RV*	EH
6073	s	**V**	E		KT
6103		**M**	WC	*WC*	CS
6107		**V**	RV	*RV*	EH
6110		**M**	DB	*SR*	TO
6115	s	**M**	WC	*WC*	CS
6117	t★	**BG**	DR		BH
6119	s	**AV**	AV		CF
6120	s	**V**	E		KT
6122	s★	**BG**	DR		BH
6134		**V**	CG		KT
6137	s pt	**AB**	AV	*AW*	CF
6139	n*	**M**	DB		EH
6141	q	**V**	RV		EH
6151	*	**V**	CG		KT
6152	*	**M**	DB		EH
6154	pt	**IC**	CG		LM
6158		**V**	RV	*RV*	EH
6162	s pt	**AV**	AV		LM
6165		**V**	DM		KT
6168	s★	**IC**	CG		WN
6170	s★	**AV**	AV		LM
6173	s★	**BG**	DR		TO
6176	t	**V**	RV	*RV*	EH
6177	s	**V**	RV	*RV*	EH
6181	wn	**V**	DM		YJ
6183	s	**AB**	AV	*AW*	CF

BRAKE GENERATOR VAN

Mark 1. Renumbered 1989 from BR departmental series. Converted from Gangwayed Brake Van in 1973 to three-phase supply brake generator van for use with HST trailers. Modified 1999 for use with loco-hauled stock. B5 bogies.

Lot No. 30400 Pressed Steel 1958.

6310	(81448, 975325)	**CH**	RV	*RV*	EH

GENERATOR VAN

Mark 1. Converted from Gangwayed Brake Vans in 1992 to Generator Vans for use on Anglo-Scottish sleeping car services. Now normally used on trains hauled by steam locomotives. B4 bogies. ETH 75.

6311. Lot No. 30162 Pressed Steel 1958. 37.25 t.
6312. Lot No. 30224 Cravens 1956. 37.25 t.
6313. Lot No. 30484 Pressed Steel 1958. 37.25 t.

6311	(80903, 92911)	**B**	DB		TO
6312	(81023, 92925)	**M**	WC	*WC*	CS
6313	(81553, 92167)	**PC**	OE	*BP*	SL

BUFFET STANDARD

Mark 2C. Converted from Open Standard by removal of one seating bay and replacing this by a counter with a space for a trolley, now replaced with a more substantial buffet. Adjacent toilet removed and converted to steward's washing area/store. Pressure ventilated. –/55 1T. B4 bogies. ETH 4.

Lot No. 30795 Derby 1969–70. 32.5 t.

6528	(5592)	**M**	WC	*WC*	CS

SLEEPER RECEPTION CAR

Mark 2F. Converted from Open First. These vehicles consist of pantry, microwave cooking facilities, seating area for passengers (with loose chairs, staff toilet plus two bars). Now refurbished again with new "sofa" seating as well as the loose chairs. Converted at RTC, Derby (6700), Ilford (6701–05) and Derby (6706–08). Air conditioned. 6700/01/03/05–08 have Stones equipment and 6702/04 have Temperature Ltd. equipment. The number of seats per coach can vary but typically is 25/– 1T (12 seats as "sofa" seating and 13 loose chairs). B4 bogies. d. ETH 5X.

6700–02/04/08. Lot No. 30859 Derby 1973–74. 33.5 t.
6703/05–07. Lot No. 30845 Derby 1973. 33.5 t.

6700	(3347)	**FS**	E	*SR*	IS
6701	(3346)	**FS**	E	*SR*	IS
6702	(3421)	**FS**	E	*SR*	IS

6703	(3308)	**FS**	E	*SR*	IS
6704	(3341)	**FS**	E	*SR*	IS
6705	(3310, 6430)	**FS**	E	*SR*	IS
6706	(3283, 6421)	**FS**	E	*SR*	IS
6707	(3276, 6418)	**FS**	E	*SR*	IS
6708	(3370)	**FS**	E	*SR*	IS

BUFFET FIRST

Mark 2D. Converted from Buffet Standard by the removal of another seating bay and fitting a more substantial buffet counter with boiler and microwave oven. Now converted to First Class with new seating and end luggage stacks. Air conditioned. Stones equipment. 30/– 1T. B4 bogies. d. ETH 5.

Lot No. 30822 Derby 1971. 33 t.

6720	(5622, 6652)	**M**	DB		EH
6722	(5736, 6661)	**FP**	RV		LM
6723	(5641, 6662)	**M**	WC	*WC*	CS
6724	(5721, 6665)	**M**	WC	*WC*	CS

OPEN BRAKE STANDARD WITH TROLLEY SPACE

Mark 2. These vehicles use the same body shell as the Mark 2 Corridor Brake First. Converted from Open Brake Standard by removal of one seating bay and replacing this with a counter with a space for a trolley. Adjacent toilet removed and converted to a steward's washing area/store. –/23. B4 bogies. ETH 4.

Lot No. 30757 Derby 1966. 31 t.

9101	(9398)	v	**CH**	VT	*VT*	TM
9104	(9401)	v	**G**	WC	*WC*	CS

OPEN BRAKE STANDARD

Mark 2. These vehicles use the same body shell as the Mark 2 Corridor Brake First and have First Class seat spacing and wider tables. Pressure ventilated. –/31 1T. B4 bogies. ETH 4.

Lot No. 30757 Derby 1966. 31.5 t.

9391		**M**	WC	*WC*	CS	9392	v	**M**	WC	*WC*	CS

OPEN BRAKE STANDARD

Mark 2C. Pressure ventilated. –/31 1T. B4 bogies. ETH 4.

Lot No. 30798 Derby 1970. 32 t.

9440	d	**M**	WC	*WC*	CS

OPEN BRAKE STANDARD

Mark 2D. Air conditioned (Stones). –/31 1T. B4 bogies. d. pg. ETH 5.

r Refurbished with new interior panelling.
s Refurbished with new seating –/22 1TD.
w Facelifted –/28 1T 1W.

Lot No. 30824 Derby 1971. 33 t.

9480	w	**FP**	E		KT
9488	s	**FP**	AV		HT
9489	r	**V**	WC		CS
9490	s	**FP**	E		KT
9492	w	**FP**	DM		YJ
9493	s	**M**	WC	*WC*	CS
9494	s	**M**	DB	*SR*	TO

OPEN BRAKE STANDARD

Mark 2E. Air conditioned (Stones). –/32 1T. B4 bogies. d. pg. ETH 5.

Lot No. 30838 Derby 1972. 33 t.

Non-standard livery: 9502 Pullman umber & cream.

r Refurbished with new interior panelling.
s Refurbished with modified design of seat headrest and new interior panelling.
w Facelifted –/28 1W 1T.

9496	r	**IC**	VT	*VT*	TM
9497	r★	**IC**	CG		WN
9498	r	**V**	E		KT
9500	r	**IC**	E		LM
9501	w	**FP**	DM		MQ
9502	s	**0**	OE	*BP*	SL
9503	s	**AV**	AV		CF
9504	s	**V**	RV		EH
9505	s★	**IC**	E		LM
9506	s★	**BG**	DR		EC
9507	s	**V**	RV	*RV*	EH
9508	s	**BG**	DR		TO
9509	s	**AV**	AV		LM

OPEN BRAKE STANDARD

Mark 2F. Air conditioned (Temperature Ltd). All now refurbished with power-operated vestibule doors, new panels and seat trim. All now further refurbished with carpets. –/32 1T. B4 bogies. d. pg. ETH 5X.

Lot No. 30861 Derby 1974. 34 t.

Advertising livery: 9537 CruiseSaver Express (dark blue).

Note: 9537 has had all its seats removed and is used to carry luggage.

9516	n	**V**	E		KT
9520	n	**AR**	RV		EH
9521	★	**AB**	AV	*AW*	CF
9522		**M**	DB	*SR*	TO
9523		**V**	E		KT
9524	n★	**AV**	AV		LM
9525		**BG**	DR		BH
9526	n★	**IC**	RV		EH
9527	n	**AR**	RV	*DR*	EH
9529	n	**M**	DB		EH
9531		**M**	DB		EH
9537	n	**AL**	RV	*RV*	EH
9538		**V**	E		KT
9539		**AB**	AV	*AW*	CF

DRIVING OPEN BRAKE STANDARD

Mark 2F. Air conditioned (Temperature Ltd.). Push & pull (tdm system). Converted from Open Brake Standard, these vehicles originally had half cabs at the brake end. They have since been refurbished and have had their cabs widened and the cab-end gangways removed. Five vehicles (9701–03/08/14) have been converted for use in Network Rail test trains and can be found in the Service Stock section of this book. –/30 1W 1T. B4 bogies. d. pg. Cowcatchers. ETH 5X.

9704–10. Lot No. 30861 Derby 1974. Converted Glasgow 1979. Disc brakes. 34 t.
9711/13. Lot No. 30861 Derby 1974. Converted Glasgow 1985. 34 t.

9704	(9512)	**AR**	BA	ZG
9705	(9519)	**AR**	BA	ZG
9707	(9511)	**AR**	BA	ZG
9709	(9515)	**AR**	BA	ZG
9710	(9518)	**1**	BA	ZG
9711	(9532)	**AR**	VT	TS
9713	(9535)	**AR**	E	ZG

OPEN BRAKE UNCLASSIFIED

Mark 2E. Converted from Open Standard with new seating for use on Anglo-Scottish overnight services by Railcare, Wolverton. Air conditioned. Stones equipment. B4 bogies. d. –/31 2T. B4 bogies. ETH 4X.

9801–03. Lot No. 30837 Derby 1972. 33.5 t.
9804–10. Lot No. 30844 Derby 1972–73. 33.5 t.

9800	(5751)	**FS**	E	*SR*	IS
9801	(5760)	**FS**	E	*SR*	IS
9802	(5772)	**FS**	E	*SR*	IS
9803	(5799)	**FS**	E	*SR*	IS
9804	(5826)	**FS**	E	*SR*	IS
9805	(5833)	**FS**	E	*SR*	IS
9806	(5840)	**FS**	E	*SR*	IS
9807	(5851)	**FS**	E	*SR*	IS
9808	(5871)	**FS**	E	*SR*	IS
9809	(5890)	**FS**	E	*SR*	IS
9810	(5892)	**FS**	E	*SR*	IS

KITCHEN BUFFET FIRST

Mark 3A. Air conditioned. Converted from HST catering vehicles and Mark 3 Open Firsts. Refurbished with table lamps and burgundy seat trim (except *). 18/– plus two seats for staff use (* 24/–, † 24/–, § 24/–, t 23/– 1W). BT10 bogies. d. ETH 14X.

10200–211. Lot No. 30884 Derby 1977. 39.8 t.
10212–229. Lot No. 30878 Derby 1975–76. 39.8 t.
10230–259. Lot No. 30890 Derby 1979. 39.8 t.

§ First Great Western Sleeper "day coaches" that have been fitted with former HST First Class seats to a 2+1 layout.

Coaches in **WS** livery were refurbished for Wrexham & Shropshire and are now in use with Chiltern Railways. Fitted with Primarius seating, new kitchen area and universal-access toilet. 30/– 1TD 1W.

Non-standard livery: 10211 EWS dark maroon.

10200	(40519)	*	**1**	P	*EA*	NC
10202	(40504)	†	**BG**	CG		BH
10203	(40506)	*	**1**	P	*EA*	NC
10206	(40507)		**V**	P		NC
10208	(40517)		**WS**	AV	*CR*	AL
10211	(40510)		**0**	DB	*DB*	TO
10212	(11049)		**VT**	P	*VW*	WB
10214	(11034)	*	**1**	P	*EA*	NC
10215	(11032)		**BG**	AV		WN
10216	(11041)	*	**1**	P	*EA*	NC
10217	(11051)		**VT**	P	*VW*	WB
10219	(11047)	§	**FD**	P	*GW*	PZ
10222	(11063)		**BG**	AV		BY
10223	(11043)	*	**1**	P	*EA*	NC
10225	(11014)	§	**FD**	P	*GW*	PZ
10226	(11015)		**V**	AV		LM
10228	(11035)	*	**1**	P	*EA*	NC
10229	(11059)	*	**1**	P	*EA*	NC
10230	(10021)		**WS**	AV	*CR*	AL
10231	(10016)		**V**	P		LM
10232	(10027)	§	**FD**	P	*GW*	PZ
10233	(10013)		**V**	AV		LM
10235	(10015)	†	**BG**	AV		WN
10236	(10018)		**WS**	AV	*CR*	AL
10237	(10022)		**DR**	AV		BY
10240	(10003)		**V**	P		LM
10241	(10009)	*	**1**	P		IL
10242	(10002)		**BG**	CG		WN
10245	(10019)		**V**	CG		ZB
10246	(10014)	†	**BG**	CG		WN
10247	(10011)	*	**NX**	P	*EA*	NC
10249	(10012)		**AB**	AV	*AW*	CF
10250	(10020)		**V**	AV		LM
10253	(10026)		**V**	P		LM
10255	(10010)		**WS**	AV	*CR*	AL
10257	(10007)	†	**BG**	AV		BY
10259	(10025)	t	**AB**	AV	*AW*	CF

KITCHEN BUFFET STANDARD

Mark 4. Air conditioned. BT41 bogies. ETH 6X. Rebuilt from First to Standard Class with bar adjacent to seating area instead of adjacent to end of coach. –/30 1T.

Lot No. 31045 Metro-Cammell 1989–92. 43.2 t.

10300	**EC**	E	*EC*	BN
10301	**GN**	E	*EC*	BN
10302	**EC**	E	*EC*	BN
10303	**EC**	E	*EC*	BN
10304	**EC**	E	*EC*	BN
10305	**GN**	E	*EC*	BN
10306	**GN**	E	*EC*	BN
10307	**EC**	E	*EC*	BN
10308	**EC**	E	*EC*	BN
10309	**EC**	E	*EC*	BN
10310	**GN**	E	*EC*	BN
10311	**GN**	E	*EC*	BN

10312	**GN**	E	*EC*	BN	10324	**EC**	E	*EC*	BN
10313	**EC**	E	*EC*	BN	10325	**GN**	E	*EC*	BN
10315	**GN**	E	*EC*	BN	10326	**EC**	E	*EC*	BN
10317	**GN**	E	*EC*	BN	10328	**GN**	E	*EC*	BN
10318	**GN**	E	*EC*	BN	10329	**GN**	E	*EC*	BN
10319	**GN**	E	*EC*	BN	10330	**GN**	E	*EC*	BN
10320	**EC**	E	*EC*	BN	10331	**EC**	E	*EC*	BN
10321	**GN**	E	*EC*	BN	10332	**EC**	E	*EC*	BN
10323	**EC**	E	*EC*	BN	10333	**EC**	E	*EC*	BN

BUFFET STANDARD

Mark 3A. Air conditioned. Converted from Mark 3 Open Standards at Derby 2006. –/52 1T (including 6 Compin Pegasus seats for "priority" use).

Lot No. 30877 Derby 1975–77. 37.8 t.

10401	(12168)	**NX**	P	*EA*	NC	10404	(12068)	**1**	P	*EA*	NC
10402	(12010)	**1**	P	*EA*	NC	10405	(12157)	**1**	P	*EA*	NC
10403	(12135)	**1**	P	*EA*	NC	10406	(12020)	**1**	P	*EA*	NC

SLEEPING CAR WITH PANTRY

Mark 3A. Air conditioned. Retention toilets. 12 compartments with a fixed lower berth and a hinged upper berth, plus an attendants compartment. 2T. BT10 bogies. d. ETH 7X.

Non-standard livery: 10546 EWS dark maroon.

Lot No. 30960 Derby 1981–83. 41 t.

10501	**FS**	P	*SR*	IS	10548	**FS**	P	*SR*	IS
10502	**FS**	P	*SR*	IS	10551	**FS**	P	*SR*	IS
10504	**FS**	P	*SR*	IS	10553	**FS**	P	*SR*	IS
10506	**FS**	P	*SR*	IS	10561	**FS**	P	*SR*	IS
10507	**FS**	P	*SR*	IS	10562	**FS**	P	*SR*	IS
10508	**FS**	P	*SR*	IS	10563	**FD**	P	*GW*	PZ
10513	**FS**	P	*SR*	IS	10565	**FS**	P	*SR*	IS
10516	**FS**	P	*SR*	IS	10580	**FS**	P	*SR*	IS
10519	**FS**	P	*SR*	IS	10584	**FD**	P	*GW*	PZ
10520	**FS**	P	*SR*	IS	10588	**BG**	CG		BH
10522	**FS**	P	*SR*	IS	10589	**FD**	P	*GW*	PZ
10523	**FS**	P	*SR*	IS	10590	**FD**	P	*GW*	PZ
10526	**FS**	P	*SR*	IS	10594	**FD**	P	*GW*	PZ
10527	**FS**	P	*SR*	IS	10596	**IC**	P		LM
10529	**FS**	P	*SR*	IS	10597	**FS**	P	*SR*	IS
10531	**FS**	P	*SR*	IS	10598	**FS**	P	*SR*	IS
10532	**FD**	P	*GW*	PZ	10600	**FS**	P	*SR*	IS
10534	**FD**	P	*GW*	PZ	10601	**FD**	P	*GW*	PZ
10542	**FS**	P	*SR*	IS	10605	**FS**	P	*SR*	IS
10543	**FS**	P	*SR*	IS	10607	**FS**	P	*SR*	IS
10544	**FS**	P	*SR*	IS	10610	**FS**	P	*SR*	IS
10546	**0**	DB	*DB*	TO	10612	**FD**	P	*GW*	PZ

10613	**FS**	P	*SR*	IS	10616	**FD**	P	*GW*	PZ
10614	**FS**	P	*SR*	IS	10617	**FS**	P	*SR*	IS

SLEEPING CAR

Mark 3A. Air conditioned. Retention toilets. 13 compartments with a fixed lower berth and a hinged upper berth (* 11 compartments with a fixed lower berth and a hinged upper berth + one compartment for a disabled person. 1TD). 2T. BT10 bogies. ETH 6X.

Note: 10734 was originally 2914 and used as a Royal Train staff sleeping car. It has 12 berths and a shower room and is ETH 11X.

10647–729. Lot No. 30961 Derby 1980–84. 43.5 t.
10734. Lot No. 31002 Derby/Wolverton 1985. 42.5 t.

10647 d	**IC**	AV		LM	10699 d*	**FS**	P	*SR*	IS
10648 d*	**FS**	P	*SR*	IS	10701 d	**IC**	AV		LM
10650 d*	**FS**	P	*SR*	IS	10703 d	**FS**	P	*SR*	IS
10666 d*	**FS**	P	*SR*	IS	10706 d*	**FS**	P	*SR*	IS
10675 d	**FS**	P	*SR*	IS	10714 d*	**FS**	P	*SR*	IS
10680 d*	**FS**	P	*SR*	IS	10718 d*	**FS**	P	*SR*	IS
10683 d	**FS**	P	*SR*	IS	10719 d*	**FS**	P	*SR*	IS
10688 d	**FS**	P	*SR*	IS	10722 d*	**FS**	P	*SR*	IS
10689 d*	**FS**	P	*SR*	IS	10723 d*	**FS**	P	*SR*	IS
10690 d	**FS**	P	*SR*	IS	10729	**VN**	OE	*NB*	CP
10693 d	**FS**	P	*SR*	IS	10734	**VN**	OE	*NB*	CP

Names:

10729 CREWE | 10734 BALMORAL

OPEN FIRST

Mark 3A. Air conditioned. All refurbished with table lamps and new seat cushions and trim. 48/– 2T (* 48/– 1T 1TD, † 47/– 2T 1W). BT10 bogies. d. ETH 6X.

§ 11029 and 11040 have been reseated with Standard Class seats. 11029 seats –/68 2T 2W and 11040 seats –/72 2T.

11006/007 were open composites 11906/907 for a time.

Non-standard livery: 11039 EWS dark maroon.

Lot No. 30878 Derby 1975–76. 34.3 t.

11006	**V**	P		LM	11029 §	**BG**	AV	*CR*	AL
11007	**VT**	P	*VW*	WB	11030 †	**DR**	AV		BY
11011 *	**V**	P		LM	11031 †	**BG**	AV	*CR*	AL
11013	**DR**	AV		LM	11033	**DR**	AV		LM
11018	**VT**	P	*VW*	WB	11039	**0**	DB	*DB*	TO
11019	**DR**	AV		BY	11040 §	**BG**	AV	*CR*	AL
11021	**V**	P		IL	11044 †	**DR**	AV		BY
11026	**V**	P		LM	11046 †	**DR**	AV		BY
11027 †	**DR**	AV		BY	11048	**VT**	P	*VW*	WB
11028	**V**	AV		ZB	11054 †	**DR**	AV		BY

OPEN FIRST

Mark 3B. Air conditioned. InterCity 80 seats. All refurbished with table lamps and new seat cushions and trim. 48/– 2T. BT10 bogies. d. ETH 6X.

† National Express East Anglia vehicles fitted with disabled toilet and reduced seating including three Compin "Pegasus" seats of the same type as used in Standard Class (but regarded as First Class!). 34/3 1T 1TD 2W.

Lot No. 30982 Derby 1985. 36.5 t.

11064	**BG**	AV		BH
11065	**BG**	AV		BH
11066	**1**	P	*EA*	NC
11067	**1**	P	*EA*	NC
11068	**1**	P	*EA*	NC
11069	**1**	P	*EA*	NC
11070	**1**	P	*EA*	NC
11071	**BG**	AV		BH
11072	**1**	P	*EA*	NC
11073	**1**	P	*EA*	NC
11074	**V**	P		NC
11075	**1**	P	*EA*	NC
11076	**1**	P	*EA*	NC
11077	**1**	P	*EA*	NC
11078 †	**1**	P	*EA*	NC
11079	**V**	AV		WN
11080	**1**	P	*EA*	NC
11081	**1**	P	*EA*	NC
11082	**1**	P	*EA*	NC
11083	**BG**	AV		BH
11084	**BG**	AV		BH
11085 †	**1**	P	*EA*	NC
11086	**BG**	AV		BH
11087 †	**NX**	P	*EA*	NC
11088 †	**1**	P	*EA*	NC
11089	**BG**	AV		WN
11090 †	**1**	P	*EA*	NC
11091	**NX**	P	*EA*	NC
11092 †	**1**	P	*EA*	NC
11093 †	**1**	P	*EA*	NC
11094 †	**1**	P	*EA*	NC
11095 †	**1**	P	*EA*	NC
11096 †	**1**	P	*EA*	NC
11097	**V**	AV		LM
11098 †	**1**	P	*EA*	NC
11099 †	**1**	P	*EA*	NC
11100 †	**1**	P	*EA*	NC
11101 †	**1**	P	*EA*	NC

OPEN FIRST

Mark 4. Air conditioned. Rebuilt with new interior by Bombardier Wakefield 2003–05 (some converted from Standard Class vehicles) 41/– 1T (plus 2 seats for staff use). BT41 bogies. ETH 6X.

11201–11273. Lot No. 31046 Metro-Cammell 1989–92. 41.3 t .
11277–11299. Lot No. 31049 Metro-Cammell 1989–92. 41.3 t .

11201		**EC**	E	*EC*	BN
11219		**EC**	E	*EC*	BN
11229		**EC**	E	*EC*	BN
11237		**GN**	E	*EC*	BN
11241		**GN**	E	*EC*	BN
11244		**GN**	E	*EC*	BN
11273		**GN**	E	*EC*	BN
11277	(12408)	**EC**	E	*EC*	BN
11278	(12479)	**EC**	E	*EC*	BN
11279	(12521)	**EC**	E	*EC*	BN
11280	(12523)	**EC**	E	*EC*	BN
11281	(12418)	**EC**	E	*EC*	BN
11282	(12524)	**EC**	E	*EC*	BN
11283	(12435)	**EC**	E	*EC*	BN
11284	(12487)	**EC**	E	*EC*	BN
11285	(12537)	**EC**	E	*EC*	BN
11286	(12482)	**GN**	E	*EC*	BN
11287	(12527)	**GN**	E	*EC*	BN
11288	(12517)	**EC**	E	*EC*	BN
11289	(12528)	**GN**	E	*EC*	BN
11290	(12530)	**GN**	E	*EC*	BN
11291	(12535)	**GN**	E	*EC*	BN
11292	(12451)	**GN**	E	*EC*	BN
11293	(12536)	**GN**	E	*EC*	BN

11294 (12529)	**GN**	E	*EC*	BN	11298 (12416)	**EC**	E	*EC*	BN
11295 (12475)	**GN**	E	*EC*	BN	11299 (12532)	**EC**	E	*EC*	BN

OPEN FIRST (DISABLED)

Mark 4. Air conditioned. Rebuilt from Open First by Bombardier Wakefield 2003–05. 42/– 1W 1TD. BT41 bogies. ETH 6X.

Lot No. 31046 Metro-Cammell 1989–92. 40.7 t.

11301 (11215)	**EC**	E	*EC*	BN	11316 (11227)	**GN**	E	*EC*	BN
11302 (11203)	**EC**	E	*EC*	BN	11317 (11223)	**EC**	E	*EC*	BN
11303 (11211)	**EC**	E	*EC*	BN	11318 (11251)	**GN**	E	*EC*	BN
11304 (11257)	**EC**	E	*EC*	BN	11319 (11247)	**GN**	E	*EC*	BN
11305 (11261)	**EC**	E	*EC*	BN	11320 (11255)	**GN**	E	*EC*	BN
11306 (11276)	**EC**	E	*EC*	BN	11321 (11245)	**GN**	E	*EC*	BN
11307 (11217)	**EC**	E	*EC*	BN	11322 (11228)	**GN**	E	*EC*	BN
11308 (11263)	**EC**	E	*EC*	BN	11323 (11235)	**GN**	E	*EC*	BN
11309 (11259)	**EC**	E	*EC*	BN	11324 (11253)	**GN**	E	*EC*	BN
11310 (11272)	**EC**	E	*EC*	BN	11325 (11231)	**GN**	E	*EC*	BN
11311 (11221)	**EC**	E	*EC*	BN	11326 (11206)	**GN**	E	*EC*	BN
11312 (11225)	**EC**	E	*EC*	BN	11327 (11236)	**GN**	E	*EC*	BN
11313 (11210)	**EC**	E	*EC*	BN	11328 (11274)	**GN**	E	*EC*	BN
11314 (11207)	**EC**	E	*EC*	BN	11329 (11243)	**GN**	E	*EC*	BN
11315 (11238)	**GN**	E	*EC*	BN	11330 (11249)	**GN**	E	*EC*	BN

OPEN FIRST

Mark 4. Air conditioned. Rebuilt from Open First by Bombardier Wakefield 2003–05. Separate area for 7 smokers, although smoking is no longer allowed. 46/– 1W 1TD. BT41 bogies. ETH 6X.

Lot No. 31046 Metro-Cammell 1989–92. 42.1 t.

11401 (11214)	**EC**	E	*EC*	BN	11416 (11254)	**GN**	E	*EC*	BN
11402 (11216)	**EC**	E	*EC*	BN	11417 (11226)	**EC**	E	*EC*	BN
11403 (11258)	**EC**	E	*EC*	BN	11418 (11222)	**GN**	E	*EC*	BN
11404 (11202)	**EC**	E	*EC*	BN	11419 (11250)	**GN**	E	*EC*	BN
11405 (11204)	**EC**	E	*EC*	BN	11420 (11242)	**GN**	E	*EC*	BN
11406 (11205)	**EC**	E	*EC*	BN	11421 (11220)	**GN**	E	*EC*	BN
11407 (11256)	**EC**	E	*EC*	BN	11422 (11232)	**GN**	E	*EC*	BN
11408 (11218)	**EC**	E	*EC*	BN	11423 (11230)	**GN**	E	*EC*	BN
11409 (11262)	**EC**	E	*EC*	BN	11424 (11239)	**GN**	E	*EC*	BN
11410 (11260)	**EC**	E	*EC*	BN	11425 (11234)	**GN**	E	*EC*	BN
11411 (11240)	**EC**	E	*EC*	BN	11426 (11252)	**GN**	E	*EC*	BN
11412 (11209)	**EC**	E	*EC*	BN	11427 (11200)	**GN**	E	*EC*	BN
11413 (11212)	**EC**	E	*EC*	BN	11428 (11233)	**GN**	E	*EC*	BN
11414 (11246)	**EC**	E	*EC*	BN	11429 (11275)	**GN**	E	*EC*	BN
11415 (11208)	**GN**	E	*EC*	BN	11430 (11248)	**GN**	E	*EC*	BN

OPEN FIRST

Mark 4. Air conditioned. Converted from Kitchen Buffet Standard with new interior by Bombardier Wakefield 2005. 46/– 1T. BT41 bogies. ETH 6X.

Lot No. 31046 Metro-Cammell 1989–92. 41.3 t.

11998 (10314)	**GN**	E	*EC*	BN	11999 (10316)	**GN**	E	*EC*	BN

OPEN STANDARD

Mark 3A. Air conditioned. All refurbished with modified seat backs and new layout and further refurbished with new seat trim. –/76 2T (s –/70 2T 1W, t –/72 2T, z –/70 1TD 1T 2W, § –/45(2) 2T 1W). BT10 bogies. d. ETH 6X.

h National Express East Anglia modified coaches with eight Compin Pegasus seats at saloon ends for "priority" use and a high density layout with more unidirectional seating. –/80 2T.

§ First Great Western Sleeper "day coaches" that have been fitted with former HST First Class seats to a 2+1 layout and are effectively unclassified.

Coaches in **WS** livery were refurbished for Wrexham & Shropshire (except 12059). Now in use with Chiltern Railways. Original InterCity 70 seats retained, but almost all arranged in a facing layout. –/72 2T or –/70 2T (12048/145).

Notes: 12169–171 were converted from open composites 11908–910, formerly Open Firsts 11008–10.

12173–175 were converted from Open Firsts 11042/052/058 respectively in 2010.

12005–167. Lot No. 30877 Derby 1975–77. 34.3 t.
12169–175. Lot No. 30878 Derby 1975–76. 34.3 t.

12005	h	**1**	P	*EA*	NC	12032	h	**1**	P	*EA*	NC
12008		**V**	P		LM	12034		**1**	P	*EA*	NC
12009	h	**1**	P	*EA*	NC	12035	h	**NX**	P	*EA*	NC
12011		**VT**	P	*VW*	WB	12036	s	**V**	P		LM
12012	h	**1**	P	*EA*	NC	12037	h	**1**	P	*EA*	NC
12013	h	**1**	P	*EA*	NC	12038	s	**BG**	AV	*CR*	AL
12014	t	**BG**	AV	*CR*	AL	12040	h	**1**	P	*EA*	NC
12015	h	**1**	P	*EA*	NC	12041	h	**1**	P	*EA*	NC
12016		**1**	P	*EA*	NC	12042	h	**1**	P	*EA*	NC
12017		**V**	AV		WN	12043	s	**BG**	AV	*CR*	AL
12019	h	**1**	P	*EA*	NC	12045		**V**	P		LM
12021		**NX**	P	*EA*	NC	12046	h	**1**	P	*EA*	NC
12022		**V**	P		LM	12047	z	**V**	P		LM
12024	h	**1**	P	*EA*	NC	12048		**WS**	AV	*CR*	AL
12026	h	**1**	P	*EA*	NC	12049		**1**	P	*EA*	NC
12027	h	**1**	P	*EA*	NC	12051	h	**NX**	P	*EA*	NC
12029		**V**	P		LM	12053	t	**BG**	AV	*CR*	AL
12030	h	**1**	P	*EA*	NC	12054	s	**V**	AV	*CR*	AL
12031		**1**	P	*EA*	NC	12056	h	**1**	P	*EA*	NC

12057 h	**1**	P	*EA*	NC
12058	**V**	AV		LM
12059 t	**WS**	AV	*CR*	AL
12060 h	**1**	P	*EA*	NC
12061 h	**1**	P	*EA*	NC
12062 h	**1**	P	*EA*	NC
12063	**1**	P		LM
12064	**1**	P	*EA*	NC
12065	**1**	P		LM
12066 h	**1**	P	*EA*	NC
12067	**1**	P	*EA*	NC
12069	**WS**	AV	*CR*	AL
12072	**WS**	AV	*CR*	AL
12073 h	**1**	P	*EA*	NC
12078	**VT**	P	*VW*	WB
12079	**1**	P	*EA*	NC
12081	**1**	P	*EA*	NC
12082 h	**1**	P	*EA*	NC
12083	**V**	P		LM
12084 h	**1**	P	*EA*	NC
12087 s	**V**	P		LM
12089	**1**	P	*EA*	NC
12090 h	**1**	P	*EA*	NC
12091 h	**1**	P	*EA*	NC
12092	**1**	P		LM
12093 h	**1**	P	*EA*	NC
12094	**V**	AV	*CR*	AL
12095	**V**	P		LM
12097 h	**1**	P	*EA*	NC
12098	**1**	P	*EA*	NC
12099 h	**1**	P	*EA*	NC
12100 §	**FD**	P	*GW*	PZ
12101 s	**V**	P		LM
12103	**1**	P	*EA*	NC
12104	**V**	AV		LM
12105 h	**1**	P	*EA*	NC
12107 h	**1**	P	*EA*	NC
12108	**1**	P	*EA*	NC
12109 h	**1**	P	*EA*	NC
12110 h	**1**	P	*EA*	NC
12111	**1**	P	*EA*	NC
12114 h	**1**	P	*EA*	NC
12115 h	**1**	P	*EA*	NC
12116 h	**1**	P	*EA*	NC
12117	**WS**	AV	*CR*	AL
12118	**1**	P	*EA*	NC
12119 t	**BG**	AV	*CR*	AL
12120 h	**1**	P	*EA*	NC
12122 z	**VT**	P	*VW*	WB
12124	**V**	AV	*CR*	AL
12125 h	**1**	P	*EA*	NC
12126 h	**1**	P	*EA*	NC
12127	**WS**	AV	*CR*	AL
12129 h	**NX**	P	*EA*	NC
12130 h	**1**	P	*EA*	NC
12131	**WS**	AV	*CR*	AL
12132	**NX**	P	*EA*	NC
12133	**VT**	P	*VW*	WB
12134	**V**	P		LM
12137 h	**1**	P	*EA*	NC
12138	**VT**	P	*VW*	WB
12139	**NC**	P	*EA*	NC
12141	**1**	P	*EA*	NC
12142 z	**V**	P		LM
12143	**1**	P	*EA*	NC
12144 s	**V**	P		LM
12145	**WS**	AV	*CR*	AL
12146	**1**	P	*EA*	NC
12147	**1**	P	*EA*	NC
12148	**1**	P	*EA*	NC
12150 h	**1**	P	*EA*	NC
12151	**1**	P	*EA*	NC
12153	**1**	P	*EA*	NC
12154 h	**1**	P	*EA*	NC
12156	**V**	P		LM
12158	**V**	P		LM
12159	**1**	P	*EA*	NC
12160 s	**V**	P		LM
12161 §	**FD**	P	*GW*	PZ
12163	**V**	P		LM
12164	**1**	P	*EA*	NC
12165	**V**	AV		LM
12166	**1**	P	*EA*	NC
12167 h	**1**	P	*EA*	NC
12169	**WS**	AV	*CR*	AL
12170	**1**	P	*EA*	NC
12171	**1**	P	*EA*	NC
12173	**WS**	AV	*CR*	AL
12174	**WS**	AV	*CR*	AL
12175	**WS**	AV	*CR*	AL

OPEN STANDARD (END)

Mark 4. Air conditioned. Rebuilt with new interior by Bombardier Wakefield 2003–05. Separate area for 26 smokers, although smoking is no longer allowed. –/76 1T. BT41 bogies. ETH 6X.

Note: 12232 was converted from the original 12405.

12200–231. Lot No. 31047 Metro-Cammell 1989–91. 39.5 t.
12232. Lot No. 31049 Metro-Cammell 1989–92. 39.5 t.

12200	**GN**	E	*EC*	BN
12201	**EC**	E	*EC*	BN
12202	**EC**	E	*EC*	BN
12203	**EC**	E	*EC*	BN
12204	**GN**	E	*EC*	BN
12205	**EC**	E	*EC*	BN
12207	**EC**	E	*EC*	BN
12208	**EC**	E	*EC*	BN
12209	**EC**	E	*EC*	BN
12210	**GN**	E	*EC*	BN
12211	**GN**	E	*EC*	BN
12212	**EC**	E	*EC*	BN
12213	**GN**	E	*EC*	BN
12214	**EC**	E	*EC*	BN
12215	**GN**	E	*EC*	BN
12216	**GN**	E	*EC*	BN
12217	**GN**	E	*EC*	BN
12218	**GN**	E	*EC*	BN
12219	**GN**	E	*EC*	BN
12220	**GN**	E	*EC*	BN
12222	**GN**	E	*EC*	BN
12223	**EC**	E	*EC*	BN
12224	**GN**	E	*EC*	BN
12225	**GN**	E	*EC*	BN
12226	**GN**	E	*EC*	BN
12227	**GN**	E	*EC*	BN
12228	**EC**	E	*EC*	BN
12229	**EC**	E	*EC*	BN
12230	**EC**	E	*EC*	BN
12231	**EC**	E	*EC*	BN
12232	**EC**	E	*EC*	BN

OPEN STANDARD (DISABLED)

Mark 4. Air conditioned. Rebuilt with new interior by Bombardier Wakefield 2003–05. –/68 2W 1TD. BT41 bogies. ETH 6X.

Note: 12331 was converted from Open Standard 12531.

12300–330. Lot No. 31048 Metro-Cammell 1989–91. 39.4 t.
12331. Lot No. 31049 Metro-Cammell 1989–92. 39.4 t.

12300	**EC**	E	*EC*	BN
12301	**EC**	E	*EC*	BN
12302	**EC**	E	*EC*	BN
12303	**EC**	E	*EC*	BN
12304	**GN**	E	*EC*	BN
12305	**EC**	E	*EC*	BN
12307	**EC**	E	*EC*	BN
12308	**EC**	E	*EC*	BN
12309	**GN**	E	*EC*	BN
12310	**GN**	E	*EC*	BN
12311	**EC**	E	*EC*	BN
12312	**EC**	E	*EC*	BN
12313	**EC**	E	*EC*	BN
12315	**EC**	E	*EC*	BN
12316	**GN**	E	*EC*	BN
12317	**GN**	E	*EC*	BN
12318	**GN**	E	*EC*	BN
12319	**GN**	E	*EC*	BN
12320	**GN**	E	*EC*	BN
12321	**GN**	E	*EC*	BN
12322	**GN**	E	*EC*	BN
12323	**GN**	E	*EC*	BN
12324	**GN**	E	*EC*	BN
12325	**GN**	E	*EC*	BN
12326	**GN**	E	*EC*	BN
12327	**EC**	E	*EC*	BN
12328	**EC**	E	*EC*	BN
12329	**EC**	E	*EC*	BN
12330	**EC**	E	*EC*	BN
12331	**GN**	E	*EC*	BN

OPEN STANDARD

Mark 4. Air conditioned. Rebuilt with new interior by Bombardier Wakefield 2003–05. –/76 1T. BT41 bogies. ETH 6X.

Note: 12405 is the second coach to carry that number. It was built from the bodyshell originally intended for 12221. The original 12405 is now 12232.

Lot No. 31049 Metro-Cammell 1989–92. 40.8 t.

12400	**GN**	E	*EC*	BN
12401	**EC**	E	*EC*	BN
12402	**EC**	E	*EC*	BN
12403	**GN**	E	*EC*	BN
12404	**EC**	E	*EC*	BN
12405	**EC**	E	*EC*	BN
12406	**EC**	E	*EC*	BN
12407	**EC**	E	*EC*	BN
12409	**GN**	E	*EC*	BN
12410	**EC**	E	*EC*	BN
12411	**EC**	E	*EC*	BN
12414	**EC**	E	*EC*	BN
12415	**EC**	E	*EC*	BN
12417	**EC**	E	*EC*	BN
12419	**EC**	E	*EC*	BN
12420	**EC**	E	*EC*	BN
12421	**EC**	E	*EC*	BN
12422	**EC**	E	*EC*	BN
12423	**EC**	E	*EC*	BN
12424	**EC**	E	*EC*	BN
12425	**GN**	E	*EC*	BN
12426	**EC**	E	*EC*	BN
12427	**EC**	E	*EC*	BN
12428	**GN**	E	*EC*	BN
12429	**GN**	E	*EC*	BN
12430	**EC**	E	*EC*	BN
12431	**EC**	E	*EC*	BN
12432	**EC**	E	*EC*	BN
12433	**GN**	E	*EC*	BN
12434	**GN**	E	*EC*	BN
12436	**EC**	E	*EC*	BN
12437	**EC**	E	*EC*	BN
12438	**GN**	E	*EC*	BN
12439	**GN**	E	*EC*	BN
12440	**GN**	E	*EC*	BN
12441	**GN**	E	*EC*	BN
12442	**GN**	E	*EC*	BN
12443	**EC**	E	*EC*	BN
12444	**EC**	E	*EC*	BN
12445	**GN**	E	*EC*	BN
12446	**GN**	E	*EC*	BN
12447	**GN**	E	*EC*	BN
12448	**EC**	E	*EC*	BN
12449	**GN**	E	*EC*	BN
12450	**EC**	E	*EC*	BN
12452	**GN**	E	*EC*	BN
12453	**GN**	E	*EC*	BN
12454	**GN**	E	*EC*	BN
12455	**GN**	E	*EC*	BN
12456	**GN**	E	*EC*	BN
12457	**GN**	E	*EC*	BN
12458	**GN**	E	*EC*	BN
12459	**EC**	E	*EC*	BN
12460	**GN**	E	*EC*	BN
12461	**GN**	E	*EC*	BN
12462	**GN**	E	*EC*	BN
12463	**GN**	E	*EC*	BN
12464	**GN**	E	*EC*	BN
12465	**GN**	E	*EC*	BN
12466	**GN**	E	*EC*	BN
12467	**GN**	E	*EC*	BN
12468	**GN**	E	*EC*	BN
12469	**EC**	E	*EC*	BN
12470	**GN**	E	*EC*	BN
12471	**GN**	E	*EC*	BN
12472	**GN**	E	*EC*	BN
12473	**GN**	E	*EC*	BN
12474	**GN**	E	*EC*	BN
12476	**GN**	E	*EC*	BN
12477	**GN**	E	*EC*	BN
12478	**EC**	E	*EC*	BN
12480	**EC**	E	*EC*	BN
12481	**EC**	E	*EC*	BN
12483	**EC**	E	*EC*	BN
12484	**EC**	E	*EC*	BN
12485	**EC**	E	*EC*	BN
12486	**EC**	E	*EC*	BN
12488	**EC**	E	*EC*	BN
12489	**EC**	E	*EC*	BN
12513	**EC**	E	*EC*	BN
12514	**EC**	E	*EC*	BN
12515	**GN**	E	*EC*	BN
12518	**EC**	E	*EC*	BN
12519	**GN**	E	*EC*	BN

12520	**EC**	E	*EC*	BN	12533	**GN** E	*EC*	BN
12522	**EC**	E	*EC*	BN	12534	**GN** E	*EC*	BN
12526	**EC**	E	*EC*	BN	12538	**GN** E	*EC*	BN

CORRIDOR FIRST

Mark 1. 42/– 2T. ETH 3.

Lot No. 30381 Swindon 1959. B4 bogies. 33 t.

13227 x	**CH**	JH	*RV*	EH	13230 xk	**M**	BK *BK*	BT
13229 xk	**M**	BK	*BK*	BT				

CORRIDOR FIRST

Mark 2A. Pressure ventilated. 42/– 2T. B4 bogies. ETH 4.

Lot No. 30774 Derby 1968. 33 t.

13440 v **G** WC *WC* CS

CORRIDOR BRAKE FIRST

Mark 1. 24/– 1T. Commonwealth bogies. ETH 2.

Lot No. 30668 Swindon 1961. 36 t.

Originally numbered in 14xxx series and then renumbered in 17xxx series.

17015 x	**CC**	RV	*RV*	EH	17018 v	**CH**	VT	TM

CORRIDOR BRAKE FIRST

Mark 2A. Pressure ventilated. 24/– 1T. B4 bogies. ETH 4.

17056–077. Lot No. 30775 Derby 1967–8. 32 t.
17080–102. Lot No. 30786 Derby 1968. 32 t.

Originally numbered 14056–102. 17080/090 were numbered 35516/503 for a time when declassified.

17056	**M**	RV	*RV*	EH	17090 v	**CH**	VT		TM
17077	**RV**	RV	*RV*	EH	17102	**M**	WC	*WC*	CS
17080	**PC**	RA	*ST*	CS					

COUCHETTE/GENERATOR COACH

Mark 2B. Formerly part of Royal Train. Converted from Corridor Brake First built 1969. Consists of luggage accommodation, guard's compartment, 350 kW diesel generator and staff sleeping accommodation. Pressure ventilated. B5 bogies. ETH 5X.

Non-standard livery: 17105 Oxford blue.

Lot No. 30888 Wolverton 1977. 46 t.

17105 (14105, 2905) **0** RV *RV* EH

CORRIDOR BRAKE FIRST

Mark 2D. Air conditioned (Stones equipment). 24/– 1T. B4 Bogies. ETH 5.

Lot No. 30823 Derby 1971–72. 33.5 t.

17159 (14159)	**DR**	DR		ZG
17167 (14167)	**VN**	OE	*NB*	CP

OPEN BRAKE UNCLASSIFIED

Mark 3B. Air conditioned. Fitted with hydraulic handbrake. Used by First Great Western as Sleeper "day coaches" that have been fitted with former HST First Class seats to a 2+1 layout and are effectively unclassified. 36/– 1T. BT10 bogies. pg. d. ETH 5X.

Lot No. 30990 Derby 1986. 35.81 t.

17173	**FD**	P	*GW*	PZ
17174	**FD**	P	*GW*	PZ
17175	**FD**	P	*GW*	PZ

CORRIDOR STANDARD

Mark 1. Each vehicle has eight compartments. All remaining vehicles have metal window frames and melamine interior panelling. Commonwealth bogies. –/48 2T. ETH 4.

Lot No. 30685 Derby 1961–62. 36 t.

t Rebuilt internally as Open Standard using components from 4936. –/64 2T.

Originally numbered 25756–862.

18756 x	**M**	WC	*WC*	CS
18767 x	**M**	WC	*WC*	CS
18806 xt	**M**	WC	*WC*	CS
18808 x	**M**	WC	*WC*	CS
18862 x	**M**	WC	*WC*	CS

CORRIDOR BRAKE COMPOSITE

Mark 1. There are two variants depending upon whether the Standard Class compartments have armrests. Each vehicle has two First Class and three Standard Class compartments. 12/18 2T (* 12/24 2T). Commonwealth bogies. ETH 2.

Non-standard livery: 21269 British racing green & cream lined out in gold.

21241–245. Lot No. 30669 Swindon 1961–62. Commonwealth bogies. 36 t.
21256. Lot No. 30731 Derby 1963. Commonwealth bogies. 37 t.
21266–272. Lot No. 30732 Derby 1964. Commonwealth bogies. 37 t.

21241 x	**CC**	BK	*BK*	BT
21245 x	**M**	RV	*RV*	EH
21256 x	**M**	WC	*WC*	CS
21266 x*	**M**	WC	*WC*	CS
21269 *	**0**	RV		EH
21272 x*	**CH**	RV	*RV*	EH

CORRIDOR BRAKE STANDARD

Mark 1. Four compartments. Lot No. 30721 has metal window frames and melamine interior panelling. –/24 1T. ETH2.

35185. Lot No. 30427 Wolverton 1959. B4 bogies. 33 t.
35459. Lot No. 30721 Wolverton 1963. Commonwealth bogies. 37 t.

35185	x	**M**	BK	*BK*	BT
35459	x	**M**	WC	*WC*	CS

CORRIDOR BRAKE GENERATOR STANDARD

Mark 1. Four compartments. Metal window frames and melamine interior panelling. Fitted with an ets generator in the former luggage compartment.

Lot No. 30721 Wolverton 1963. Commonwealth bogies. 37 t.

35469	x	**CC**	RV	*RV*	EH

BRAKE/POWER KITCHEN

Mark 2C. Pressure ventilated. Converted from Corridor Brake First (declassified to Corridor Brake Standard) built 1970. Converted at West Coast Railway Company 2000–01. Consists of 60 kVA generator, guard's compartment and electric kitchen. B5 bogies. ETH 4.

Non-standard livery: British Racing Green with gold lining.

Lot No. 30796 Derby 1969–70. 32.5 t.

35511 (14130, 17130)	**0**	RA	Railway Restorations North-East, Shildon

KITCHEN CAR

Mark 1. Converted 1989/2006 from Kitchen Buffet Unclassified. Buffet and seating area replaced with additional kitchen and food preparation area. Fluorescent lighting. Commonwealth bogies. ETH 2X.

Lot No. 30628 Pressed Steel 1960–61. 39 t.

80041 (1690)	x	**M**	RV	*RV*	EH
80042 (1646)		**BG**	RV	*RV*	EH

DRIVING BRAKE VAN (110 mph)

Mark 3B. Air conditioned. T4 bogies. dg. ETH 5X.

Lot No. 31042 Derby 1988. 45.18 t.

Non-standard livery: 82146 EWS silver.

82101	**V**	P	*VW*	WB
82102	**1**	P	*EA*	NC
82103	**1**	P	*EA*	NC
82104	**V**	CG		NC
82105	**1**	P	*EA*	NC
82106	**V**	AV		LM
82107	**NX**	P	*EA*	NC
82110	**V**	AV		LM

82111	**V**	P		LM
82112	**1**	P	*EA*	NC
82113	**V**	AV		LM
82114	**1**	P	*EA*	NC
82115	**B**	NR		ZN
82116	**V**	AV		LM
82118	**1**	P	*EA*	NC
82120	**V**	AV		LM
82121	**1**	P	*EA*	NC
82122	**V**	AV		LM
82123	**V**	AV		LM
82124	**V**	P		LB
82125	**V**	P		LM
82126	**VT**	P	*VW*	WB
82127	**1**	P	*EA*	NC
82128	**V**	P		LM
82129	**V**	P		LM
82132	**1**	P	*EA*	NC
82133	**1**	P	*EA*	NC
82136	**1**	P	*EA*	NC
82137	**V**	AV		LM
82138	**V**	AV		LM
82139	**1**	P	*EA*	NC
82140	**V**	P		LM
82141	**V**	AV		LM
82143	**1**	P	*EA*	NC
82145	**V**	P		LM
82146	**0**	DB	*DB*	TO
82148	**V**	AV		LM
82150	**V**	AV		LM
82152	**1**	P	*EA*	NC

DRIVING BRAKE VAN (140 mph)

Mark 4. Air conditioned. Swiss-built (SIG) bogies. dg. ETH 6X.

Lot No. 31043 Metro-Cammell 1988. 43.5 t.

Advertising livery: 82205 Flying Scotsman (purple).

82200	**GN**	E	*EC*	BN
82201	**GN**	E	*EC*	BN
82202	**EC**	E	*EC*	BN
82203	**GN**	E	*EC*	BN
82204	**EC**	E	*EC*	BN
82205	**AL**	E	*EC*	BN
82206	**EC**	E	*EC*	BN
82207	**EC**	E	*EC*	BN
82208	**EC**	E	*EC*	BN
82209	**EC**	E	*EC*	BN
82210	**EC**	E	*EC*	BN
82211	**EC**	E	*EC*	BN
82212	**EC**	E	*EC*	BN
82213	**GN**	E	*EC*	BN
82214	**GN**	E	*EC*	BN
82215	**EC**	E	*EC*	BN
82216	**GN**	E	*EC*	BN
82217	**GN**	E	*EC*	BN
82218	**EC**	E	*EC*	BN
82219	**EC**	E	*EC*	BN
82220	**GN**	E	*EC*	BN
82222	**GN**	E	*EC*	BN
82223	**GN**	E	*EC*	BN
82224	**GN**	E	*EC*	BN
82225	**EC**	E	*EC*	BN
82226	**GN**	E	*EC*	BN
82227	**GN**	E	*EC*	BN
82228	**GN**	E	*EC*	BN
82229	**GN**	E	*EC*	BN
82230	**GN**	E	*EC*	BN
82231	**GN**	E	*EC*	BN

DRIVING BRAKE VAN (110 mph)

Mark 3B. Air conditioned. T4 bogies. dg. ETH 6X.

Lot No. 31042 Derby 1988. 45.2 t.

82301–305 originally converted for use on Wrexham & Shropshire services. Now operated by Chiltern Railways. Converted to work in push-pull mode with 67001/010/012–015/018/029.

g Fitted with diesel generator.

82301 (82117)	g	**WS**	AV	*CR*	AL
82302 (82151)		**CR**	AV	*CR*	AL
82303 (82135)		**WS**	AV	*CR*	AL
82304 (82130)		**WS**	AV	*CR*	AL
82305 (82134)		**WS**	AV	*CR*	AL
82306 (82144)		**AB**	AV	*AW*	CF
82307 (82131)		**AB**	AV		LB
82308 (82108)		**AB**	AV		LB

GANGWAYED BRAKE VAN (100 mph)

Mark 1. Short frame (57 ft). Load 10 t. Adapted 199? for use as Brake Luggage Van. Guard's compartment retained and former baggage area adapted for secure stowage of passengers' luggage. B4 bogies. 100 mph. ETH 1X.

Lot No. 30162 Pressed Steel 1956–57. 30.5 t.

92904 (80867, 99554)		**VN**	OE	*NB*	CP

HIGH SECURITY BRAKE VAN (110 mph)

Mark 1. Short frame (57 ft). Load 10 t. Modified 1994 with sealed gangways, new floor, built in tail lights and roller shutter doors. Adapted 2010 for use as baggage vans. ETH 1X.

94515. Lot No. 30162 Pressed Steel 1956–57. 31.4 t. B4 bogies. Composition brake blocks.
94538. Lot No. 30323 Pressed Steel 1957. 31.4 t. B4 bogies. Composition brake blocks.

94515 (80916, 92513)		**M**	DB		EH
94538 (81283, 94426)		**M**	DB		EH

GENERAL UTILITY VAN (100 mph)

Mark 1. Short frame. Load 14 t. Screw couplers. Adapted 2010 for use as a water carrier with 3000 gallon capacity.

Lot No. 30403 York/Glasgow 1958–60. 30 t. Commonwealth bogies.

96175 (86628, 93628)	x	**M**	WC	*WC*	CS

KITCHEN CAR

Mark 1 converted from Corridor First/Corridor Standard in 2008/2011 with staff accommodation. Commonwealth bogies. ETH 3.

99316. Lot No. 30667 Swindon 1961. 35 t.
99712. Lot No. 30685 Derby 1961–62. 34 t.

99316 (13321)	x	**M**	WC	*WC*	CS
99712 (18893)	x	**M**	WC	*WC*	CS

NYMR REGISTERED COACHES

These coaches are permitted to operate on the national railway network but may only be used to convey fare-paying passengers between Middlesbrough and Whitby on the Esk Valley branch line as an extension of North Yorkshire Moors Railway services between Pickering and Grosmont. Only those coaches currently registered for use on the national railway network are listed here.

RESTAURANT FIRST

Mark 1. –/44 2T. Commonwealth bogies. 24/–. ETH 2.

Lot No. 30633 Swindon 1961. 42.5 t.

324	x	**PC**	NY	*NY*	NY	JOS de CRAU

BUFFET STANDARD

Mark 1. –/44 2T. BR Mark 1 bogies. Commonwealth bogies. ETH 3.

Lot No. 30520 Wolverton 1960. 38 t.

1823	v	**M**	NY	*NY*	NY

OPEN STANDARD

Mark 1. –/64 2T (* –/60 2W 2T, † –/60 3W 1T). BR Mark 1 bogies. ETH 4.

3798. Lot No. 30079 York 1953. 33 t.
3860/72. Lot No. 30080 York 1954. 33 t.
3948. Lot No. 30086 Eastleigh 1954–55. 33 t.
4198/4252. Lot No. 30172 York 1956. 33 t.
4286/90. Lot No. 30207 BRCW 1956. 33 t.
4455. Lot No. 30226 BRCW 1957. 33 t.

3798	v	**M**	NY	*NY*	NY
3860	v*	**M**	NY	*NY*	NY
3872	v†	**BG**	NY	*NY*	NY
3948	v	**CC**	NY	*NY*	NY
4198	v	**CC**	NY	*NY*	NY
4252	v*	**CC**	NY	*NY*	NY
4286	v	**CC**	NY	*NY*	NY
4290	v	**M**	NY	*NY*	NY
4455	v	**CC**	NY	*NY*	NY

OPEN STANDARD

Mark 1. –/48 2T. BR Mark 1 bogies. ETH 4.

4786. Lot No. 30376 York 1957. 33 t.
4817. Lot No. 30473 BRCW 1959. 33 t.

4786	v	**CH**	NY	*NY*	NY
4817	v	**M**	NY	*NY*	NY

OPEN STANDARD

Mark 1. Later vehicles built with Commonwealth bogies. –/64 2T. ETH 4.

Lot No. 30690 Wolverton 1961–62. Aluminium window frames. 37 t.

5000	v	**M**	NY	*NY*	NY	5029	v	**CH**	NY	*NY*	NY

OPEN BRAKE STANDARD

Mark 1. –/39 1T. BR Mark 1 bogies. ETH 4.

Lot No. 30170 Doncaster 1956. 34 t.

9267	v	**BG**	NY	*NY*	NY	9274	v	**M**	NY	*NY*	NY

CORRIDOR COMPOSITE

Mark 1. 24/18 1T. BR Mark 1 bogies. ETH 2.

15745. Lot No. 30179 Metro Cammell 1956. 36 t.
16156. Lot No. 30665 Derby 1961. 36 t.

15745	v	**M**	NY	*NY*	NY	16156	v	**CC**	NY	*NY*	NY

CORRIDOR BRAKE COMPOSITE

Mark 1. Two First Class and three Standard Class compartments. 12/18 2T. BR Mark 1 bogies.

Lot No. 30185 Metro Cammell 1956. 36 t.

21100	v	**CC**	NY	*NY*	NY

CORRIDOR BRAKE STANDARD

Mark 1. –/24 1T. BR Mark 1 bogies. ETH 2.

Lot No. 30233 Gloucester 1957. 35 t.

35089	v	**CC**	NY	*NY*	NY

PULLMAN BRAKE THIRD

Built 1928 by Metropolitan Carriage & Wagon Company. Gresley bogies. –/30. 37.5 t.

232	v	**PC**	NY	*NY*	NY	CAR No. 79

PULLMAN KITCHEN FIRST

Built by Metro-Cammell 1960–61 for ECML services. Commonwealth bogies. 20/– 2T. ETH 4. 41.2 t.

318	x	**PC**	NY	*NY*	NY	ROBIN

PULLMAN PARLOUR FIRST

Built by Metro-Cammell 1960–61 for ECML services. Commonwealth bogies. 29/– 2T. 38.5 t.

328	x	**PC**	NY	*NY*	NY	OPAL

2.2. HIGH SPEED TRAIN TRAILER CARS

HSTs consist of a number of trailer cars (usually seven to nine) with a power car at each end. All trailer cars are classified Mark 3 and have BT10 bogies with disc brakes and central door locking. Heating is by a 415 V three-phase supply and vehicles have air conditioning. Maximum speed is 125 mph.

The trailer cars have one standard bodyshell for both First and Standard Class, thus facilitating easy conversion from one class to the other. As built all cars had facing seating around tables with Standard Class coaches having nine bays of seats per side which did not line up with the eight windows per side. This created a new unwelcome trend in British rolling stock of seats not lining up with windows.

All vehicles underwent a mid-life refurbishment in the 1980s with Standard Class seating layouts revised to incorporate unidirectional seating in addition to facing, in a somewhat higgledy-piggledy layout where seats did not line up either side of the aisle.

A further refurbishment programme was completed in November 2000, with each Train Operating Company having a different scheme as follows:

Great Western Trains (later First Great Western). Green seat covers and extra partitions between seat bays.

Great North Eastern Railway. New ceiling lighting panels and brown seat covers. First Class vehicles have table lamps and imitation walnut plastic end panels.

Virgin CrossCountry. Green seat covers. Standard Class vehicles had four seats in the centre of each carriage replaced with a luggage stack. All have now passed to other operators.

Midland Mainline. Grey seat covers, redesigned seat squabs, side carpeting and two seats in the centre of each Standard Class carriage and one in First Class carriages replaced with a luggage stack.

Since then the remaining three operators of HSTs have embarked on separate, and very different, refurbishment projects:

Midland Mainline was first to refurbish its vehicles a second time during 2003–04. This involved fitting new fluorescent and halogen ceiling lighting, although the original seats were retained in First and Standard Class, but with blue upholstery.

London St Pancras–Sheffield/Leeds and Nottingham services are now operated by **East Midlands Trains** and in late summer 2009 this operator embarked on another, less radical, refurbishment which included retention of the original seats but with red upholstery in Standard Class and blue in First Class. This programme was completed in 2010.

First Great Western started a major rebuild of its HST sets in late 2006, with the programme completed in 2008. With an increased fleet of 54 sets (since reduced to 53) the new interiors feature new lighting and seating throughout. First Class seats have leather upholstery, and are made by

Primarius UK. Standard Class seats are of high-back design by Grammer. A number of sets operate without a full buffet or kitchen car, instead using one of 19 TS vehicles converted to include a "mini buffet" counter for use on shorter distance services. During 2012 15 402xx or 407xx buffet vehicles are to be converted to Trailer Standards to make the rakes currently formed as 7-cars up to 8-cars.

GNER modernised its buffet cars with new corner bars in 2004 and at the same time each HST set was made up to 9-cars with an extra Standard Class vehicle added with a disabled person's toilet.

At the end of 2006 **GNER** embarked on a major rebuild of its sets, with the work being carried out at Wabtec, Doncaster. All vehicles will have similar interiors to the Mark 4 "Mallard" fleet, with new Primarius seats throughout. The refurbishment of 13 sets was completed in late 2009, now operated by **East Coast**.

Ten sets ex-Virgin CrossCountry, and some spare vehicles, were temporarily allocated to Midland Mainline for the interim service to Manchester during 2003–04 and had a facelift. Buffet cars were converted from TSB to TFKB and renumbered in the 408xx series. These vehicles are now in use with First Great Western or East Coast.

Open access operator **Grand Central** started operation in December 2007 with a new service from Sunderland to London King's Cross. This operator has three sets mostly using stock converted from loco-hauled Mark 3s. The seats in Standard Class have First Class spacing and in most vehicles are all facing.

CrossCountry reintroduced HSTs to the Cross-Country network from 2008. Five sets were refurbished at Wabtec, Doncaster principally for use on the Plymouth–Edinburgh route. Three of these sets use stock mostly converted from loco-hauled Mark 3s and two are sets ex-Midland Mainline. The interiors are similar to refurbished East Coast sets, although the seating layout is different and one toilet per coach has been removed in favour of a luggage stack.

Operator Codes

Operator codes are shown in the heading before each set of vehicles. The first letter is always "T" for HST coaches, denoting a Trailer vehicle. The second letter denotes the passenger accommodation in that vehicle, for example "F" for First. "GS" denotes Guards accommodation and Standard Class seating. This is followed by catering provision, with "B" for buffet, and "K" for a kitchen and buffet:

TCK	Trailer Composite Kitchen
TF	Trailer First
TFB	Trailer Buffet First
TGS	Trailer Guard's Standard
TFKB	Trailer Kitchen Buffet First
TSB	Trailer Buffet Standard
TS	Trailer Standard

TRAILER STANDARD BUFFET TSB

19 vehicles converted at Laira 2009–10 from HST TSs for First Great Western. Refurbished with Grammer seating.

40101–119. For Lot No. details see TS. –/70 1T. 35.5 t.

40101 (42170)	**FD**	P	*GW*	OO
40102 (42223)	**FD**	P	*GW*	OO
40103 (42316)	**FD**	P	*GW*	OO
40104 (42254)	**FD**	P	*GW*	OO
40105 (42084)	**FD**	P	*GW*	OO
40106 (42162)	**FD**	P	*GW*	OO
40107 (42334)	**FD**	P	*GW*	OO
40108 (42314)	**FD**	P	*GW*	OO
40109 (42262)	**FD**	P	*GW*	OO
40110 (42187)	**FD**	P	*GW*	OO
40111 (42248)	**FD**	P	*GW*	OO
40112 (42336)	**FD**	P	*GW*	OO
40113 (42309)	**FD**	P	*GW*	OO
40114 (42086)	**FD**	P	*GW*	OO
40115 (42320)	**FD**	P	*GW*	OO
40116 (42147)	**FD**	P	*GW*	OO
40117 (42249)	**FD**	P	*GW*	OO
40118 (42338)	**FD**	P	*GW*	OO
40119 (42090)	**FD**	P	*GW*	OO

TRAILER BUFFET FIRST TFB

Converted from TSB by fitting First Class seats. Renumbered from 404xx series by subtracting 200. 23/–.

40204–228. Lot No. 30883 Derby 1976–77. 36.12 t.
40231. Lot No. 30899 Derby 1978–79. 36.12 t.

* Refurbished First Great Western vehicles. Primarius leather seating.

40204 *	**FD**	A	*GW*	LA
40205 *	**FD**	A	*GW*	LA
40207 *	**FD**	A	*GW*	LA
40208	**FG**	A		ZK
40209	**FG**	A		ZK
40210 *	**FD**	A	*GW*	LA
40221 *	**FD**	A	*GW*	LA
40228	**FG**	A		ZK
40231 *	**FD**	A	*GW*	LA

TRAILER BUFFET STANDARD TSB

Renumbered from 400xx series by adding 400. –/33 1W.

40402–426. Lot No. 30883 Derby 1976–77. 36.12 t.
40433/434. Lot No. 30899 Derby 1978–79. 36.12 t.

Note: 40433/434 were numbered 40233/234 for a time when fitted with 23 First Class seats.

40402	**V**	AV		LM	40424	**GC**	A	*GC*	HT
40403	**V**	AV		LM	40426	**GC**	A	*GC*	HT
40416	**V**	AV		LM	40433	**GC**	A	*GC*	HT
40419	**V**	AV		LM	40434	**V**	AV		LM

TRAILER KITCHEN BUFFET FIRST TFKB

These vehicles have larger kitchens than the 402xx and 404xx series vehicles, and are used in trains where a full meal service is required. They were renumbered from the 403xx series (in which the seats were unclassified) by adding 400 to the previous number. 17/–.

40700–721. Lot No. 30921 Derby 1978–79. 38.16 t.
40722–735. Lot No. 30940 Derby 1979–80. 38.16 t.
40736–753. Lot No. 30948 Derby 1980–81. 38.16 t.
40754–757. Lot No. 30966 Derby 1982. 38.16 t.

* Refurbished First Great Western vehicles. Primarius leather seating.
m Refurbished East Coast vehicles with Primarius seating.

40700		**ST**	P	*EM*	NL
40701	m	**NX**	P	*EC*	EC
40702	m	**NX**	P	*EC*	EC
40703	*	**FD**	A	*GW*	LA
40704	m	**NX**	A	*EC*	EC
40705	m	**NX**	A	*EC*	EC
40706	m	**NX**	A	*EC*	EC
40707	*	**FD**	A	*GW*	LA
40708	m	**NX**	P	*EC*	EC
40709		**FG**	A		ZK
40710	*	**FD**	A	*GW*	LA
40711	m	**NX**	A	*EC*	EC
40712		**FD**	A		ZK
40713	*	**FD**	A	*GW*	LA
40714		**FD**	A		ZK
40715	*	**FD**	A	*GW*	LA
40716	*	**FD**	A	*GW*	LA
40717		**FD**	A		ZK
40718	*	**FD**	A	*GW*	OO
40720	m	**NX**	A	*EC*	EC
40721	*	**FD**	A	*GW*	LA
40722	*	**FD**	A	*GW*	LA
40723		**MN**	A		LM
40724		**FD**	A		ZK
40725		**FD**	A		ZK
40726		**FD**	A		ZK
40727	*	**FD**	A	*GW*	LA
40728		**ST**	P	*EM*	NL
40730		**ST**	P	*EM*	NL
40731		**FD**	A		ZK
40732		**ST**	P	*EC*	EC
40733	*	**FD**	A	*GW*	LA
40734	*	**FD**	A	*GW*	LA
40735	m	**NX**	A	*EC*	EC
40736		**FD**	A		ZK
40737	m	**NX**	A	*EC*	EC
40738		**FD**	A		ZK
40739	*	**FD**	A	*GW*	LA
40740	m	**NX**	A	*EC*	EC
40741		**ST**	P	*EM*	NL
40742	m	**NX**	A	*EC*	EC
40743	*	**FD**	A	*GW*	LA
40744		**FD**	A		ZK
40745		**FG**	A		ZG
40746		**ST**	P	*EM*	NL
40747		**FD**	A		ZK
40748	m	**NX**	A	*EC*	EC
40749		**ST**	P	*EM*	NL
40750	m	**NX**	A	*EC*	EC
40751		**ST**	P	*EM*	NL
40752	*	**FD**	A	*GW*	LA
40753		**ST**	P	*EM*	NL
40754		**ST**	P	*EM*	NL
40755	*	**FD**	A	*GW*	LA
40756		**ST**	P	*EM*	NL
40757	*	**FD**	A	*GW*	LA

TRAILER KITCHEN BUFFET FIRST TFKB

These vehicles have been converted from TSBs in the 404xx series to be similar to the 407xx series vehicles. 17/–.

40801–803/805/808/809/811. Lot No. 30883 Derby 1976–77. 38.16 t.
40804/806/807/810. Lot No. 30899 Derby 1978–79. 38.16 t.

Note: 40802/804/811 were numbered 40212/232/211 for a time when fitted with 23 First Class seats.

* Refurbished First Great Western vehicles. Primarius leather seating.
m Refurbished East Coast vehicle with Primarius seating.

40801	(40027, 40427)	*	**FD**	P	*GW*	OO
40802	(40012, 40412)	*	**FD**	P	*GW*	OO
40803	(40018, 40418)	*	**FD**	P	*GW*	OO
40804	(40032, 40432)	*	**FD**	P	*GW*	OO
40805	(40020, 40420)	m	**NX**	P	*EC*	EC
40806	(40029, 40429)	*	**FD**	P	*GW*	OO
40807	(40035, 40435)	*	**FD**	P	*GW*	OO
40808	(40015, 40415)	*	**FD**	P	*GW*	OO
40809	(40014, 40414)	*	**FD**	P	*GW*	OO
40810	(40030, 40430)	*	**FD**	P	*GW*	OO
40811	(40011, 40411)	*	**FD**	P	*GW*	OO

TRAILER BUFFET FIRST TFB

Vehicles owned by First Group. Converted from TSB by First Great Western. Refurbished with Primarius leather seating. 23/–.

40900/902/904. Lot No. 30883 Derby 1976–77. 36.12 t.
40901/903. Lot No. 30899 Derby 1978–79. 36.12 t.

40900	(40022, 40422)	**FD**	FG	*GW*	LA
40901	(40036, 40436)	**FD**	FG	*GW*	LA
40902	(40023, 40423)	**FD**	FG	*GW*	LA
40903	(40037, 40437)	**FD**	FG	*GW*	LA
40904	(40001, 40401)	**FD**	FG	*GW*	LA

TRAILER FIRST TF

41003–056. Lot No. 30881 Derby 1976–77. 33.66 t.
41057–120. Lot No. 30896 Derby 1977–78. 33.66 t.
41121–148. Lot No. 30938 Derby 1979–80. 33.66 t.
41149–166. Lot No. 30947 Derby 1980. 33.66 t.
41167–169. Lot No. 30963 Derby 1982. 33.66 t.
41170. Lot No. 30967 Derby 1982. Former prototype vehicle. 33.66 t.
41176. Lot No. 30897 Derby 1977. 33.66 t.
41179/180. Lot No. 30884 Derby 1976–77. 33.66 t.
41181–184/189. Lot No. 30939 Derby 1979–80. 33.66 t.
41185–187/191. Lot No. 30969 Derby 1982. 33.66 t.

41190. Lot No. 30882 Derby 1976–77. 33.60 t.
41192. Lot No. 30897 Derby 1977–79. 33.60 t.
41193–195/41201–206. Lot No. 30878 Derby 1975–76. 34.3 t. Converted from Mark 3A Open First.

As built and m 48/– 2T (m† 48/– 1T – one toilet removed for trolley space).
- * Refurbished First Great Western vehicles. Primarius leather seating.
- c Refurbished CrossCountry vehicles with Primarius seating and 2 tip-up seats. One toilet removed. 40/– 1TD 1W.
- m Refurbished East Coast vehicles with Primarius seating.
- s Fitted with centre luggage stack, disabled toilet and wheelchair space. 46/– 1T 1TD 1W.
- w Wheelchair space. 47/– 2T 1W. (41154 47/– 1TD 1T 1W).
- x Toilet removed for trolley space (FGW). 48/– 1T.

41003	*x	**FD**	A	*GW*	LA
41004	*x	**FD**	A	*GW*	OO
41005	*x	**FD**	A	*GW*	OO
41006	*w	**FD**	A	*GW*	OO
41007	*x	**FD**	A	*GW*	OO
41008	*w	**FD**	A	*GW*	OO
41009	*x	**FD**	A	*GW*	LA
41010	*w	**FD**	A	*GW*	LA
41011	*x	**FD**	A	*GW*	LA
41012	*w	**FD**	A	*GW*	LA
41015	*x	**FD**	A	*GW*	LA
41016	*w	**FD**	A	*GW*	LA
41017	*x	**FD**	A	*GW*	OO
41018	*w	**FD**	A	*GW*	OO
41019	*x	**FD**	A	*GW*	LA
41020	*w	**FD**	A	*GW*	LA
41021	*x	**FD**	A	*GW*	LA
41022	*w	**FD**	A	*GW*	LA
41023	*x	**FD**	A	*GW*	LA
41024	*w	**FD**	A	*GW*	LA
41026	c	**XC**	A	*XC*	EC
41027	*x	**FD**	A	*GW*	OO
41028	*w	**FD**	A	*GW*	OO
41029	*x	**FD**	A	*GW*	OO
41030	*w	**FD**	A	*GW*	OO
41031	*x	**FD**	A	*GW*	LA
41032	*w	**FD**	A	*GW*	LA
41033	*x	**FD**	A	*GW*	OO
41034	*w	**FD**	A	*GW*	OO
41035	c	**XC**	A	*XC*	EC
41037	*x	**FD**	A	*GW*	LA
41038	*w	**FD**	A	*GW*	LA
41039	m†	**NX**	A	*EC*	EC
41040	mw	**NX**	A	*EC*	EC
41041	s	**ST**	P	*EM*	NL
41044	mw	**NX**	A	*EC*	EC
41045	*x	**FD**	FG	*GW*	LA
41046	s	**ST**	P	*EM*	NL
41051	*x	**FD**	A	*GW*	LA
41052	*w	**FD**	A	*GW*	LA
41055	*x	**FD**	A	*GW*	OO
41056	*w	**FD**	A	*GW*	OO
41057		**ST**	P	*EM*	NL
41059	*w	**FD**	FG	*GW*	LA
41061	w	**ST**	P	*EM*	NL
41062		**ST**	P	*EC*	EC
41063		**ST**	P	*EM*	NL
41064	s	**ST**	P	*EM*	NL
41065	*x	**FD**	A	*GW*	OO
41066	m†	**NX**	A	*EC*	EC
41067	s	**ST**	P	*EM*	NL
41068	s	**ST**	P	*EM*	NL
41069	s	**ST**	P	*EM*	NL
41070	s	**ST**	P	*EM*	NL
41071		**ST**	P	*EM*	NL
41072	s	**ST**	P	*EM*	NL
41075		**ST**	P	*EM*	NL
41076	s	**ST**	P	*EM*	NL
41077		**ST**	P	*EM*	NL
41079		**ST**	P	*EM*	NL
41081	*x	**FD**	P	*GW*	OO
41083	mw	**NX**	P	*EC*	EC
41084	s	**ST**	P	*EM*	NL
41085	*x	**FD**	FG	*GW*	LA
41086	*x	**FD**	FG	*GW*	LA
41087	m†	**NX**	A	*EC*	EC
41088	mw	**NX**	A	*EC*	EC
41089	*w	**FD**	A	*GW*	OO
41090	m†	**NX**	A	*EC*	EC
41091	m†	**NX**	A	*EC*	EC
41092	mw	**NX**	A	*EC*	EC
41093	*x	**FD**	A	*GW*	LA
41094	*w	**FD**	A	*GW*	LA
41095	mw	**NX**	P	*EC*	EC

41096	*x	**FD**	P	*GW*	OO
41097	m†	**NX**	A	*EC*	EC
41098	mw	**NX**	A	*EC*	EC
41099	m†	**NX**	A	*EC*	EC
41100	mw	**NX**	A	*EC*	EC
41101	*x	**FD**	A	*GW*	OO
41102	*w	**FD**	A	*GW*	OO
41103	*x	**FD**	A	*GW*	LA
41104	*w	**FD**	A	*GW*	LA
41105	*x	**FD**	A	*GW*	OO
41106	*w	**FD**	A	*GW*	OO
41108	*w	**FD**	P	*GW*	OO
41109	*x	**FD**	P	*GW*	OO
41110	*w	**FD**	A	*GW*	OO
41111		**ST**	P	*EM*	NL
41112		**ST**	P	*EM*	NL
41113	s	**ST**	P	*EM*	NL
41114	*x	**FD**	FG	*GW*	LA
41115	m†	**NX**	P	*EC*	EC
41116	*x	**FD**	A	*GW*	LA
41117		**ST**	P	*EM*	NL
41118	mw	**NX**	A	*EC*	EC
41119	*x	**FD**	P	*GW*	OO
41120	m†	**NX**	A	*EC*	EC
41121	*x	**FD**	A	*GW*	LA
41122	*w	**FD**	A	*GW*	LA
41123	*x	**FD**	A	*GW*	LA
41124	*w	**FD**	A	*GW*	LA
41125	*x	**FD**	A	*GW*	OO
41126	*w	**FD**	A	*GW*	OO
41127	*x	**FD**	A	*GW*	OO
41128	*w	**FD**	A	*GW*	OO
41129	*x	**FD**	A	*GW*	LA
41130	*w	**FD**	A	*GW*	LA
41131	*x	**FD**	A	*GW*	OO
41132	*w	**FD**	A	*GW*	OO
41133	*x	**FD**	A	*GW*	LA
41134	*w	**FD**	A	*GW*	LA
41135	*w	**FD**	A	*GW*	LA
41136	*w	**FD**	A	*GW*	LA
41137	*x	**FD**	A	*GW*	OO
41138	*w	**FD**	A	*GW*	OO
41139	*x	**FD**	A	*GW*	OO
41140	*w	**FD**	A	*GW*	OO
41141	*x	**FD**	A	*GW*	LA
41142	*w	**FD**	A	*GW*	LA
41143	*x	**FD**	A	*GW*	LA
41144	*w	**FD**	A	*GW*	LA
41145	*x	**FD**	A	*GW*	LA
41146	*w	**FD**	A	*GW*	LA
41147	*w	**FD**	P	*GW*	OO
41148	*x	**FD**	P	*GW*	OO
41149	*w	**FD**	P	*GW*	OO
41150	mw	**NX**	A	*EC*	EC
41151	m†	**NX**	A	*EC*	EC
41152	mw	**NX**	A	*EC*	EC
41153	*x	**FD**	P	*GW*	OO
41154	w	**ST**	P	*EC*	EC
41155	*x	**FD**	P	*GW*	OO
41156		**ST**	P	*EM*	NL
41157	*x	**FD**	A	*GW*	LA
41158	*w	**FD**	A	*GW*	LA
41159	m†	**NX**	P	*EC*	EC
41160	*w	**FD**	FG	*GW*	LA
41161	*w	**FD**	P	*GW*	OO
41162	*w	**FD**	FG	*GW*	LA
41163	*x	**FD**	FG	*GW*	LA
41164	mw	**NX**	A	*EC*	EC
41165	mw	**NX**	P	*EC*	EC
41166	*w	**FD**	FG	*GW*	LA
41167	*w	**FD**	FG	*GW*	LA
41168	*x	**FD**	P	*GW*	OO
41169	*w	**FD**	P	*GW*	OO

41170	(41001)	m†	**NX**	A	*EC*	EC
41176	(42142, 42352)	*w	**FD**	P	*GW*	OO
41179	(40505)	*x	**FD**	A	*GW*	OO
41180	(40511)	*w	**FD**	A	*GW*	OO
41181	(42282)	*x	**FD**	P	*GW*	OO
41182	(42278)	*w	**FD**	P	*GW*	OO
41183	(42274)	*w	**FD**	P	*GW*	OO
41184	(42270)	*x	**FD**	P	*GW*	OO
41185	(42313)	m†	**NX**	P	*EC*	EC
41186	(42312)	*x	**FD**	P	*GW*	OO
41187	(42311)	*w	**FD**	P	*GW*	OO
41189	(42298)	*w	**FD**	P	*GW*	OO
41190	(42088)	m†	**NX**	P	*EC*	EC

41191 (42318)	*x	**FD**	P	*GW*	OO
41192 (42246)	*w	**FD**	P	*GW*	OO

The following coaches have been converted from loco-hauled Mark 3 vehicles for CrossCountry.

41193 (11060)	c	**XC**	P	*XC*	EC
41194 (11016)	c	**XC**	P	*XC*	EC
41195 (11020)	c	**XC**	P	*XC*	EC

The following coaches have been converted from loco-hauled Mark 3 vehicles for Grand Central. 48/– 2T.

41201 (11045)	**GC**	A	*GC*	HT
41202 (11017)	**GC**	A	*GC*	HT
41203 (11038)	**GC**	A	*GC*	HT
41204 (11023)	**GC**	A	*GC*	HT
41205 (11036)	**GC**	A	*GC*	HT
41206 (11055)	**GC**	A	*GC*	HT

TRAILER STANDARD TS

42003–089/362. Lot No. 30882 Derby 1976–77. 33.60 t.
42091–250. Lot No. 30897 Derby 1977–79. 33.60 t.
42251–305. Lot No. 30939 Derby 1979–80. 33.60 t.
42306–322. Lot No. 30969 Derby 1982. 33.60 t.
42323–341. Lot No. 30983 Derby 1984–85. 33.60 t.
42342/360. Lot No. 30949 Derby 1982. 33.47 t. Converted from TGS.
42343/345. Lot No. 30970 Derby 1982. 33.47 t. Converted from TGS.
42344/361. Lot No. 30964 Derby 1982. 33.47 t. Converted from TGS.
42346/347/350/351/379/380. Lot No. 30881 Derby 1976–77. 33.66 t. Converted from TF.
42348/349/363–365/381. Lot No. 30896 Derby 1977–78. 33.66 t. Converted from TF.
42354. Lot No. 30897 Derby 1977. Was TF from 1983 to 1992. 33.66 t.
42353/355–357. Lot No. 30967 Derby 1982. Ex-prototype vehicles. 33.66 t.
42366–378/382/383/401–409. Lot No. 30877 Derby 1975–77. 34.3 t. Converted from Mark 3A Open Standard.
42384. Lot No. 30896 Derby 1977–78. 33.66 t.

Notes: 42158 was numbered 41177 for a time when fitted with First Class seats. 42310 was numbered 41188 for a time when fitted with First Class seats.

Standard seating and m –/76 2T.

- * Refurbished First Great Western vehicles. Grammer seating. –/80 2T (unless h – high density).
- c Refurbished CrossCountry vehicles with Primarius seating. One toilet removed. –/82 1T.
- §c Refurbished CrossCountry vehicles with Primarius seating and 2 tip-up seats. One toilet removed. –/66 1TD 2W. Note 42379/380 are –/71 1TD 1T 2W.
- d FGW vehicles with disabled persons toilet and 5, 6 or 7 tip-up seats. –/68 1T 1TD 2W.
- h "High density" FGW vehicles. –/84 2T.

k “High density” FGW refurbished vehicle with disabled persons toilet and 5, 6 or 7 tip-up seats. –/72 1T 1TD 2W.
m Refurbished East Coast vehicles with Primarius seating.
u Centre luggage stack (EMT) –/74 2T.
v First Great Western Volo entertainment coach. TV screens fitted to most seat backs.
w Centre luggage stack and wheelchair space (EMT) –72 2T 1W.
† Disabled persons toilet (East Coast) –/62 1T 1TD 1W.

42003	*hv	**FD**	A	*GW*	OO
42004	*d	**FD**	A	*GW*	LA
42005	*hv	**FD**	A	*GW*	LA
42006	*h	**FD**	A	*GW*	LA
42007	*d	**FD**	A	*GW*	LA
42008	*k	**FD**	A	*GW*	OO
42009	*hv	**FD**	A	*GW*	LA
42010	*hv	**FD**	A	*GW*	LA
42012	*k	**FD**	A	*GW*	LA
42013	*h	**FD**	A	*GW*	LA
42014	*h	**FD**	A	*GW*	LA
42015	*k	**FD**	A	*GW*	LA
42016	*h	**FD**	A	*GW*	LA
42019	*v	**FD**	A	*GW*	LA
42021	*k	**FD**	A	*GW*	LA
42023	*h	**FD**	A	*GW*	LA
42024	*k	**FD**	A	*GW*	OO
42025	*h	**FD**	A	*GW*	OO
42026	*h	**FD**	A	*GW*	OO
42027	*hv	**FD**	A	*GW*	OO
42028	*h	**FD**	A	*GW*	LA
42029	*h	**FD**	A	*GW*	LA
42030	*k	**FD**	A	*GW*	LA
42031	*h	**FD**	A	*GW*	LA
42032	*h	**FD**	A	*GW*	LA
42033	*v	**FD**	A	*GW*	LA
42034	*	**FD**	A	*GW*	LA
42035	*	**FD**	A	*GW*	LA
42036	c	**XC**	A	*XC*	EC
42037	c	**XC**	A	*XC*	EC
42038	c	**XC**	A	*XC*	EC
42039	*hv	**FD**	A	*GW*	OO
42040	*h	**FD**	A	*GW*	OO
42041	*h	**FD**	A	*GW*	OO
42042	*hv	**FD**	A	*GW*	OO
42043	*h	**FD**	A	*GW*	OO
42044	*h	**FD**	A	*GW*	OO
42045	*v	**FD**	A	*GW*	LA
42046	*	**FD**	A	*GW*	LA
42047	*	**FD**	A	*GW*	LA
42048	*hv	**FD**	A	*GW*	OO
42049	*h	**FD**	A	*GW*	LA

42050	*h	**FD**	A	*GW*	OO
42051	c	**XC**	A	*XC*	EC
42052	c	**XC**	A	*XC*	EC
42053	c	**XC**	A	*XC*	EC
42054	*v	**FD**	A	*GW*	LA
42055	*	**FD**	A	*GW*	LA
42056	*	**FD**	A	*GW*	LA
42057	m	**NX**	A	*EC*	EC
42058	m	**NX**	A	*EC*	EC
42059	m	**NX**	A	*EC*	EC
42060	*h	**FD**	A	*GW*	OO
42061	*h	**FD**	A	*GW*	OO
42062	*k	**FD**	A	*GW*	OO
42063	m	**NX**	A	*EC*	EC
42064	m	**NX**	A	*EC*	EC
42065	m	**NX**	A	*EC*	EC
42066	*k	**FD**	A	*GW*	OO
42067	*h	**FD**	A	*GW*	OO
42068	*h	**FD**	A	*GW*	OO
42069	*k	**FD**	A	*GW*	OO
42070	*hv	**FD**	A	*GW*	OO
42071	*h	**FD**	A	*GW*	OO
42072	*	**FD**	A	*GW*	LA
42073	*hv	**FD**	A	*GW*	OO
42074	*hv	**FD**	A	*GW*	OO
42075	*v	**FD**	A	*GW*	LA
42076	*v	**FD**	A	*GW*	LA
42077	*	**FD**	A	*GW*	LA
42078	*	**FD**	A	*GW*	LA
42079	*h	**FD**	A	*GW*	OO
42080	*h	**FD**	A	*GW*	OO
42081	*k	**FD**	A	*GW*	OO
42083	*h	**FD**	A	*GW*	OO
42085	*hv	**FD**	P	*GW*	OO
42087	*h	**FD**	P	*GW*	OO
42089	*h	**FD**	A	*GW*	OO
42091	m†	**NX**	A	*EC*	EC
42092	*d	**FD**	FG	*GW*	LA
42093	*hv	**FD**	FG	*GW*	LA
42094	*h	**FD**	FG	*GW*	LA
42095	*	**FD**	FG	*GW*	LA
42096	*hv	**FD**	A	*GW*	LA

42097	c	**XC**	A	*XC*	EC
42098	*hv	**FD**	A	*GW*	OO
42099	*hv	**FD**	A	*GW*	OO
42100	u	**ST**	P	*EM*	NL
42101	*h	**FD**	P	*GW*	OO
42102	*hv	**FD**	P	*GW*	OO
42103	*k	**FD**	FG	*GW*	LA
42104	m	**NX**	A	*EC*	EC
42105	*d	**FD**	FG	*GW*	LA
42106	m	**NX**	A	*EC*	EC
42107	*	**FD**	A	*GW*	LA
42108	*h	**FD**	FG	*GW*	LA
42109	m	**NX**	P	*EC*	EC
42110	m	**NX**	P	*EC*	EC
42111	u	**ST**	P	*EM*	NL
42112	u	**ST**	P	*EM*	NL
42113	u	**ST**	P	*EM*	NL
42115	*hv	**FD**	P	*GW*	OO
42116	m†	**NX**	A	*EC*	EC
42117	m	**NX**	P	*EC*	EC
42118	*h	**FD**	A	*GW*	OO
42119	u	**ST**	P	*EM*	NL
42120	u	**ST**	P	*EM*	NL
42121	u	**ST**	P	*EM*	NL
42122	m	**NX**	A	*EC*	EC
42123		**ST**	P	*EC*	EC
42124	u	**ST**	P	*EM*	NL
42125		**ST**	P	*EC*	EC
42126	*h	**FD**	A	*GW*	OO
42127	m†	**NX**	A	*EC*	EC
42128	m†	**NX**	A	*EC*	EC
42129	*v	**FD**	A	*GW*	LA
42130	m	**NX**	P	*EC*	EC
42131	u	**ST**	P	*EM*	NL
42132	u	**ST**	P	*EM*	NL
42133	u	**ST**	P	*EM*	NL
42134	m	**NX**	A	*EC*	EC
42135	u	**ST**	P	*EM*	NL
42136	u	**ST**	P	*EM*	NL
42137	u	**ST**	P	*EM*	NL
42138	*k	**FD**	A	*GW*	OO
42139	u	**ST**	P	*EM*	NL
42140	u	**ST**	P	*EM*	NL
42141	u	**ST**	P	*EM*	NL
42143	*v	**FD**	A	*GW*	LA
42144	*	**FD**	A	*GW*	LA
42145	*	**FD**	A	*GW*	LA
42146	m	**NX**	A	*EC*	EC
42148	u	**ST**	P	*EM*	NL
42149	u	**ST**	P	*EM*	NL
42150	m	**NX**	A	*EC*	EC
42151	w	**ST**	P	*EM*	NL
42152	u	**ST**	P	*EM*	NL
42153	u	**ST**	P	*EM*	NL
42154	m	**NX**	A	*EC*	EC
42155	w	**ST**	P	*EM*	NL
42156	u	**ST**	P	*EM*	NL
42157	u	**ST**	P	*EM*	NL
42158	m	**NX**	A	*EC*	EC
42159	m†	**NX**	P	*EC*	EC
42160	m	**NX**	P	*EC*	EC
42161	m†	**NX**	A	*EC*	EC
42163	m	**NX**	P	*EC*	EC
42164		**ST**	P	*EM*	NL
42165		**ST**	P	*EM*	NL
42166	*h	**FD**	P	*GW*	OO
42167	*h	**FD**	FG	*GW*	LA
42168	*hv	**FD**	FG	*GW*	LA
42169	*h	**FD**	FG	*GW*	LA
42171	m	**NX**	A	*EC*	EC
42172	m	**NX**	A	*EC*	EC
42173	*k	**FD**	P	*GW*	OO
42174	*k	**FD**	P	*GW*	OO
42175	*h	**FD**	FG	*GW*	LA
42176	*hv	**FD**	FG	*GW*	LA
42177	*h	**FD**	FG	*GW*	LA
42178	*hv	**FD**	P	*GW*	OO
42179	m	**NX**	A	*EC*	EC
42180	m	**NX**	A	*EC*	EC
42181	m	**NX**	A	*EC*	EC
42182	m	**NX**	A	*EC*	EC
42183	*d	**FD**	A	*GW*	LA
42184	*v	**FD**	A	*GW*	LA
42185	*	**FD**	A	*GW*	LA
42186	m	**NX**	A	*EC*	EC
42188	m†	**NX**	A	*EC*	EC
42189	m†	**NX**	A	*EC*	EC
42190	m	**NX**	A	*EC*	EC
42191	m	**NX**	A	*EC*	EC
42192	m	**NX**	A	*EC*	EC
42193	m	**NX**	A	*EC*	EC
42194	w	**ST**	P	*EM*	NL
42195	*k	**FD**	P	*GW*	OO
42196	*hv	**FD**	A	*GW*	OO
42197	*hv	**FD**	A	*GW*	OO
42198	m	**NX**	A	*EC*	EC
42199	m	**NX**	A	*EC*	EC
42200	*d	**FD**	A	*GW*	LA
42201	*k	**FD**	A	*GW*	OO
42202	*k	**FD**	A	*GW*	OO
42203	*h	**FD**	A	*GW*	OO
42204	*h	**FD**	A	*GW*	OO

42205		**ST**	P	*EC*	EC
42206	*d	**FD**	A	*GW*	LA
42207	*d	**FD**	A	*GW*	LA
42208	*	**FD**	A	*GW*	LA
42209	*	**FD**	A	*GW*	LA
42210		**ST**	P	*EC*	EC
42211	*k	**FD**	A	*GW*	OO
42212	*hv	**FD**	A	*GW*	OO
42213	*h	**FD**	A	*GW*	OO
42214	*h	**FD**	A	*GW*	OO
42215	m	**NX**	A	*EC*	EC
42216	*hv	**FD**	A	*GW*	OO
42217	*k	**FD**	P	*GW*	OO
42218	*d	**FD**	P	*GW*	OO
42219	m	**NX**	A	*EC*	EC
42220	w	**ST**	P	*EM*	NL
42221	*hv	**FD**	A	*GW*	OO
42222	*hv	**FD**	P	*GW*	OO
42224	*k	**FD**	P	*GW*	OO
42225	u	**ST**	P	*EM*	NL
42226	m	**NX**	A	*EC*	EC
42227	u	**ST**	P	*EM*	NL
42228	m	**NX**	P	*EC*	EC
42229	u	**ST**	P	*EM*	NL
42230	u	**ST**	P	*EM*	NL
42231	*h	**FD**	FG	*GW*	LA
42232	*hv	**FD**	FG	*GW*	LA
42233	*h	**FD**	FG	*GW*	LA
42234	c	**XC**	P	*XC*	EC
42235	m	**NX**	A	*EC*	EC
42236	*hv	**FD**	A	*GW*	OO
42237	m	**NX**	P	*EC*	EC
42238	m†	**NX**	A	*EC*	EC
42239	m†	**NX**	A	*EC*	EC
42240	m	**NX**	A	*EC*	EC
42241	m	**NX**	A	*EC*	EC
42242	m	**NX**	A	*EC*	EC
42243	m	**NX**	A	*EC*	EC
42244	m	**NX**	A	*EC*	EC
42245	*	**FD**	A	*GW*	LA
42247	*hv	**FD**	P	*GW*	OO
42250	*	**FD**	A	*GW*	LA
42251	*k	**FD**	A	*GW*	OO
42252	*	**FD**	A	*GW*	LA
42253	*	**FD**	A	*GW*	LA
42255	*d	**FD**	A	*GW*	LA
42256	*	**FD**	A	*GW*	LA
42257	*	**FD**	A	*GW*	LA
42258	*hv	**FD**	P	*GW*	OO
42259	*k	**FD**	A	*GW*	LA
42260	*h	**FD**	A	*GW*	OO

42261	*h	**FD**	A	*GW*	OO
42263	*v	**FD**	A	*GW*	LA
42264	*k	**FD**	A	*GW*	OO
42265	*v	**FD**	A	*GW*	LA
42266	*k	**FD**	P	*GW*	OO
42267	*d	**FD**	A	*GW*	LA
42268	*d	**FD**	A	*GW*	LA
42269	*	**FD**	A	*GW*	LA
42271	*k	**FD**	A	*GW*	OO
42272	*h	**FD**	A	*GW*	OO
42273	*h	**FD**	A	*GW*	OO
42275	*d	**FD**	A	*GW*	LA
42276	*	**FD**	A	*GW*	LA
42277	*	**FD**	A	*GW*	LA
42279	*d	**FD**	A	*GW*	LA
42280	*	**FD**	A	*GW*	LA
42281	*	**FD**	A	*GW*	LA
42283	*h	**FD**	A	*GW*	OO
42284	*h	**FD**	A	*GW*	OO
42285	*h	**FD**	A	*GW*	OO
42286	m†	**NX**	P	*EC*	EC
42287	*k	**FD**	A	*GW*	OO
42288	*h	**FD**	A	*GW*	OO
42289	*h	**FD**	A	*GW*	OO
42290	c	**XC**	P	*XC*	EC
42291	*d	**FD**	A	*GW*	LA
42292	*d	**FD**	A	*GW*	LA
42293	*	**FD**	A	*GW*	LA
42294	*	**FD**	P	*GW*	OO
42295	*d	**FD**	A	*GW*	LA
42296	*	**FD**	A	*GW*	LA
42297	*	**FD**	A	*GW*	LA
42299	*d	**FD**	A	*GW*	LA
42300	*	**FD**	A	*GW*	LA
42301	*	**FD**	A	*GW*	LA
42302	*k	**FD**	FG	*GW*	LA
42303	*hv	**FD**	FG	*GW*	LA
42304	*h	**FD**	FG	*GW*	LA
42305	*h	**FD**	FG	*GW*	LA
42306	m	**NX**	P	*EC*	EC
42307	m	**NX**	P	*EC*	EC
42308	*hv	**FD**	P	*GW*	OO
42310	*k	**FD**	P	*GW*	OO
42315	*h	**FD**	P	*GW*	OO
42317	*k	**FD**	P	*GW*	OO
42319	*hv	**FD**	P	*GW*	OO
42321	*h	**FD**	P	*GW*	OO
42322	m	**NX**	P	*EC*	EC
42323	m	**NX**	A	*EC*	EC
42325	*v	**FD**	A	*GW*	LA
42326	m	**NX**	P	*EC*	EC

42327	w	**ST**	P	*EM*	NL
42328	w	**ST**	P	*EM*	NL
42329	w	**ST**	P	*EM*	NL
42330	m	**NX**	P	*EC*	EC
42331	w	**ST**	P	*EM*	NL
42332	*v	**FD**	A	*GW*	LA
42333	*	**FD**	A	*GW*	LA
42335	w	**ST**	P	*EC*	EC
42337	w	**ST**	P	*EM*	NL
42339	w	**ST**	P	*EM*	NL
42340	m	**NX**	A	*EC*	EC
42341	u	**ST**	P	*EM*	NL

42342	(44082)	c	**XC**	A	*XC*	EC
42343	(44095)	*v	**FD**	A	*GW*	LA
42344	(44092)	*k	**FD**	A	*GW*	OO
42345	(44096)	*d	**FD**	A	*GW*	LA
42346	(41053)	*h	**FD**	A	*GW*	OO
42347	(41054)	*k	**FD**	A	*GW*	OO
42348	(41073)	*k	**FD**	A	*GW*	OO
42349	(41074)	*hv	**FD**	A	*GW*	OO
42350	(41047)	*v	**FD**	A	*GW*	LA
42351	(41048)	*v	**FD**	A	*GW*	LA
42353	(42001, 41171)	*k	**FD**	FG	*GW*	LA
42354	(42114, 41175)	m	**NX**	A	*EC*	EC
42355	(42000, 41172)	m	**NX**	A	*EC*	EC
42356	(42002, 41173)	*k	**FD**	A	*GW*	OO
42357	(41002, 41174)	m	**NX**	A	*EC*	EC
42360	(44084, 45084)	*hv	**FD**	A	*GW*	LA
42361	(44099, 42000)	*h	**FD**	A	*GW*	LA
42362	(42011, 41178)	*hv	**FD**	A	*GW*	OO
42363	(41082)	m†	**NX**	A	*EC*	EC
42364	(41080)	*k	**FD**	P	*GW*	OO
42365	(41107)	*h	**FD**	P	*GW*	OO

42366–378 have been converted from loco-hauled Mark 3 vehicles for CrossCountry and 42382/383 for First Great Western.

42366	(12007)	c	**XC**	P	*XC*	EC
42367	(12025)	c	**XC**	P	*XC*	EC
42368	(12028)	c	**XC**	P	*XC*	EC
42369	(12050)	c	**XC**	P	*XC*	EC
42370	(12086)	c	**XC**	P	*XC*	EC
42371	(12052)	§c	**XC**	P	*XC*	EC
42372	(12055)	c	**XC**	P	*XC*	EC
42373	(12071)	c	**XC**	P	*XC*	EC
42374	(12075)	c	**XC**	P	*XC*	EC
42375	(12113)	c	**XC**	P	*XC*	EC
42376	(12085)	§c	**XC**	P	*XC*	EC
42377	(12102)	c	**XC**	P	*XC*	EC
42378	(12123)	c	**XC**	P	*XC*	EC
42379	(41036)	§c	**XC**	A	*XC*	EC
42380	(41025)	§c	**XC**	A	*XC*	EC
42381	(41058)	*k	**FD**	P	*GW*	OO
42382	(12128)	*h	**FD**	P	*GW*	OO
42383	(12172)	*h	**FD**	P	*GW*	OO
42384	(41078)	w	**ST**	P	*EM*	NL

The following coaches have been converted from loco-hauled Mark 3 vehicles for Grand Central. They have a lower density seating layout (most seats arranged around tables). –/64 2T († –/60 1TD 1T 2W).

42401	(12149)		**GC**	A	*GC*	HT
42402	(12155)		**GC**	A	*GC*	HT
42403	(12033)	†	**GC**	A	*GC*	HT
42404	(12152)		**GC**	A	*GC*	HT
42405	(12136)		**GC**	A	*GC*	HT
42406	(12112)	†	**GC**	A	*GC*	HT
42407	(12044)		**GC**	A	*GC*	HT
42408	(12121)		**GC**	A	*GC*	HT
42409	(12088)	†	**GC**	A	*GC*	HT

TRAILER GUARD'S STANDARD TGS

44000. Lot No. 30953 Derby 1980. 33.47 t.
44001–090. Lot No. 30949 Derby 1980–82. 33.47 t.
44091–094. Lot No. 30964 Derby 1982. 33.47 t.
44097–101. Lot No. 30970 Derby 1982. 33.47 t.

As built and m –/65 1T.
- * Refurbished First Great Western vehicles. Grammer seating and toilet removed for trolley store. –/67 (unless h).
- † Contains a mix of original and new Grammer seating. –/65 1T.
- c Refurbished CrossCountry vehicles with Primarius seating. –/67 1T.
- h "High density" FGW vehicles. –/71.
- m Refurbished East Coast vehicles with Primarius seating.
- s Fitted with centre luggage stack (EMT) –/63 1T.
- t Fitted with centre luggage stack –/61 1T.

44000	*h	**FD**	P	*GW*	OO
44001	*	**FD**	A	*GW*	LA
44002	*h	**FD**	A	*GW*	OO
44003	*h	**FD**	A	*GW*	OO
44004	*h	**FD**	A	*GW*	LA
44005	*h	**FD**	A	*GW*	LA
44007	*h	**FD**	A	*GW*	LA
44008	*h	**FD**	A	*GW*	OO
44009	*h	**FD**	A	*GW*	LA
44010	*h	**FD**	A	*GW*	LA
44011	*	**FD**	A	*GW*	LA
44012	c	**XC**	A	*XC*	EC
44013	*h	**FD**	A	*GW*	OO
44014	*h	**FD**	A	*GW*	OO
44015	*	**FD**	A	*GW*	LA
44016	*h	**FD**	A	*GW*	OO
44017	c	**XC**	A	*XC*	EC
44018	*	**FD**	A	*GW*	LA
44019	m	**NX**	A	*EC*	EC
44020	*h	**FD**	A	*GW*	OO
44021	c	**XC**	P	*XC*	EC
44022	*h	**FD**	A	*GW*	OO
44023	*h	**FD**	A	*GW*	OO
44024	*h	**FD**	A	*GW*	OO
44025	*	**FD**	A	*GW*	LA
44026	*h	**FD**	A	*GW*	OO
44027	s	**ST**	P	*EM*	NL
44028	*	**FD**	A	*GW*	LA
44029	*	**FD**	A	*GW*	LA
44030	*h	**FD**	A	*GW*	OO
44031	m	**NX**	A	*EC*	EC
44032	*	**FD**	A	*GW*	LA
44033	*h	**FD**	A	*GW*	OO
44034	*	**FD**	A	*GW*	LA
44035	*	**FD**	A	*GW*	LA
44036	*h	**FD**	A	*GW*	OO
44037	*h	**FD**	A	*GW*	OO
44038	*	**FD**	A	*GW*	LA
44039	*	**FD**	A	*GW*	LA
44040	*	**FD**	A	*GW*	LA
44041	s	**ST**	P	*EM*	NL
44042	*h	**FD**	P	*GW*	OO

▲ **Mark 1s:** In all over Riviera blue livery, Mark 1 Unclassified Kitchen Buffet 1699 is seen at Girvan on 12/02/11. **Robert Pritchard**

▼ BR Maroon-liveried Mark 1 Open First 3136 "DIANA" is seen near Scarborough on 02/07/11. **Andrew Mason**

▲ BR Chocolate & Cream-liveried Mark 1 Open Standard 5009 is seen at Sheffield on 29/01/11. **Robert Pritchard**

▼ BR Maroon-liveried Mark 1 Kitchen Car 99712 (ex-18893) is seen at Stoneycombe, near Newton Abbot, on 23/04/11. **Stewart Armstrong**

▲ **Mark 2s:** Riviera Trains-liveried Mark 2F Buffet First 1200 "AMBER" is seen at Colton Junction on 05/08/11. **Andrew Mason**

▼ VSOE Northern Belle-liveried Mark 2E Open First 3273 "ALNWICK" is seen at Old Linslade on 02/07/11. **Mark Beal**

▲ BR Carmine & Cream-liveried Mark 2A Open Standard 5341 at Sheffield on 29/01/11. **Robert Pritchard**

▼ Arriva Trains Wales "executive"-liveried Mark 2F Open Standard 5965 is seen near Yorton on 28/04/11. **Robert Pritchard**

▲ BR Maroon-liveried Mark 2C Buffet Standard 6528 is seen in Goodrington Sidings, Paignton on 09/07/11. **Steve Widdowson**

▼ BR Maroon-liveried Mark 2 Open Brake Standard 9392 is seen at Preston on 14/08/11. **Robin Ralston**

▲ Mark 2F Open Brake Standard 9537 is seen near Swinton (South Yorks) on 19/04/11 in an advertising livery for CruiseSaver Express. All seats have been removed to provide luggage space. **Ross Byers**

▼ **Mark 3s:** First Great Western Dynamic Lines-liveried Mark 3A Kitchen Buffet First 10225 is seen at Truro on 13/07/11 formed in the "Night Riviera" Sleeper service. **Robert Pritchard**

▲ Royal Train Queen's Saloon 2903, converted from Mark 3 Open First 11001, is seen at Chelmscote on 22/06/11. **Mark Beal**

▼ BR Blue & Grey-liveried Mark 3B Open First 11086 is seen at Meadowhall on 25/08/10. **Robert Pritchard**

▲ In "One" livery with a National Express white stripe, Mark 3A Open Standard 12067 is seen at Great Yarmouth on 15/07/11. **Robert Pritchard**

▼ **Mark 3 Sleeping cars:** First Group-liveried Mark 3A Sleeping Car 10693 at London Euston in the formation of the ScotRail Highland Sleeper on 12/07/11. **Robert Pritchard**

▲ **Mark 3 HST vehicles:** First Great Western "Dynamic Lines" liveried HST TSB 40119 at Hollicombe, near Paignton, on 02/09/11. **Robin Ralston**

▼ Stagecoach East Midlands Trains-liveried HST TS 42384 (a spare carriage) at Dore & Totley on 10/04/11. **Robert Pritchard**

▲ CrossCountry-liveried HST TGS 44021 at Sheffield on 14/03/11.
Robert Pritchard

▼ **Mark 4s:** East Coast silver-liveried Mark 4 Open Standard 12478 is seen at Doncaster on 24/07/11. **Robert Pritchard**

▲ **Pullman cars, saloons and other stock:** Royal Scotsman-liveried LNER General Managers Saloon 1999, used with the Royal Scotsman as "Dining Car No. 2" is seen at Carlisle on 10/07/11. **Robert Pritchard**

▼ Maroon-liveried LMS Club Car 99993 is seen at Preston on 14/08/11. **Robin Ralston**

▲ VSOE Pullman Kitchen First 280 "AUDREY" stands at Folkestone West on 29/09/11.
Brian Denton

▼ BR Maroon-liveried Metro-Cammell Pullman Parlour Second 348 (numbered 99348 and used as an Open First) is seen at Heeley, Sheffield on 12/06/10.
Robert Pritchard

▲ **DVTs:** In unbranded Chiltern livery, Mark 3B DVT 82302 arrives at Bicester North leading the 18.06 London Marylebone–Banbury on 28/06/11. **John Binch**

▼ East Coast-liveried Mark 4 DVT 82219 passes Moorhouse, near South Elmsall, leading the 12.05 Leeds–London King's Cross on 24/07/11. **Robert Pritchard**

▲ **Service stock:** Painted in all-over red livery, former DMU Translator Vehicle 6360 (converted from Mark 2A Open Brake Standard 9420) is used as a barrier vehicle at Neville Hill depot, where it is seen on 30/04/11. **Jason Rogers**

▼ In Arlington Fleet Services green livery, Mark 1 EMU Translator Vehicle 975974 "Paschar" is seen at Milton Keynes Central on 18/07/11. **Mark Beal**

▲ Network Rail yellow-liveried Generator Van 6261 is seen at Scarborough behind 37087 on 14/06/11. **Andrew Mason**

▼ One of the five Network Rail Driving Trailer Coaches, 9701, leads a Derby–Skegness test train at Great Hale Drove on 19/01/11. The train was powered by 31465 and also included 999508. **Lindsay Atkinson**

▲ New Measurement Train Conference Coach 975814 (converted from the prototype HST TF 41000) is seen at Sheffield on 10/07/10. **Robert Pritchard**

▼ Network Rail Track Inspection Coach 999508 is seen at Ipswich on 15/07/11. **Robert Pritchard**

44043	*h	**FD**	A	*GW*	OO
44044	s	**ST**	P	*EM*	NL
44045	m	**NX**	A	*EC*	EC
44046	s	**ST**	P	*EM*	NL
44047	s	**ST**	P	*EM*	NL
44048	s	**ST**	P	*EM*	NL
44049	*	**FD**	A	*GW*	LA
44050	m	**NX**	P	*EC*	EC
44051	s	**ST**	P	*EM*	NL
44052	c	**XC**	P	*XC*	EC
44054	s	**ST**	P	*EM*	NL
44055	*h	**FD**	FG	*GW*	LA
44056	m	**NX**	A	*EC*	EC
44057	m	**NX**	P	*EC*	EC
44058	m	**NX**	A	*EC*	EC
44059	*	**FD**	A	*GW*	LA
44060	*h	**FD**	P	*GW*	OO
44061	m	**NX**	A	*EC*	EC
44063	m	**NX**	A	*EC*	EC
44064	*h	**FD**	A	*GW*	OO
44065	t	**V**	AV		LM
44066	*	**FD**	A	*GW*	LA
44067	*h	**FD**	A	*GW*	OO
44068	*h	**FD**	FG	*GW*	LA
44069	*h	**FD**	P	*GW*	OO
44070	s	**ST**	P	*EM*	NL
44071	s	**ST**	P	*EM*	NL
44072	c	**XC**	P	*XC*	EC
44073	†	**ST**	P	*EC*	EC
44074	*h	**FD**	FG	*GW*	LA
44075	m	**NX**	P	*EC*	EC
44076	*h	**FD**	FG	*GW*	LA
44077	m	**NX**	A	*EC*	EC
44078	*h	**FD**	P	*GW*	OO
44079	*h	**FD**	P	*GW*	OO
44080	m	**NX**	A	*EC*	EC
44081	*h	**FD**	FG	*GW*	LA
44083	*h	**FD**	P	*GW*	OO
44085	s	**ST**	P	*EM*	NL
44086	*	**FD**	A	*GW*	LA
44088	t	**V**	AV		LM
44089	t	**V**	AV		LM
44090	*h	**FD**	P	*GW*	OO
44091	*h	**FD**	P	*GW*	OO
44093	*h	**FD**	A	*GW*	OO
44094	m	**NX**	A	*EC*	EC
44097	*h	**FD**	P	*GW*	OO
44098	m	**NX**	A	*EC*	EC
44100	*h	**FD**	FG	*GW*	PM
44101	*h	**FD**	P	*GW*	OO

TRAILER COMPOSITE KITCHEN TCK

45001–005. Lot No. 30877 Derby 1975–77. 34.3 t. Converted from Mark 3A Open Standard. Refurbished CrossCountry vehicles with Primarius seating. Small kitchen for the preparation of hot food and stowage space for two trolleys between First and Standard Class sections. One toilet removed. 30/10 1T.

45001	(12004)	**XC**	P	*XC*	EC
45002	(12106)	**XC**	P	*XC*	EC
45003	(12076)	**XC**	P	*XC*	EC
45004	(12077)	**XC**	P	*XC*	EC
45005	(12080)	**XC**	P	*XC*	EC

2.3. HST SET FORMATIONS

FIRST GREAT WESTERN

The largest operator of HSTs is First Great Western with 53 sets to cover 49 diagrams (of these one is a "hot spare" at Old Oak Common and one a "hot spare" at Bristol St Philip's Marsh). There are 16 "low density" sets with more seats arranged around tables in Standard Class, designed for mainly working longer distance West Country services. The rest of the sets are "high density". Volo TV screens are fitted to Coach D TS vehicles. The 14 7-car sets are to be increased to 8-cars during summer 2012 with the addition of converted former TFB/TFKB vehicles.

Number of sets: 53.
Maximum number of daily diagrams: 49.
Formations: 8-cars or 7-cars (with 401xx TSB vehicle).
Allocation: Laira (Plymouth) or Old Oak Common (London).
Other maintenance and servicing depots: Landore (Swansea), St Philip's Marsh (Bristol), Long Rock (Penzance).
Operation: London Paddington–Exeter/Paignton/Plymouth/(Newquay in the summer)/Penzance, Bristol, Cardiff/Swansea/West Wales, Oxford/Hereford/Malvern/Cheltenham Spa.

Set	*H*	*G*	*F*	*E*	*D*	*C*	*B*	*A*	*density*
LA01	41023	41024	40755	42034	42033	42007	42035	44011	L
LA02	41031	41032	40727	42046	42045	42207	42047	44015	L
LA03	41037	41038	40757	42055	42343	42292	42056	44018	L
LA04	41051	41052	40710	42077	42076	42004	42078	44025	L
LA05	41093	41094	40707	42185	42184	42183	42107	44001	L
LA06	41103	41104	40713	42208	42054	42206	42209	44066	L
LA07	41121	41122	40722	42252	42019	42345	42253	44028	L
LA08	41123	41124	40739	42256	42263	42255	42257	44029	L
LA09	41129	41130	40716	42072	42325	42267	42269	44032	L
LA10	41133	41134	40721	42276	42332	42275	42277	44034	L
LA11	41116	41135	40703	42280	42265	42279	42281	44035	L
LA12	41003	41136	40752	42144	42143	42268	42145	44049	L
LA13	41141	41142	40734	42333	42075	42291	42293	44038	L
LA14	41143	41144	40733	42296	42350	42295	42297	44039	L
LA15	41145	41146	40715	42300	42351	42299	42301	44040	L
LA16	41157	41158	40743	42245	42129	42200	42250	44086	L
OC30	41007	41008	40807	42079	42236	42251	42080	44026	H
OC31	41127	41128	40804	42060	42197	42347	42061	44020	H
OC32	41017	41018	40801	42025	42362	42024	42026	44008	H
OC33	41027	41028	40806	42040	42039	42348	42041	44013	H
OC34	41101	41102	40803	42203	42027	42201	42204	44064	H
OC35	41105	41106	40808	42213	42212	42211	42214	44067	H
OC36	41004	41110	40809	42346	42349	42138	42089	44003	H
OC37	41131	41132	40802	42272	42073	42271	42273	44033	H
OC38	41137	41138	40810	42284	42003	42202	42285	44036	H
OC40	41181	41149	40106		42166	42218	42071	44079	H

OC41	41109	41182	40107		42222	42224	42382	44101	H
OC42	41168	41183	40108		42315	42317	42383	44090	H
OC43	41147	41186	40109		42258	42266	42365	44000	H
OC44	41191	41192	40110		42115	42174	42288	44097	H
OC45	41119	41187	40111		42247	42173	42260	44078	H
OC46	41096	41161	40112		42178	42195	42043	44042	H
OC47	41081	41108	40113	42101	42308	42217	42067	44060	H
OC48	41184	41189	40114	42294	42085	42310	42087	44069	H
OC49	41148	41169	40115	42102	42319	42364	42321	44091	H
OC50	41179	41180	40101	42196	42098	42264	42283	44093	H
OC51	41005	41006	40103		42070	42069	42118	44023	H
OC52	41029	41030	40102		42042	42008	42044	44014	H
OC53	41033	41034	40118		42048	42066	42050	44016	H
OC54	41055	41056	40117		42074	42081	42126	44043	H
OC55	41065	41089	40104		42221	42062	42068	44022	H
OC56	41125	41126	40116		42216	42344	42261	44030	H
OC57	41139	41140	40105		42099	42287	42289	44037	H
LA60	41114	41162	40900	42231	42232	42353	42233	44074	H
LA61	41086	41160	40901	42304	42303	42302	42305	44068	H
LA62	41085	41167	40902	42167	42168	42103	42169	44055	H
LA63	41045	41059	40903	42175	42176	42105	42177	44081	H
LA64	41163	41166	40904	42094	42093	42092	42108	44076	H
LA71	41009	41010	40204	42013	42360	42012	42014	44004	H
LA72	41011	41012	40205	42016	42005	42015	42361	44005	H
LA73	41015	41016	40207	42006	42096	42021	42023	44007	H
LA74	41019	41020	40221	42028	42009	42259	42029	44009	H
LA75	41021	41022	40210	42031	42010	42030	42032	44010	H

Spares:

OO: 40119 40811 41153* 41155 41176 42083 42356 42381
44002 44024 44083
LA: 40231 40718 42049 42095 44059
PM: 44100
* To be reseated as Standard Class

Undergoing conversion to TS:

40208 40209 40228 40709 40712 40714 40717 40724 40725
40726 40731 40736 40738 40744 40747

NETWORK RAIL: NEW MEASUREMENT TRAIN

The Network Rail "New Measurement Train" is used to test and evaluate Britain's main railway lines. Can run in 4-, 5- or 6-car formation depending on routes being taken (6-car formation is shown below).

977995 975984 977994 977993 975814 977984

EAST COAST

East Coast operates 14 refurbished HST sets on the ECML. As well as serving non-electrified destinations such as Hull and Inverness the East Coast HSTs also work alongside Class 91s and Mark 4 sets on services to Leeds, Newcastle and Edinburgh. Set EC64 (ex-NL05) transferred from East Midlands Trains in 2011.

Number of sets: 14.
Maximum number of daily diagrams: 13.
Formations: 9-cars.
Allocation: Craigentinny (Edinburgh).
Other maintenance depot: Neville Hill (Leeds).
Operation: London King's Cross–Leeds/Harrogate/Skipton/Hull/Lincoln/Newcastle/Edinburgh/Aberdeen/Inverness.

Set	*M*	*L*	*J*	*G*	*F*	*E*	*D*	*C*	*B*
EC51	41120	41150	40748	42215	42091	42146	42150	42154	44094
EC52	41039	41040	40735	42323	42189	42057	42058	42059	44019
EC53	41090	41044	40737	42340	42127	42063	42064	42065	44045
EC54	41087	41088	40706	42104	42161	42171	42172	42219	44056
EC55	41091	41092	40704	42179	42188	42180	42181	42106	44058
EC56	41170	41118	40720	42241	42363	42242	42243	42244	44098
EC57	41151	41152	40740	42226	42128	42182	42186	42190	44080
EC58	41097	41098	40750	42158	42238	42191	42192	42193	44061
EC59	41099	41100	40711	42235	42239	42240	42198	42199	44063
EC60	41066	41164	40742	42122	42116	42357	42134	42355	44031
EC61	41115	41165	40702	42117	42159	42160	42109	42110	44057
EC62	41185	41095	40701	42306	42326	42330	42237	42307	44075
EC63	41159	41083	40708	42163	42286	42228	42130	42322	44050
EC64	41062	41154	40732	42125	42335	42123	42205	42210	44073

Spares:

EC: 40705 40805 41190 42354 44077

GRAND CENTRAL

GC operates HSTs between Sunderland and King's Cross. The formations are flexible, but are shown below as formed at the time of going to press.

Number of sets: 3.
Maximum number of daily diagrams: 3.
Formations: 5-cars or 6-cars.
Allocation: Heaton (Newcastle).
Operation: London King's Cross–Sunderland.

Set	*TF*	*TSB*	*TS*	*TS*	*TS*	*TF**
GC01	41205	40424	42403	42401		41204*
GC02	41202	40433	42406	42404	42407	
GC03	41203	40426	42409	42408		41201* * declassified

Spares:

HT: 41206 42402 42405

EAST MIDLANDS TRAINS

East Midlands Trains HSTs are concentrated on the Nottingham corridor during the day, with early morning and evening services to Leeds for servicing at Neville Hill.

Number of sets: 10.
Maximum number of daily diagrams: 9.
Formations: 8-cars.
Allocation: Neville Hill (Leeds).
Other maintenance depot: Derby Etches Park.
Operation: London St Pancras–Nottingham, Sheffield/Leeds.

Set	*J*	*G*	*F*	*E*	*D*	*C*	*B*	*A*
NL01	41057	41084	40730	42327	42111	42112	42113	44041
NL02	41112	41067	40754	42194	42229	42227	42225	44027
NL03	41061	41068	40741	42337	42119	42120	42121	44054
NL04	41077	41064	40749	42151	42164	42165	42153	44047
NL06	41156	41041	40746	42132	42131	42331	42133	44046
NL07	41111	41070	40751	42339	42135	42136	42137	44044
NL08	41071	41072	40753	42329	42139	42140	42141	44048
NL10	41075	41076	40756	42328	42341	42148	42149	44051
NL11	41117	41046	40728	42220	42100	42230	42124	44085
NL12	41079	41069	40700	42155	42156	42157	42152	44070

Spares:

NL: 41063 41113 42384 44071

CROSSCOUNTRY

CrossCountry reintroduced regular HST diagrams on its services from the December 2008 timetable. Trains run in 7-car formation with TS coaches "C", "D" and "E" rotated in service (rakes below are shown as 8-cars).

Number of sets: 5.
Maximum number of daily diagrams: 4.
Formations: 7-cars (one TS spare).
Allocation: Craigentinny (Edinburgh).
Other maintenance depots: Laira (Plymouth) or Neville Hill (Leeds).
Operation: Edinburgh–Leeds–Plymouth is the core route with some services extending to Dundee or Penzance.

Set	*A*	*B*	*C*	*D*	*E*	*F*	*G*	*H*
XC01	41193	45001	42368	42369	42370	42367	42366	44021
XC02	41194	45002	42375	42374	42373	42372	42371	44072
XC03	41195	45003	42290	42234	42378	42377	42376	44052
XC04	41026	45004	42038	42097	42037	42036	42380	44012
XC05	41035	45005	42051	42342	42053	42052	42379	44017

2.4. SALOONS

Several specialist passenger carrying vehicles, normally referred to as saloons are permitted to run on the National Rail system. Many of these are to pre-nationalisation designs.

WCJS FIRST CLASS SALOON

Built 1892 by LNWR, Wolverton. Originally dining saloon mounted on six-wheel bogies. Rebuilt with new underframe with four-wheel bogies in 1927. Rebuilt 1960 as observation saloon with DMU end. Gangwayed at other end. The interior has a saloon, kitchen, guards vestibule and observation lounge. Gresley bogies. 19/– 1T. 28.5 t. 75 mph.

Non-standard livery: London & North Western Railway.

41 (484, 45018) x **0** WC *WC* CS

LNWR DINING SALOON

Built 1890 by LNWR, Wolverton. Mounted on the underframe of LMS General Utility Van 37908 in the 1980s. Contains kitchen and dining area seating 12 at tables for two. Gresley bogies. 10/–. 75 mph. 25.4 t.

Non-standard livery: London & North Western Railway.

159 (5159) x **0** WC *WC* CS

GNR FIRST CLASS SALOON

Built 1912 by GNR, Doncaster. Contains entrance vestibule, lavatory, two separate saloons, library and luggage space. Gresley bogies. 19/– 1T. 75 mph. 29.4 t.

Non-standard livery: Teak.

807 (4807) x **0** WC *WC* CS

LNER GENERAL MANAGERS SALOON

Built 1945 by LNER, York. Gangwayed at one end with a veranda at the other. The interior has a dining saloon seating 12, kitchen, toilet, office and nine seat lounge. 21/– 1T. B4 bogies. 75 mph. ETH 3. 35.7 t.

1999 (902260) **M** OE *RS* CS DINING CAR No. 2

GENERAL MANAGER'S SALOON

Renumbered 1989 from London Midland Region departmental series. Formerly the LMR General Manager's saloon. Rebuilt from LMS period 1 Corridor Brake First M 5033 M to dia 1654 and mounted on the underframe of BR suburban Brake Standard M 43232. Screw couplings have been removed. B4 bogies. 100 mph. ETH 2X.

LMS Lot No. 326 Derby 1927. 27.5 t.

6320 (5033, DM 395707) x **M** 62 *62* SK

GWR FIRST CLASS SALOON

Built 1930 by GWR, Swindon. Contains saloons at either end with body end observation windows, staff compartment, central kitchen and pantry/bar. Numbered DE321011 when in departmental service with British Railways. 14/– 1T. GWR bogies. 75 mph. 34 t.

GWR Lot No. 1431 1930.

9004 **CH** RA *WC* CS

BRITISH PULLMAN SUPPORT CAR

Converted 199? from Courier vehicle converted from Mark 1 Corridor Brake Standard 1986–87. Toilet retained and former compartment area replaced with train manager's office, crew locker room, linen store and dry goods store. The former luggage area has been adapted for use as an engineers' compartment and workshop. Commonwealth bogies. 100 mph. ETH 2.

Lot No. 30721 Wolverton 1963. 37 t.

99545 (35466, 80207) **PC** OE *BP* SL BAGGAGE CAR No. 11

SERVICE CAR

Converted from BR Mark 1 Corridor Brake Standard. Commonwealth bogies. 100 mph. ETH 2.

Non-standard livery: London & North Western Railway.

Lot No. 30721 Wolverton 1963.

99886 (35407) x **0** WC *WC* CS SERVICE CAR No. 1

ROYAL SCOTSMAN SALOONS

Built 1960 by Metro-Cammell as Pullman Parlour First (§ Pullman Kitchen First) for East Coast Main Line services. Rebuilt 1990 as sleeping cars with four twin sleeping rooms (*§ three twin sleeping rooms and two single sleeping rooms at each end). Commonwealth bogies. 38.5 t.

99961 (324 AMBER)	*	**M**	OE	*RS*	CS	STATE CAR 1
99962 (329 PEARL)		**M**	OE	*RS*	CS	STATE CAR 2
99963 (331 TOPAZ)		**M**	OE	*RS*	CS	STATE CAR 3
99964 (313 FINCH)	§	**M**	OE	*RS*	CS	STATE CAR 4

Built 1960 by Metro-Cammell as Pullman Kitchen First for East Coast Main Line services. Rebuilt 1990 as observation car with open verandah seating 32. Commonwealth bogies. 38.5 t.

99965 (319 SNIPE)	**M**	OE	*RS*	CS	OBSERVATION CAR

Built 1960 by Metro-Cammell as Pullman Kitchen First for East Coast Main Line services. Rebuilt 1993 as dining car. Commonwealth bogies. 38.5 t.

99967 (317 RAVEN)	**M**	OE	*RS*	CS	DINING CAR No. 1

Mark 3A. Converted from a Sleeping Car at Carnforth Railway Restoration and Engineering Services in 1997. BT10 bogies. Attendant's and adjacent two sleeping compartments converted to generator room containing a 160 kW Volvo unit. In 99968 four sleeping compartments remain for staff use with another converted for use as a staff shower and toilet. The remaining five sleeping compartments have been replaced by two passenger cabins. In 99969 seven sleeping compartments remain for staff use. A further sleeping compartment, along with one toilet, have been converted to store rooms. The other two sleeping compartments have been combined to form a crew mess. ETH 7X. 41.5 t.

Lot. No. 30960 Derby 1981–83.

99968 (10541)	**M**	OE	*RS*	CS	STATE CAR 5
99969 (10556)	**M**	OE	*RS*	CS	SERVICE CAR

RAILFILMS "LMS CLUB CAR"

Converted from BR Mark 1 Open Standard at Carnforth Railway Restoration & Engineering Services in 1994. Contains kitchen, pantry and two dining saloons. 20/– 1T. Commonwealth bogies. 100 mph. ETH 4.

Lot. No. 30724 York 1963. 37 t.

99993 (5067)	**M**	RA	*WC*	CS	LMS CLUB CAR

BR INSPECTION SALOON

Mark 1. Short frames. Non-gangwayed. Observation windows at each end. The interior layout consists of two saloons interspersed by a central lavatory/kitchen/guards/luggage section. 90 mph.

BR Wagon Lot No. 3095 Swindon 1957. B4 bogies. 30.5 t.

999506	**M**	WC	*WC*	CS

2.5. PULLMAN CAR COMPANY SERIES

Pullman cars have never generally been numbered as such, although many have carried numbers, instead they have carried titles. However, a scheme of schedule numbers exists which generally lists cars in chronological order. In this section those numbers are shown followed by the car's title. Cars described as "kitchen" contain a kitchen in addition to passenger accommodation and have gas cooking unless otherwise stated. Cars described as "parlour" consist entirely of passenger accommodation. Cars described as "brake" contain a compartment for the use of the guard and a luggage compartment in addition to passenger accommodation.

PULLMAN PARLOUR FIRST

Built 1927 by Midland Carriage & Wagon Company. Gresley bogies. 26/– 2T. ETH 2. 41 t.

213	MINERVA	**PC**	OE	*BP*	SL

PULLMAN PARLOUR FIRST

Built 1928 by Metropolitan Carriage & Wagon Company. Gresley bogies. 24/– 2T. ETH 4. 40 t.

239	AGATHA	**PC**	OE		SL
243	LUCILLE	**PC**	OE	*BP*	SL

PULLMAN KITCHEN FIRST

Built 1925 by BRCW. Rebuilt by Midland Carriage & Wagon Company in 1928. Gresley bogies. 20/– 1T. ETH 4. 41 t.

245	IBIS	**PC**	OE	*BP*	SL

PULLMAN PARLOUR FIRST

Built 1928 by Metropolitan Carriage & Wagon Company. Gresley bogies. 24/– 2T. ETH 4.

254	ZENA	**PC**	OE	*BP*	SL

PULLMAN KITCHEN FIRST

Built 1928 by Metropolitan Carriage & Wagon Company. Gresley bogies. 20/– 1T. ETH 4. 42 t.

255	IONE	**PC**	OE	*BP*	SL

PULLMAN KITCHEN COMPOSITE

Built 1932 by Metropolitan Carriage & Wagon Company. Originally included in 6-Pul EMU. Electric cooking. EMU bogies. 12/16 1T.

264	RUTH		**PC**	OE		SL

PULLMAN KITCHEN FIRST

Built 1932 by Metropolitan Carriage & Wagon Company. Originally included in "Brighton Belle" EMUs but now used as hauled stock. Electric cooking. B5 (SR) bogies (§ EMU bogies). 20/– 1T. ETH 2. 44 t.

280	AUDREY		**PC**	OE	*BP*	SL
281	GWEN		**PC**	OE	*BP*	SL
283	MONA	§	**PC**	OE		SL
284	VERA		**PC**	OE	*BP*	SL

PULLMAN PARLOUR THIRD

Built 1932 by Metropolitan Carriage & Wagon Company. Originally included in "Brighton Belle" EMUs. EMU bogies. –/56 2T.

286	CAR No. 86	**PC**	OE		SL

PULLMAN BRAKE THIRD

Built 1932 by Metropolitan Carriage & Wagon Company. Originally driving motor cars in "Brighton Belle" EMUs. Traction and control equipment removed for use as hauled stock. EMU bogies. –/48 1T.

292	CAR No. 92	**PC**	OE		SL
293	CAR No. 93	**PC**	OE		SL

PULLMAN PARLOUR FIRST

Built 1951 by Birmingham Railway Carriage & Wagon Company. Gresley bogies. 32/– 2T. ETH 3. 39 t.

301	PERSEUS	**PC**	OE	*BP*	SL

Built 1952 by Pullman Car Company, Preston Park using underframe and bogies from 176 RAINBOW, the body of which had been destroyed by fire. Gresley bogies. 26/– 2T. ETH 4. 38 t.

302	PHOENIX	**PC**	OE	*BP*	SL

PULLMAN PARLOUR FIRST

Built 1951 by Birmingham Railway Carriage & Wagon Company. Gresley bogies. 32/– 2T. ETH 3. 39 t.

308	CYGNUS		**PC**	OE	*BP*	SL

PULLMAN BAR FIRST

Built 1951 by Birmingham Railway Carriage & Wagon Company. Rebuilt 1999 by Blake Fabrications, Edinburgh with original timber-framed body replaced by a new fabricated steel body. Contains kitchen, bar, dining saloon and coupé. Electric cooking. Gresley bogies. 14/– 1T. ETH 3.

310	PEGASUS	x	**PC**	RA	*ST*	CS

Also carries "THE TRIANON BAR" branding.

PULLMAN KITCHEN SECOND

Built 1960–61 by Metro-Cammell for East Coast Main Line services. Commonwealth bogies. –/30 1T. 40 t.

335	CAR No. 335	x	**PC**	VT	*VT*	TM

PULLMAN PARLOUR SECOND

Built 1960–61 by Metro-Cammell for East Coast Main Line services. Commonwealth bogies. 347, 348, 350 and 352 are used as Open Firsts. –/42 2T. 38.5 t.

347	CAR No. 347	x	**M**	WC	*WC*	CS
348	CAR No. 348	x	**M**	WC	*WC*	CS
349	CAR No. 349	x	**PC**	VT	*VT*	TM
350	CAR No. 350	x	**M**	WC	*WC*	CS
352	CAR No. 352	x	**M**	WC	*WC*	CS
353	CAR No. 353	x	**PC**	VT	*VT*	TM

PULLMAN SECOND BAR

Built 1960–61 by Metro-Cammell for East Coast Main Line services. Commonwealth bogies. –/24 + 17 bar seats. 38.5 t.

354	THE HADRIAN BAR	x	**PC**	WC	*WC*	CS

2.6. LOCOMOTIVE SUPPORT COACHES

These carriages have been adapted from Mark 1s and Mark 2s for use as support coaches for heritage steam locomotives. Some seating is retained for the use of personnel supporting the locos operation with the remainder of the carriage adapted for storage, workshop, dormitory and catering purposes. These carriages can spend considerable periods of time off the national railway system when the locos they support are not being used on that system. After the depot code, the loco(s) each carriage is usually used to support is given. Seating capacities refer to the original vehicle as running in normal service.

CORRIDOR BRAKE FIRST

Mark 1. 24/– 1T. Commonwealth bogies. ETH 2.

14007. Lot No. 30382 Swindon 1959. 35 t.
17013/019. Lot No. 30668 Swindon 1961. 36 t.
17025. Lot No. 30718 Swindon 1963. Metal window frames. 36 t.

14007	(14007, 17007)	x	**M**	B1	BH	LNER 61264	
17013	(14013)	x	**PC**	JH	SH	LNER 60019	BOTAURUS
17019	(14019)	x	**M**	92	CS	SR 30777/LMS 45305/BR 70013	
17025	(14025)	v	**M**	JU	CS	LMS 45690	

CORRIDOR BRAKE FIRST

Mark 2. Pressure ventilated. 24/– 1T. B4 bogies. ETH 4.

Lot No. 30756 Derby 1966. 31.5 t.

17041	(14041)		**M**	DG	BQ	BR 71000

CORRIDOR BRAKE FIRST

Mark 2A. Pressure ventilated. 24/– 1T. B4 bogies. ETH 4.

14064. Lot No. 30775 Derby 1967–68. 32 t.
14099/17096. Lot No. 30786 Derby 1968. 32 t.

14064	(14064, 17064)	x	**M**	53	CS	SR 30777/LMS 45305/BR 70013	
14099	(14099, 17099)	v	**M**	53	CS	SR 30777/LMS 45305/BR 70013	
17096	(14096)		**PC**	MN	SL	SR 35028	MERCATOR

CORRIDOR BRAKE COMPOSITE

Mark 1. Two First Class and three Standard Class compartments. 12/18 2T (* 12/24 2T). ETH 2.

21096. Lot No. 30185 Metro-Cammell 1956. BR Mark 1 bogies. 32.5 t.
21232. Lot No. 30574 GRCW 1960. B4 bogies. 34 t.
21268. Lot No. 30732 Derby 1964. Commonwealth bogies. 37 t.

21096	x	**M**	A4	NY	LNER 60007

21232	x	**M**	62	CQ	LMS 46201
21268	*	**M**	BS	YK	New Build 60163

CORRIDOR BRAKE STANDARD

Mark 1. Four compartments. Metal window frames and melamine interior panelling. –/24 1T. ETH 2.

35322/333. Lot No. 30699 Wolverton 1962–63. Commonwealth bogies. 37 t.
35449. Lot No. 30728 Wolverton 1963. Commonwealth bogies. 37 t.
35461–486. Lot No. 30721 Wolverton 1963. Commonwealth bogies. 37 t.

35322	x	**M**	WC	CS	GWR 5972/LMS 44932/LMS 46115/LMS 48151
35333	x	**CH**	24	MI	GWR 6024
35449	x	**M**	HR	BQ	LMS 45231
35461	x	**CH**	JH	TM	GWR 5029
35463	v	**M**	WC	CS	GWR 5972/LMS 44932/LMS 46115/LMS 48151
35465	x	**CC**	JH	CQ	BR 70000
35468	x	**M**	NM	YK	National Railway Museum locomotives
35470	v	**CH**	VT	TM	Tyseley Locomotive Works-based locomotives
35476	x	**M**	62	SK	LMS 46233
35486	x	**M**	JC	TN	LNER 60009/61994

CORRIDOR BRAKE FIRST

Mark 2C. Pressure ventilated. Renumbered when declassified. –/24 1T. B4 bogies. ETH 4.

Lot No. 30796 Derby 1969–70. 32.5 t.

35508 (14128, 17128)		**M**	IR	BQ	LMS 44871/45407

CORRIDOR BRAKE FIRST

Mark 2A. Pressure ventilated. Renumbered when declassified. –/24 1T. B4 bogies. Cage removed from brake compartment. ETH 4.

Lot No. 30786 Derby 1968. 32 t.

35517 (14088, 17088)	b	**M**	IR	BQ	LMS 44871/45407
35518 (14097, 17097)	b	**G**	WC	SH	SR 34067

COURIER VEHICLE

Mark 1. Converted 1986–87 from Corridor Brake Standards. One compartment and toilet retained for courier use. One set of roller shutter doors inserted on each side. ETH 2.

80204/217. Lot No. 30699 Wolverton 1962. Commonwealth bogies. 37 t.
80220. Lot No. 30573 Gloucester 1960. B4 bogies. 33 t.

80204 (35297)	**M**	WC	CS	GWR 5972/LMS 44932/LMS 46115/LMS 48151
80217 (35299)	**M**	WC	CS	GWR 5972/LMS 44932/LMS 46115/LMS 48151
80220 (35276)	**M**	NE	NY	LNER 62005

2.7. 99xxx RANGE NUMBER CONVERSION TABLE

The following table is presented to help readers identify vehicles which may carry numbers in the 99xxx range, the former private owner number series which is no longer in general use.

99xxx	*BR No.*
99035	35322
99040	21232
99041	35476
99052	Saloon 41
99121	3105
99122	3106
99125	3113
99127	3117
99128	3130
99131	1999
99141	17041
99241	35449
99304	21256
99311	1882
99312	35463
99317	3766
99318	4912
99326	4954
99327	5044
99328	5033
99329	4931
99347	Pullman 347
99348	Pullman 348
99349	Pullman 349
99350	Pullman 350
99352	Pullman 352
99353	Pullman 353
99354	Pullman 354
99361	Pullman 355
99371	3128
99530	Pullman 301
99531	Pullman 302
99532	Pullman 308
99534	Pullman 245
99535	Pullman 213
99536	Pullman 254
99537	Pullman 280
99539	Pullman 255
99541	Pullman 243
99543	Pullman 284
99546	Pullman 281
99547	Pullman 292
99548	Pullman 293
99670	546
99671	548
99672	549
99673	550
99674	551
99675	552
99676	553
99677	586
99678	504
99679	506
99680	17102
99710	18767
99716	18808
99718	18862
99721	18756
99722	18806
99723	35459
99792	17019
99880	159
99881	807
99953	35468
99970	Pullman 232
99972	Pullman 318
99973	324
99974	Pullman 328

2.8. SET FORMATIONS

CHILTERN MARK 3 SET FORMATIONS

Chiltern Railways uses a number of loco-hauled rakes on services principally between London Marylebone and Birmingham Moor Street. Rake AL02 is used on a commuter train between Marylebone and Banbury. These coaches are currently being refurbished at Wabtec, Doncaster and fitted with sliding plug doors.

Set							*DVT*
AL01	12069	12048	12014	12038	10208		82301
AL02	12094	12124	12043	11029	12119	12054	82302
AL03	12059	12145	12117	12173	10230		82303
AL04	11040	12053	12072	12131	10236		82304
AL05	12174	12169	12175	12127	10255		82305
Spare	11027	11031					

EAST COAST MARK 4 SET FORMATIONS

The East Coast Mark 4 sets generally run in fixed formations since their refurbishment at Bombardier, Wakefield in 2003–05. These rakes are listed below. Class 91 locomotives are positioned next to Coach B.

Set	*B*	*C*	*D*	*E*	*F*	*H*	*K*	*L*	*M*	*DVT*
BN01	12207	12417	12415	12414	12307	10307	11298	11301	11401	82207
BN02	12232	12402	12450	12448	12302	10302	11299	11302	11402	82202
BN03	12201	12401	12459	12478	12301	10320	11277	11303	11403	82219
BN04	12202	12480	12421	12518	12327	10303	11278	11304	11404	82209
BN05	12209	12486	12520	12522	12300	10326	11219	11305	11405	82210
BN06	12208	12406	12420	12422	12313	10309	11279	11306	11406	82208
BN07	12231	12411	12405	12489	12329	10323	11280	11307	11407	82204
BN08	12205	12481	12485	12407	12328	10300	11229	11308	11408	82211
BN09	12230	12513	12483	12514	12308	10304	11281	11309	11409	82215
BN10	12214	12419	12488	12443	12305	10331	11282	11310	11410	82205
BN11	12203	12437	12436	12484	12315	10308	11283	11311	11411	82218
BN12	12212	12431	12404	12426	12330	10333	11284	11312	11412	82212
BN13	12228	12469	12430	12424	12311	10313	11285	11313	11413	82213
BN14	12229	12410	12526	12423	12312	10332	11201	11314	11414	82206
BN15	12226	12442	12409	12515	12309	10306	11286	11315	11415	82214
BN16	12213	12428	12445	12433	12304	10315	11287	11316	11416	82222
BN17	12223	12444	12427	12432	12303	10324	11288	11317	11417	82225
BN18	12215	12453	12468	12467	12324	10305	11289	11318	11418	82220
BN19	12211	12434	12400	12470	12310	10318	11290	11319	11419	82201
BN20	12224	12477	12439	12440	12326	10321	11241	11320	11420	82200
BN21	12222	12461	12441	12476	12323	10330	11244	11321	11421	82227
BN22	12210	12452	12460	12473	12316	10301	11291	11322	11422	82230
BN23	12225	12454	12456	12455	12318	10325	11292	11323	11423	82226
BN24	12219	12447	12425	12403	12319	10328	11293	11324	11424	82229
BN25	12217	12446	12519	12464	12322	10312	11294	11325	11425	82216
BN26	12220	12474	12465	12429	12325	10311	11295	11326	11426	82223
BN27	12216	12449	12466	12538	12317	10319	11237	11327	11427	82228
BN28	12218	12458	12463	12533	12320	10310	11273	11328	11428	82217
BN29	12204	12462	12457	12438	12321	10317	11998	11329	11429	82231
BN30	12227	12471	12534	12472	12331	10329	11999	11330	11430	82203
Spare	12200									82224

Note: The Mark 4 sets are currently being overhauled at Wabtec, Doncaster and at the same time are being repainted into East Coast livery. Sets BN01–BN06 were repainted into the silver livery whilst sets from BN07 onwards are being repainted into a similar grey scheme.

2.9. SERVICE STOCK

Most vehicles in this section are numbered in the former BR departmental number series. They are used for internal purposes within the railway industry, ie they do not generate revenue from outside the industry.

BARRIER, ESCORT & TRANSLATOR VEHICLES

These vehicles are used to move multiple unit, HST and other vehicles around the national railway system.

Desiro EMU Barrier Vehicles. Mark 1. Converted from General Utility Vans with bodies removed. Fitted with B4 bogies for use as Eurostar barrier vehicles but modified in 2003 by LNWR, Crewe for current use.

6321. Lot No. 30343 York 1957.
6322/23. Lot No. 30616 Pressed Steel 1959–60.
6324. Lot No. 30403 Glasgow 1958–60.
6325. Lot No. 30417 Pressed Steel 1958–59.

6321	(86515, 96385)	**U**	SM	NN
6322	(86859, 96386)	**U**	SM	NN
6323	(86973, 96387)	**U**	SM	NN
6324	(86562, 96388)	**U**	SM	CP
6325	(86135, 96389)	**U**	SM	NN

HST Barrier Vehicles. Mark 1/2A. Renumbered from BR departmental series, or converted from various types. B4 bogies (* Commonwealth bogies).

6330. Mark 2A. Lot No. 30786 Derby 1968.
6336/38/44. Mark 1. Lot No. 30715 Gloucester 1962.
6340. Mark 1. Lot No. 30669 Swindon 1962.
6346. Mark 2A. Lot No. 30777 Derby 1967.
6348. Mark 1. Lot No. 30163 Pressed Steel 1957.

Non-standard livery: 6340, 6344, 6346 All over dark blue.

6330	(14084, 975629)		**FB**	A	*GW*	LA
6336	(81591, 92185)		**FB**	A	*GW*	LA
6338	(81581, 92180)		**FB**	A	*GW*	LA
6340	(21251, 975678)	*	**0**	A	*EC*	EC
6344	(81263, 92080)		**0**	A	*EC*	EC
6346	(9422)		**0**	A	*EC*	EC
6348	(81233, 92963)		**FB**	A	*GW*	LA

Mark 4 Barrier Vehicles. Mark 2A/2C. Converted from * FK or BSO. B4 bogies.

6352/53. Mark 2A. Lot No. 30774 Derby 1968.
6354/55. Mark 2C. Lot No. 30820 Derby 1970.
6358/59. Mark 2A. Lot No. 30788 Derby 1968.

6352	(13465, 19465)	*	**GN**	E	*EC*	BN
6353	(13478, 19478)	*	**GN**	E	*EC*	BN
6354	(9459)		**GN**	E	*EC*	BN

6355	(9477)	**GN**	E	*EC*	BN
6358	(9432)	**GN**	E	*EC*	BN
6359	(9429)	**GN**	E	*EC*	BN

EMU Translator Vehicles. Mark 1. Converted 1980 from Restaurant Unclassified Opens. Commonwealth bogies.

Lot No. 30647 Wolverton 1959–61.

6376	(1021, 975973)	**PB**	P	*GB*	PG
6377	(1042, 975975)	**PB**	P	*GB*	PG
6378	(1054, 975971)	**PB**	P	*GB*	PG
6379	(1059, 975972)	**PB**	P	*GB*	PG

HST Barrier Vehicles. Mark 1. Converted from Gangwayed Brake Vans in 1994–95. B4 bogies.

6392. Lot No. 30715 Gloucester 1962.
6393/97. Lot No. 30716 Gloucester 1962.
6394. Lot No. 30162 Pressed Steel 1956–57.
6395. Lot No. 30484 Pressed Steel 1958.
6398/99. Lot No. 30400 Pressed Steel 1957–58.

6392	(81588, 92183)	**PB**	P	*EM*	NL
6393	(81609, 92196)	**PB**	P	*EC*	EC
6394	(80878, 92906)	**P**	P	*EC*	EC
6395	(81506, 92148)	**P**	EM	*EM*	NL
6397	(81600, 92190)	**PB**	P	*EM*	NL
6398	(81471, 92126)	**PB**	EM	*EM*	NL
6399	(81367, 92994)	**PB**	EM	*EM*	NL

Escort Coaches. Converted from Mark 2A Open Brake Standards. These vehicles use the same bodyshell as the Mark 2A Corridor Brake First. B4 bogies.

9419. Lot No.30777 Derby 1970.
9428. Lot No.30820 Derby 1970.

9419	**DS**	DR	*DR*	KM
9428	**DS**	DR	*DR*	KM

Eurostar Barrier Vehicles. Mark 1. Converted from General Utility Vans. Bodies removed. B4 bogies.

96380–381. Lot No. 30417 Pressed Steel 1958–59.
96383. Lot No. 30565 Pressed Steel 1959.
96384. Lot No. 30616 Pressed Steel 1959–60.

96380	(86386, 6380)	**B**	EU	*EU*	TI
96381	(86187, 6381)	**B**	EU	*EU*	TI
96383	(86664, 6383)	**B**	EU	*EU*	TI
96384	(86955, 6384)	**B**	EU	*EU*	TI

EMU Translator Vehicles. Converted from various Mark 1s.

975864. Lot No. 30054 Eastleigh 1951–54. Commonwealth bogies.
975867. Lot No. 30014 York 1950–51. Commonwealth bogies.
975875. Lot No. 30143 Charles Roberts 1954–55. Commonwealth bogies.

975974/978. Lot No. 30647 Wolverton 1959–61. B4 bogies.
977087. Lot No. 30229 Metro–Cammell 1955–57. Commonwealth bogies.
977942/948. Lot No. 30417 Pressed Steel 1958–59. B5 bogies.
977943/949. Lot No. 30565 Pressed Steel 1959. B5 bogies.

Non-standard livery: All over blue.

975864	(3849)	**HB**	E	*GB*	ZH	
975867	(1006)	**HB**	E	*GB*	ZH	
975875	(34643)	**0**	E		SE	
975974	(1030)	**AG**	A	*GB*	PG	Paschar
975978	(1025)	**AG**	A	*GB*	PG	Perpetiel
977087	(34971)	**0**	E		SE	
977942	(86467, 80251)	**E**	DB	*DB*	TO	
977943	(86718, 80252)	**E**	DB	*DB*	TO	
977948	(86733, 94028)	**E**	DB	*DB*	TO	
977949	(86377, 94025)	**E**	DB	*DB*	TO	

LABORATORY, TESTING & INSPECTION COACHES

These coaches are used for research, development, testing and inspection on the national railway system. Many are fitted with sophisticated technical equipment.

Staff Coaches. Mark 2F. Converted from BR Mark 2F Open First later converted to Buffet First and Open Standard. B4 bogies.

1256. Lot No. 30845 Derby 1973.
5981. Lot No. 30860 Derby 1973–74.

1256	(3296)	**Y**	NR	*DB*	ZA
5981		**Y**	NR	*DB*	ZA

Generator Vans. Mark 1. Converted from BR Mark 1 Gangwayed Brake Vans. B5 bogies.

6261. Lot No. 30323 Pressed Steel 1957.
6262. Lot No. 30228 Metro-Cammell 1957–58.
6263. Lot No. 30163 Pressed Steel 1957.
6264. Lot No. 30173 York 1956.

6261	(81284, 92988)	**Y**	NR	*DB*	ZA
6262	(81064, 92928)	**Y**	NR	*DB*	ZA
6263	(81231, 92961)	**Y**	NR	*DB*	ZA
6264	(80971, 92923)	**Y**	NR	*DB*	ZA

Staff Coach. Mark 2D. Converted from BR Mark 2D Open Brake Standard. B4 bogies.

Lot No. 30824 Derby 1971.

9481	**Y**	NR	*DB*	ZA

Driving Trailer Coaches. Converted 2008 at Serco, Derby from Mark 2F Driving Open Brake Standards. Modified to work in Blue Star push-pull mode. Disc brakes. B4 bogies.

9701–08. Lot No. 30861 Derby 1974. Converted to Driving Open Brake Standard Glasgow 1974.
9714. Lot No. 30861 Derby 1974. Converted to Driving Open Brake Standard Glasgow 1986.

9701	(9528)	**Y**	NR	*DB*	ZA
9702	(9510)	**Y**	NR	*DB*	ZA
9703	(9517)	**Y**	NR	*DB*	ZA
9708	(9530)	**Y**	NR	*DB*	ZA
9714	(9536)	**Y**	NR	*DB*	ZA

Structure Gauging Train Coach. Converted from BR Mark 2E Open First then converted to exhibition van. Lot No. 30843 Derby 1972–73. B4 bogies.

99666 (3250) **Y** NR *DB* ZA

Inspection Saloon. Converted from Class 202 DEMU TRB at Stewarts Lane for use as a BR Southern Region General Manager's Saloon. Overhauled at FM Rail, Derby in 2004–05 for use as a New Trains Project Saloon. Can be used in push-pull mode with suitably equipped locomotives. Eastleigh 1958. SR Mk 4 bogies.

975025 (60755) **G** NR *DB* ZA CAROLINE

Structure Gauging Train Coach. Originally used as a Driving Trailer. Converted from BR Mark 1 Corridor Brake Standard. Lot No. 30699 Wolverton 1961–63. B4 bogies.

975081 (35313) **Y** NR *DB* ZA

Overhead Line Equipment Test Coach ("MENTOR"). Converted from BR Mark 1 Corridor Brake Standard. Lot No. 30142 Gloucester 1954–55. Fitted with pantograph. B4 bogies.

975091 (34615) **Y** NR *DB* ZA

Structure Gauging Train Dormitory and Generator Coach. Converted from BR Mark 1 Corridor Brake Composite. Lot No. 30732 Derby 1962–64. B4 bogies.

975280 (21263) **Y** NR *DB* ZA

New Measurement Train Conference Coach. Converted from prototype HST TF Lot No. 30848 Derby 1972. BT10 bogies.

975814 (11000, 41000) **Y** NR *DB* EC

New Measurement Train Lecture Coach. Converted from prototype HST catering vehicle. Lot No. 30849 Derby 1972–73. BT10 bogies.

975984 (10000, 40000) **Y** NR *DB* EC

Radio Survey Coaches. Converted from BR Mark 2E Open Standard. Lot No. 30844 Derby 1972–73. B4 bogies.

977868 (5846)	**Y**	NR	*DB*	ZA
977869 (5858)	**Y**	NR	*DB*	ZA

Track Recording Train Staff Coach. Converted from Royal Household couchette Lot No. 30889, which in turn had been converted from BR Mark 2B Corridor Brake First. Lot No. 30790 Derby 1969. B5 bogies.

977969 (14112, 2906)	**Y**	NR	*DB*	ZA

ERTMS Laboratory Coach. Converted from BR Mark 2E Open Standard. Lot No. 30844 Derby 1972–73. B4 bogies.

977974 (5854)	**Y**	NR	*DB*	ZA

Track Recording Train Electrification Measurement Coach. Converted from BR Mark 2F Open First converted to Class 488/2 EMU TFOH. Lot No. 30859 Derby 1973–74. B4 bogies.

977983 (3407, 72503)	**Y**	NR	*DB*	ZA

New Measurement Train Staff Coach. Converted from HST catering vehicle. Lot No. 30884 Derby 1976–77. BT10 bogies.

977984 (40501)	**Y**	P	*DB*	EC

Structure Gauging Train Coach. Converted from BR Mark 2D Open First subsequently declassified to Open Standard and then converted to exhibition van. Lot No. 30821 Derby 1971.

977986 (3189, 99664)	**Y**	NR		ZA

New Measurement Train Overhead Line Equipment Test Coach. Converted from HST TGS. Lot No. 30949 Derby 1982. Fitted with pantograph. BT10 bogies.

977993 (44053)	**Y**	P	*DB*	EC

New Measurement Train Track Recording Coach. Converted from HST TGS. Lot No. 30949 Derby 1982. BT10 bogies.

977994 (44087)	**Y**	P	*DB*	EC

New Measurement Train Coach. Converted from HST catering vehicle. Lot No. 30921 Derby 1978–79. BT10 bogies. Fitted with generator.

977995 (40719, 40619)	**Y**	P	*DB*	EC

Radio Survey Coach. Converted from Mark 2F Open Standard converted to Class 488/3 EMU TSOLH. Lot No. 30860 Derby 1973–74.

977997 (72613, 6126)	**Y**	NR	*DB*	ZA

Track Inspection Coach. Converted from BR Inspection Saloon. BR Wagon Lot No. 3379. Swindon 1960. B4 bogies.

999508	**Y**	NR	*DB*	ZA

Track Recording Coach. Purpose built Mark 2. B4 bogies.

999550	**Y**	NR	*DB*	ZA

Ultrasonic Test Coaches. Converted from Class 421 EMU MBSO and Class 432 EMU MSO.

999602/605. Lot No. 30862 York 1974. SR Mk 6 bogies.
999606/(62384). Lot No. 30816. York 1970. SR Mk 6 bogies.

999602	(62483)	**Y**	NR	*DB*	ZA
999605	(62482)	**Y**	NR	*DB*	ZA
999606	(62356)	**Y**	NR	*DB*	ZA
	(62384)	**Y**	NR		ZA

TEST TRAIN BRAKE FORCE RUNNERS

Converted from Class 488/3 ex-Gatwick Express locomotive-hauled stock (formerly Mark 2 coaches). These vehicles are included in test trains to provide brake force and are not used for any other purposes. B4 bogies.

72612–639/977985. Lot No. 30860 Derby 1973–74.
72708. Lot No. 30860 Derby 1973–74.

72612	(6156)	**Y**	NR	*DB*	ZA
72616	(6007)	**Y**	NR	*DB*	ZA
72630	(6094)	**Y**	NR	*DB*	ZA
72631	(6096)	**Y**	NR	*DB*	ZA
72639	(6070)	**Y**	NR	*DB*	ZA
977985	(6019, 72715)	**Y**	NR	*DB*	ZA

BREAKDOWN TRAIN COACHES

These coaches are formed in trains used for the recovery of derailed railway vehicles and were converted from BR Mark 1 Corridor Brake Standard and General Utility Van. The current use of each vehicle is given.

971001/003/004. Lot No. 30403 York/Glasgow 1958–60. Commonwealth bogies.
971002. Lot No. 30417 Pressed Steel 1958–59. Commonwealth bogies.
975087. Lot No. 30032 Wolverton 1951–52. BR Mark 1 bogies.
975464. Lot No. 30386 Charles Roberts 1956–58. Commonwealth bogies.
975471. Lot No. 30095 Wolverton 1953–55. Commonwealth bogies.
975477. Lot No. 30233 GRCW 1955–57. BR Mark 1 bogies.
975486. Lot No. 30025 Wolverton 1950–52. Commonwealth bogies.

971001	(86560, 94150)	**Y**	NR	*DB*	BS	Tool & Generator Van
971002	(86624, 94190)	**Y**	NR	*DB*	WT	Tool Van
971003	(86596, 94191)	**Y**	NR	*DB*	BS	Tool Van

971004	(86194, 94168)	**Y**	NR	*DB*	KY	Tool Van
975087	(34289)	**Y**	NR	*DB*	KY	Tool & Generator Van
975464	(35171)	**Y**	NR	*DB*	WT	Staff Coach
975471	(34543)	**Y**	NR	*DB*	BS	Staff Coach
975477	(35108)	**Y**	NR	*DB*	KY	Staff Coach
975486	(34100)	**Y**	NR	*DB*	WT	Tool & Generator Van

INFRASTRUCTURE MAINTENANCE COACHES

Generator Van. Mark 1. Converted from BR Mark 1 Gangwayed Brake Van. B5 bogies.

Lot No. 30400 Pressed Steel 1957–58.

6260	(81450, 92116)	**NR**	NR	*DB*	LU

De-Icing Coaches

These coaches are used for removing ice from the conductor rail of DC lines. They were converted from Class 489 DMLVs that had originally been Class 414/3 DMBSOs.

Lot No. 30452 Ashford/Eastleigh 1959. Mk 4 bogies.

68501	(61281)	**Y**	NR	*GB*	TW
68504	(61286)	**Y**	NR	*GB*	TW
68505	(61299)	**Y**	NR	*GB*	TW
68508	(61272)	**Y**	NR		ZG

INTERNAL USER VEHICLES

These vehicles are confined to yards and depots or do not normally move at all. Details are given of the internal user number (if allocated), type, former identity, current use and location. Many no longer see regular use.

041379	LMS CCT 35527	Stores van	Leeman Road EY, York
041898	BR BG 84608	Stores van	Leeman Road EY, York
041947	BR GUV 93425	Stores van	IL
041963	LMS milk tank 44047	Storage tank	DR
042154	BR GUV 93975	Stores van	Ipswich Upper Yard
061061	BR CCT 94135	Stores van	Oxford Station
061223	BR GUV 93714	Stores van	Oxford Station
083439	BR CCT 94752	Stores van	WD
083602	BR CCT 94494	Stores van	Three Bridges Station
083637	BR NW 99203	Stores van	SL
083644	BR Ferry Van 889201	Stores van	EH
083664	BR Ferry Van 889203	Stores van	EH
–	BR Open First 3186	Instruction Coach	DY
–	BR Open First 3381	Instruction Coach	HE
–	BR Open Standard 5636	Instruction Coach	PM
–	BR BV 6360	Barrier vehicle	NL
–	BR BV 6396	Stores van	MA
–	BR RFKB 10256	Instruction Coach	Yoker
–	BR RFKB 10260	Instruction Coach	Yoker
–	BR BFK 17156	Instruction Coach	DY
–	BR TSOLH 72614	Instruction Coach	DY
–	BR TSOLH 72615	Instruction Coach	DY
–	BR TSOL 72707	Instruction Coach	DY
–	BR BG 92901	Stores van	WB
–	BR NL 94003	Stores van	OO
–	BR NL 94006	Stores van	OO
–	BR NK 94121	Stores van	TO
–	BR CCT 94181	Stores van	SL
–	BR NB 94438	Stores van	TO
–	BR GUV 96139	Stores van	MA
–	BR Ferry Van 889017	Stores van	SL
–	BR Ferry Van 889200	Stores van	SL
–	BR Ferry Van 889202	Stores van	SL
–	BR Open Standard 975403	Cinema Coach	PM

Notes: BFK = Corridor Brake First
BG = Gangwayed Brake Van
BV = Barrier Vehicle
CCT = Covered Carriage Truck (a 4-wheeled van similar to a GUV)
GUV = General Utility Van
NB = High Security Brake Van (converted from BG)
NK= High Security General Utility Van
NL = Newspaper Van (converted from a GUV)
NW = Bullion Van (converted from a Corridor Brake Standard)
RFKB = Kitchen Buffet First

2.10. COACHING STOCK AWAITING DISPOSAL

This list contains the last known locations of coaching stock awaiting disposal. The definition of which vehicles are "awaiting disposal" is somewhat vague, but generally speaking these are vehicles of types not now in normal service or vehicles which have been damaged by fire, vandalism or collision.

1205	ZA
1644	CS
1650	CS
1652	CS
1655	CS
1663	CS
1670	CS
2127	CS
3181	CD
4860	CS
4932	CS
4997	CS
5647	CD
5754	KT
5756	CS
5905	KT
5908	ZG
5943	SH
5978	SH
6009	SH
6012	SH
6016	ZG
6021	SH
6029	SH
6050	SH
6136	ZG
6175	SH
6178	HM
6179	SH
6361	NL
6364	SO
6365	SO
10201	LM
10540	LM
10554	LM
10681	LM
10682	LM
10709	LM
10710	LM
10727	LM
10731	LM
11005	LM
12096	ZN
13306	CS
13320	CS
13323	CS
13508	BO
17168	CS
34525	CS
40729	NL
41043	ZB
80211	ZA
80403	CS
80404	CS
84519	CD
92111	CD
92114	ZA
92159	CS
92303	CD
92400	CD
92908	CS
92929	CD
92936	CD
93723	BY
94101	CS
94103	Cardiff Tidal
94104	TO
94106	MH
94116	TY
94137	ME
94147	ME
94153	WE
94160	MH
94166	BS
94170	MH
94176	BS
94177	TO
94192	ME
94195	BS
94196	MH
94197	BS
94199	MH
94207	TO
94208	TO
94209	Cardiff Tidal
94213	ME
94214	MH
94217	MH
94221	ME
94222	MH
94224	CD
94225	MH
94227	Tees Yard
94229	MH
94302	TY
94303	TY
94304	MH
94306	TY
94307	Cardiff Tidal
94308	MH
94310	WE
94311	WE
94313	WE
94316	TO
94317	TO
94318	Cardiff Tidal
94322	MH
94323	TY
94326	TY
94331	Cardiff Tidal
94332	TY
94333	TY
94334	CD
94335	TY
94336	TY
94337	WE
94338	WE
94340	CD
94343	MH
94344	TO
94400	Cardiff Tidal
94401	MH
94406	MH
94408	TY
94410	WE
94411	Cardiff Tidal
94412	ME
94413	ME
94416	ME
94420	MH
94422	TO
94423	BS
94427	WE
94428	ME
94429	Tees Yard
94431	MH
94432	ME
94433	MH
94434	TY
94435	TO
94440	ME
94445	WE
94450	WE
94451	WE
94458	Cardiff Tidal
94462	CD
94463	TY
94470	TO
94476	CD
94479	TO
94481	Cardiff Tidal
94482	MH
94488	CD
94490	MH
94492	WE
94495	TY
94497	ME
94498	MH
94499	CD
94501	TO

94504	TY	94545	Tees Yard	96372	LM	975687	Portobello
94512	TY	94546	TY	96373	LM	975688	Portobello
94514	ME	94547	MH	96374	ZB	975918	ME
94517	CD	94548	TY	96375	LM	975920	Portobello
94518	ME	95300	MH	96602	RU	975991	CD
94519	ME	95301	MH	96603	ZG	977077	**
94520	TY	95400	MH	96604	ZG	977085	BO
94521	CD	95410	MH	96605	ZG	977095	CS
94522	TY	95727	WE	96606	RU	977111	**
94525	TY	95754	TY	96607	ZG	977112	**
94526	TY	95761	WE	96608	RU	977163	AP
94527	TY	95763	BS	96609	RU	977165	AP
94528	ME	96100	TM	99019	ZR	977166	AP
94529	CD	96110	CS	889400	ZA	977167	AP
94530	ME	96132	CS	975290	ZG	977618	BY
94531	TY	96135	CS	975454	TO	977905	ZG
94534	ME	96164	CS	975463	ZA	977989	ZA
94536	ME	96165	CS	975482	ZA	977990	ZA
94539	MH	96170	CS	975484	CS	977991	ZA
94540	TJ	96178	CS	975639	CS		
94541	ME	96182	CS	975681	Portobello		
94542	TY	96191	CS	975682	Portobello	024909	CD
94543	ME	96192	CS	975685	Portobello	025000	CD
94544	MH	96371	WB	975686	Portobello	DS 70220	**

** Other locations:

977077	Ripple Lane Yard
977111	Ripple Lane Yard
977112	Ripple Lane Yard
DS 70220	Western Trading Estate Siding, North Acton

3. DIESEL MULTIPLE UNITS

INTRODUCTION

DMU CLASSES

DMU Classes are listed in class number order. Principal details and dimensions are quoted for each class in metric and/or imperial units as considered appropriate bearing in mind common usage in the UK.

All dimensions and weights are quoted for vehicles in an "as new" condition with all necessary supplies (eg oil, water, sand) on board. Dimensions are quoted in the order Length – Width. All lengths quoted are over buffers or couplers as appropriate. Where two lengths are quoted, the first refers to outer vehicles in a set and the second to inner vehicles. All width dimensions quoted are maxima. All weights are shown as metric tonnes (t = tonnes).

NUMERICAL LISTINGS

DMUs are listed in numerical order of set – using current numbers as allocated by the RSL. Individual "loose" vehicles are listed in numerical order after vehicles formed into fixed formations. Where sets or vehicles have been renumbered in recent years, former numbering detail is shown in parentheses. Each entry is laid out as in the following example:

RSL Set No.	*Detail*	*Livery*	*Owner*	*Operator*	*Depot*	*Formation*	*Name*
142 073	v	**AV**	A	*AW*	CF	55723 55769	Myfanwy

Detail Differences. Detail differences which currently affect the areas and types of train which vehicles may work are shown, plus differences in interior layout. Where such differences occur within a class, these are shown either in the heading information or alongside the individual set or vehicle number. The following standard abbreviations are used:

- e European Railway Traffic Management System (ERTMS) signalling equipment fitted.
- r Radio Electric Token Block signalling equipment fitted.

Use of the above abbreviations indicates the equipment fitted is normally operable. Meaning of non-standard abbreviations is detailed in individual class headings.

Set Formations. Regular set formations are shown where these are normally maintained. Readers should note set formations might be temporarily varied from time to time to suit maintenance and/or operational requirements. Vehicles shown as "spare" are not formed in any regular set formation.

Codes. Codes are used to denote the livery, owner, operation and depot of each unit. Details of these will be found in section 7 of this book. Where a unit or spare car is off-lease, the operator column will be left blank.

Names. Only names carried with official sanction are listed. As far as possible names are shown in UPPER/lower case characters as actually shown on the name carried on the vehicle(s). Unless otherwise shown, complete units are regarded as named rather than just the individual car(s) which carry the name.

GENERAL INFORMATION

CLASSIFICATION AND NUMBERING

First generation ("Heritage") DMUs were classified in the series 100–139.
Parry People Movers (not technically DMUs) are classified in the series 139.
Second generation DMUs are classified in the series 140–199.
Diesel-electric multiple units are classified in the series 200–249.
Service units are classified in the series 930–999.

First and second generation individual cars are numbered in the series 50000–59999 and 79000–79999.

Parry People Mover cars are numbered in the 39000 series.

DEMU individual cars are numbered in the series 60000–60999, except for a few former EMU vehicles which retain their EMU numbers.

Service stock individual cars are numbered in the series 975000–975999 and 977000–977999, although this series is not exclusively used for DMU vehicles.

OPERATING CODES

These codes are used by train operating company staff to describe the various different types of vehicles and normally appear on data panels on the inner (ie non driving) ends of vehicles.

The first part of the code describes whether or not the car has a motor or a driving cab as follows:

DM Driving motor.
M Motor
DT Driving trailer
T Trailer

The next letter is a "B" for cars with a brake compartment.

This is followed by the saloon details:

F First
S Standard
C Composite
so denotes a semi-open vehicle (part compartments, part open). All other vehicles are assumed to consist solely of open saloons.

L denotes a vehicle with a toilet.
W denotes a wheelchair space.

Finally vehicles with a buffet are suffixed RB or RMB for a miniature buffet.

Where two vehicles of the same type are formed within the same unit, the above codes may be suffixed by (A) and (B) to differentiate between the vehicles.

A composite is a vehicle containing both First and Standard Class accommodation, whilst a brake vehicle is a vehicle containing separate specific accommodation for the conductor.

Where vehicles have been declassified, the correct operating code which describes the actual vehicle layout is quoted in this publication.

BUILD DETAILS

Lot Numbers
Vehicles ordered under the auspices of BR were allocated a lot (batch) number when ordered and these are quoted in class headings and sub-headings.

Builders
These are shown in class headings. Abbreviations used are found in section 7.7.

Information on sub-contracting works which built parts of vehicles eg the underframes etc is not shown.

ACCOMMODATION

The information given in class headings and sub-headings is in the form F/S nT (or TD) nW. For example 12/54 1T 1W denotes 12 First Class and 54 Standard Class seats, one toilet and one space for a wheelchair. A number in brackets (ie (2)) denotes tip-up seats (in addition to the fixed seats). Tip-up seats in vestibules do not count. The seating layout of open saloons is shown as 2+1, 2+2 or 3+2 as the case may be. Where units have First Class accommodation as well as Standard Class and the layout is different for each class then these are shown separately prefixed by "1:" and "2:". TD denotes a toilet suitable for use by a disabled person.

3.1. DIESEL MECHANICAL & DIESEL HYDRAULIC UNITS

FIRST GENERATION UNITS

CLASS 121 PRESSED STEEL SUBURBAN

First generation units used by Chiltern Railways on peak-hour Aylesbury–Princes Risborough services (121 020 and 121 034) and by Arriva Trains Wales on Cardiff Queen Street–Cardiff Bay shuttles (121 032).
Construction: Steel.
Engines: Two Leyland 1595 of 112 kW (150 hp) at 1800 rpm.
Transmission: Mechanical. Cardan shaft and freewheel to a four-speed epicyclic gearbox and final drive.
Bogies: DD10.
Brakes: Vacuum.
Couplers: Screw.
Dimensions: 20.45 x 2.82 m.
Gangways: Non gangwayed single cars with cabs at each end.
Wheel arrangement: 1-A + A-1.
Doors: Manually-operated slam.
Maximum Speed: 70 mph.
Seating Layout: 3+2 facing.
Multiple Working: "Blue Square" coupling code. First Generation vehicles cannot be coupled to Second Generation units.

55020/032/034. DMBS. Lot No. 30518 1960–61. –/65. 38.0 t.

Non-standard livery: 121 020 All over Chiltern blue with a silver stripe.

Notes: Fitted with central door locking.

121 020 formerly in departmental use as unit 960 002 (977722).

121 032 formerly in departmental use as 977842, and more recently in preservation at The Railway Age, Crewe.

121 034 returned to use with Chiltern Railways in 2011. Formerly in departmental use as 977828.

121 020	**0**	CR	*CR*	AL	55020
121 032	**AV**	AV	*AW*	CF	55032
121 034	**G**	CR	*CR*	AL	55034

3.1.2. PARRY PEOPLE MOVERS

CLASS 139 PPM-60

Gas/flywheel hybrid drive Railcars used on the Stourbridge Junction–Stourbridge Town branch.
Body construction: Stainless steel framework.
Chassis construction: Welded mild steel box section.
Primary Drive: Ford MVH420 2.3 litre 64 kW (86 hp) LPG fuel engine driving through Newage marine gearbox, Tandler bevel box and 4 "V" belt driver to flywheel.
Flywheel Energy Store: 500 kg, 1 m diameter, normal operational speed range 1000–1500 rpm.
Final transmission: 4 "V" belt driver from flywheel to Tandler bevel box, Linde hydrostatic transmission and spiral bevel gearbox at No. 2 end axle.
Braking: Normal service braking by regeneration to flywheel (1 m/s/s); emergency/parking braking by sprung-on, air-off disc brakes (3 m/s/s).
Maximum Speed: 45 mph.
Dimensions: 8.7 x 2.4 m.
Doors: Deans powered doors, double-leaf folding (one per side).
Seating Layout: 1+1 unidirectional/facing.
Multiple Working: Not applicable.

39001–002. DMS. Main Road Sheet Metal, Leyland 2007–08. –/17(4) 1W. 12.5 t.

139 001	**LM**	P	*LM*	SJ	39001
139 002	**LM**	P	*LM*	SJ	39002

3.1.3. SECOND GENERATION UNITS

All units in this section have air brakes and are equipped with public address, with transmission equipment on driving vehicles and flexible diaphragm gangways. Except where otherwise stated, transmission is Voith 211r hydraulic with a cardan shaft to a Gmeinder GM190 final drive.

CLASS 142 PACER BREL DERBY/LEYLAND

DMS–DMSL.

Construction: Steel underframe, rivetted steel body and roof. Built from Leyland National bus parts on Leyland Bus four-wheeled underframes.
Engines: One Cummins LT10-R of 165 kW (225 hp) at 1950 rpm.
Couplers: BSI at outer ends, bar within unit.
Dimensions: 15.55 x 2.80 m.
Gangways: Within unit only.
Wheel Arrangement: 1-A + A-1.
Doors: Twin-leaf inward pivoting.
Maximum Speed: 75 mph.
Seating Layout: 3+2 mainly unidirectional bus/bench style unless stated.
Multiple Working: Within class and with Classes 143, 144, 150, 153, 155, 156, 158 and 159.

55542–591. DMS. Lot No. 31003 1985–86. –/62 (c –/46(6) 2W, s –/56, t –/53 or 55 1W, u –/52 or 54 1W). 24.5 t.
55592–641. DMSL. Lot No. 31004 1985–86. –/59 1T (c –/44(6) 1T 2W, s –/50 1T, u –/60 1T). 25.0 t.
55701–746. DMS. Lot No. 31013 1986–87. –/62 (c –/46(6) 2W, s –/56, t –/53 or 55 1W, u –/52 or 54 1W). 24.5 t.
55747–792. DMSL. Lot No. 31014 1986–87. –/59 1T (c –/44(6) 1T 2W, s –/50 1T, u –/60 1T). 25.0 t.

Notes:

c Refurbished Arriva Trains Wales units. Fitted with 2+2 individual Chapman seating.
s Fitted with 2+2 individual high-back seating.
t Former First North Western facelifted units – DMS fitted with a luggage/bicycle rack and wheelchair space.
u Merseytravel units – Fitted with 3+2 individual low-back seating.

142 001	t	**NO**	A	*NO*	NH	55542	55592
142 002	c	**AV**	A	*AW*	CF	55543	55593
142 003		**NO**	A	*NO*	NH	55544	55594
142 004	t	**NO**	A	*NO*	NH	55545	55595
142 005	t	**NO**	A	*NO*	NH	55546	55596
142 006	c	**AV**	A	*AW*	CF	55547	55597
142 007	t	**NO**	A	*NO*	NH	55548	55598
142 009	t	**NO**	A	*NO*	HT	55550	55600
142 010	c	**AV**	A	*AW*	CF	55551	55601
142 011	t	**NO**	A	*NO*	NH	55552	55602
142 012	t	**NO**	A	*NO*	NH	55553	55603
142 013		**NO**	A	*NO*	NH	55554	55604
142 014	t	**NO**	A	*NO*	NH	55555	55605
142 015	s	**NO**	A	*NO*	HT	55556	55606
142 016	s	**NO**	A	*NO*	HT	55557	55607
142 017	s	**NO**	A	*NO*	HT	55558	55608
142 018	s	**NO**	A	*NO*	HT	55559	55609
142 019	s	**NO**	A	*NO*	HT	55560	55610
142 020	s	**NO**	A	*NO*	HT	55561	55611
142 021	s	**NO**	A	*NO*	HT	55562	55612
142 022	s	**NO**	A	*NO*	HT	55563	55613
142 023	t	**NO**	A	*NO*	HT	55564	55614
142 024	s	**NO**	A	*NO*	HT	55565	55615
142 025	s	**NO**	A	*NO*	HT	55566	55616
142 026	s	**NO**	A	*NO*	HT	55567	55617
142 027	t	**NO**	A	*NO*	HT	55568	55618
142 028	t	**NO**	A	*NO*	NH	55569	55619
142 029		**NO**	A	*NO*	HT	55570	55620
142 030		**NO**	A	*NO*	NH	55571	55621
142 031	t	**NO**	A	*NO*	NH	55572	55622
142 032	t	**NO**	A	*NO*	NH	55573	55623
142 033	t	**NO**	A	*NO*	NH	55574	55624
142 033	t	**NO**	A	*NO*	NH	55574	55624
142 034	t	**NO**	A	*NO*	NH	55575	55625

142 035	t	**NO**	A	*NO*	NH	55576	55626	
142 036	t	**NO**	A	*NO*	NH	55577	55627	
142 037	t	**NO**	A	*NO*	NH	55578	55628	
142 038	t	**NO**	A	*NO*	NH	55579	55629	
142 039	t	**NO**	A	*NO*	NH	55580	55630	
142 040	t	**NO**	A	*NO*	NH	55581	55631	
142 041	u	**NO**	A	*NO*	NH	55582	55632	
142 042	u	**NO**	A	*NO*	NH	55583	55633	
142 043	u	**NO**	A	*NO*	NH	55584	55634	
142 044	u	**NO**	A	*NO*	NH	55585	55635	
142 045	u	**NO**	A	*NO*	NH	55586	55636	
142 046	u	**NO**	A	*NO*	NH	55587	55637	
142 047	u	**NO**	A	*NO*	NH	55588	55638	
142 048	u	**NO**	A	*NO*	NH	55589	55639	
142 049	u	**NO**	A	*NO*	NH	55590	55640	
142 050	s	**NO**	A	*NO*	HT	55591	55641	
142 051	u	**NO**	A	*NO*	NH	55701	55747	
142 052	u	**NO**	A	*NO*	NH	55702	55748	
142 053	u	**NO**	A	*NO*	NH	55703	55749	
142 054	u	**NO**	A	*NO*	NH	55704	55750	
142 055	u	**NO**	A	*NO*	NH	55705	55751	
142 056	u	**NO**	A	*NO*	NH	55706	55752	
142 057	u	**NO**	A	*NO*	NH	55707	55753	
142 058	u	**NO**	A	*NO*	NH	55708	55754	
142 060	t	**NO**	A	*NO*	NH	55710	55756	
142 061	t	**NO**	A	*NO*	NH	55711	55757	
142 062	t	**NO**	A	*NO*	NH	55712	55758	
142 063	t	**NO**	A	*NO*	NH	55713	55759	
142 064	t	**NO**	A	*NO*	HT	55714	55760	
142 065	s	**NO**	A	*NO*	HT	55715	55761	
142 066	s	**NO**	A	*NO*	HT	55716	55762	
142 067		**NO**	A	*NO*	HT	55717	55763	
142 068	t	**NO**	A	*NO*	HT	55718	55764	
142 069	c	**AV**	A	*AW*	CF	55719	55765	
142 070	t	**NO**	A	*NO*	HT	55720	55766	
142 071	s	**NO**	A	*NO*	HT	55721	55767	
142 072	c	**AV**	A	*AW*	CF	55722	55768	
142 073	c	**AV**	A	*AW*	CF	55723	55769	Myfanwy
142 074	c	**AV**	A	*AW*	CF	55724	55770	
142 075	c	**AV**	A	*AW*	CF	55725	55771	
142 076	c	**AV**	A	*AW*	CF	55726	55772	
142 077	c	**AV**	A	*AW*	CF	55727	55773	
142 078	s	**NO**	A	*NO*	HT	55728	55774	
142 079	s	**NO**	A	*NO*	HT	55729	55775	
142 080	c	**AV**	A	*AW*	CF	55730	55776	
142 081	c	**AV**	A	*AW*	CF	55731	55777	
142 082	c	**AV**	A	*AW*	CF	55732	55778	
142 083	c	**AV**	A	*AW*	CF	55733	55779	
142 084	s	**NO**	A	*NO*	HT	55734	55780	
142 085	c	**AV**	A	*AW*	CF	55735	55781	
142 086	s	**NO**	A	*NO*	HT	55736	55782	

▲ In London Midland livery, Parry People Mover 139 002 arrives at Stourbridge Junction with the 09.44 from Stourbridge Town on 02/08/11. **Robert Pritchard**

▼ In 2011 Chiltern restored a second Class 121, BR Green-liveried 121 034, to work peak-time services between Aylesbury and Princes Risborough. On its first day in traffic it stands at Princes Risborough on 25/05/11. **Robert Pritchard**

▲ Northern-liveried 142 041 is seen between Hathersage and Grindleford with the 12.45 Sheffield–Manchester Piccadilly on 09/04/11. **Robert Pritchard**

▼ Arriva Trains-liveried 143 614 arrives at Llanbradach with the 14.25 Bargoed–Penarth on 14/07/11. **Robert Pritchard**

▲ Northern-liveried 144 009 at Sheffield with the 08.27 Lincoln–Adwick on 14/03/11. **Robert Pritchard**

▼ The 150/1s transferring to FGW from London Overground and London Midland have been receiving the all over blue livery. On 25/06/11 150 121 is seen near Parsons Tunnel, Teignmouth with the 08.06 Paignton–Exmouth. **Stacey Thew**

▲ Northern-liveried 153 358 and London Midland 153 366 (on hire to Northern) pass Moorhouse, near South Elmsall, with an empty stock working on 01/05/11. **Robert Pritchard**

▼ In Northern livery with promotional vinyls, 155 344 emerges from Horbury Cutting with the 12.34 Huddersfield–Wakefield Westgate on 27/06/11. **Gavin Morrison**

▲ ScotRail "Saltire"-liveried 156 431 arrives at Whifflet with the 14.10 Cumbernauld–Motherwell on 04/08/10. **Ian Lothian**

▼ One of the refurbished Arriva Trains Wales 158s, 158 840, arrives at Tywyn with the 11.38 Pwllheli–Birmingham International on 09/05/11. **Robert Pritchard**

▲ South West Trains-liveried 159 019/008 pass Raynes Park with the 07.22 Yeovil Junction–London Waterloo on 06/04/11. **Alex Dasi-Sutton**

▼ Chiltern Railways-liveried 165 022/007 (nearest camera) pause at Haddenham & Thame Parkway with the 07.53 London Marylebone–Bicester North on 25/05/11. **Robert Pritchard**

▲ First Great Western Dynamic Lines-liveried 166 210 and 165 106 arrive at Reading with the 10.50 Oxford–London Paddington on 26/09/10. **Robert Pritchard**

▼ One of the original build of five 168/0s, 168 002, passes Kings Sutton with the 16.34 London Marylebone–Birmingham Snow Hill on 16/06/11. **Dave Gommersall**

▲ CrossCountry-liveried 170 106 leaves Newport with the 08.08 Nottingham–Cardiff Central on 26/04/11. **Robert Pritchard**

▼ Southern-liveried 171 725 passes London Road (Brighton) with the 16.32 Ashford International–Brighton Marshlink service on 24/05/10. **Robert Pritchard**

▲ The London Midland Class 172s entered service in September 2011. Just prior to this 172 211/345 pass Henley-in-Arden on 15/08/11 with a crew training run.
John Binch

▼ Arriva Trains-liveried 175 106 leaves Haverfordwest with the 09.03 Newport–Milford Haven on 14/06/11.
Paul Biggs

▲ First TransPennine Express "Dynamic Lines"-liveried 185 143 is seen near Hathersage with the 13.55 Manchester Airport–Cleethorpes on 09/04/11. **Robert Pritchard**

▲ First Hull Trains "Dynamic Lines"-liveried 180 113 leaves Doncaster with the 18.30 Hull–London King's Cross on 14/08/11. **Robert Pritchard**

▼ CrossCountry Voyagers 220 019/015 pass Moorhouse, near South Elmsall, with the 08.50 Edinburgh–Penzance on 23/07/11. **Robert Pritchard**

▲ Virgin Trains-liveried 221 113 "Sir Walter Raleigh" passes Rugby at speed with the 13.10 London Euston–Chester on 04/03/11. **Robert Pritchard**

▼ East Midlands Trains-liveried 222 003 "TORNADO" passes Heeley on the approaches to Sheffield with the 06.37 from London St Pancras on 22/06/10. **Robert Pritchard**

▲ The Network Rail yellow-liveried Track Assessment Unit 950 001 can be seen nationwide. On 09/08/11 it is seen passing Rearsby, Leicestershire with a test train from Derby. **Joshua Day**

▼ Balfour Beatty Matisa B 41 UE Tamper DR 75408 heads north on the West Anglia Main Line at Stansted Mountfitchet on 22/08/11. **Robert Pritchard**

▲ Swietelsky Babcock Rail Plasser & Theurer AFM 2000-RT Finishing Machine DR 77002 heads north on the West Coast Main Line at Docker working a 6J41 10.01 Wigan–Tebay on 19/02/10. **Andrew Wills**

▼ Colas Rail Plasser & Theurer USP 5000-RT Regulator DR 77901 is seen at Exeter St Davids on 02/03/11. **Stacey Thew**

▲ Balfour Beatty Plasser & Theurer Self-Propelled Heavy Duty Twin Jib Track Relayer DRP 78221 at Whitemoor Yard, March on 14/08/11. **Harry Savage**

▼ Network Rail Harsco Track Technologies RGH20C Rail Grinder DR 79272+ DR 79262 is seen stabled at Warrington Bank Quay on 03/07/11. **Cliff Beeton**

▲ Balfour Beatty Kirow KRC1200UK 125 tonne Heavy Duty Diesel Hydraulic Crane DRK 81611 unloads a track panel during an engineering possession at Faversham on 02/10/10. **William Turvill**

▼ Network Rail Windhoff Multi Vehicle Master & Slave DR 98959+DR 98909 passes Croome Perry Wood, Besford, on 24/05/11 whilst on weedkilling duties. **Dave Gommersall**

142 087	s	**NO**	A	*NO*	HT	55737	55783
142 088	s	**NO**	A	*NO*	HT	55738	55784
142 089	s	**NO**	A	*NO*	HT	55739	55785
142 090	s	**NO**	A	*NO*	HT	55740	55786
142 091	s	**NO**	A	*NO*	HT	55741	55787
142 092	s	**NO**	A	*NO*	HT	55742	55788
142 093	s	**NO**	A	*NO*	HT	55743	55789
142 094	s	**NO**	A	*NO*	HT	55744	55790
142 095	s	**NO**	A	*NO*	HT	55745	55791
142 096	s	**NO**	A	*NO*	HT	55746	55792

CLASS 143 PACER ALEXANDER/BARCLAY

DMS–DMSL. Similar design to Class 142, but bodies built by W. Alexander with Barclay underframes.

Construction: Steel underframe, aluminium alloy body and roof. Alexander bus bodywork on four-wheeled underframes.
Engines: One Cummins LT10-R of 165 kW (225 hp) at 1950 rpm.
Couplers: BSI at outer ends, bar within unit.
Dimensions: 15.45 x 2.80 m.
Gangways: Within unit only. **Wheel Arrangement:** 1-A + A-1.
Doors: Twin-leaf inward pivoting. **Maximum Speed:** 75 mph.
Seating Layout: 2+2 high-back Chapman seating, mainly unidirectional.
Multiple Working: Within class and with Classes 142, 144, 150, 153, 155, 156, 158 and 159.

DMS. Lot No. 31005 Andrew Barclay 1985–86. –/48(6) 2W. 24.0 t.
DMSL. Lot No. 31006 Andrew Barclay 1985–86. –/44(6) 1T 2W. 24.5 t.

143 601	**AV**	MG	*AW*	CF	55642	55667	
143 602	**AV**	P	*AW*	CF	55651	55668	
143 603	**FI**	P	*GW*	EX	55658	55669	
143 604	**AV**	P	*AW*	CF	55645	55670	
143 605	**AV**	P	*AW*	CF	55646	55671	
143 606	**AV**	P	*AW*	CF	55647	55672	
143 607	**AV**	P	*AW*	CF	55648	55673	
143 608	**AV**	P	*AW*	CF	55649	55674	
143 609	**AV**	SG	*AW*	CF	55650	55675	Sir Tom Jones
143 610	**AV**	MG	*AW*	CF	55643	55676	
143 611	**FI**	P	*GW*	EX	55652	55677	
143 612	**FI**	P	*GW*	EX	55653	55678	
143 614	**AV**	MG	*AW*	CF	55655	55680	
143 616	**AV**	P	*AW*	CF	55657	55682	
143 617	**FI**	FW	*GW*	EX	55644	55683	
143 618	**FI**	FW	*GW*	EX	55659	55684	
143 619	**FI**	FW	*GW*	EX	55660	55685	
143 620	**FI**	P	*GW*	EX	55661	55686	
143 621	**FI**	P	*GW*	EX	55662	55687	
143 622	**AV**	P	*AW*	CF	55663	55688	
143 623	**AV**	P	*AW*	CF	55664	55689	
143 624	**AV**	P	*AW*	CF	55665	55690	
143 625	**AV**	P	*AW*	CF	55666	55691	

CLASS 144 PACER ALEXANDER/BREL DERBY

DMS–DMSL or DMS–MS–DMSL. As Class 143, but underframes built by BREL.

Construction: Steel underframe, aluminium alloy body and roof. Alexander bus bodywork on four-wheeled underframes.
Engines: One Cummins LT10-R of 165 kW (225 hp) at 1950 rpm.
Couplers: BSI at outer ends, bar within unit.
Dimensions: 15.45/15.43 x 2.80 m.
Gangways: Within unit only. **Wheel Arrangement:** 1-A + A-1.
Doors: Twin-leaf inward pivoting. **Maximum Speed:** 75 mph.
Seating Layout: 2+2 high-back Richmond seating, mainly unidirectional.
Multiple Working: Within class and with Classes 142, 143, 150, 153, 155, 156, 158 and 159.

DMS. Lot No. 31015 BREL Derby 1986–87. –/45(3) 1W 24.0 t.
MS. Lot No. BREL Derby 31037 1987. –/58. 23.5 t.
DMSL. Lot No. BREL Derby 31016 1986–87. –/41(3) 1T. 24.5 t.

144 001	**NO**	P	*NO*	NL	55801		55824
144 002	**NO**	P	*NO*	NL	55802		55825
144 003	**NO**	P	*NO*	NL	55803		55826
144 004	**NO**	P	*NO*	NL	55804		55827
144 005	**NO**	P	*NO*	NL	55805		55828
144 006	**NO**	P	*NO*	NL	55806		55829
144 007	**NO**	P	*NO*	NL	55807		55830
144 008	**NO**	P	*NO*	NL	55808		55831
144 009	**NO**	P	*NO*	NL	55809		55832
144 010	**NO**	P	*NO*	NL	55810		55833
144 011	**NO**	P	*NO*	NL	55811		55834
144 012	**NO**	P	*NO*	NL	55812		55835
144 013	**NO**	P	*NO*	NL	55813		55836
144 014	**NO**	P	*NO*	NL	55814	55850	55837
144 015	**NO**	P	*NO*	NL	55815	55851	55838
144 016	**NO**	P	*NO*	NL	55816	55852	55839
144 017	**NO**	P	*NO*	NL	55817	55853	55840
144 018	**NO**	P	*NO*	NL	55818	55854	55841
144 019	**NO**	P	*NO*	NL	55819	55855	55842
144 020	**NO**	P	*NO*	NL	55820	55856	55843
144 021	**NO**	P	*NO*	NL	55821	55857	55844
144 022	**NO**	P	*NO*	NL	55822	55858	55845
144 023	**NO**	P	*NO*	NL	55823	55859	55846

Name: 144 001 THE PENISTONE LINE PARTNERSHIP

CLASS 150/0 SPRINTER BREL YORK

DMSL–MS–DMS. Prototype Sprinter.

Construction: Steel.
Engines: One Cummins NT855R5 of 213 kW (285 hp) at 2100 rpm.
Bogies: BX8P (powered), BX8T (non-powered).
Couplers: BSI at outer end of driving vehicles, bar non-driving ends.

Dimensions: 19.93/19.92 x 2.73 m.
Gangways: Within unit only.
Wheel Arrangement: 2-B + 2-B + B-2.
Doors: Twin-leaf sliding.
Maximum Speed: 75 mph.
Seating Layout: 3+2 (mainly unidirectional).
Multiple Working: Within class and with Classes 142, 143, 144, 153, 155, 156, 158, 159, 170 and 172.

DMSL. Lot No. 30984 1984. –/72 1T. 35.4 t.
MS. Lot No. 30986 1984. –/92. 35.0 t.
DMS. Lot No. 30985 1984. –/69(6). 34.7 t.

150 001	**CI**	A	*GW*	RG	55200	55400	55300
150 002	**CI**	A	*GW*	RG	55201	55401	55301

CLASS 150/1 SPRINTER BREL YORK

DMSL–DMS or DMSL–DMSL–DMS or DMSL–DMS–DMS.

Construction: Steel.
Engines: One Cummins NT855R5 of 213 kW (285 hp) at 2100 rpm.
Bogies: BP38 (powered), BT38 (non-powered).
Couplers: BSI.
Dimensions: 19.74 x 2.82 m.
Gangways: Within unit only.
Wheel Arrangement: 2-B (+ 2-B) + B-2.
Doors: Twin-leaf sliding.
Maximum Speed: 75 mph.
Seating Layout: 3+2 facing as built but Centro units were reseated with mainly unidirectional seating.
Multiple Working: Within class and with Classes 142, 143, 144, 153, 155, 156, 158, 159, 170 and 172.

DMSL. Lot No. 31011 1985–86. –/72 1T (c –/59 1TD (except 52144 which is –/62 1TD), t –/71 1T, u –/71 1T). 38.3 t.
DMS. Lot No. 31012 1985–86. –/76 (c –/65, t –/73, u –/70). 38.1 t.

c 3+2 Chapman seating.

150 101	u	**CI**	A	*GW*	PM	52101	57101
150 102	u	**CI**	A	*GW*	PM	52102	57102
150 103	u	**WM**	A	*NO*	NH	52103	57103
150 104	u	**CI**	A	*GW*	PM	52104	57104
150 105	u	**CI**	A	*LM*	TS	52105	57105
150 106	u	**CI**	A	*GW*	PM	52106	57106
150 107	u	**CI**	A	*LM*	TS	52107	57107
150 108	u	**CI**	A	*GW*	PM	52108	57108
150 109	u	**CI**	A	*LM*	TS	52109	57109
150 110	u	**WM**	A	*NO*	NH	52110	57110
150 111	u	**CI**	A	*NO*	NH	52111	57111
150 112	u	**CI**	A	*NO*	NH	52112	57112
150 113	u	**CI**	A	*NO*	NH	52113	57113
150 114	u	**CI**	A	*NO*	NH	52114	57114
150 115	u	**CI**	A	*NO*	NH	52115	57115
150 116	u	**CI**	A	*NO*	NH	52116	57116
150 117	u	**NO**	A	*NO*	NH	52117	57117
150 118	u	**WM**	A	*NO*	NH	52118	57118

150 119	u	**CI**	A	*NO*	NH	52119	57119
150 120	t	**FB**	A	*GW*	EX	52120	57120
150 121	u	**FB**	A	*GW*	EX	52121	57121
150 122	u	**CI**	A	*GW*	PM	52122	57122
150 123	t	**FB**	A	*GW*	PM	52123	57123
150 124	u	**CI**	A	*GW*	PM	52124	57124
150 125	u	**FB**	A	*GW*	EX	52125	57125
150 126	u	**FB**	A	*GW*	EX	52126	57126
150 127	t	**FB**	A	*GW*	EX	52127	57127
150 128	t	**FB**	A	*GW*	EX	52128	57128
150 129	t	**FB**	A	*GW*	EX	52129	57129
150 130	t	**FB**	A	*GW*	PM	52130	57130
150 131	t	**FB**	A	*GW*	EX	52131	57131
150 132	u	**WM**	A	*NO*	NH	52132	57132
150 133	c	**NO**	A	*NO*	NH	52133	57133
150 134	c	**NO**	A	*NO*	NH	52134	57134
150 135	c	**NO**	A	*NO*	NH	52135	57135
150 136	c	**NO**	A	*NO*	NH	52136	57136
150 137	c	**NO**	A	*NO*	NH	52137	57137
150 138	c	**NO**	A	*NO*	NH	52138	57138
150 139	c	**NO**	A	*NO*	NH	52139	57139
150 140	c	**NO**	A	*NO*	NH	52140	57140
150 141	c	**NO**	A	*NO*	NH	52141	57141
150 142	c	**NO**	A	*NO*	NH	52142	57142
150 143	c	**NO**	A	*NO*	NH	52143	57143
150 144	c	**NO**	A	*NO*	NH	52144	57144
150 145	c	**NO**	A	*NO*	NH	52145	57145
150 146	c	**NO**	A	*NO*	NH	52146	57146
150 147	c	**NO**	A	*NO*	NH	52147	57147
150 148	c	**NO**	A	*NO*	NH	52148	57148
150 149	c	**NO**	A	*NO*	NH	52149	57149
150 150	c	**NO**	A	*NO*	NH	52150	57150

Names:

150 129 Devon & Cornwall RAIL PARTNERSHIP
150 130 Severnside Community Rail Partnership

CLASS 150/2 SPRINTER BREL YORK

DMSL–DMS.

Construction: Steel.
Engines: One Cummins NT855R5 of 213 kW (285 hp) at 2100 rpm.
Bogies: BP38 (powered), BT38 (non-powered).
Couplers: BSI.
Dimensions: 19.74 x 2.82 m.
Gangways: Throughout. **Wheel Arrangement:** 2-B + B-2.
Doors: Twin-leaf sliding. **Maximum Speed:** 75 mph.
Seating Layout: 3+2 mainly unidirectional seating as built, but most units have now been refurbished with new 2+2 seating (see notes below).

Multiple Working: Within class and with Classes 142, 143, 144, 153, 155, 156, 158, 159, 170 and 172.

DMSL. Lot No. 31017 1986–87. –/73 1T (c –/62 1TD, p –/60(4) 1T, u –/71 1T), v –/60(8) 1T, w –/60(8) 1T). 37.5 t.
DMS. Lot No. 31018 1986–87. –/76 (c –/70, p –/56(10) 1W, u –/70), v –/56(15) 2W, w –/56(17) 2W, z –/68). 36.5 t.

Northern promotional vinyls: 150 203/205/207/215/218/222/223/225/228/268–271/273–277 Welcome to Yorkshire
150 272 R&B Festival week, Colne

Notes:

c 3+2 Chapman seating (former First North Western units).
p Refurbished Arriva Trains Wales units with 2+2 Primarius seating.
v Units refurbished for Valley Lines with 2+2 Chapman seating.
w Units refurbished for First Great Western with 2+2 Chapman seating.

150 209 is formed of two toiletless vehicles which were spare once they had been disbanded from London Midland 3-car 150/0 sets. These two vehicles are to be formed into 150 121/127 to make 3-car sets.

Units 150 210/220/226 carry a different livery on each vehicle.

150 280 is on sub-lease from Arriva Trains Wales to National Express East Anglia.

150 201	c	**NO**	A	*NO*	NH	52201	57201
150 202	u	**CI**	A	*GW*	PM	52202	57202
150 203	c	**NO**	A	*NO*	NH	52203	57203
150 204	u	**CI**	A	*NO*	NH	52204	57204
150 205	c	**NO**	A	*NO*	NH	52205	57205
150 206	u	**CI**	A	*NO*	NH	52206	57206
150 207	c	**NO**	A	*NO*	NH	52207	57207
150 208	p	**AV**	P	*AW*	CF	52208	57208
150 209	u	**CI**	A		PM	57209	57212
150 210	u	**CI/WM**	A	*NO*	NH	52210	57210
150 211	c	**NO**	A	*NO*	NH	52211	57211
150 213	p	**AV**	P	*AW*	CF	52213	57213
150 214	u	**CI**	A	*NO*	NH	52214	57214
150 215	c	**NO**	A	*NO*	NH	52215	57215
150 216	u	**CI**	A	*GW*	PM	52216	57216
150 217	p	**AV**	P	*AW*	CF	52217	57217
150 218	c	**NO**	A	*NO*	NH	52218	57218
150 219	w	**FI**	P	*GW*	PM	52219	57219
150 220	u	**WM/CI**	A	*NO*	NH	52220	57220
150 221	w	**FI**	P	*GW*	PM	52221	57221
150 222	c	**NO**	A	*NO*	NH	52222	57222
150 223	c	**NO**	A	*NO*	NH	52223	57223
150 224	c	**NO**	A	*NO*	NH	52224	57224
150 225	c	**NO**	A	*NO*	NH	52225	57225
150 226	u	**CI/WM**	A	*NO*	NH	52226	57226
150 227	p	**AV**	P	*AW*	CF	52227	57227
150 228		**NO**	P	*NO*	NH	52228	57228
150 229	p	**AV**	P	*AW*	CF	52229	57229

150 230	w	**AV**	P	*AW*	CF	52230	57230
150 231	p	**AV**	P	*AW*	CF	52231	57231
150 232	w	**FI**	P	*GW*	PM	52232	57232
150 233	w	**FI**	P	*GW*	PM	52233	57233
150 234	w	**FI**	P	*GW*	PM	52234	57234
150 235	p	**AV**	P	*AW*	CF	52235	57235
150 236	w	**AV**	P	*AW*	CF	52236	57236
150 237	p	**AV**	P	*AW*	CF	52237	57237
150 238	w	**FI**	P	*GW*	PM	52238	57238
150 239	w	**FI**	P	*GW*	PM	52239	57239
150 240	w	**AV**	P	*AW*	CF	52240	57240
150 241	w	**AV**	P	*AW*	CF	52241	57241
150 242	w	**AV**	P	*AW*	CF	52242	57242
150 243	w	**FI**	P	*GW*	PM	52243	57243
150 244	w	**FI**	P	*GW*	PM	52244	57244
150 245	p	**AV**	P	*AW*	CF	52245	57245
150 246	w	**FI**	P	*GW*	PM	52246	57246
150 247	w	**FI**	P	*GW*	PM	52247	57247
150 248	w	**FI**	P	*GW*	PM	52248	57248
150 249	w	**FI**	P	*GW*	PM	52249	57249
150 250	p	**AV**	P	*AW*	CF	52250	57250
150 251	w	**AV**	P	*AW*	CF	52251	57251
150 252	p	**AV**	P	*AW*	CF	52252	57252
150 253	w	**AV**	P	*AW*	CF	52253	57253
150 254	w	**AV**	P	*AW*	CF	52254	57254
150 255	p	**AV**	P	*AW*	CF	52255	57255
150 256	p	**AV**	P	*AW*	CF	52256	57256
150 257	p	**AV**	P	*AW*	CF	52257	57257
150 258	p	**AV**	P	*AW*	CF	52258	57258
150 259	p	**AV**	P	*AW*	CF	52259	57259
150 260	p	**AV**	P	*AW*	CF	52260	57260
150 261	w	**FI**	P	*GW*	PM	52261	57261
150 262	p	**AV**	P	*AW*	CF	52262	57262
150 263	w	**FI**	P	*GW*	PM	52263	57263
150 264	p	**AV**	P	*AW*	CF	52264	57264
150 265	w	**FI**	P	*GW*	PM	52265	57265
150 266	w	**FI**	P	*GW*	PM	52266	57266
150 267	v	**AV**	P	*AW*	CF	52267	57267
150 268		**NO**	P	*NO*	NH	52268	57268
150 269		**NO**	P	*NO*	NH	52269	57269
150 270		**NO**	P	*NO*	NH	52270	57270
150 271		**NO**	P	*NO*	NH	52271	57271
150 272		**NO**	P	*NO*	NH	52272	57272
150 273		**NO**	P	*NO*	NH	52273	57273
150 274		**NO**	P	*NO*	NH	52274	57274
150 275		**NO**	P	*NO*	NH	52275	57275
150 276		**NO**	P	*NO*	NH	52276	57276
150 277		**NO**	P	*NO*	NH	52277	57277
150 278	v	**AV**	P	*AW*	CF	52278	57278
150 279	v	**AV**	P	*AW*	CF	52279	57279
150 280	v	**AV**	P	*EA*	NC	52280	57280

150 281	v	**AV**	P	*AW*	CF	52281	57281
150 282	v	**AV**	P	*AW*	CF	52282	57282
150 283	p	**AV**	P	*AW*	CF	52283	57283
150 284	p	**AV**	P	*AW*	CF	52284	57284
150 285	p	**AV**	P	*AW*	CF	52285	57285

CLASS 153 SUPER SPRINTER LEYLAND BUS

DMSL. Converted by Hunslet-Barclay, Kilmarnock from Class 155 2-car units.

Construction: Steel underframe, rivetted steel body and roof. Built from Leyland National bus parts on Leyland Bus bogied underframes.
Engine: One Cummins NT855R5 of 213 kW (285 hp) at 2100 rpm.
Bogies: One P3-10 (powered) and one BT38 (non-powered).
Couplers: BSI.
Dimensions: 23.21 x 2.70 m.
Gangways: Throughout.
Wheel Arrangement: 2-B.
Doors: Single-leaf sliding plug.
Maximum Speed: 75 mph.
Seating Layout: 2+2 facing/unidirectional.
Multiple Working: Within class and with Classes 142, 143, 144, 150, 155, 156, 158, 159, 170 and 172.

52301–52335. DMSL. Lot No. 31026 1987–88. Converted under Lot No. 31115 1991–92. –/72(3) 1T 1W. (s –/72 1T 1W, t –/72(2) 1T 1W). 41.2 t.
57301–57335. DMSL. Lot No. 31027 1987–88. Converted under Lot No. 31115 1991–92. –/72(3) 1T 1W (s –/72 1T 1W). 41.2 t.

Notes: Cars numbered in the 573xx series were renumbered by adding 50 to their original number so that the last two digits correspond with the set number.

† Uprated Cummins engine fitted (231 kW – 310 hp)
c Chapman seating.
d Richmond seating.

153 301	d	**NO**	A	*NO*	NL	52301	
153 302	c	**EM**	A	*EM*	NM	52302	
153 303	c	**AV**	A	*AW*	CF	52303	
153 304	ds	**NO**	A	*NO*	NL	52304	
153 305	d	**FI**	A	*GW*	EX	52305	
153 306	cr	**1**	P	*EA*	NC	52306	
153 307	d	**NO**	A	*NO*	NL	52307	
153 308	c	**EM**	A	*EM*	NM	52308	
153 309	cr	**AR**	P	*EA*	NC	52309	GERARD FIENNES
153 310	c	**EM**	P	*EM*	NM	52310	
153 311	c	**EM**	P	*EM*	NM	52311	
153 312	s	**AV**	A	*AW*	CF	52312	
153 313	cs	**EM**	P	*EM*	NM	52313	
153 314	cr	**1**	P	*EA*	NC	52314	
153 315	ds	**NO**	A	*NO*	NL	52315	
153 316	c	**NO**	P	*NO*	NL	52316	
153 317	ds	**NO**	A	*NO*	NL	52317	
153 318	d	**FI**	A	*GW*	EX	52318	
153 319	d	**EM**	A	*EM*	NM	52319	

153 320	†c	**AV**	P	*AW*	CF	52320	
153 321	ct	**EM**	P	*EM*	NM	52321	
153 322	cr	**AR**	P	*EA*	NC	52322	BENJAMIN BRITTEN
153 323	c	**AV**	P	*AW*	CF	52323	
153 324	c	**NO**	P	*NO*	NL	52324	
153 325	c	**LM**	P	*GW*	EX	52325	
153 326	c	**EM**	P	*EM*	NM	52326	
153 327	c	**AV**	A	*AW*	CF	52327	
153 328	ds	**NO**	A	*NO*	NL	52328	
153 329	c	**FI**	P	*GW*	EX	52329	
153 330	cs	**NO**	P	*NO*	NL	52330	
153 331	d	**NO**	A	*NO*	NL	52331	
153 332	c	**NO**	P	*NO*	NL	52332	
153 333	cs	**LM**	P	*GW*	EX	52333	
153 334	ct	**LM**	P	*LM*	TS	52334	
153 335	cr	**AR**	P	*EA*	NC	52335	MICHAEL PALIN
153 351	d	**NO**	A	*NO*	NL	57351	
153 352	ds	**NO**	A	*NO*	NL	57352	
153 353	c	**AV**	A	*AW*	CF	57353	
153 354	c	**LM**	P	*LM*	TS	57354	
153 355	c	**EM**	A	*EM*	NM	57355	
153 356	c	**LM**	P	*LM*	TS	57356	
153 357	c	**EM**	A	*EM*	NM	57357	
153 358	c	**NO**	P	*NO*	NL	57358	
153 359	c	**NO**	P	*NO*	NL	57359	
153 360	c	**NO**	P	*NO*	NL	57360	
153 361	cs	**FI**	P	*GW*	EX	57361	
153 362	cs	**AV**	A	*AW*	CF	57362	Dylan Thomas 1914–1953
153 363	cs	**NO**	P	*NO*	NL	57363	
153 364	c	**LM**	P	*LM*	TS	57364	
153 365	c	**LM**	P	*LM*	TS	57365	
153 366	c	**LM**	P	*LM*	TS	57366	
153 367	cs	**AV**	P	*AW*	CF	57367	
153 368	d	**FI**	A	*GW*	EX	57368	
153 369	c	**FI**	P	*GW*	EX	57369	
153 370	d	**FI**	A	*GW*	EX	57370	
153 371	c	**LM**	P	*LM*	TS	57371	
153 372	d	**FI**	A	*GW*	EX	57372	
153 373	d	**FI**	A	*GW*	EX	57373	
153 374	c	**EM**	A	*EM*	NM	57374	
153 375	c	**LM**	P	*LM*	TS	57375	
153 376	c	**CT**	P	*EM*	NM	57376	
153 377	d	**FI**	A	*GW*	EX	57377	
153 378	d	**NO**	A	*NO*	NL	57378	
153 379	c	**CT**	P	*EM*	NM	57379	
153 380	d	**FI**	A	*GW*	EX	57380	
153 381	c	**EM**	P	*EM*	NM	57381	
153 382	d	**FI**	A	*GW*	EX	57382	
153 383	c	**EM**	P	*EM*	NM	57383	
153 384	c	**CT**	P	*EM*	NM	57384	
153 385	c	**EM**	P	*EM*	NM	57385	

CLASS 155 SUPER SPRINTER LEYLAND BUS

DMSL–DMS.

Construction: Steel underframe, rivetted steel body and roof. Built from Leyland National bus parts on Leyland Bus bogied underframes.
Engines: One Cummins NT855R5 of 213 kW (285 hp) at 2100 rpm.
Bogies: One P3-10 (powered) and one BT38 (non-powered).
Couplers: BSI.
Dimensions: 23.21 x 2.70 m.
Gangways: Throughout.
Wheel Arrangement: 2-B + B-2.
Doors: Single-leaf sliding plug.
Maximum Speed: 75 mph.
Seating Layout: 2+2 facing/unidirectional Chapman seating.
Multiple Working: Within class and with Classes 142, 143, 144, 150, 153, 156, 158, 159, 170 and 172.

DMSL. Lot No. 31057 1988. –/76 1TD 1W. 39.0 t.
DMS. Lot No. 31058 1988. –/80. 38.6 t.

Northern promotional vinyls:

155 341–347 Leeds–Bradford–Manchester route (the "Calder Valley").

155 341	**NO**	P	*NO*	NL	52341	57341
155 342	**NO**	P	*NO*	NL	52342	57342
155 343	**NO**	P	*NO*	NL	52343	57343
155 344	**NO**	P	*NO*	NL	52344	57344
155 345	**NO**	P	*NO*	NL	52345	57345
155 346	**NO**	P	*NO*	NL	52346	57346
155 347	**NO**	P	*NO*	NL	52347	57347

CLASS 156 SUPER SPRINTER METRO-CAMMELL

DMSL–DMS.

Construction: Steel.
Engines: One Cummins NT855R5 of 213 kW (285 hp) at 2100 rpm.
Bogies: One P3-10 (powered) and one BT38 (non-powered).
Couplers: BSI.
Dimensions: 23.03 x 2.73 m.
Gangways: Throughout.
Wheel Arrangement: 2-B + B-2.
Doors: Single-leaf sliding.
Maximum Speed: 75 mph.
Seating Layout: 2+2 facing/unidirectional.
Multiple Working: Within class and with Classes 142, 143, 144, 150, 153, 155, 158, 159, 170 and 172.

DMSL. Lot No. 31028 1988–89. –/74 († * –/72, c, t –/70, u –/68) 1TD 1W. 38.6 t.
DMS. Lot No. 31029 1987–89. –/76 (d –/78, † –/74, t, u –/72) 36.1 t.

Advertising livery: 156 402 Chapelfield Shopping Centre (white & blue).

Northern promotional vinyls:

156 448 Hadrians Wall Country (Newcastle–Carlisle line).
156 461 Ravenglass & Eskdale Railway.
156 464 Lancashire DalesRail

156 469 Bishop Auckland branch.
156 484 Settle & Carlisle line.
156 490 National Railway Museum.

Notes:

c Chapman seating.
d Richmond seating.

156 401	c*	**EM**	P	*EM*	DY	52401	57401
156 402	cr	**AL**	P	*EA*	NC	52402	57402
156 403	c*	**EM**	P	*EM*	DY	52403	57403
156 404	c*	**EM**	P	*EM*	DY	52404	57404
156 405	c*	**EM**	P	*EM*	DY	52405	57405
156 406	c*	**EM**	P	*EM*	DY	52406	57406
156 407	cr	**1**	P	*EA*	NC	52407	57407
156 408	c*	**EM**	P	*EM*	DY	52408	57408
156 409	cr	**1**	P	*EA*	NC	52409	57409
156 410	c*	**EM**	P	*EM*	DY	52410	57410
156 411	c*	**EM**	P	*EM*	DY	52411	57411
156 412	cr	**CT**	P	*EA*	NC	52412	57412
156 413	c*	**EM**	P	*EM*	DY	52413	57413
156 414	c*	**EM**	P	*EM*	DY	52414	57414
156 415	c*	**EM**	P	*EM*	DY	52415	57415
156 416	cr	**1**	P	*EA*	NC	52416	57416
156 417	cr	**1**	P	*EA*	NC	52417	57417
156 418	cr	**CT**	P	*EA*	NC	52418	57418
156 419	cr	**NX**	P	*EA*	NC	52419	57419
156 420	c	**NO**	P	*NO*	AN	52420	57420
156 421	c	**NO**	P	*NO*	AN	52421	57421
156 422	cr	**1**	P	*EA*	NC	52422	57422
156 423	c	**NO**	P	*NO*	AN	52423	57423
156 424	c	**NO**	P	*NO*	AN	52424	57424
156 425	c	**NO**	P	*NO*	AN	52425	57425
156 426	c	**NO**	P	*NO*	AN	52426	57426
156 427	c	**NO**	P	*NO*	AN	52427	57427
156 428	c	**NO**	P	*NO*	AN	52428	57428
156 429	c	**NO**	P	*NO*	AN	52429	57429
156 430	t	**SR**	A	*SR*	CK	52430	57430
156 431	t	**SR**	A	*SR*	CK	52431	57431
156 432	t	**SR**	A	*SR*	CK	52432	57432
156 433	t	**SR**	A	*SR*	CK	52433	57433
156 434	t	**SR**	A	*SR*	CK	52434	57434
156 435	t	**SR**	A	*SR*	CK	52435	57435
156 436	†	**SR**	A	*SR*	CK	52436	57436
156 437	t	**SR**	A	*SR*	CK	52437	57437
156 438	d	**NO**	A	*NO*	HT	52438	57438
156 439	t	**SR**	A	*SR*	CK	52439	57439
156 440	c	**NO**	P	*NO*	AN	52440	57440
156 441	c	**NO**	P	*NO*	AN	52441	57441
156 442	t	**SR**	A	*SR*	CK	52442	57442
156 443	d	**NO**	A	*NO*	HT	52443	57443

156 444	d	**NO**	A	*NO*	HT	52444	57444
156 445	u	**SR**	A	*SR*	CK	52445	57445
156 446	t	**FS**	A	*SR*	CK	52446	57446
156 447	ru	**FS**	A	*SR*	CK	52447	57447
156 448	d	**NO**	A	*NO*	HT	52448	57448
156 449	u	**FS**	A	*SR*	CK	52449	57449
156 450	ru	**FS**	A	*SR*	CK	52450	57450
156 451	d	**NO**	A	*NO*	HT	52451	57451
156 452	c	**NO**	P	*NO*	AN	52452	57452
156 453	ru	**FS**	A	*SR*	CK	52453	57453
156 454	d	**NO**	A	*NO*	HT	52454	57454
156 455	c	**NO**	P	*NO*	AN	52455	57455
156 456	rt	**FS**	A	*SR*	CK	52456	57456
156 457	rt	**FS**	A	*SR*	CK	52457	57457
156 458	rt	**FS**	A	*SR*	CK	52458	57458
156 459	c	**NO**	P	*NO*	AN	52459	57459
156 460	c	**NO**	P	*NO*	AN	52460	57460
156 461	c	**NO**	P	*NO*	AN	52461	57461
156 462		**FS**	A	*SR*	CK	52462	57462
156 463	d	**NO**	A	*NO*	HT	52463	57463
156 464	c	**NO**	P	*NO*	AN	52464	57464
156 465	ru	**FS**	A	*SR*	CK	52465	57465
156 466	c	**NO**	P	*NO*	AN	52466	57466
156 467	r	**FS**	A	*SR*	CK	52467	57467
156 468	d	**NO**	A	*NO*	AN	52468	57468
156 469	d	**NO**	A	*NO*	HT	52469	57469
156 470	d	**NO**	A	*EM*	DY	52470	57470
156 471	d	**NO**	A	*NO*	AN	52471	57471
156 472	d	**NO**	A	*NO*	AN	52472	57472
156 473	d	**EM**	A	*EM*	DY	52473	57473
156 474	rt	**FS**	A	*SR*	CK	52474	57474
156 475	d	**NO**	A	*NO*	HT	52475	57475
156 476	rt	**FS**	A	*SR*	CK	52476	57476
156 477	t	**FS**	A	*SR*	CK	52477	57477
156 478	rt	**FS**	A	*SR*	CK	52478	57478
156 479	d	**NO**	A	*NO*	HT	52479	57479
156 480	d	**NO**	A	*NO*	HT	52480	57480
156 481	d	**NO**	A	*NO*	HT	52481	57481
156 482	d	**NO**	A	*NO*	AN	52482	57482
156 483	d	**NO**	A	*NO*	AN	52483	57483
156 484	d	**NO**	A	*NO*	HT	52484	57484
156 485	ru	**FS**	A	*SR*	CK	52485	57485
156 486	d	**NO**	A	*NO*	AN	52486	57486
156 487	d	**NO**	A	*NO*	AN	52487	57487
156 488	d	**NO**	A	*NO*	AN	52488	57488
156 489	d	**NO**	A	*NO*	AN	52489	57489
156 490	d	**NO**	A	*NO*	HT	52490	57490
156 491	d	**NO**	A	*NO*	AN	52491	57491
156 492	r†	**FS**	A	*SR*	CK	52492	57492
156 493	rt	**FS**	A	*SR*	CK	52493	57493
156 494	u	**SR**	A	*SR*	CK	52494	57494

156 495	u	**SR**	A	*SR*	CK	52495	57495
156 496	u	**FS**	A	*SR*	CK	52496	57496
156 497	d	**NO**	A	*EM*	DY	52497	57497
156 498	d	**NO**	A	*EM*	DY	52498	57498
156 499	rt	**FS**	A	*SR*	CK	52499	57499
156 500	u	**SR**	A	*SR*	CK	52500	57500
156 501		**SR**	A	*SR*	CK	52501	57501
156 502		**SR**	A	*SR*	CK	52502	57502
156 503		**SR**	A	*SR*	CK	52503	57503
156 504		**SR**	A	*SR*	CK	52504	57504
156 505		**SR**	A	*SR*	CK	52505	57505
156 506		**SR**	A	*SR*	CK	52506	57506
156 507		**SR**	A	*SR*	CK	52507	57507
156 508		**SR**	A	*SR*	CK	52508	57508
156 509		**SR**	A	*SR*	CK	52509	57509
156 510		**SR**	A	*SR*	CK	52510	57510
156 511		**SR**	A	*SR*	CK	52511	57511
156 512		**SR**	A	*SR*	CK	52512	57512
156 513		**SR**	A	*SR*	CK	52513	57513
156 514		**SR**	A	*SR*	CK	52514	57514

Names:

156 409	Cromer Pier Seaside Special
156 416	Saint Edmund
156 420	LA' AL RATTY Ravenglass & Eskdale Railway
156 441	William Huskisson MP
156 444	Councillor Bill Cameron
156 459	Benny Rothman – The Manchester Rambler
156 460	Driver John Axon G.C.
156 464	Lancashire DalesRail
156 466	Gracie Fields

CLASS 158/0 BREL

DMSL(B)–DMSL(A) or DMCL–DMSL or DMSL–MSL–DMSL.

Construction: Welded aluminium.
Engines: 158 701–813/158 880–890/158 950–959: One Cummins NTA855R of 260 kW (350 hp) at 1900 rpm.
158 815–862: One Perkins 2006-TWH of 260 kW (350 hp) at 1900 rpm.
158 863–872: One Cummins NTA855R of 300 kW (400 hp) at 2100 rpm.
Bogies: One BREL P4 (powered) and one BREL T4 (non-powered) per car.
Couplers: BSI.
Dimensions: 22.57 x 2.70 m.
Gangways: Throughout.
Wheel Arrangement: 2-B + B-2.
Doors: Twin-leaf swing plug.
Maximum Speed: 90 mph.
Seating Layout: 2+2 facing/unidirectional in all Standard and First Class except 2+1 in South West Trains First Class.
Multiple Working: Within class and with Classes 142, 143, 144, 150, 153, 155, 156, 159, 170 and 172.

DMSL(B). Lot No. 31051 BREL Derby 1989–92. –/68 1TD 1W. († –/72 1TD 1W, c, w –/66 1TD 1W, s –/64(4) 1TD 2W, t –/64 1TD 1W). 38.5 t.
MSL. Lot No. 31050 BREL Derby 1991. –/66(3) 1T. 38.5 t.
DMSL(A). Lot No. 31052 BREL Derby 1989–92. –/70 1T († –/74, c, w –/68 1T, * –/64(2) 1T plus cycle stowage area, s –/70 1T, t –/66 1T). 38.5 t.

The above details refer to the "as built" condition. The following DMSL(B) have now been converted to DMCL as follows:

52701–736/52738–741 (ScotRail). 15/53 1TD 1W (* refurbished sets 14/46(6) 1TD 1W plus cycle stowage area).
52786/789 (Former South West Trains units). 13/44 1TD 1W.

Northern promotional vinyls:

158 784 PTEG: 40 years.
158 787, 158 792–796 Sheffield–Leeds fast service.
158 790 Rugby League (Northern Rail Cup).
158 860 Keighley & Brontë Country.
158 861 Welcome to Yorkshire.
158 901–910 Leeds–Bradford–Manchester route (the "Calder Valley").

Notes:

* Refurbished ScotRail units fitted with Grammer seating, additional luggage racks and cycle stowage areas.
ScotRail units 158 726–741 are fitted with Richmond seating.
† Refurbished East Midlands Trains units with Primarius seating.
c Chapman seating.
s Refurbished Arriva Trains Wales units with Grammer seating.
t Arriva Trains Wales and Northern units with some seats removed for additional luggage space.
u Refurbished former South West Trains units with Class 159-style interiors, including First Class seating.
w Refurbished First Great Western units. Units 158 745–751 & 158 762 (now formed into 3-car sets) have been fitted with Richmond seating.

ScotRail 158s 158 701–741 are "fitted" for RETB. When a unit arrives at Inverness the cab display unit is clipped on and plugged in. Similarly Arriva Trains Wales units have RETB plugged in at Shrewsbury for working the Cambrian Lines.

158 701	*	**FS**	P	*SR*	IS	52701	57701
158 702	*	**FS**	P	*SR*	IS	52702	57702
158 703	*	**FS**	P	*SR*	IS	52703	57703
158 704	*	**FS**	P	*SR*	IS	52704	57704
158 705	*	**FS**	P	*SR*	IS	52705	57705
158 706	*	**FS**	P	*SR*	IS	52706	57706
158 707	*	**FS**	P	*SR*	IS	52707	57707
158 708	*	**FS**	P	*SR*	IS	52708	57708
158 709	*	**FS**	P	*SR*	IS	52709	57709
158 710	*	**FS**	P	*SR*	IS	52710	57710
158 711	*	**FS**	P	*SR*	IS	52711	57711
158 712	*	**FS**	P	*SR*	IS	52712	57712
158 713	*	**FS**	P	*SR*	IS	52713	57713

158 714	*	**FS**	P	*SR*	IS	52714	57714	
158 715	*	**FS**	P	*SR*	IS	52715	57715	
158 716	*	**FS**	P	*SR*	IS	52716	57716	
158 717	*	**FS**	P	*SR*	IS	52717	57717	
158 718	*	**FS**	P	*SR*	IS	52718	57718	
158 719	*	**FS**	P	*SR*	IS	52719	57719	
158 720	*	**FS**	P	*SR*	IS	52720	57720	
158 721	*	**FS**	P	*SR*	IS	52721	57721	
158 722	*	**FS**	P	*SR*	IS	52722	57722	
158 723	*	**FS**	P	*SR*	IS	52723	57723	
158 724	*	**FS**	P	*SR*	IS	52724	57724	
158 725	*	**FS**	P	*SR*	IS	52725	57725	
158 726		**FS**	P	*SR*	HA	52726	57726	
158 727		**FS**	P	*SR*	HA	52727	57727	
158 728		**FS**	P	*SR*	HA	52728	57728	
158 729		**FS**	P	*SR*	HA	52729	57729	
158 730		**FS**	P	*SR*	HA	52730	57730	
158 731		**FS**	P	*SR*	HA	52731	57731	
158 732		**FS**	P	*SR*	HA	52732	57732	
158 733		**FS**	P	*SR*	HA	52733	57733	
158 734		**FS**	P	*SR*	HA	52734	57734	
158 735		**FS**	P	*SR*	HA	52735	57735	
158 736		**FS**	P	*SR*	HA	52736	57736	
158 738		**FS**	P	*SR*	HA	52738	57738	
158 739		**FS**	P	*SR*	HA	52739	57739	
158 740		**FS**	P	*SR*	HA	52740	57740	
158 741		**FS**	P	*SR*	HA	52741	57741	
158 752		**NO**	P	*NO*	NL	52752	58716	57752
158 753		**NO**	P	*NO*	NL	52753	58710	57753
158 754		**NO**	P	*NO*	NL	52754	58708	57754
158 755		**NO**	P	*NO*	NL	52755	58702	57755
158 756		**NO**	P	*NO*	NL	52756	58712	57756
158 757		**NO**	P	*NO*	NL	52757	58706	57757
158 758		**NO**	P	*NO*	NL	52758	58714	57758
158 759		**NO**	P	*NO*	NL	52759	58713	57759
158 763	w	**FI**	P	*GW*	PM	52763	57763	
158 766	w	**FI**	P	*GW*	PM	52766	57766	
158 770	†	**ST**	P	*EM*	NM	52770	57770	
158 773	†	**ST**	P	*EM*	NM	52773	57773	
158 774	†	**ST**	P	*EM*	NM	52774	57774	
158 777	†	**ST**	P	*EM*	NM	52777	57777	
158 780	†	**ST**	A	*EM*	NM	52780	57780	
158 782		**SR**	A	*SR*	HA	52782	57782	
158 783	†	**ST**	A	*EM*	NM	52783	57783	
158 784	t	**NO**	A	*NO*	NL	52784	57784	
158 785	†	**ST**	A	*EM*	NM	52785	57785	
158 786	u	**SR**	A	*SR*	HA	52786	57786	
158 787		**NO**	A	*NO*	NL	52787	57787	
158 788	†	**ST**	A	*EM*	NM	52788	57788	
158 789	u	**SR**	A	*SR*	HA	52789	57789	
158 790	t	**NO**	A	*NO*	NL	52790	57790	

158 791	t	**NO**	A	*NO*	NL	52791	57791	
158 792		**NO**	A	*NO*	NL	52792	57792	
158 793		**NO**	A	*NO*	NL	52793	57793	
158 794		**NO**	A	*NO*	NL	52794	57794	
158 795		**NO**	A	*NO*	NL	52795	57795	
158 796		**NO**	A	*NO*	NL	52796	57796	
158 797	t	**NO**	A	*NO*	NL	52797	57797	
158 798	w	**FI**	P	*GW*	PM	52798	58715	57798
158 799	†	**ST**	P	*EM*	NM	52799	57799	
158 806	†	**ST**	P	*EM*	NM	52806	57806	
158 810	†	**ST**	P	*EM*	NM	52810	57810	
158 812	†	**ST**	P	*EM*	NM	52812	57812	
158 813	†	**ST**	P	*EM*	NM	52813	57813	
158 815	c	**NO**	A	*NO*	NL	52815	57815	
158 816	c	**NO**	A	*NO*	NL	52816	57816	
158 817	c	**NO**	A	*NO*	NL	52817	57817	
158 818	ce	**AV**	A	*AW*	MN	52818	57818	
158 819	ce	**WB**	A	*AW*	MN	52819	57819	
158 820	es	**AB**	A	*AW*	MN	52820	57820	
158 821	es	**AB**	A	*AW*	MN	52821	57821	
158 822	es	**AB**	A	*AW*	MN	52822	57822	
158 823	ce	**AV**	A	*AW*	MN	52823	57823	
158 824	ce	**AV**	A	*AW*	MN	52824	57824	
158 825	ce	**WB**	A	*AW*	MN	52825	57825	
158 826	ce	**WB**	A	*AW*	MN	52826	57826	
158 827	es	**AB**	A	*AW*	MN	52827	57827	
158 828	es	**AB**	A	*AW*	MN	52828	57828	
158 829	ce	**AV**	A	*AW*	MN	52829	57829	
158 830	ce	**WB**	A	*AW*	MN	52830	57830	
158 831	ce	**WB**	A	*AW*	MN	52831	57831	
158 832	es	**AB**	A	*AW*	MN	52832	57832	
158 833	es	**AB**	A	*AW*	MN	52833	57833	
158 834	es	**AB**	A	*AW*	MN	52834	57834	
158 835	ce	**WB**	A	*AW*	MN	52835	57835	
158 836	ce	**WB**	A	*AW*	MN	52836	57836	
158 837	es	**AB**	A	*AW*	MN	52837	57837	
158 838	es	**AB**	A	*AW*	MN	52838	57838	
158 839	ce	**WB**	A	*AW*	MN	52839	57839	
158 840	es	**AB**	A	*AW*	MN	52840	57840	
158 841	ce	**WB**	A	*AW*	MN	52841	57841	
158 842	c	**NO**	A	*NO*	NL	52842	57842	
158 843	c	**NO**	A	*NO*	NL	52843	57843	
158 844	t	**NO**	A	*NO*	NL	52844	57844	
158 845	t	**NO**	A	*NO*	NL	52845	57845	
158 846	†	**ST**	A	*EM*	NM	52846	57846	
158 847	†	**ST**	A	*EM*	NM	52847	57847	
158 848	t	**NO**	A	*NO*	NL	52848	57848	
158 849	t	**NO**	A	*NO*	NL	52849	57849	
158 850	t	**NO**	A	*NO*	NL	52850	57850	
158 851	t	**NO**	A	*NO*	NL	52851	57851	
158 852	†	**ST**	A	*EM*	NM	52852	57852	

158 853	t	**NO**	A	*NO*	NL	52853	57853
158 854	†	**ST**	A	*EM*	NM	52854	57854
158 855		**NO**	A	*NO*	NL	52855	57855
158 856	†	**ST**	A	*EM*	NM	52856	57856
158 857	†	**ST**	A	*EM*	NM	52857	57857
158 858	†	**ST**	A	*EM*	NM	52858	57858
158 859		**NO**	A	*NO*	NL	52859	57859
158 860		**NO**	A	*NO*	NL	52860	57860
158 861		**NO**	A	*NO*	NL	52861	57861
158 862	†	**ST**	A	*EM*	NM	52862	57862
158 863	†	**ST**	A	*EM*	NM	52863	57863
158 864	†	**ST**	A	*EM*	NM	52864	57864
158 865	†	**ST**	A	*EM*	NM	52865	57865
158 866	†	**ST**	A	*EM*	NM	52866	57866
158 867	c	**SR**	A	*SR*	HA	52867	57867
158 868	c	**SR**	A	*SR*	HA	52868	57868
158 869	c	**SR**	A	*SR*	HA	52869	57869
158 870	c	**SR**	A	*SR*	HA	52870	57870
158 871	c	**SR**	A	*SR*	HA	52871	57871
158 872	c	**NO**	A	*NO*	NL	52872	57872

Names (ScotRail units carry their names on the unit ends):

158 702	BBC Scotland 75 years
158 707	Far North Line 125th ANNIVERSARY
158 715	Haymarket
158 720	Inverness & Nairn Railway – 150 years
158 784	Barbara Castle
158 791	County of Nottinghamshire
158 796	Fred Trueman Cricketing Legend
158 797	Jane Tomlinson
158 860	Ian Dewhirst

Class 158/8. Refurbished South West Trains units. Converted from former TransPennine Express units at Wabtec, Doncaster in 2007. 2+1 seating in First Class. Details as Class 158/0 except:

DMCL. Lot No. 31051 BREL Derby 1989–92. 13/44 1TD 1W. 38.5 t.
DMSL. Lot No. 31052 BREL Derby 1989–92. –/70 1T. 38.5 t.

158 880	(158 737)	**ST**	P	*SW*	SA	52737	57737
158 881	(158 742)	**ST**	P	*SW*	SA	52742	57742
158 882	(158 743)	**ST**	P	*SW*	SA	52743	57743
158 883	(158 744)	**ST**	P	*SW*	SA	52744	57744
158 884	(158 772)	**ST**	P	*SW*	SA	52772	57772
158 885	(158 775)	**ST**	P	*SW*	SA	52775	57775
158 886	(158 779)	**ST**	P	*SW*	SA	52779	57779
158 887	(158 781)	**ST**	P	*SW*	SA	52781	57781
158 888	(158 802)	**ST**	P	*SW*	SA	52802	57802
158 889	(158 808)	**ST**	P	*SW*	SA	52808	57808
158 890	(158 814)	**ST**	P	*SW*	SA	52814	57814

CLASS 158/9 BREL

DMSL–DMS. Units leased by West Yorkshire PTE but managed by Eversholt Rail. Details as Class 158/0 except for seating and toilets.

DMSL. Lot No. 31051 BREL Derby 1990–92. –/70 1TD 1W. 38.5 t.
DMS. Lot No. 31052 BREL Derby 1990–92. –/72 and parcels area. 38.5 t.

158 901	**NO**	E	*NO*	NL	52901	57901	
158 902	**NO**	E	*NO*	NL	52902	57902	
158 903	**NO**	E	*NO*	NL	52903	57903	
158 904	**NO**	E	*NO*	NL	52904	57904	
158 905	**NO**	E	*NO*	NL	52905	57905	
158 906	**NO**	E	*NO*	NL	52906	57906	
158 907	**NO**	E	*NO*	NL	52907	57907	
158 908	**NO**	E	*NO*	NL	52908	57908	
158 909	**NO**	E	*NO*	NL	52909	57909	
158 910	**NO**	E	*NO*	NL	52910	57910	William Wilberforce

CLASS 158/0 BREL

DMSL–DMSL–DMSL. Refurbished units reformed for First Great Western. For vehicle details see above. Formations can be flexible depending on when unit exams become due.

158 950	w	**FI**	P	*GW*	PM	57751	52761	57761
158 951	w	**FI**	P	*GW*	PM	52751	52764	57764
158 952	w	**FI**	P	*GW*	PM	57745	52762	57762
158 953	w	**FI**	P	*GW*	PM	52745	52750	57750
158 954	w	**FI**	P	*GW*	PM	57747	52760	57760
158 955	w	**FI**	P	*GW*	PM	52747	52765	57765
158 956	w	**FI**	P	*GW*	PM	52748	52768	57768
158 957	w	**FI**	P	*GW*	PM	57748	52771	57771
158 958	w	**FI**	P	*GW*	PM	57746	52776	57776
158 959	w	**FI**	P	*GW*	PM	52746	52778	57778
158 960	w	**FI**	P	*GW*	PM	57749	52769	57769
158 961	w	**FI**	P	*GW*	PM	52749	52767	57767

CLASS 159/0 BREL

DMCL–MSL–DMSL. Built as Class 158. Converted before entering passenger service to Class 159 by Rosyth Dockyard.

Construction: Welded aluminium.
Engines: One Cummins NTA855R of 300 kW (400 hp) at 2100 rpm.
Bogies: One BREL P4 (powered) and one BREL T4 (non-powered) per car.
Couplers: BSI.
Dimensions: 22.16 x 2.70 m.
Gangways: Throughout.
Doors: Twin-leaf swing plug.
Wheel Arrangement: 2-B + B-2 + B-2.
Maximum Speed: 90 mph.

Seating Layout: 1: 2+1 facing, 2: 2+2 facing/unidirectional.
Multiple Working: Within class and with Classes 142, 143, 144, 150, 153, 155, 156, 158 and 170.

DMCL. Lot No. 31051 BREL Derby 1992–93. 23/28 1TD 1W. 38.5 t.
MSL. Lot No. 31050 BREL Derby 1992–93. –/70(6) 1T. 38.5 t.
DMSL. Lot No. 31052 BREL Derby 1992–93. –/72 1T. 38.5 t.

159 001	**ST**	P	*SW*	SA	52873	58718	57873	CITY OF EXETER
159 002	**ST**	P	*SW*	SA	52874	58719	57874	CITY OF SALISBURY
159 003	**ST**	P	*SW*	SA	52875	58720	57875	TEMPLECOMBE
159 004	**ST**	P	*SW*	SA	52876	58721	57876	BASINGSTOKE AND DEANE
159 005	**ST**	P	*SW*	SA	52877	58722	57877	
159 006	**ST**	P	*SW*	SA	52878	58723	57878	
159 007	**ST**	P	*SW*	SA	52879	58724	57879	
159 008	**ST**	P	*SW*	SA	52880	58725	57880	
159 009	**ST**	P	*SW*	SA	52881	58726	57881	
159 010	**ST**	P	*SW*	SA	52882	58727	57882	
159 011	**ST**	P	*SW*	SA	52883	58728	57883	
159 012	**ST**	P	*SW*	SA	52884	58729	57884	
159 013	**ST**	P	*SW*	SA	52885	58730	57885	
159 014	**ST**	P	*SW*	SA	52886	58731	57886	
159 015	**ST**	P	*SW*	SA	52887	58732	57887	
159 016	**ST**	P	*SW*	SA	52888	58733	57888	
159 017	**ST**	P	*SW*	SA	52889	58734	57889	
159 018	**ST**	P	*SW*	SA	52890	58735	57890	
159 019	**ST**	P	*SW*	SA	52891	58736	57891	
159 020	**ST**	P	*SW*	SA	52892	58737	57892	
159 021	**ST**	P	*SW*	SA	52893	58738	57893	
159 022	**ST**	P	*SW*	SA	52894	58739	57894	

CLASS 159/1 BREL

DMCL–MSL–DMSL. Units converted from Class 158s at Wabtec, Doncaster in 2006–07 for South West Trains.

Details as Class 158/0 except:
Seating Layout: 1: 2+1 facing, 2: 2+2 facing/unidirectional.

DMCL. Lot No. 31051 BREL Derby 1989–92. 24/28 1TD 1W. 38.5 t.
MSL. Lot No. 31050 BREL Derby 1989–92. –/70 1T. 38.5 t.
DMSL. Lot No. 31052 BREL Derby 1989–92. –/72 1T.38.5 t.

159 101	(158 800)	**ST**	P	*SW*	SA	52800	58717	57800
159 102	(158 803)	**ST**	P	*SW*	SA	52803	58703	57803
159 103	(158 804)	**ST**	P	*SW*	SA	52804	58704	57804
159 104	(158 805)	**ST**	P	*SW*	SA	52805	58705	57805
159 105	(158 807)	**ST**	P	*SW*	SA	52807	58707	57807
159 106	(158 809)	**ST**	P	*SW*	SA	52809	58709	57809
159 107	(158 811)	**ST**	P	*SW*	SA	52811	58711	57811
159 108	(158 801)	**ST**	P	*SW*	SA	52801	58701	57801

CLASS 165/0 NETWORK TURBO BREL

DMSL–DMS and DMSL–MS–DMS. Chiltern Railways units. Refurbished 2003–05 with First Class seats removed and air conditioning fitted.
Construction: Welded aluminium.
Engines: One Perkins 2006-TWH of 260 kW (350 hp) at 1900 rpm.
Bogies: BREL P3-17 (powered), BREL T3-17 (non-powered).
Couplers: BSI.
Dimensions: 23.50/23.25 x 2.81 m.
Gangways: Within unit only.
Wheel Arrangement: 2-B (+ B-2) + B-2.
Doors: Twin-leaf swing plug.
Maximum Speed: 75 mph.
Seating Layout: 2+2/3+2 facing/unidirectional.
Multiple Working: Within class and with Classes 166, 168, 170 and 172.

Fitted with tripcocks for working over London Underground tracks between Harrow-on-the-Hill and Amersham.

58801–822/58873–878. DMSL. Lot No. 31087 BREL York 1990. –/82(7) 1T 2W. 40.1 t.
58823–833. DMSL. Lot No. 31089 BREL York 1991–92. –/82(7) 1T 2W. 40.1 t.
MS. Lot No. 31090 BREL York 1991–92. –/106. 37.0 t.
DMS. Lot No. 31088 BREL York 1991–92. –/94. 39.4 t.

165 001	**CR**	A	*CR*	AL	58801		58834
165 002	**CR**	A	*CR*	AL	58802		58835
165 003	**CR**	A	*CR*	AL	58803		58836
165 004	**CR**	A	*CR*	AL	58804		58837
165 005	**CR**	A	*CR*	AL	58805		58838
165 006	**CR**	A	*CR*	AL	58806		58839
165 007	**CR**	A	*CR*	AL	58807		58840
165 008	**CR**	A	*CR*	AL	58808		58841
165 009	**CR**	A	*CR*	AL	58809		58842
165 010	**CR**	A	*CR*	AL	58810		58843
165 011	**CR**	A	*CR*	AL	58811		58844
165 012	**CR**	A	*CR*	AL	58812		58845
165 013	**CR**	A	*CR*	AL	58813		58846
165 014	**CR**	A	*CR*	AL	58814		58847
165 015	**CR**	A	*CR*	AL	58815		58848
165 016	**CR**	A	*CR*	AL	58816		58849
165 017	**CR**	A	*CR*	AL	58817		58850
165 018	**CR**	A	*CR*	AL	58818		58851
165 019	**CR**	A	*CR*	AL	58819		58852
165 020	**CR**	A	*CR*	AL	58820		58853
165 021	**CR**	A	*CR*	AL	58821		58854
165 022	**CR**	A	*CR*	AL	58822		58855
165 023	**CR**	A	*CR*	AL	58873		58867
165 024	**CR**	A	*CR*	AL	58874		58868
165 025	**CR**	A	*CR*	AL	58875		58869
165 026	**CR**	A	*CR*	AL	58876		58870
165 027	**CR**	A	*CR*	AL	58877		58871
165 028	**CR**	A	*CR*	AL	58878		58872
165 029	**CR**	A	*CR*	AL	58823	55404	58856

165 030	**CR**	A	*CR*	AL	58824	55405	58857
165 031	**CR**	A	*CR*	AL	58825	55406	58858
165 032	**CR**	A	*CR*	AL	58826	55407	58859
165 033	**CR**	A	*CR*	AL	58827	55408	58860
165 034	**CR**	A	*CR*	AL	58828	55409	58861
165 035	**CR**	A	*CR*	AL	58829	55410	58862
165 036	**CR**	A	*CR*	AL	58830	55411	58863
165 037	**CR**	A	*CR*	AL	58831	55412	58864
165 038	**CR**	A	*CR*	AL	58832	55413	58865
165 039	**CR**	A	*CR*	AL	58833	55414	58866

CLASS 165/1 NETWORK TURBO BREL

First Great Western units. DMCL–MS–DMS or DMCL–DMS.

Construction: Welded aluminium.
Engines: One Perkins 2006-TWH of 260 kW (350 hp) at 1900 rpm.
Bogies: BREL P3-17 (powered), BREL T3-17 (non-powered).
Couplers: BSI.
Dimensions: 23.50/23.25 x 2.81 m.
Gangways: Within unit only. **Wheel Arrangement**: 2-B (+ B-2) + B-2.
Doors: Twin-leaf swing plug. **Maximum Speed**: 90 mph.
Seating Layout: 1: 2+2 facing, 2: 3+2 facing/unidirectional.
Multiple Working: Within class and with Classes 166, 168, 170 and 172.

58953–969. DMCL. Lot No. 31098 BREL York 1992. 16/66 1T. 38.0 t.
58879–898. DMCL. Lot No. 31096 BREL York 1992. 16/72 1T. 38.0 t.
MS. Lot No. 31099 BREL 1992. –/106. 37.0 t.
DMS. Lot No. 31097 BREL 1992. –/98. 37.0 t.

165 101	**FD**	A	*GW*	RG	58953	55415	58916
165 102	**FD**	A	*GW*	RG	58954	55416	58917
165 103	**FD**	A	*GW*	RG	58955	55417	58918
165 104	**FD**	A	*GW*	RG	58956	55418	58919
165 105	**FD**	A	*GW*	RG	58957	55419	58920
165 106	**FD**	A	*GW*	RG	58958	55420	58921
165 107	**FD**	A	*GW*	RG	58959	55421	58922
165 108	**FD**	A	*GW*	RG	58960	55422	58923
165 109	**FD**	A	*GW*	RG	58961	55423	58924
165 110	**FD**	A	*GW*	RG	58962	55424	58925
165 111	**FD**	A	*GW*	RG	58963	55425	58926
165 112	**FD**	A	*GW*	RG	58964	55426	58927
165 113	**FD**	A	*GW*	RG	58965	55427	58928
165 114	**FD**	A	*GW*	RG	58966	55428	58929
165 116	**FD**	A	*GW*	RG	58968	55430	58931
165 117	**FD**	A	*GW*	RG	58969	55431	58932
165 118	**FD**	A	*GW*	RG	58879		58933
165 119	**FD**	A	*GW*	RG	58880		58934
165 120	**FD**	A	*GW*	RG	58881		58935
165 121	**FD**	A	*GW*	RG	58882		58936
165 122	**FD**	A	*GW*	RG	58883		58937
165 123	**FD**	A	*GW*	RG	58884		58938

165 124	**FD**	A	*GW*	RG	58885	58939
165 125	**FD**	A	*GW*	RG	58886	58940
165 126	**FD**	A	*GW*	RG	58887	58941
165 127	**FD**	A	*GW*	RG	58888	58942
165 128	**FD**	A	*GW*	RG	58889	58943
165 129	**FD**	A	*GW*	RG	58890	58944
165 130	**FD**	A	*GW*	RG	58891	58945
165 131	**FD**	A	*GW*	RG	58892	58946
165 132	**FD**	A	*GW*	RG	58893	58947
165 133	**FD**	A	*GW*	RG	58894	58948
165 134	**FD**	A	*GW*	RG	58895	58949
165 135	**FD**	A	*GW*	RG	58896	58950
165 136	**FD**	A	*GW*	RG	58897	58951
165 137	**FD**	A	*GW*	RG	58898	58952

CLASS 166 NETWORK EXPRESS TURBO ABB

DMCL(A)–MS–DMCL(B). First Great Western units, built for Paddington–Oxford/Newbury services. Air conditioned and with additional luggage space compared to the Class 165s.

Construction: Welded aluminium.
Engines: One Perkins 2006-TWH of 260 kW (350 hp) at 1900 rpm.
Bogies: BREL P3-17 (powered), BREL T3-17 (non-powered).
Couplers: BSI.
Dimensions: 23.50 x 2.81 m.
Gangways: Within unit only. **Wheel Arrangement:** 2-B + B-2 + B-2.
Doors: Twin-leaf swing plug. **Maximum Speed:** 90 mph.
Seating Layout: 1: 2+2 facing, 2: 2+2/3+2 facing/unidirectional.
Multiple Working: Within class and with Classes 165, 168, 170 and 172.

DMCL (A). Lot No. 31116 ABB York 1992–93. 16/68 1T. 39.6 t.
MS. Lot No. 31117 ABB York 1992–93. –/91. 38.0 t.
DMCL (B). Lot No. 31116 ABB York 1992–93. 16/68 1T. 39.6 t.

166 201	**FD**	A	*GW*	RG	58101	58601	58122
166 202	**FD**	A	*GW*	RG	58102	58602	58123
166 203	**FD**	A	*GW*	RG	58103	58603	58124
166 204	**FD**	A	*GW*	RG	58104	58604	58125
166 205	**FD**	A	*GW*	RG	58105	58605	58126
166 206	**FD**	A	*GW*	RG	58106	58606	58127
166 207	**FD**	A	*GW*	RG	58107	58607	58128
166 208	**FD**	A	*GW*	RG	58108	58608	58129
166 209	**FD**	A	*GW*	RG	58109	58609	58130
166 210	**FD**	A	*GW*	RG	58110	58610	58131
166 211	**FD**	A	*GW*	RG	58111	58611	58132
166 212	**FD**	A	*GW*	RG	58112	58612	58133
166 213	**FD**	A	*GW*	RG	58113	58613	58134
166 214	**FD**	A	*GW*	RG	58114	58614	58135
166 215	**FD**	A	*GW*	RG	58115	58615	58136
166 216	**FD**	A	*GW*	RG	58116	58616	58137
166 217	**FD**	A	*GW*	RG	58117	58617	58138

166 218	**FD**	A	*GW*	RG	58118	58618	58139
166 219	**FD**	A	*GW*	RG	58119	58619	58140
166 220	**FD**	A	*GW*	RG	58120	58620	58141
166 221	**FD**	A	*GW*	RG	58121	58621	58142

CLASS 168 CLUBMAN ADTRANZ/BOMBARDIER

Air conditioned.

Construction: Welded aluminium bodies with bolt-on steel ends.
Engines: One MTU 6R183TD13H of 315 kW (422 hp) at 1900 rpm.
Transmission: Hydraulic. Voith T211rzze to ZF final drive.
Bogies: One Adtranz P3–23 and one BREL T3–23 per car.
Couplers: BSI at outer ends, bar within unit.
Dimensions: Class 168/0: 24.1/23.61 x 2.69 m. Others: 23.62/23.61 x 2.69 m.
Gangways: Within unit only. **Wheel Arrangement:** 2-B (+ B-2 + B-2) + B-2.
Doors: Twin-leaf swing plug. **Maximum Speed:** 100 mph.
Seating Layout: 2+2 facing/unidirectional.
Multiple Working: Within class and with Classes 165 and 166.

Fitted with tripcocks for working over London Underground tracks between Harrow-on-the-Hill and Amersham.

Class 168/0. Original Design. DMSL(A)–MS–MSL–DMSL(B) or DMSL(A)–MSL–MS–DMSL(B).

58151–155. DMSL(A). Adtranz Derby 1997–98. –/57 1TD 1W. 44.0 t.
58651–655. MSL. Adtranz Derby 1998. –/73 1T. 41.0 t.
58451–455. MS. Adtranz Derby 1998. –/77. 41.0 t.
58251–255. DMSL(B). Adtranz Derby 1998. –/68 1T. 43.6 t.

Note: 58451–455 were numbered 58656–660 for a time when used in 168 106–110.

168 001	**CR**	P	*CR*	AL	58151	58451	58651	58251
168 002	**CR**	P	*CR*	AL	58152	58652	58452	58252
168 003	**CR**	P	*CR*	AL	58153	58653	58453	58253
168 004	**CR**	P	*CR*	AL	58154	58654	58454	58254
168 005	**CR**	P	*CR*	AL	58155	58655	58455	58255

Class 168/1. These units are effectively Class 170s. DMSL(A)–MSL–MS–DMSL(B) or DMSL(A)–MS–DMSL(B).

58156–163. DMSL(A). Adtranz Derby 2000. –/57 1TD 2W. 45.2 t.
58456–460. MS. Bombardier Derby 2002. –/76. 41.8 t.
58756–757. MSL. Bombardier Derby 2002. –/73 1T. 42.9 t.
58461–463. MS. Adtranz Derby 2000. –/76. 42.4 t.
58256–263. DMSL(B). Adtranz Derby 2000. –/69 1T. 45.2 t.

Notes: 58461–463 have been renumbered from 58661–663.

168 106	**CR**	P	*CR*	AL	58156	58456	58756	58256
168 107	**CR**	P	*CR*	AL	58157	58757	58457	58257
168 108	**CR**	P	*CR*	AL	58158		58458	58258
168 109	**CR**	P	*CR*	AL	58159		58459	58259
168 110	**CR**	P	*CR*	AL	58160		58460	58260

168 111	**CR**	E	*CR*	AL	58161		58461	58261
168 112	**CR**	E	*CR*	AL	58162		58462	58262
168 113	**CR**	E	*CR*	AL	58163		58463	58263

Class 168/2. These units are effectively Class 170s. DMSL(A)–(MS)–MS–DMSL(B).

58164–169. DMSL(A). Bombardier Derby 2003–04. –/57 1TD 2W. 45.4 t.
58365–367. MS. Bombardier Derby 2006. –/76. 43.3 t.
58464/468/469. MS. Bombardier Derby 2003–04. –/76. 44.0 t.
58465–467. MS. Bombardier Derby 2006. –/76. 43.3 t.
58264–269. DMSL(B). Bombardier Derby 2003–04. –/69 1T. 45.5 t.

168 214	**CR**	P	*CR*	AL	58164		58464	58264
168 215	**CR**	P	*CR*	AL	58165	58365	58465	58265
168 216	**CR**	P	*CR*	AL	58166	58366	58466	58266
168 217	**CR**	P	*CR*	AL	58167	58367	58467	58267
168 218	**CR**	P	*CR*	AL	58168		58468	58268
168 219	**CR**	P	*CR*	AL	58169		58469	58269

CLASS 170 TURBOSTAR ADTRANZ/BOMBARDIER

Various formations. Air conditioned.

Construction: Welded aluminium bodies with bolt-on steel ends.
Engines: One MTU 6R183TD13H of 315 kW (422 hp) at 1900 rpm.
Transmission: Hydraulic. Voith T211rzze to ZF final drive.
Bogies: One Adtranz P3–23 and one BREL T3–23 per car.
Couplers: BSI at outer ends, bar within later build units.
Dimensions: 23.62/23.61 x 2.69 m.
Gangways: Within unit only.
Wheel Arrangement: 2-B (+ B-2) + B-2.
Doors: Twin-leaf sliding plug.
Maximum Speed: 100 mph.
Seating Layout: 1: 2+1 facing/unidirectional. 2: 2+2 unidirectional/facing.
Multiple Working: Within class and with Classes 150, 153, 155, 156, 158, 159 and 172.

Class 170/1. CrossCountry (former Midland Mainline) units. Lazareni seating. DMSL–MS–DMCL/DMSL–DMCL.

DMSL. Adtranz Derby 1998–99. –/59 1TD 2W. 45.0 t.
MS. Adtranz Derby 2001. –/80. 43.0 t.
DMCL. Adtranz Derby 1998–99. 9/52 1T. 44.8 t

170 101	**XC**	P	*XC*	TS	50101	55101	79101
170 102	**XC**	P	*XC*	TS	50102	55102	79102
170 103	**XC**	P	*XC*	TS	50103	55103	79103
170 104	**XC**	P	*XC*	TS	50104	55104	79104
170 105	**XC**	P	*XC*	TS	50105	55105	79105
170 106	**XC**	P	*XC*	TS	50106	55106	79106
170 107	**XC**	P	*XC*	TS	50107	55107	79107
170 108	**XC**	P	*XC*	TS	50108	55108	79108
170 109	**XC**	P	*XC*	TS	50109	55109	79109
170 110	**XC**	P	*XC*	TS	50110	55110	79110

170 111	**XC**	P	*XC*	TS	50111		79111
170 112	**XC**	P	*XC*	TS	50112		79112
170 113	**XC**	P	*XC*	TS	50113		79113
170 114	**XC**	P	*XC*	TS	50114		79114
170 115	**XC**	P	*XC*	TS	50115		79115
170 116	**XC**	P	*XC*	TS	50116		79116
170 117	**XC**	P	*XC*	TS	50117		79117

Class 170/2. National Express East Anglia 3-car units. Chapman seating. DMCL–MSL–DMSL.

DMCL. Adtranz Derby 1999. 7/39 1TD 2W. 45.0 t.
MSL. Adtranz Derby 1999. –/68 1T. Guard's office. 45.3 t.
DMSL. Adtranz Derby 1999. –/66 1T. 43.4 t.

170 201	r	**1**	P	*EA*	NC	50201	56201	79201
170 202	r	**1**	P	*EA*	NC	50202	56202	79202
170 203	r	**1**	P	*EA*	NC	50203	56203	79203
170 204	r	**1**	P	*EA*	NC	50204	56204	79204
170 205	r	**1**	P	*EA*	NC	50205	56205	79205
170 206	r	**1**	P	*EA*	NC	50206	56206	79206
170 207	r	**1**	P	*EA*	NC	50207	56207	79207
170 208	r	**1**	P	*EA*	NC	50208	56208	79208

Class 170/2. National Express East Anglia 2-car units. Chapman seating. DMSL–DMCL.

DMSL. Bombardier Derby 2002. –/57 1TD 2W. 45.7 t.
DMCL. Bombardier Derby 2002. 9/53 1T. 45.7 t.

170 270	r	**1**	P	*EA*	NC	50270	79270
170 271	r	**AN**	P	*EA*	NC	50271	79271
170 272	r	**AN**	P	*EA*	NC	50272	79272
170 273	r	**AN**	P	*EA*	NC	50273	79273

Class 170/3. TransPennine Express units. Chapman seating. DMCL–DMSL. 170 309 renumbered from 170 399.

50301–308/399. DMCL. Adtranz Derby 2000–01. 8/43 1TD 2W. 45.8 t.
79301–308/399. DMSL. Adtranz Derby 2000–01. –/65 1T. 45.8 t.

170 301	**FT**	P	*TP*	XW	50301	79301
170 302	**FT**	P	*TP*	XW	50302	79302
170 303	**FT**	P	*TP*	XW	50303	79303
170 304	**FT**	P	*TP*	XW	50304	79304
170 305	**FT**	P	*TP*	XW	50305	79305
170 306	**FT**	P	*TP*	XW	50306	79306
170 307	**FT**	P	*TP*	XW	50307	79307
170 308	**FT**	P	*TP*	XW	50308	79308
170 309	**FT**	P	*TP*	XW	50399	79399

Class 170/3. Units built for Hull Trains, now in use with ScotRail. Chapman seating. DMCL–MSLRB–DMSL.

DMCL. Bombardier Derby 2004. 7/41 1TD 2W. 46.5 t.
MSLRB. Bombardier Derby 2004. –/57 1T. Buffet and guard's office 44.7 t.

DMSL. Bombardier Derby 2004. –/67 1T. 47.0 t.

170 393	**FS**	P	*SR*	HA	50393	56393	79393
170 394	**FS**	P	*SR*	HA	50394	56394	79394
170 395	**FS**	P	*SR*	HA	50395	56395	79395
170 396	**FS**	P	*SR*	HA	50396	56396	79396

Class 170/3. CrossCountry units. Lazareni seating. DMSL–MS–DMCL.

DMSL. Bombardier Derby 2002. –/59 1TD 2W. 45.4 t.
MS. Bombardier Derby 2002. –/80. 43.0 t.
DMCL. Bombardier Derby 2002. 9/52 1T. 45.8 t.

170 397	**XC**	P	*XC*	TS	50397	56397	79397
170 398	**XC**	P	*XC*	TS	50398	56398	79398

Class 170/4. ScotRail "express" units. Chapman seating. DMCL–MS–DMCL.

DMCL(A). Adtranz Derby 1999–2001. 9/43 1TD 2W. 45.2 t.
MS. Adtranz Derby 1999–2001. –/76. 42.5 t.
DMCL(B). Adtranz Derby 1999–2001. 9/49 1T. 45.2 t.

170 401	**FS**	P	*SR*	HA	50401	56401	79401
170 402	**FS**	P	*SR*	HA	50402	56402	79402
170 403	**FS**	P	*SR*	HA	50403	56403	79403
170 404	**FS**	P	*SR*	HA	50404	56404	79404
170 405	**FS**	P	*SR*	HA	50405	56405	79405
170 406	**FS**	P	*SR*	HA	50406	56406	79406
170 407	**FS**	P	*SR*	HA	50407	56407	79407
170 408	**FS**	P	*SR*	HA	50408	56408	79408
170 409	**FS**	P	*SR*	HA	50409	56409	79409
170 410	**FS**	P	*SR*	HA	50410	56410	79410
170 411	**FS**	P	*SR*	HA	50411	56411	79411
170 412	**FS**	P	*SR*	HA	50412	56412	79412
170 413	**FS**	P	*SR*	HA	50413	56413	79413
170 414	**FS**	P	*SR*	HA	50414	56414	79414
170 415	**FS**	P	*SR*	HA	50415	56415	79415
170 416	**FS**	E	*SR*	HA	50416	56416	79416
170 417	**FS**	E	*SR*	HA	50417	56417	79417
170 418	**FS**	E	*SR*	HA	50418	56418	79418
170 419	**FS**	E	*SR*	HA	50419	56419	79419
170 420	**FS**	E	*SR*	HA	50420	56420	79420
170 421	**FS**	E	*SR*	HA	50421	56421	79421
170 422	**FS**	E	*SR*	HA	50422	56422	79422
170 423	**FS**	E	*SR*	HA	50423	56423	79423
170 424	**FS**	E	*SR*	HA	50424	56424	79424

Names (carried on end cars):

170 401	Sir Moir Lockhead OBE
170 405	Riverside Museum
170 407	UNIVERSITY OF ABERDEEN

Class 170/4. ScotRail "express" units. Chapman seating. DMCL–MS–DMCL.

DMCL. Bombardier Derby 2003–05. 9/43 1TD 2W. 46.8 t.
MS. Bombardier Derby 2003–05. –/76. 43.7 t.
DMCL. Bombardier Derby 2003–05. 9/49 1T. 46.5 t.

Note: * 170 431 & 170 432 have new uprated engines fitted: MTU 6H1800R83 of 360 kW (483 hp) at 1800 rpm.

170 425		**SR**	P	*SR*	HA	50425	56425	79425	
170 426		**SR**	P	*SR*	HA	50426	56426	79426	
170 427		**FS**	P	*SR*	HA	50427	56427	79427	
170 428		**FS**	P	*SR*	HA	50428	56428	79428	
170 429		**FS**	P	*SR*	HA	50429	56429	79429	
170 430		**FS**	P	*SR*	HA	50430	56430	79430	
170 431	*	**FS**	P	*SR*	HA	50431	56431	79431	
170 432	*	**FS**	P	*SR*	HA	50432	56432	79432	
170 433		**FS**	P	*SR*	HA	50433	56433	79433	Investor in People
170 434		**SR**	P	*SR*	HA	50434	56434	79434	

Class 170/4. ScotRail units. Originally built as Standard Class only units. 170 450–457 have been retro-fitted with First Class. Chapman seating. DMSL–MS–DMSL or † DMCL–MS–DMCL.

DMSL. Bombardier Derby 2004–05. –/55 1TD 2W († 9/47 1TD 2W). 46.3 t.
MS. Bombardier Derby 2004–05. –/76. 43.4 t.
DMSL. Bombardier Derby 2004–05. –/67 1T († 9/49 1T 1W). 46.4 t.

170 450	†	**FS**	P	*SR*	HA	50450	56450	79450
170 451	†	**FS**	P	*SR*	HA	50451	56451	79451
170 452	†	**FS**	P	*SR*	HA	50452	56452	79452
170 453	†	**FS**	P	*SR*	HA	50453	56453	79453
170 454	†	**FS**	P	*SR*	HA	50454	56454	79454
170 455	†	**FS**	P	*SR*	HA	50455	56455	79455
170 456	†	**FS**	P	*SR*	HA	50456	56456	79456
170 457	†	**FS**	P	*SR*	HA	50457	56457	79457
170 458		**FS**	P	*SR*	HA	50458	56458	79458
170 459		**FS**	P	*SR*	HA	50459	56459	79459
170 460		**FS**	P	*SR*	HA	50460	56460	79460
170 461		**FS**	P	*SR*	HA	50461	56461	79461

Class 170/4. ScotRail units. Standard Class only units. Chapman seating. DMSL–MS–DMSL.

50470–471. DMSL(A). Adtranz Derby 2001. –/55 1TD 2W. 45.1 t.
50472–478. DMSL(A). Bombardier Derby 2004–05. –/57 1TD 2W. 46.3 t.
56470–471. MS. Adtranz Derby 2001. –/76. 42.4 t.
56472–478. MS. Bombardier Derby 2004–05. –/76. 43.4 t.
79470–471. DMSL(B). Adtranz Derby 2001. –/67 1T. 45.1 t.
79472–478. DMSL(B). Bombardier Derby 2004–05. –/67 1T. 46.4 t.

170 470	**SR**	P	*SR*	HA	50470	56470	79470
170 471	**SR**	P	*SR*	HA	50471	56471	79471
170 472	**SP**	P	*SR*	HA	50472	56472	79472
170 473	**SP**	P	*SR*	HA	50473	56473	79473

170 474		**SP**	P	*SR*	HA	50474	56474	79474
170 475		**SP**	P	*SR*	HA	50475	56475	79475
170 476		**SP**	P	*SR*	HA	50476	56476	79476
170 477		**SP**	P	*SR*	HA	50477	56477	79477
170 478		**SP**	P	*SR*	HA	50478	56478	79478

Class 170/5. London Midland and CrossCountry 2-car units. Lazareni seating. DMSL–DMSL or * DMSL–DMCL (CrossCountry).

DMSL(A). Adtranz Derby 1999–2000. –/55 1TD 2W (* –/59 1TD 2W). 45.8 t.
DMSL(B). Adtranz Derby 1999–2000. –/67 1T (* DMCL 9/52 1T). 45.9 t.

170 501		**LM**	P	*LM*	TS	50501	79501
170 502		**LM**	P	*LM*	TS	50502	79502
170 503		**LM**	P	*LM*	TS	50503	79503
170 504		**LM**	P	*LM*	TS	50504	79504
170 505		**LM**	P	*LM*	TS	50505	79505
170 506		**LM**	P	*LM*	TS	50506	79506
170 507		**LM**	P	*LM*	TS	50507	79507
170 508		**LM**	P	*LM*	TS	50508	79508
170 509		**LM**	P	*LM*	TS	50509	79509
170 510		**LM**	P	*LM*	TS	50510	79510
170 511		**LM**	P	*LM*	TS	50511	79511
170 512		**LM**	P	*LM*	TS	50512	79512
170 513		**LM**	P	*LM*	TS	50513	79513
170 514		**LM**	P	*LM*	TS	50514	79514
170 515		**LM**	P	*LM*	TS	50515	79515
170 516		**LM**	P	*LM*	TS	50516	79516
170 517		**LM**	P	*LM*	TS	50517	79517
170 518	*	**XC**	P	*XC*	TS	50518	79518
170 519	*	**XC**	P	*XC*	TS	50519	79519
170 520	*	**XC**	P	*XC*	TS	50520	79520
170 521	*	**XC**	P	*XC*	TS	50521	79521
170 522	*	**XC**	P	*XC*	TS	50522	79522
170 523	*	**XC**	P	*XC*	TS	50523	79523

Class 170/6. London Midland and CrossCountry 3-car units. Lazareni seating. DMSL–MS–DMSL or * DMSL–MS–DMCL (CrossCountry).

DMSL(A). Adtranz Derby 2000. –/55 1TD 2W (* –/59 1TD 2W). 45.8 t.
MS. Adtranz Derby 2000. –/74 (* –/80). 42.4 t.
DMSL(B). Adtranz Derby 2000. –/67 1T (* DMCL 9/52 1T). 45.9 t.

170 630		**LM**	P	*LM*	TS	50630	56630	79630
170 631		**LM**	P	*LM*	TS	50631	56631	79631
170 632		**LM**	P	*LM*	TS	50632	56632	79632
170 633		**LM**	P	*LM*	TS	50633	56633	79633
170 634		**LM**	P	*LM*	TS	50634	56634	79634
170 635		**LM**	P	*LM*	TS	50635	56635	79635
170 636	*	**XC**	P	*XC*	TS	50636	56636	79636
170 637	*	**XC**	P	*XC*	TS	50637	56637	79637
170 638	*	**XC**	P	*XC*	TS	50638	56638	79638
170 639	*	**XC**	P	*XC*	TS	50639	56639	79639

CLASS 171 TURBOSTAR BOMBARDIER

DMCL–DMSL or DMCL–MS–MS–DMCL. Southern units. Air conditioned. Chapman seating.

Construction: Welded aluminium bodies with bolt-on steel ends.
Engines: One MTU 6R183TD13H of 315 kW (422 hp) at 1900 rpm.
Transmission: Hydraulic. Voith T211rzze to ZF final drive.
Bogies: One Adtranz P3–23 and one BREL T3–23 per car.
Couplers: Dellner 12 at outer ends, bar within unit (Class 171/8s).
Dimensions: 23.62/23.61 x 2.69 m.
Gangways: Within unit only. **Wheel Arrangement:** 2-B (+ B-2 + B-2) + B-2.
Doors: Twin-leaf swing plug. **Maximum Speed:** 100 mph.
Seating Layout: 1: 2+1 facing/unidirectional. 2: 2+2 facing/unidirectional.
Multiple Working: Within class and with EMU Classes 375 and 377 in an emergency.

Class 171/7. 2-car units. DMCL–DMSL.

50721–726. DMCL. Bombardier Derby 2003. 9/43 1TD 2W. 47.6 t.
50727–729. DMCL. Bombardier Derby 2005. 9/43 1TD 2W. 46.3 t.
50392. DMCL. Bombardier Derby 2003. 9/43 1TD 2W. 46.6 t.
79721–726. DMSL. Bombardier Derby 2003. –/64 1T. 47.8 t.
79727–729. DMSL. Bombardier Derby 2005. –/64 1T. 46.2 t.
79392. DMSL. Bombardier Derby 2003. –/64 1T. 46.5 t.

Notes: 171 721–726 were built as Class 170s (170 721–726), but renumbered as Class 171s on fitting with Dellner couplers.
171 730 was formerly South West Trains unit 170 392, before transferring to Southern in 2007.

171 721	**SN**	P	*SN*	SU	50721	79721
171 722	**SN**	P	*SN*	SU	50722	79722
171 723	**SN**	P	*SN*	SU	50723	79723
171 724	**SN**	P	*SN*	SU	50724	79724
171 725	**SN**	P	*SN*	SU	50725	79725
171 726	**SN**	P	*SN*	SU	50726	79726
171 727	**SN**	P	*SN*	SU	50727	79727
171 728	**SN**	P	*SN*	SU	50728	79728
171 729	**SN**	P	*SN*	SU	50729	79729
171 730	**SN**	P	*SN*	SU	50392	79392

Class 171/8. 4-car units. DMCL(A)–MS–MS–DMCL(B).

DMCL(A). Bombardier Derby 2004. 9/43 1TD 2W. 46.5 t.
MS. Bombardier Derby 2004. –/74. 43.7 t.
DMCL(B). Bombardier Derby 2004. 9/50 1T. 46.5 t.

171 801	**SN**	P	*SN*	SU	50801	54801	56801	79801
171 802	**SN**	P	*SN*	SU	50802	54802	56802	79802
171 803	**SN**	P	*SN*	SU	50803	54803	56803	79803
171 804	**SN**	P	*SN*	SU	50804	54804	56804	79804
171 805	**SN**	P	*SN*	SU	50805	54805	56805	79805
171 806	**SN**	P	*SN*	SU	50806	54806	56806	79806

CLASS 172 TURBOSTAR BOMBARDIER

New generation London Overground, Chiltern Railways and London Midland Turbostars. Air conditioned.

Construction: Welded aluminium bodies with bolt-on steel ends.
Engines: One MTU 6H1800R83 of 360 kW (483 hp) at 1800 rpm.
Transmission: Mechanical. Supplied by ZF, Germany.
Bogies: B5006 type "lightweight" bogies.
Couplers: BSI at outer ends, bar within unit.
Dimensions: 23.62/23.0 x 2.69 m.
Gangways: London Overground & Chiltern units: Within unit only. London Midland units: Throughout.
Wheel Arrangement: 2-B (+ B-2) + B-2.
Doors: Twin-leaf sliding plug.
Maximum Speed: 100 mph (London Overground units 75 mph).
Seating Layout: 2+2 facing/unidirectional.
Multiple Working: Within class and with Classes 150, 153, 155, 156, 158, 159, 165, 166 and 170.

Class 172/0. London Overground units. Used on the Gospel Oak–Barking line. DMS–DMS.

59311–318. DMS(W). Bombardier Derby 2009–10. –/60 2W. 41.6 t.
59411–418. DMS. Bombardier Derby 2009–10. –/64. 41.5 t.

172 001	**LO**	A	*LO*	WN	59311	59411
172 002	**LO**	A	*LO*	WN	59312	59412
172 003	**LO**	A	*LO*	WN	59313	59413
172 004	**LO**	A	*LO*	WN	59314	59414
172 005	**LO**	A	*LO*	WN	59315	59415
172 006	**LO**	A	*LO*	WN	59316	59416
172 007	**LO**	A	*LO*	WN	59317	59417
172 008	**LO**	A	*LO*	WN	59318	59418

Class 172/1. Chiltern Railways units. DMSL–DMS.

59111–114. DMSL. Bombardier Derby 2009–10. –/60(5) 1TD 2W. 42.4 t.
59211–214. DMS. Bombardier Derby 2009–10. –/80. 41.8 t.

172 101	**CR**	A	*CR*	AL	59111	59211
172 102	**CR**	A	*CR*	AL	59112	59212
172 103	**CR**	A	*CR*	AL	59113	59213
172 104	**CR**	A	*CR*	AL	59114	59214

Class 172/2. London Midland 2-car units. DMSL–DMS. Used on local services via Birmingham Snow Hill.

50211–222. DMSL. Bombardier Derby 2010–11. –/52(11) 1TD 2W. 42.5 t.
79211–222. DMS. Bombardier Derby 2010–11. –/68(8). 41.9 t.

172 211	**LM**	P	*LM*	TS	50211	79211
172 212	**LM**	P	*LM*	TS	50212	79212
172 213	**LM**	P	*LM*	TS	50213	79213
172 214	**LM**	P	*LM*	TS	50214	79214

172 215	**LM**	P	*LM*	TS	50215		79215
172 216	**LM**	P	*LM*	TS	50216		79216
172 217	**LM**	P	*LM*	TS	50217		79217
172 218	**LM**	P	*LM*	TS	50218		79218
172 219	**LM**	P	*LM*	TS	50219		79219
172 220	**LM**	P	*LM*	TS	50220		79220
172 221	**LM**	P	*LM*	TS	50221		79221
172 222	**LM**	P	*LM*	TS	50222		79222

Class 172/3. London Midland 3-car units. DMSL–MS–DMS. Used on local services via Birmingham Snow Hill.

50331–345. DMSL. Bombardier Derby 2010–11. –/52(11) 1TD 2W. 42.5 t.
56331–345. MS. Bombardier Derby 2010–11. –/72(8). 38.8 t.
79331–345. DMS. Bombardier Derby 2010–11. –/68(8). 41.9 t.

172 331	**LM**	P	*LM*	TS	50331	56331	79331
172 332	**LM**	P	*LM*	TS	50332	56332	79332
172 333	**LM**	P	*LM*	TS	50333	56333	79333
172 334	**LM**	P	*LM*	TS	50334	56334	79334
172 335	**LM**	P	*LM*	TS	50335	56335	79335
172 336	**LM**	P	*LM*	TS	50336	56336	79336
172 337	**LM**	P	*LM*	TS	50337	56337	79337
172 338	**LM**	P	*LM*	TS	50338	56338	79338
172 339	**LM**	P	*LM*	TS	50339	56339	79339
172 340	**LM**	P	*LM*	TS	50340	56340	79340
172 341	**LM**	P	*LM*	TS	50341	56341	79341
172 342	**LM**	P	*LM*	TS	50342	56342	79342
172 343	**LM**	P	*LM*	TS	50343	56343	79343
172 344	**LM**	P	*LM*	TS	50344	56344	79344
172 345	**LM**	P	*LM*	TS	50345	56345	79345

CLASS 175 CORADIA 1000 ALSTOM

Air conditioned.

Construction: Steel.
Engines: One Cummins N14 of 335 kW (450 hp).
Transmission: Hydraulic. Voith T211rzze to ZF Voith final drive.
Bogies: ACR (Alstom FBO) – LTB-MBS1, TB-MB1, MBS1-LTB.
Couplers: Scharfenberg outer ends and bar within unit (Class 175/1).
Dimensions: 23.7 x 2.73 m.
Gangways: Within unit only.
Doors: Single-leaf swing plug.
Wheel Arrangement: 2-B (+ B-2) + B-2.
Maximum Speed: 100 mph.
Seating Layout: 2+2 facing/unidirectional.
Multiple Working: Within class and with Class 180.

Class 175/0. DMSL–DMSL. 2-car units.

DMSL(A). Alstom Birmingham 1999–2000. –/54 1TD 2W. 48.8 t.
DMSL(B). Alstom Birmingham 1999–2000. –/64 1T. 50.7 t.

175 001	**AV**	A	*AW*	CH	50701	79701
175 002	**AV**	A	*AW*	CH	50702	79702
175 003	**AV**	A	*AW*	CH	50703	79703
175 004	**AV**	A	*AW*	CH	50704	79704
175 005	**AV**	A	*AW*	CH	50705	79705
175 006	**AV**	A	*AW*	CH	50706	79706
175 007	**AV**	A	*AW*	CH	50707	79707
175 008	**AV**	A	*AW*	CH	50708	79708
175 009	**AV**	A	*AW*	CH	50709	79709
175 010	**AV**	A	*AW*	CH	50710	79710
175 011	**AV**	A	*AW*	CH	50711	79711

Class 175/1. DMSL–MSL–DMSL. 3-car units.

DMSL(A). Alstom Birmingham 1999–2001. –/54 1TD 2W. 50.7 t.
MSL. Alstom Birmingham 1999–2001. –/68 1T. 47.5 t.
DMSL(B). Alstom Birmingham 1999–2001. –/64 1T. 49.5 t.

175 101	**AV**	A	*AW*	CH	50751	56751	79751
175 102	**AV**	A	*AW*	CH	50752	56752	79752
175 103	**AV**	A	*AW*	CH	50753	56753	79753
175 104	**AV**	A	*AW*	CH	50754	56754	79754
175 105	**AV**	A	*AW*	CH	50755	56755	79755
175 106	**AV**	A	*AW*	CH	50756	56756	79756
175 107	**AV**	A	*AW*	CH	50757	56757	79757
175 108	**AV**	A	*AW*	CH	50758	56758	79758
175 109	**AV**	A	*AW*	CH	50759	56759	79759
175 110	**AV**	A	*AW*	CH	50760	56760	79760
175 111	**AV**	A	*AW*	CH	50761	56761	79761
175 112	**AV**	A	*AW*	CH	50762	56762	79762
175 113	**AV**	A	*AW*	CH	50763	56763	79763
175 114	**AV**	A	*AW*	CH	50764	56764	79764
175 115	**AV**	A	*AW*	CH	50765	56765	79765
175 116	**AV**	A	*AW*	CH	50766	56766	79766

CLASS 180 ADELANTE ALSTOM

Air conditioned.

Construction: Steel.
Engines: One Cummins QSK19 of 560 kW (750 hp) at 2100 rpm.
Transmission: Hydraulic. Voith T312br to Voith final drive.
Bogies: ACR (Alstom FBO): LTB1-MBS2, TB1-MB2, TB1-MB2, TB2-MB2, MBS2-LTB1.
Couplers: Scharfenberg outer ends, bar within unit.
Dimensions: 23.71/23.03 x 2.73 m.
Gangways: Within unit only.
Wheel Arrangement: 2-B + B-2 + B-2 + B-2 + B-2.
Doors: Single-leaf swing plug. **Maximum Speed:** 125 mph.
Seating Layout: 1: 2+1 facing/unidirectional, 2: 2+2 facing/unidirectional.
Multiple Working: Within class and with Class 175.

DMSL(A). Alstom Birmingham 2000–01. –/46 2W 1TD. 51.7 t.
MFL. Alstom Birmingham 2000–01. 42/– 1T 1W + catering point. 49.6 t.
MSL. Alstom Birmingham 2000–01. –/68 1T. 49.5 t.
MSLRB. Alstom Birmingham 2000–01. –/56 1T. 50.3 t.
DMSL(B). Alstom Birmingham 2000–01. –/56 1T. 51.4 t.

Note: Five units, 180 102–104/106/108, are to be used by First Great Western on Cotswold Line services from summer 2012. At the time of writing 180 102 is being used by Grand Central on a short-term basis.

180 101	**GC**	A	*GC*	HT	50901	54901	55901	56901	59901
180 102	**FG**	A	*GC*	HT	50902	54902	55902	56902	59902
180 103	**FB**	A		ZK	50903	54903	55903	56903	59903
180 104	**FG**	A		LB	50904	54904	55904	56904	59904
180 105	**GC**	A	*GC*	HT	50905	54905	55905	56905	59905
180 106	**FB**	A		OO	50906	54906	55906	56906	59906
180 107	**GC**	A	*GC*	HT	50907	54907	55907	56907	59907
180 108	**FB**	A		OO	50908	54908	55908	56908	59908
180 109	**FD**	A	*HT*	OO	50909	54909	55909	56909	59909
180 110	**FD**	A	*HT*	OO	50910	54910	55910	56910	59910
180 111	**FD**	A	*HT*	OO	50911	54911	55911	56911	59911
180 112	**GC**	A	*GC*	HT	50912	54912	55912	56912	59912
180 113	**FD**	A	*HT*	OO	50913	54913	55913	56913	59913
180 114	**GC**	A	*GC*	HT	50914	54914	55914	56914	59914

Names (carried on DMSL(A):

180 105 THE YORKSHIRE ARTIST ASHLEY JACKSON
180 107 HART OF THE NORTH
180 112 JAMES HERRIOT

CLASS 185 DESIRO UK SIEMENS

Air conditioned. Grammer seating.

Construction: Aluminium.
Engines: One Cummins QSK19 of 560 kW (750 hp) at 2100 rpm.
Transmission: Voith.
Bogies: Siemens.
Couplers: Dellner 12.
Dimensions: 23.76/23.75 x 2.66 m.
Gangways: Within unit only. **Wheel Arrangement:** 2-B + 2-B + B-2.
Doors: Double-leaf sliding plug. **Maximum Speed:** 100 mph.
Seating Layout: 1: 2+1 facing/unidirectional, 2: 2+2 facing/unidirectional.
Multiple Working: Within class only.

DMCL. Siemens Krefeld 2005–06. 15/18(8) 2W 1TD + catering point. 55.4 t.
MSL. Siemens Krefeld 2005–06. –/72 1T. 52.7 t.
DMS. Siemens Krefeld 2005–06. –/64(4). 54.9 t.

185 101	**FT**	E	*TP*	AK	51101	53101	54101
185 102	**FT**	E	*TP*	AK	51102	53102	54102
185 103	**FT**	E	*TP*	AK	51103	53103	54103
185 104	**FT**	E	*TP*	AK	51104	53104	54104

185 105	**FT**	E	*TP*	AK	51105	53105	54105
185 106	**FT**	E	*TP*	AK	51106	53106	54106
185 107	**FT**	E	*TP*	AK	51107	53107	54107
185 108	**FT**	E	*TP*	AK	51108	53108	54108
185 109	**FT**	E	*TP*	AK	51109	53109	54109
185 110	**FT**	E	*TP*	AK	51110	53110	54110
185 111	**FT**	E	*TP*	AK	51111	53111	54111
185 112	**FT**	E	*TP*	AK	51112	53112	54112
185 113	**FT**	E	*TP*	AK	51113	53113	54113
185 114	**FT**	E	*TP*	AK	51114	53114	54114
185 115	**FT**	E	*TP*	AK	51115	53115	54115
185 116	**FT**	E	*TP*	AK	51116	53116	54116
185 117	**FT**	E	*TP*	AK	51117	53117	54117
185 118	**FT**	E	*TP*	AK	51118	53118	54118
185 119	**FT**	E	*TP*	AK	51119	53119	54119
185 120	**FT**	E	*TP*	AK	51120	53120	54120
185 121	**FT**	E	*TP*	AK	51121	53121	54121
185 122	**FT**	E	*TP*	AK	51122	53122	54122
185 123	**FT**	E	*TP*	AK	51123	53123	54123
185 124	**FT**	E	*TP*	AK	51124	53124	54124
185 125	**FT**	E	*TP*	AK	51125	53125	54125
185 126	**FT**	E	*TP*	AK	51126	53126	54126
185 127	**FT**	E	*TP*	AK	51127	53127	54127
185 128	**FT**	E	*TP*	AK	51128	53128	54128
185 129	**FT**	E	*TP*	AK	51129	53129	54129
185 130	**FT**	E	*TP*	AK	51130	53130	54130
185 131	**FT**	E	*TP*	AK	51131	53131	54131
185 132	**FT**	E	*TP*	AK	51132	53132	54132
185 133	**FT**	E	*TP*	AK	51133	53133	54133
185 134	**FT**	E	*TP*	AK	51134	53134	54134
185 135	**FT**	E	*TP*	AK	51135	53135	54135
185 136	**FT**	E	*TP*	AK	51136	53136	54136
185 137	**FT**	E	*TP*	AK	51137	53137	54137
185 138	**FT**	E	*TP*	AK	51138	53138	54138
185 139	**FT**	E	*TP*	AK	51139	53139	54139
185 140	**FT**	E	*TP*	AK	51140	53140	54140
185 141	**FT**	E	*TP*	AK	51141	53141	54141
185 142	**FT**	E	*TP*	AK	51142	53142	54142
185 143	**FT**	E	*TP*	AK	51143	53143	54143
185 144	**FT**	E	*TP*	AK	51144	53144	54144
185 145	**FT**	E	*TP*	AK	51145	53145	54145
185 146	**FT**	E	*TP*	AK	51146	53146	54146
185 147	**FT**	E	*TP*	AK	51147	53147	54147
185 148	**FT**	E	*TP*	AK	51148	53148	54148
185 149	**FT**	E	*TP*	AK	51149	53149	54149
185 150	**FT**	E	*TP*	AK	51150	53150	54150
185 151	**FT**	E	*TP*	AK	51151	53151	54151

3.2. DIESEL ELECTRIC UNITS

CLASS 201/202 PRESERVED "HASTINGS" UNIT BR

DMBS–TSL–TSL–TSRB–TSL–DMBS.

Preserved unit made up from two Class 201 short-frame cars and three Class 202 long-frame cars. The "Hastings" units were made with narrow body-profiles for use on the section between Tonbridge and Battle which had tunnels of restricted loading gauge. These tunnels were converted to single track operation in the 1980s thus allowing standard loading gauge stock to be used. The set also contains a Class 411 EMU trailer (not Hastings line gauge) and a Class 422 EMU buffet car.

Construction: Steel.
Engine: One English Electric 4SRKT Mk. 2 of 450 kW (600 hp) at 850 rpm.
Main Generator: English Electric EE824.
Traction Motors: Two English Electric EE507 mounted on the inner bogie.
Bogies: SR Mk. 4. (Former EMU TSL vehicles have Commonwealth bogies).
Couplers: Drophead buckeye.
Dimensions: 18.40 x 2.50 m (60000), 20.35 x 2.50 m (60116/118/529), 18.36 x 2.50 m (60501), 20.35 x 2.82 (69337), 20.30 x 2.82 (70262).
Gangways: Within unit only. **Doors**: Manually operated slam.
Brakes: Electro-pneumatic and automatic air.
Maximum Speed: 75 mph. **Seating Layout**: 2+2 facing.
Multiple Working: Other ex-BR Southern Region DEMU vehicles.

60000. DMBS. Lot No. 30329 Eastleigh 1957. –/22. 55.0 t.
60116. DMBS. Lot No. 30395 Eastleigh 1957. –/31. 56.0 t.
60118. DMBS. Lot No. 30395 Eastleigh 1957. –/30. 56.0 t.
60501. TSL. Lot No. 30331 Eastleigh 1957. –/52 2T. 29.5 t.
60529. TSL. Lot No. 30397 Eastleigh 1957. –/60 2T. 30.5 t.
69337. TSRB (ex-Class 422 EMU). Lot No. 30805 York 1970. –/40. 35.0 t.
70262. TSL (ex-Class 411/5 EMU). Lot No. 30455 Eastleigh 1958. –/64 2T. 31.5 t.

201 001	**G**	HD	*HD*	SE	60116 60529 70262 69337 60501 60118
Spare	**G**	HD	*HD*	SE	60000

Names:

60000	Hastings
60116	Mountfield
60118	Tunbridge Wells

CLASS 220 VOYAGER BOMBARDIER

DMS–MS–MS–DMF.

Construction: Steel.
Engine: Cummins QSK19 of 560 kW (750 hp) at 1800 rpm.
Transmission: Two Alstom Onix 800 three-phase traction motors of 275 kW.
Braking: Rheostatic and electro-pneumatic.
Bogies: Bombardier B5005.
Couplers: Dellner 12 at outer ends, bar within unit.
Dimensions: 23.85/23.00 (602xx) x 2.73 m.
Gangways: Within unit only.
Wheel Arrangement: 1A-A1 + 1A-A1 + 1A-A1 + 1A-A1.
Doors: Single-leaf swing plug.
Maximum Speed: 125 m.p.h.
Seating Layout: 1: 2+1 facing/unidirectional, 2: 2+2 mainly unidirectional.
Multiple Working: Within class and with Classes 221 and 222 (in an emergency). Also can be controlled from Class 57/3 locomotives.

DMS. Bombardier Bruges/Wakefield 2000–01. –/42 1TD 1W. 51.1 t.
MS(A). Bombardier Bruges/Wakefield 2000–01. –/66. 45.9 t.
MS(B). Bombardier Bruges/Wakefield 2000–01. –/66 1TD. 46.7 t.
DMF. Bombardier Bruges/Wakefield 2000–01. 26/– 1TD 1W. 50.9 t.

220 001	**XC**	VL	*XC*	CZ	60301	60701	60201	60401
220 002	**XC**	VL	*XC*	CZ	60302	60702	60202	60402
220 003	**XC**	VL	*XC*	CZ	60303	60703	60203	60403
220 004	**XC**	VL	*XC*	CZ	60304	60704	60204	60404
220 005	**XC**	VL	*XC*	CZ	60305	60705	60205	60405
220 006	**XC**	VL	*XC*	CZ	60306	60706	60206	60406
220 007	**XC**	VL	*XC*	CZ	60307	60707	60207	60407
220 008	**XC**	VL	*XC*	CZ	60308	60708	60208	60408
220 009	**XC**	VL	*XC*	CZ	60309	60709	60209	60409
220 010	**XC**	VL	*XC*	CZ	60310	60710	60210	60410
220 011	**XC**	VL	*XC*	CZ	60311	60711	60211	60411
220 012	**XC**	VL	*XC*	CZ	60312	60712	60212	60412
220 013	**XC**	VL	*XC*	CZ	60313	60713	60213	60413
220 014	**XC**	VL	*XC*	CZ	60314	60714	60214	60414
220 015	**XC**	VL	*XC*	CZ	60315	60715	60215	60415
220 016	**XC**	VL	*XC*	CZ	60316	60716	60216	60416
220 017	**XC**	VL	*XC*	CZ	60317	60717	60217	60417
220 018	**XC**	VL	*XC*	CZ	60318	60718	60218	60418
220 019	**XC**	VL	*XC*	CZ	60319	60719	60219	60419
220 020	**XC**	VL	*XC*	CZ	60320	60720	60220	60420
220 021	**XC**	VL	*XC*	CZ	60321	60721	60221	60421
220 022	**XC**	VL	*XC*	CZ	60322	60722	60222	60422
220 023	**XC**	VL	*XC*	CZ	60323	60723	60223	60423
220 024	**XC**	VL	*XC*	CZ	60324	60724	60224	60424
220 025	**XC**	VL	*XC*	CZ	60325	60725	60225	60425
220 026	**XC**	VL	*XC*	CZ	60326	60726	60226	60426
220 027	**XC**	VL	*XC*	CZ	60327	60727	60227	60427
220 028	**XC**	VL	*XC*	CZ	60328	60728	60228	60428

220 029	**XC**	VL	*XC*	CZ	60329	60729	60229	60429
220 030	**XC**	VL	*XC*	CZ	60330	60730	60230	60430
220 031	**XC**	VL	*XC*	CZ	60331	60731	60231	60431
220 032	**XC**	VL	*XC*	CZ	60332	60732	60232	60432
220 033	**XC**	VL	*XC*	CZ	60333	60733	60233	60433
220 034	**XC**	VL	*XC*	CZ	60334	60734	60234	60434

CLASS 221 SUPER VOYAGER BOMBARDIER

* DMS–MS–MS–MSRMB–DMF (Virgin Trains units) or DMS–MS–MS–MS–DMF (CrossCountry units). Built as tilting units but tilt now isolated on CrossCountry sets.

Construction: Steel.
Engine: Cummins QSK19 of 560 kW (750 hp) at 1800 rpm.
Transmission: Two Alstom Onix 800 three-phase traction motors of 275 kW.
Braking: Rheostatic and electro-pneumatic.
Bogies: Bombardier HVP.
Couplers: Dellner 12 at outer ends, bar within unit.
Dimensions: 23.67 x 2.73 m.
Gangways: Within unit only.
Wheel Arrangement: 1A-A1 + 1A-A1 + 1A-A1 (+ 1A-A1) + 1A-A1.
Doors: Single-leaf swing plug.
Maximum Speed: 125 mph.
Seating Layout: 1: 2+1 facing/unidirectional, 2: 2+2 mainly unidirectional.
Multiple Working: Within class and with Classes 220 and 222 (in an emergency). Also can be controlled from Class 57/3 locomotives.
DMS. Bombardier Bruges/Wakefield 2001–02. –/42 1TD 1W. 58.5 t (* 58.9 t.)
60751–794 MS (* MSRMB). Bombardier Bruges/Wakefield 2001–02. –/66 (* –/52). 54.1 t (* 55.9 t.)
60951–994. MS. Bombardier Bruges/Wakefield 2001–02. –/66 1TD (* –/68 1TD). 54.8 t (* 54.3 t.)
60851–890. MS. Bombardier Bruges/Wakefield 2001–02. –/62 1TD (* –/68 1TD). 54.4 t (* 55.0 t.)
DMF. Bombardier Bruges/Wakefield 2001–02. 26/– 1TD 1W. 58.9 t (* 59.1 t.)

Advertising livery: 221 115 Dark grey Bombardier branding on end vehicles.

Note: * Virgin Trains units. MSRMB moved adjacent to the DMF. The seating in this vehicle (2+2 facing) can be used by First or Standard Class passengers depending on demand.

221 101	*	**VT**	VL	*VW*	CZ	60351	60951	60851	60751	60451
221 102	*	**VT**	VL	*VW*	CZ	60352	60952	60852	60752	60452
221 103	*	**VT**	VL	*VW*	CZ	60353	60953	60853	60753	60453
221 104	*	**VT**	VL	*VW*	CZ	60354	60954	60854	60754	60454
221 105	*	**VT**	VL	*VW*	CZ	60355	60955	60855	60755	60455
221 106	*	**VT**	VL	*VW*	CZ	60356	60956	60856	60756	60456
221 107	*	**VT**	VL	*VW*	CZ	60357	60957	60857	60757	60457
221 108	*	**VT**	VL	*VW*	CZ	60358	60958	60858	60758	60458
221 109	*	**VT**	VL	*VW*	CZ	60359	60959	60859	60759	60459
221 110	*	**VT**	VL	*VW*	CZ	60360	60960	60860	60760	60460

221 111	*	**VT**	VL	*VW*	CZ	60361	60961	60861	60761	60461
221 112	*	**VT**	VL	*VW*	CZ	60362	60962	60862	60762	60462
221 113	*	**VT**	VL	*VW*	CZ	60363	60963	60863	60763	60463
221 114	*	**VT**	VL	*VW*	CZ	60364	60764	60964	60864	60464
221 115	*	**AL**	VL	*VW*	CZ	60365	60765	60965	60865	60465
221 116	*	**VT**	VL	*VW*	CZ	60366	60766	60966	60866	60466
221 117	*	**VT**	VL	*VW*	CZ	60367	60767	60967	60867	60467
221 118	*	**VT**	VL	*VW*	CZ	60368	60768	60968	60868	60468
221 119		**XC**	VL	*XC*	CZ	60369	60769	60969	60869	60469
221 120		**XC**	VL	*XC*	CZ	60370	60770	60970	60870	60470
221 121		**XC**	VL	*XC*	CZ	60371	60771	60971	60871	60471
221 122		**XC**	VL	*XC*	CZ	60372	60772	60972	60872	60472
221 123		**XC**	VL	*XC*	CZ	60373	60773	60973	60873	60473
221 124		**XC**	VL	*XC*	CZ	60374	60774	60974	60874	60474
221 125		**XC**	VL	*XC*	CZ	60375	60775	60975	60875	60475
221 126		**XC**	VL	*XC*	CZ	60376	60776	60976	60876	60476
221 127		**XC**	VL	*XC*	CZ	60377	60777	60977	60877	60477
221 128		**XC**	VL	*XC*	CZ	60378	60778	60978	60878	60478
221 129		**XC**	VL	*XC*	CZ	60379	60779	60979	60879	60479
221 130		**XC**	VL	*XC*	CZ	60380	60780	60980	60880	60480
221 131		**XC**	VL	*XC*	CZ	60381	60781	60981	60881	60481
221 132		**XC**	VL	*XC*	CZ	60382	60782	60982	60882	60482
221 133		**XC**	VL	*XC*	CZ	60383	60783	60983	60883	60483
221 134		**XC**	VL	*XC*	CZ	60384	60784	60984	60884	60484
221 135		**XC**	VL	*XC*	CZ	60385	60785	60985	60885	60485
221 136		**XC**	VL	*XC*	CZ	60386	60786	60986	60886	60486
221 137		**XC**	VL	*XC*	CZ	60387	60787	60987	60887	60487
221 138		**XC**	VL	*XC*	CZ	60388	60788	60988	60888	60488
221 139		**XC**	VL	*XC*	CZ	60389	60789	60989	60889	60489
221 140		**XC**	VL	*XC*	CZ	60390	60790	60990	60890	60490
221 141		**XC**	VL	*XC*	CZ	60391	60791	60991		60491
221 142	*	**VT**	VL	*VW*	CZ	60392	60992	60994	60792	60492
221 143	*	**VT**	VL	*VW*	CZ	60393	60993	60794	60793	60493
Spare	*	**VT**	VL		CZ	60394				60494

Names (carried on MS No. 609xx):

221 101	Louis Bleriot
221 102	John Cabot
221 103	Christopher Columbus
221 104	Sir John Franklin
221 105	William Baffin
221 106	Willem Barents
221 107	Sir Martin Frobisher
221 108	Sir Ernest Shackleton
221 109	Marco Polo
221 110	James Cook
221 111	Roald Amundsen
221 112	Ferdinand Magellan
221 113	Sir Walter Raleigh
221 115	Polmadie Depot
221 142	BOMBARDIER Voyager
221 143	Auguste Picard

CLASS 222 MERIDIAN BOMBARDIER

Construction: Steel.
Engine: Cummins QSK19 of 560 kW (750 hp) at 1800 rpm.
Transmission: Two Alstom Onix 800 three-phase traction motors of 275 kW.
Braking: Rheostatic and electro-pneumatic.
Bogies: Bombardier B5005. **Dimensions:** 23.85/23.00 x 2.73 m.
Couplers: Dellner at outer ends, bar within unit.
Gangways: Within unit only. **Wheel Arrangement:** All cars 1A-A1.
Doors: Single-leaf swing plug. **Maximum Speed:** 125 mph.
Seating Layout: 1: 2+1, 2: 2+2 facing/unidirectional.
Multiple Working: Within class and with Classes 220 and 221 (in an emergency).

222 001–006. 7-car units. DMF–MF–MF–MSRMB–MS–MS–DMS.

Note: The 7-car units were built as 9-car units, before being reduced to 8-car sets and then later to 7-car sets to strengthen all 4-car units to 5-cars. 222 007 was built as a 9-car unit but later reduced to a 5-car unit.

DMF. Bombardier Bruges 2004–05. 22/– 1TD 1W. 52.8 t.
MF. Bombardier Bruges 2004–05. 42/– 1T. 46.8 t.
MSRMB. Bombardier Bruges 2004–05. –/62. 48.0 t.
MS. Bombardier Bruges 2004–05. –/68 1T. 47.0 t.
DMS. Bombardier Bruges 2004–05. –/38 1TD 1W. 49.4 t.

222 001	**ST**	E	*EM*	DY	60241	60445	60341	60621
					60561	60551	60161	
222 002	**ST**	E	*EM*	DY	60242	60346	60342	60622
					60562	60544	60162	
222 003	**ST**	E	*EM*	DY	60243	60446	60343	60623
					60563	60553	60163	
222 004	**ST**	E	*EM*	DY	60244	60345	60344	60624
					60564	60554	60164	
222 005	**ST**	E	*EM*	DY	60245	60347	60443	60625
					60565	60555	60165	
222 006	**ST**	E	*EM*	DY	60246	60447	60441	60626
					60566	60556	60166	

Names (carried on MSRMB or DMS (222 003)):

222 001 THE ENTREPRENEUR EXPRESS
222 002 THE CUTLERS' COMPANY
222 003 TORNADO
222 006 THE CARBON CUTTER

222 007–023. 5-car units. DMF–MC–MSRMB–MS–DMS.

DMF. Bombardier Bruges 2003–04. 22/– 1TD 1W. 52.8 t.
MC. Bombardier Bruges 2003–04. 28/22 1T. 48.6 t.
MSRMB. Bombardier Bruges 2003–04. –/62. 49.6 t.
MS. Bombardier Bruges 2004–05. –/68 1T. 47.0 t.
DMS. Bombardier Bruges 2003–04. –/40 1TD 1W. 51.0 t.

222 007	**ST**	E	*EM*	DY	60247	60442	60627	60567	60167
222 008	**ST**	E	*EM*	DY	60248	60918	60628	60545	60168

222 009	**ST**	E	*EM*	DY	60249	60919	60629	60557	60169
222 010	**ST**	E	*EM*	DY	60250	60920	60630	60546	60170
222 011	**ST**	E	*EM*	DY	60251	60921	60631	60531	60171
222 012	**ST**	E	*EM*	DY	60252	60922	60632	60532	60172
222 013	**ST**	E	*EM*	DY	60253	60923	60633	60533	60173
222 014	**ST**	E	*EM*	DY	60254	60924	60634	60534	60174
222 015	**ST**	E	*EM*	DY	60255	60925	60635	60535	60175
222 016	**ST**	E	*EM*	DY	60256	60926	60636	60536	60176
222 017	**ST**	E	*EM*	DY	60257	60927	60637	60537	60177
222 018	**ST**	E	*EM*	DY	60258	60928	60638	60444	60178
222 019	**ST**	E	*EM*	DY	60259	60929	60639	60547	60179
222 020	**ST**	E	*EM*	DY	60260	60930	60640	60543	60180
222 021	**ST**	E	*EM*	DY	60261	60931	60641	60552	60181
222 022	**ST**	E	*EM*	DY	60262	60932	60642	60542	60182
222 023	**ST**	E	*EM*	DY	60263	60933	60643	60541	60183

Name (carried on MSRMB): 222 022 INVEST IN NOTTINGHAM

222 101–104. 4-car former Hull Trains units. DMF–MC–MSRMB–DMS.

DMF. Bombardier Bruges 2005. 22/– 1TD 1W. 52.8 t.
MC. Bombardier Bruges 2005. 11/46 1T. 47.1 t.
MSRMB. Bombardier Bruges 2005. –/62. 48.0 t.
DMS. Bombardier Bruges 2005. –/40 1TD 1W. 49.4 t.

222 101	**ST**	E	*EM*	DY	60271	60571	60681	60191
222 102	**ST**	E	*EM*	DY	60272	60572	60682	60192
222 103	**ST**	E	*EM*	DY	60273	60573	60683	60193
222 104	**ST**	E	*EM*	DY	60274	60574	60684	60194

3.3. SERVICE DMUS

This section lists vehicles not used for passenger-carrying purposes. Vehicles are numbered in the special service stock number series.

CLASS 950 TRACK ASSESSMENT UNIT

DM–DM. Purpose built service unit based on the Class 150/1 design. Gangwayed within unit.

Construction: Steel.
Engine: One Cummins NT-855-RT5 of 213 kW (285 hp) at 2100 rpm per power car.
Transmission: Hydraulic. Voith T211r with cardan shafts to Gmeinder GM190 final drive.
Maximum Speed: 75 mph. **Couplers:** BSI automatic.
Bogies: BP38 (powered), BT38 (non-powered).
Brakes: Electro-pneumatic. **Dimensions:** 20.06 x 2.82 m.
Doors: Manually operated slam & power operated sliding.
Multiple Working: Classes 142, 143, 144, 150, 153, 155, 156, 158, 159 and 170.

999600. DM. Lot No. 4060 BREL York 1987. 35.0 t.
999601. DM. Lot No. 4061 BREL York 1987. 35.0 t.

950 001	**Y**	NR	*DB*	ZA	999600	999601

CLASS 960 ROUTE LEARNING UNIT

DMB. Converted from Class 121. Non-gangwayed.

For details see Page 189.

This unit is available for hire to other operators for route learning if required.

Lot No. 30518 Pressed Steel 1960. 38.0 t.

960 014	**BG**	CR	*CR*	AL	977873	(55022)

CLASS 960 WATER-JETTING UNIT

DMB–MS–DMB. Converted 2003–2004 from Class 117. Non-gangwayed.

Construction: Steel.
Engines: Two Leyland 1595 of 112 kW (150 hp) at 1800 rpm.
Transmission: Mechanical. Cardan shaft and freewheel to a four-speed epicyclic gearbox with a further cardan shaft to the final drive, each engine driving the inner axle of one bogie.
Maximum Speed: 70 mph.
Bogies: DD10.
Brakes: Twin pipe vacuum.
Doors: Manually operated slam.
Couplings: Screw.
Multiple Working: Blue Square.
Dimensions: 20.45 x 2.84 m.

977987/988. DMB. Lot No. 30546/30548 Pressed Steel 1959–60. 36.5 t.
977992. MS. Lot No. 30548 Pressed Steel 1959–60. 36.5 t.

960 301	**G**	CR	*CR*	AL	977987	(51371)	977992	(51375)
					977988	(51413)		

3.4. DMUS AWAITING DISPOSAL

The list below comprises vehicles awaiting disposal which are stored on the National Railway network.

Class 101

Spare	**RR**	X	SN	51432	51498

Class 960

Converted from Class 121 or 122. 960 302/303 converted for use as Severn Tunnel Emergency Train units, but not actually used as such.

960 011	**RK**	CR	TM	977859	(55025)
960 302	**Y**	AV	CF	977975	(55027)
960 303	**Y**	AV	CF	977976	(55031)

4. ELECTRIC MULTIPLE UNITS

INTRODUCTION

EMU CLASSES

Principal details and dimensions are quoted for each class in metric and/or imperial units as considered appropriate bearing in mind common UK usage.

All dimensions and weights are quoted for vehicles in an "as new" condition with all necessary supplies on board. Dimensions are quoted in the order length x overall width. All lengths quoted are over buffers or couplers as appropriate. Where two lengths are quoted, the first refers to outer vehicles in a set and the second to inner vehicles. All weights are shown as metric tonnes (t = tonnes).

Bogie Types are quoted in the format motored/non-motored (eg BP20/BT13 denotes BP20 motored bogies and BT non-motored bogies).

Unless noted to the contrary, all vehicles listed have bar couplers at non-driving ends.

Vehicles ordered under the auspices of BR were allocated a Lot (batch) number when ordered and these are quoted in class headings and sub-headings. Vehicles ordered since 1995 have no Lot Numbers, but the manufacturer and location that they were built is given.

NUMERICAL LISTINGS

25 kV AC 50 Hz overhead Electric Multiple Units (EMUs) and dual voltage EMUs are listed in numerical order of set numbers. Individual "loose" vehicles are listed in numerical order after vehicles formed into fixed formations.

750 V DC third rail EMUs are listed in numerical order of class number, then in numerical order of set number. Some of these use the former Southern Region four-digit set numbers. These are derived from theoretical six digit set numbers which are the four-digit set number prefixed by the first two numbers of the class.

Where sets or vehicles have been renumbered in recent years, former numbering detail is shown alongside current detail. Each entry is laid out as in the following example:

Set No.	*Detail*	*Livery*	*Owner*	*Operator*	*Allocation*	*Formation*
320314	*	**SR**	E	*SR*	GW	77912 63034 77934

Detail Differences. Only detail differences which currently affect the areas and types of train which vehicles may work are shown. All other detail differences are specifically excluded. Where such differences occur within a class or part class, these are shown alongside the individual set or vehicle number. Meaning of abbreviations are detailed in individual class headings.

Set Formations. Set formations shown are those normally maintained. Readers should note some set formations might be temporarily varied from time to time to suit maintenance and/or operational requirements. Vehicles shown as "Spare" are not formed in any regular set formation.

Codes. Codes are used to denote the livery, owner, operator and depot of each unit. Details of these will be found in section 7 of this book. Where a unit or spare car is off-lease, the operator column will be left blank.

Names. Only names carried with official sanction are listed. As far as possible names are shown in UPPER/lower case characters as actually shown on the name carried on the vehicle(s). Unless otherwise shown, complete units are regarded as named rather than just the individual car(s) which carry the name.

GENERAL INFORMATION

CLASSIFICATION AND NUMBERING

25 kV AC 50 Hz overhead and "Versatile" EMUs are classified in the series 300–399.

750 V DC third rail EMUs are classified in the series 400–599.

Service units are classified in the series 900–949.

EMU individual cars are numbered in the series 61000–78999, except for vehicles used on the Isle of Wight – which are numbered in a separate series, and for the Class 378s, 380s and 395s, which take up new 38xxx and 39xxx series'.

Any vehicle constructed or converted to replace another vehicle following accident damage and carrying the same number as the original vehicle is denoted by the suffix" in this publication.

OPERATING CODES

These codes are used by train operating company staff to describe the various different types of vehicles and normally appear on data panels on the inner (ie non driving) ends of vehicles.

A "B" prefix indicates a battery vehicle.
A "P" prefix indicates a trailer vehicle on which is mounted the pantograph, instead of the default case where the pantograph is mounted on a motor vehicle.

The first part of the code describes whether or not the car has a motor or a driving cab as follows:

DM Driving motor.
M Motor
DT Driving trailer
T Trailer

The next letter is a "B" for cars with a brake compartment.
This is followed by the saloon details:

F First
S Standard
C Composite

The next letter denotes the style of accommodation as follows:

O Open
K Side compartment with lavatory
so Semi-open (part compartments, part open). All other vehicles are assumed to consist solely of open saloons.

Finally vehicles with a buffet are suffixed RB or RMB for a miniature buffet.

Where two vehicles of the same type are formed within the same unit, the above codes may be suffixed by (A) and (B) to differentiate between the vehicles.

A composite is a vehicle containing both First and Standard Class accommodation, whilst a brake vehicle is a vehicle containing separate specific accommodation for the conductor.

BUILD DETAILS

Lot Numbers

Vehicles ordered under the auspices of BR were allocated a Lot (batch) number when ordered and these are quoted in class headings and sub-headings.

Builders

These are shown in class headings. Abbreviations used are found in section 7.6.

Information on sub-contracting works which built parts of vehicles eg the underframes etc is not shown.

ACCOMMODATION

The information given in class headings and sub-headings is in the form F/S nT (or TD) nW. For example 12/54 1T 1W denotes 12 First Class and 54 Standard Class seats, one toilet and one space for a wheelchair. A number in brackets (ie (2)) denotes tip-up seats (in addition to the fixed seats). Tip-up seats in vestibules do not count. The seating layout of open saloons is shown as 2+1, 2+2 or 3+2 as the case may be. Where units have first class accommodation as well as standard and the layout is different for each class then these are shown separately prefixed by "1:" and "2:". Compartments are three seats a side in First Class and mostly four a side in Standard Class in EMUs. TD denotes a toilet suitable for use by a disabled person.

4.1. 25 kV AC 50 Hz OVERHEAD & DUAL VOLTAGE UNITS

Except where otherwise stated, all units in this section operate on 25kV AC 50Hz overhead only.

CLASS 313 BREL YORK

Inner suburban units.

Formation: DMSO–PTSO–BDMSO or DMSO–TSO–BDMSO.
Systems: 25 kV AC overhead/750 V DC third rail.
Construction: Steel underframe, aluminium alloy body and roof.
Traction Motors: Four GEC G310AZ of 82.125 kW.
Wheel Arrangement: Bo-Bo + 2-2 + Bo-Bo.
Braking: Disc & rheostatic.
Dimensions: 20.33/20.18 x 2.82 m.
Bogies: BX1.
Couplers: Tightlock.
Gangways: Within unit + end doors.
Control System: Camshaft.
Doors: Sliding.
Maximum Speed: 75 mph.
Seating Layouts: 313/0: Refurbished with high back seats (3+2 facing).
313/1: low back seats (3+2 facing).
313/2: refurbished with 2+2 mainly facing high-back seating.
Multiple Working: Within class.

DMSO. Lot No. 30879 1976–77. –/74. 36.0 t.
PTSO. Lot No. 30880 1976–77. –/83. 31.0 t.
BDMSO. Lot No. 30885 1976–77. –/74. 37.5 t.

Class 313/0. Standard Design.

313018	**FU**	E	*FC*	HE	62546	71230	62610
313024	**FU**	E	*FC*	HE	62552	71236	62616
313025	**FU**	E	*FC*	HE	62553	71237	62617
313026	**FU**	E	*FC*	HE	62554	71238	62618
313027	**FU**	E	*FC*	HE	62555	71239	62619
313028	**FU**	E	*FC*	HE	62556	71240	62620
313029	**FU**	E	*FC*	HE	62557	71241	62621
313030	**FU**	E	*FC*	HE	62558	71242	62622
313031	**FU**	E	*FC*	HE	62559	71243	62623
313032	**FU**	E	*FC*	HE	62560	71244	62643
313033	**FU**	E	*FC*	HE	62561	71245	62625
313035	**FU**	E	*FC*	HE	62563	71247	62627
313036	**FU**	E	*FC*	HE	62564	71248	62628
313037	**FU**	E	*FC*	HE	62565	71249	62629
313038	**FU**	E	*FC*	HE	62566	71250	62630
313039	**FU**	E	*FC*	HE	62567	71251	62631
313040	**FU**	E	*FC*	HE	62568	71252	62632
313041	**FU**	E	*FC*	HE	62569	71253	62633
313042	**FU**	E	*FC*	HE	62570	71254	62634
313043	**FU**	E	*FC*	HE	62571	71255	62635
313044	**FU**	E	*FC*	HE	62572	71256	62636

313045	**FU**	E	*FC*	HE	62573	71257	62637
313046	**FU**	E	*FC*	HE	62574	71258	62638
313047	**FU**	E	*FC*	HE	62575	71259	62639
313048	**FU**	E	*FC*	HE	62576	71260	62640
313049	**FU**	E	*FC*	HE	62577	71261	62641
313050	**FU**	E	*FC*	HE	62578	71262	62649
313051	**FU**	E	*FC*	HE	62579	71263	62624
313052	**FU**	E	*FC*	HE	62580	71264	62644
313053	**FU**	E	*FC*	HE	62581	71265	62645
313054	**FU**	E	*FC*	HE	62582	71266	62646
313055	**FU**	E	*FC*	HE	62583	71267	62647
313056	**FU**	E	*FC*	HE	62584	71268	62648
313057	**FU**	E	*FC*	HE	62585	71269	62642
313058	**FU**	E	*FC*	HE	62586	71270	62650
313059	**FU**	E	*FC*	HE	62587	71271	62651
313060	**FU**	E	*FC*	HE	62588	71272	62652
313061	**FU**	E	*FC*	HE	62589	71273	62653
313062	**FU**	E	*FC*	HE	62590	71274	62654
313063	**FU**	E	*FC*	HE	62591	71275	62655
313064	**FU**	E	*FC*	HE	62592	71276	62656

Name (carried on PTSO): 313054 Captain William Leefe Robinson V.C.

Class 313/1. Former London Overground units. Details as Class 313/0.

313121	**SL**	H		ZN	62549	71233	62613
313122	**FU**	E	*FC*	HE	62550	71234	62614
313123	**FU**	E	*FC*	HE	62551	71235	62615
313134	**FU**	E	*FC*	HE	62562	71246	62626

Name (carried on PTSO): 313134 City of London

Class 313/2. Southern units. Units refurbished for Southern for Brighton Coastway services. 750 V DC only (pantographs removed).

DMSO. Lot No. 30879 1976–77. –/64. 36.0 t.
TSO. Lot No. 30880 1976–77. –/68. . t.
BDMSO. Lot No. 30885 1976–77. –/64. 37.5 t.

313201	(313101)	**SN**	H	*SN*	BI	62529	71213	62593
313202	(313102)	**SN**	H	*SN*	BI	62530	71214	62594
313203	(313103)	**SN**	H	*SN*	BI	62531	71215	62595
313204	(313104)	**SN**	H	*SN*	BI	62532	71216	62596
313205	(313105)	**SN**	H	*SN*	BI	62533	71217	62597
313206	(313106)	**SN**	H	*SN*	BI	62534	71218	62598
313207	(313107)	**SN**	H	*SN*	BI	62535	71219	62599
313208	(313108)	**SN**	H	*SN*	BI	62536	71220	62600
313209	(313109)	**SN**	H	*SN*	BI	62537	71221	62601
313210	(313110)	**SN**	H	*SN*	BI	62538	71222	62602
313211	(313111)	**SN**	H	*SN*	BI	62539	71223	62603
313212	(313112)	**SN**	H	*SN*	BI	62540	71224	62604
313213	(313113)	**SN**	H	*SN*	BI	62541	71225	62605
313214	(313114)	**SN**	H	*SN*	BI	62542	71226	62606
313215	(313115)	**SN**	H	*SN*	BI	62543	71227	62607

313216	(313116)	**SN**	H	*SN*	BI	62544	71228	62608
313217	(313117)	**SN**	H	*SN*	BI	62545	71229	62609
313219	(313119)	**SN**	H	*SN*	BI	62547	71231	62611
313220	(313120)	**SN**	H	*SN*	BI	62548	71232	62612

CLASS 314 BREL YORK

Inner suburban units.

Formation: DMSO–PTSO–DMSO.
Construction: Steel underframe, aluminium alloy body and roof.
Traction Motors: Four GEC G310AZ (* Brush TM61-53) of 82.125 kW.
Wheel Arrangement: Bo-Bo + 2-2 + Bo-Bo.
Braking: Disc & rheostatic.
Dimensions: 20.33/20.18 x 2.82 m.
Bogies: BX1.
Couplers: Tightlock.
Gangways: Within unit + end doors.
Control System: Thyristor.
Doors: Sliding.
Maximum Speed: 70 mph.
Seating Layout: 3+2 low-back facing.
Multiple Working: Within class and with Class 315.

DMSO. Lot No. 30912 1979. –/68. 34.5 t.
64588ˡˡ. DMSO. Lot No. 30908 1978–80. Rebuilt Railcare Glasgow 1996 from Class 507 No. 64426. The original 64588 has been scrapped. –/74. 34.5 t.
PTSO. Lot No. 30913 1979. –/76. 33.0 t.

314201	*	**SC**	A	*SR*	GW	64583	71450	64584
314202	*	**SC**	A	*SR*	GW	64585	71451	64586
314203	*	**SR**	A	*SR*	GW	64587	71452	64588ˡˡ
314204	*	**SC**	A	*SR*	GW	64589	71453	64590
314205	*	**SC**	A	*SR*	GW	64591	71454	64592
314206	*	**SC**	A	*SR*	GW	64593	71455	64594
314207		**SC**	A	*SR*	GW	64595	71456	64596
314208		**SC**	A	*SR*	GW	64597	71457	64598
314209		**SC**	A	*SR*	GW	64599	71458	64600
314210		**SC**	A	*SR*	GW	64601	71459	64602
314211		**SC**	A	*SR*	GW	64603	71460	64604
314212		**SR**	A	*SR*	GW	64605	71461	64606
314213		**SC**	A	*SR*	GW	64607	71462	64608
314214		**SC**	A	*SR*	GW	64609	71463	64610
314215		**SC**	A	*SR*	GW	64611	71464	64612
314216		**SC**	A	*SR*	GW	64613	71465	64614

CLASS 315 BREL YORK

Inner suburban units.

Formation: DMSO–TSO–PTSO–DMSO.
Construction: Steel underframe, aluminium alloy body and roof.
Traction Motors: Four Brush TM61-53 (* GEC G310AZ) of 82.125 kW.
Wheel Arrangement: Bo-Bo + 2-2 + 2-2 + Bo-Bo.
Braking: Disc & rheostatic.
Dimensions: 20.33/20.18 x 2.82 m.
Bogies: BX1.
Couplers: Tightlock.

Gangways: Within unit + end doors. **Control System:** Thyristor.
Doors: Sliding. **Maximum Speed:** 75 mph.
Seating Layout: 3+2 low-back facing.
Multiple Working: Within class and with Class 314.

DMSO. Lot No. 30902 1980–81. –/74. 35.0 t.
TSO. Lot No. 30904 1980–81. –/86. 25.5 t.
PTSO. Lot No. 30903 1980–81. –/84. 32.0 t.

315801		**1**	E	*EA*	IL	64461	71281	71389	64462
315802		**1**	E	*EA*	IL	64463	71282	71390	64464
315803		**1**	E	*EA*	IL	64465	71283	71391	64466
315804		**1**	E	*EA*	IL	64467	71284	71392	64468
315805		**1**	E	*EA*	IL	64469	71285	71393	64470
315806		**1**	E	*EA*	IL	64471	71286	71394	64472
315807		**1**	E	*EA*	IL	64473	71287	71395	64474
315808		**1**	E	*EA*	IL	64475	71288	71396	64476
315809		**1**	E	*EA*	IL	64477	71289	71397	64478
315810		**1**	E	*EA*	IL	64479	71290	71398	64480
315811		**1**	E	*EA*	IL	64481	71291	71399	64482
315812		**1**	E	*EA*	IL	64483	71292	71400	64484
315813		**1**	E	*EA*	IL	64485	71293	71401	64486
315814		**1**	E	*EA*	IL	64487	71294	71402	64488
315815		**1**	E	*EA*	IL	64489	71295	71403	64490
315816		**1**	E	*EA*	IL	64491	71296	71404	64492
315817		**1**	E	*EA*	IL	64493	71297	71405	64494
315818		**1**	E	*EA*	IL	64495	71298	71406	64496
315819		**1**	E	*EA*	IL	64497	71299	71407	64498
315820		**1**	E	*EA*	IL	64499	71300	71408	64500
315821		**1**	E	*EA*	IL	64501	71301	71409	64502
315822		**1**	E	*EA*	IL	64503	71302	71410	64504
315823		**1**	E	*EA*	IL	64505	71303	71411	64506
315824		**1**	E	*EA*	IL	64507	71304	71412	64508
315825		**1**	E	*EA*	IL	64509	71305	71413	64510
315826		**1**	E	*EA*	IL	64511	71306	71414	64512
315827		**1**	E	*EA*	IL	64513	71307	71415	64514
315828		**1**	E	*EA*	IL	64515	71308	71416	64516
315829		**1**	E	*EA*	IL	64517	71309	71417	64518
315830		**1**	E	*EA*	IL	64519	71310	71418	64520
315831		**1**	E	*EA*	IL	64521	71311	71419	64522
315832		**1**	E	*EA*	IL	64523	71312	71420	64524
315833		**1**	E	*EA*	IL	64525	71313	71421	64526
315834		**1**	E	*EA*	IL	64527	71314	71422	64528
315835		**1**	E	*EA*	IL	64529	71315	71423	64530
315836		**1**	E	*EA*	IL	64531	71316	71424	64532
315837		**1**	E	*EA*	IL	64533	71317	71425	64534
315838		**1**	E	*EA*	IL	64535	71318	71426	64536
315839		**1**	E	*EA*	IL	64537	71319	71427	64538
315840		**1**	E	*EA*	IL	64539	71320	71428	64540
315841		**1**	E	*EA*	IL	64541	71321	71429	64542
315842	*	**1**	E	*EA*	IL	64543	71322	71430	64544
315843	*	**1**	E	*EA*	IL	64545	71323	71431	64546

315844	*	**1**	E	*EA*	IL	64547	71324	71432	64548
315845	*	**1**	E	*EA*	IL	64549	71325	71433	64550
315846	*	**1**	E	*EA*	IL	64551	71326	71434	64552
315847	*	**1**	E	*EA*	IL	64553	71327	71435	64554
315848	*	**1**	E	*EA*	IL	64555	71328	71436	64556
315849	*	**1**	E	*EA*	IL	64557	71329	71437	64558
315850	*	**1**	E	*EA*	IL	64559	71330	71438	64560
315851	*	**1**	E	*EA*	IL	64561	71331	71439	64562
315852	*	**1**	E	*EA*	IL	64563	71332	71440	64564
315853	*	**1**	E	*EA*	IL	64565	71333	71441	64566
315854	*	**1**	E	*EA*	IL	64567	71334	71442	64568
315855	*	**1**	E	*EA*	IL	64569	71335	71443	64570
315856	*	**1**	E	*EA*	IL	64571	71336	71444	64572
315857	*	**1**	E	*EA*	IL	64573	71337	71445	64574
315858	*	**1**	E	*EA*	IL	64575	71338	71446	64576
315859	*	**1**	E	*EA*	IL	64577	71339	71447	64578
315860	*	**1**	E	*EA*	IL	64579	71340	71448	64580
315861	*	**1**	E	*EA*	IL	64581	71341	71449	64582

Names (carried on DMSO):

315817 Transport for London
315829 London Borough of Havering Celebrating 40 years
315845 Herbie Woodward
315857 Stratford Connections

CLASS 317 BREL YORK/DERBY

Outer suburban units.

Formation: Various, see sub-class headings.
Construction: Steel.
Traction Motors: Four GEC G315BZ of 247.5 kW.
Wheel Arrangement: 2-2 + Bo-Bo + 2-2 + 2-2.
Braking: Disc.
Dimensions: 20.13/20.18 x 2.82 m.
Bogies: BP20 (MSO), BT13 (others).
Couplers: Tightlock.
Gangways: Throughout
Control System: Thyristor.
Doors: Sliding.
Maximum Speed: 100 mph.
Seating Layout: Various, see sub-class headings.
Multiple Working: Within class & with Classes 318, 319, 320, 321, 322 and 323.

Class 317/1. Pressure ventilated.

Formation: DTSO–MSO–TCO–DTSO.
Seating Layout: 1: 2+2 facing, 2: 3+2 facing.

DTSO(A) Lot No. 30955 York 1981–82. –/74. 29.5 t.
MSO. Lot No. 30958 York 1981–82. –/79. 49.0 t.
TCO. Lot No. 30957 Derby 1981–82. 22/46 2T. 29.0 t.
DTSO(B) Lot No. 30956 York 1981–82. –/71. 29.5 t.

317337	**FU**	A	*FC*	HE	77036	62671	71613	77084
317338	**FU**	A	*FC*	HE	77037	62698	71614	77085
317339	**FU**	A	*FC*	HE	77038	62699	71615	77086

317 340	**FU**	A	*FC*	HE	77039	62700	71616	77087
317 341	**FU**	A	*FC*	HE	77040	62701	71617	77088
317 342	**FU**	A	*FC*	HE	77041	62702	71618	77089
317 343	**FU**	A	*FC*	HE	77042	62703	71619	77090
317 344	**FU**	A	*FC*	HE	77029	62690	71620	77091
317 345	**FU**	A	*FC*	HE	77044	62705	71621	77092
317 346	**FU**	A	*FC*	HE	77045	62706	71622	77093
317 347	**FU**	A	*FC*	HE	77046	62707	71623	77094
317 348	**FU**	A	*FC*	HE	77047	62708	71624	77095

Names (carried on TCO):

317 345 Driver John Webb | 317 348 Richard A Jenner

Class 317/5. Pressure ventilated. Units renumbered from Class 317/1 in 2005 for West Anglia Metro services. Refurbished with new upholstery and Passenger Information Systems. Details as Class 317/1.

Note: The original DTSO 77048 was written off after the Cricklewood accident of 1983. A replacement vehicle was built (at Wolverton) in 1987 and given the same number.

317 501	**NX**	A	*EA*	IL	77024	62661	71577	77048
317 502	**NX**	A	*EA*	IL	77001	62662	71578	77049
317 503	**NX**	A	*EA*	IL	77002	62663	71579	77050
317 504	**NX**	A	*EA*	IL	77003	62664	71580	77051
317 505	**NX**	A	*EA*	IL	77004	62665	71581	77052
317 506	**NX**	A	*EA*	IL	77005	62666	71582	77053
317 507	**NX**	A	*EA*	IL	77006	62667	71583	77054
317 508	**NX**	A	*EA*	IL	77010	62697	71587	77058
317 509	**NX**	A	*EA*	IL	77011	62672	71588	77059
317 510	**NX**	A	*EA*	IL	77012	62673	71589	77060
317 511	**NC**	A	*EA*	IL	77014	62675	71591	77062
317 512	**NC**	A	*EA*	IL	77015	62676	71592	77063
317 513	**NX**	A	*EA*	IL	77016	62677	71593	77064
317 514	**NX**	A	*EA*	IL	77017	62678	71594	77065
317 515	**NX**	A	*EA*	IL	77019	62680	71596	77067

Name (carried on TCO):

317 507 University of Cambridge 800 Years 1209–2009

Class 317/6. Convection heating. Units converted from Class 317/2 by Railcare, Wolverton 1998–99 with new seating layouts.

Formation: DTSO–MSO–TSO–DTCO.
Seating Layout: 2+2 facing.

77200–219. DTSO. Lot No. 30994 York 1985–86. –/64. 29.5 t.
77280–283. DTSO. Lot No. 31007 York 1987. –/64. 29.5 t.
62846–865. MSO. Lot No. 30996 York 1985–86. –/70. 49.0 t.
62886–889. MSO. Lot No. 31009 York 1987. –/70. 49.0 t.
71734–753. TSO. Lot No. 30997 York 1985–86. –/62 2T. 29.0 t.
71762–765. TSO. Lot No. 31010 York 1987. –/62 2T. 29.0 t.
77220–239. DTCO. Lot No. 30995 York 1985–86. 24/48. 29.5 t.
77284–287. DTCO. Lot No. 31008 York 1987. 24/48. 29.5 t.

317649	**NC**	A	*EA*	IL	77200	62846	71734	77220
317650	**NC**	A	*EA*	IL	77201	62847	71735	77221
317651	**NC**	A	*EA*	IL	77202	62848	71736	77222
317652	**NC**	A	*EA*	IL	77203	62849	71739	77223
317653	**NC**	A	*EA*	IL	77204	62850	71738	77224
317654	**NC**	A	*EA*	IL	77205	62851	71737	77225
317655	**NC**	A	*EA*	IL	77206	62852	71740	77226
317656	**1**	A	*EA*	IL	77207	62853	71742	77227
317657	**NC**	A	*EA*	IL	77208	62854	71741	77228
317658	**NC**	A	*EA*	IL	77209	62855	71743	77229
317659	**1**	A	*EA*	IL	77210	62856	71744	77230
317660	**1**	A	*EA*	IL	77211	62857	71745	77231
317661	**1**	A	*EA*	IL	77212	62858	71746	77232
317662	**1**	A	*EA*	IL	77213	62859	71747	77233
317663	**1**	A	*EA*	IL	77214	62860	71748	77234
317664	**1**	A	*EA*	IL	77215	62861	71749	77235
317665	**1**	A	*EA*	IL	77216	62862	71750	77236
317666	**NC**	A	*EA*	IL	77217	62863	71752	77237
317667	**1**	A	*EA*	IL	77218	62864	71751	77238
317668	**1**	A	*EA*	IL	77219	62865	71753	77239
317669	**NC**	A	*EA*	IL	77280	62886	71762	77284
317670	**1**	A	*EA*	IL	77281	62887	71763	77285
317671	**1**	A	*EA*	IL	77282	62888	71764	77286
317672	**1**	A	*EA*	IL	77283	62889	71765	77287

Name (carried on DTCO):

317654 Richard Wells

Class 317/7. Units converted from Class 317/1 by Railcare, Wolverton 2000 for Stansted Express services between London Liverpool Street and Stansted. Air conditioning. Fitted with luggage stacks. Displaced from Stansted services in 2011 by Class 379s.

Formation: DTSO–MSO–TSO–DTCO.
Seating Layout: 1: 2+1 facing, 2: 2+2 facing.

DTSO Lot No. 30955 York 1981–82. –/52 + catering point. 31.4 t.
MSO. Lot No. 30958 York 1981–82. –/62. 51.3 t.
TSO. Lot No. 30957 Derby 1981–82. –/42(5) 1W 1T 1TD. 30.2 t.
DTCO Lot No. 30956 York 1981–82. 22/16 + catering point. 31.6 t.

317708	**NX**	A	*EA*	IL	77007	62668	71584	77055
317709	**NX**	A	*EA*	IL	77008	62669	71585	77056
317710	**NX**	A	*EA*	IL	77009	62670	71586	77057
317714	**NX**	A	*EA*	IL	77013	62674	71590	77061
317719	**NX**	A	*EA*	IL	77018	62679	71595	77066
317722	**NX**	A	*EA*	IL	77021	62682	71598	77069
317723	**NX**	A	*EA*	IL	77022	62683	71599	77070
317729	**NX**	A	*EA*	IL	77028	62689	71605	77076
317732	**NX**	A	*EA*	IL	77031	62692	71608	77079

Names (carried on DTCO):

317709 Len Camp | 317723 The Tottenham Flyer

Class 317/8. Pressure Ventilated. Units refurbished and renumbered from Class 317/1 in 2005–06 at Wabtec, Doncaster for use on Stansted Express services. Fitted with luggage stacks. Displaced from Stansted services in 2011 by Class 379s.

Formation: DTSO–MSO–TCO–DTSO.
Seating Layout: 1: 2+2 facing, 2: 3+2 facing.

DTSO(A) Lot No. 30955 York 1981–82. –/66. 29.5 t.
MSO. Lot No. 30958 York 1981–82. –/71. 49.0 t.
TCO. Lot No. 30957 Derby 1981–82. 20/42 2T. 29.0 t.
DTSO(B) Lot No. 30956 York 1981–82. –/66. 29.5 t.

317881	**NX**	A	*EA*	IL	77020	62681	71597	77068	
317882	**NC**	A	*EA*	IL	77023	62684	71600	77071	
317883	**NC**	A	*EA*	IL	77000	62685	71601	77072	
317884	**NC**	A	*EA*	IL	77025	62686	71602	77073	
317885	**NC**	A	*EA*	IL	77026	62687	71603	77074	
317886	**NC**	A	*EA*	IL	77027	62688	71604	77075	
317887	**NX**	A	*EA*	IL	77043	62704	71606	77077	
317888	**NX**	A	*EA*	IL	77030	62691	71607	77078	
317889	**NX**	A	*EA*	IL	77032	62693	71609	77080	
317890	**NX**	A	*EA*	IL	77033	62694	71610	77081	
317891	**NX**	A	*EA*	IL	77034	62695	71611	77082	
317892	**NX**	A	*EA*	IL	77035	62696	71612	77083	Ilford Depot

CLASS 318 BREL YORK

Outer suburban units.

Formation: DTSO–MSO–DTSO.
Construction: Steel.
Traction Motors: Four Brush TM 2141 of 268 kW.
Wheel Arrangement: 2-2 + Bo-Bo + 2-2.
Braking: Disc.
Dimensions: 19.83/19.92 x 2.82 m.
Bogies: BP20 (MSO), BT13 (others).
Couplers: Tightlock.
Gangways: Within unit.
Control System: Thyristor.
Doors: Sliding.
Maximum Speed: 90 mph.
Seating Layout: 3+2 facing.
Multiple Working: Within class & with Classes 317, 319, 320, 321, 322 and 323.

77240–259. DTSO. Lot No. 30999 1985–86. –/64 1T. 30.0 t.
77288. DTSO. Lot No. 31020 1987. –/64 1T. 30.0 t.
62866–885. MSO. Lot No. 30998 1985–86. –/77. 50.9 t.
62890. MSO. Lot No. 31019 1987. –/77. 50.9 t.
77260–279. DTSO. Lot No. 31000 1985–86. –/72. 29.6 t.
77289. DTSO. Lot No. 31021 1987. –/72. 29.6 t.

318250	**SC**	E	*SR*	GW	77240	62866	77260
318251	**SC**	E	*SR*	GW	77241	62867	77261
318252	**SC**	E	*SR*	GW	77242	62868	77262
318253	**SC**	E	*SR*	GW	77243	62869	77263
318254	**SC**	E	*SR*	GW	77244	62870	77264
318255	**SC**	E	*SR*	GW	77245	62871	77265

318 256	**SC**	E	*SR*	GW	77246	62872	77266	
318 257	**SC**	E	*SR*	GW	77247	62873	77267	
318 258	**SC**	E	*SR*	GW	77248	62874	77268	
318 259	**SC**	E	*SR*	GW	77249	62875	77269	Citizens' Network
318 260	**SC**	E	*SR*	GW	77250	62876	77270	
318 261	**SC**	E	*SR*	GW	77251	62877	77271	
318 262	**SC**	E	*SR*	GW	77252	62878	77272	
318 263	**SC**	E	*SR*	GW	77253	62879	77273	
318 264	**SC**	E	*SR*	GW	77254	62880	77274	
318 265	**SC**	E	*SR*	GW	77255	62881	77275	
318 266	**SC**	E	*SR*	GW	77256	62882	77276	STRATHCLYDER
318 267	**SC**	E	*SR*	GW	77257	62883	77277	
318 268	**SC**	E	*SR*	GW	77258	62884	77278	
318 269	**SC**	E	*SR*	GW	77259	62885	77279	
318 270	**SC**	E	*SR*	GW	77288	62890	77289	

CLASS 319 — BREL YORK

Express and outer suburban units.

Formation: Various, see sub-class headings.
Systems: 25 kV AC overhead/750 V DC third rail.
Construction: Steel.
Traction Motors: Four GEC G315BZ of 268 kW.
Wheel Arrangement: 2-2 + Bo-Bo + 2-2 + 2-2.
Braking: Disc.
Bogies: P7-4 (MSO), T3-7 (others).
Gangways: Within unit + end doors.
Doors: Sliding.
Dimensions: 20.17/20.16 x 2.82 m.
Couplers: Tightlock.
Control System: GTO chopper.
Maximum Speed: 100 mph.
Seating Layout: Various, see sub-class headings.
Multiple Working: Within class & with Classes 317, 318, 320, 321, 322 and 323.

Class 319/0. DTSO–MSO–TSO–DTSO.

Seating Layout: 3+2 facing.

DTSO(A). Lot No. 31022 (odd nos.) 1987–88. –/82. 28.2 t.
MSO. Lot No. 31023 1987–88. –/82. 49.2 t.
TSO. Lot No. 31024 1987–88. –/77 2T. 31.0 t.
DTSO(B). Lot No. 31025 (even nos.) 1987–88. –/78. 28.1 t.

319 001	**FU**	P	*FC*	BF	77291	62891	71772	77290
319 002	**FU**	P	*FC*	BF	77293	62892	71773	77292
319 003	**FU**	P	*FC*	BF	77295	62893	71774	77294
319 004	**FU**	P	*FC*	BF	77297	62894	71775	77296
319 005	**FU**	P	*FC*	BF	77299	62895	71776	77298
319 006	**FU**	P	*FC*	BF	77301	62896	71777	77300
319 007	**FU**	P	*FC*	BF	77303	62897	71778	77302
319 008	**SN**	P	*FC*	BF	77305	62898	71779	77304
319 009	**SN**	P	*FC*	BF	77307	62899	71780	77306
319 010	**FU**	P	*FC*	BF	77309	62900	71781	77308
319 011	**SN**	P	*FC*	BF	77311	62901	71782	77310
319 012	**SN**	P	*FC*	BF	77313	62902	71783	77312
319 013	**SN**	P	*FC*	BF	77315	62903	71784	77314

Names (carried on TSO):

319008 Cheriton
319011 John Ruskin College
319013 The Surrey Hills

Class 319/2. DTSO–MSO–TSO–DTCO. Units converted from Class 319/0.

Seating Layout: 1: 2+1 facing, 2: 2+2 facing.

DTSO. Lot No. 31022 (odd nos.) 1987–88. –/64. 28.2 t.
MSO. Lot No. 31023 1987–88. –/73 2T. 49.2 t.
TSO. Lot No. 31024 1987–88. –/52 1T 1TD. 31.0 t.
DTCO. Lot No. 31025 (even nos.) 1987–88. 18/36. 28.1 t.

Advertising livery: 319215 Visit Switzerland (red).

319214	**SN**	P	*FC*	BF	77317	62904	71785	77316	
319215	**AL**	P	*FC*	BF	77319	62905	71786	77318	
319216	**SN**	P	*FC*	BF	77321	62906	71787	77320	
319217	**SN**	P	*FC*	BF	77323	62907	71788	77322	Brighton
319218	**SN**	P	*FC*	BF	77325	62908	71789	77324	Croydon
319219	**SN**	P	*FC*	BF	77327	62909	71790	77326	
319220	**SN**	P	*FC*	BF	77329	62910	71791	77328	

Class 319/3. DTSO–MSO–TSO–DTSO. Converted from Class 319/1 by replacing First Class seats with Standard Class seats. Used mainly on the Luton–Sutton/Wimbledon routes.

Seating Layout: 3+2 facing.
Dimensions: 19.33 x 2.82 m.

Advertising livery: 319364 & 319365 Thameslink Programme (multi-coloured horizontal stripes with pink ends).

DTSO(A). Lot No. 31063 1990. –/70. 29.0 t.
MSO. Lot No. 31064 1990. –/78. 50.6 t.
TSO. Lot No. 31065 1990. –/74 2T. 31.0 t.
DTSO(B). Lot No. 31066 1990. –/75. 29.7 t.

319361	**FU**	P	*FC*	BF	77459	63043	71929	77458
319362	**FU**	P	*FC*	BF	77461	63044	71930	77460
319363	**FU**	P	*FC*	BF	77463	63045	71931	77462
319364	**AL**	P	*FC*	BF	77465	63046	71932	77464
319365	**AL**	P	*FC*	BF	77467	63047	71933	77466
319366	**FU**	P	*FC*	BF	77469	63048	71934	77468
319367	**FU**	P	*FC*	BF	77471	63049	71935	77470
319368	**FU**	P	*FC*	BF	77473	63050	71936	77472
319369	**FU**	P	*FC*	BF	77475	63051	71937	77474
319370	**FU**	P	*FC*	BF	77477	63052	71938	77476
319371	**FU**	P	*FC*	BF	77479	63053	71939	77478
319372	**FU**	P	*FC*	BF	77481	63054	71940	77480
319373	**FU**	P	*FC*	BF	77483	63055	71941	77482
319374	**FU**	P	*FC*	BF	77485	63056	71942	77484
319375	**FU**	P	*FC*	BF	77487	63057	71943	77486
319376	**FU**	P	*FC*	BF	77489	63058	71944	77488
319377	**FU**	P	*FC*	BF	77491	63059	71945	77490

319378	**FU**	P	*FC*	BF	77493	63060	71946	77492
319379	**FU**	P	*FC*	BF	77495	63061	71947	77494
319380	**FU**	P	*FC*	BF	77497	63062	71948	77496
319381	**FU**	P	*FC*	BF	77973	63093	71979	77974
319382	**FU**	P	*FC*	BF	77975	63094	71980	77976
319383	**FU**	P	*FC*	BF	77977	63095	71981	77978
319384	**FU**	P	*FC*	BF	77979	63096	71982	77980
319385	**FU**	P	*FC*	BF	77981	63097	71983	77982
319386	**FU**	P	*FC*	BF	77983	63098	71984	77984

Names (carried on TSO):

319364 Transforming Blackfriars
319365 Transforming Farringdon
319374 Bedford Cauldwell TMD

Class 319/4. DTCO–MSO–TSO–DTSO. Converted from Class 319/0. Refurbished with carpets. DTSO(A) converted to composite. Used mainly on the Bedford–Gatwick–Brighton route.

Seating Layout: 1: 2+1 facing 2: 2+2/3+2 facing.

77331–381. DTCO. Lot No. 31022 (odd nos.) 1987–88. 12/51. 28.2t.
77431–457. DTCO. Lot No. 31038 (odd nos.) 1988. 12/51. 28.2t.
62911–936. MSO. Lot No. 31023 1987–88. –/74. 49.2t.
62961–974. MSO. Lot No. 31039 1988. –/74. 49.2t.
71792–817. TSO. Lot No. 31024 1987–88. –/67 2T. 31.0t.
71866–879. TSO. Lot No. 31040 1988. –67 2T. 31.0t.
77330–380. DTSO. Lot No. 31025 (even nos.) 1987–88. –/71 1W. 28.1t.
77430–456. DTSO. Lot No. 31041 (even nos.) 1988. –/71 1W. 28.1t.

319421	**FU**	P	*FC*	BF	77331	62911	71792	77330
319422	**FU**	P	*FC*	BF	77333	62912	71793	77332
319423	**FU**	P	*FC*	BF	77335	62913	71794	77334
319424	**FU**	P	*FC*	BF	77337	62914	71795	77336
319425	**FU**	P	*FC*	BF	77339	62915	71796	77338
319426	**FU**	P	*FC*	BF	77341	62916	71797	77340
319427	**FU**	P	*FC*	BF	77343	62917	71798	77342
319428	**FU**	P	*FC*	BF	77345	62918	71799	77344
319429	**FU**	P	*FC*	BF	77347	62919	71800	77346
319430	**FU**	P	*FC*	BF	77349	62920	71801	77348
319431	**FU**	P	*FC*	BF	77351	62921	71802	77350
319432	**FU**	P	*FC*	BF	77353	62922	71803	77352
319433	**FU**	P	*FC*	BF	77355	62923	71804	77354
319434	**FU**	P	*FC*	BF	77357	62924	71805	77356
319435	**FU**	P	*FC*	BF	77359	62925	71806	77358
319436	**FU**	P	*FC*	BF	77361	62926	71807	77360
319437	**FU**	P	*FC*	BF	77363	62927	71808	77362
319438	**FU**	P	*FC*	BF	77365	62928	71809	77364
319439	**FU**	P	*FC*	BF	77367	62929	71810	77366
319440	**FU**	P	*FC*	BF	77369	62930	71811	77368
319441	**FU**	P	*FC*	BF	77371	62931	71812	77370
319442	**FU**	P	*FC*	BF	77373	62932	71813	77372
319443	**FU**	P	*FC*	BF	77375	62933	71814	77374

319444	**FU**	P	*FC*	BF	77377	62934	71815	77376
319445	**FU**	P	*FC*	BF	77379	62935	71816	77378
319446	**FU**	P	*FC*	BF	77381	62936	71817	77380
319447	**FU**	P	*FC*	BF	77431	62961	71866	77430
319448	**FU**	P	*FC*	BF	77433	62962	71867	77432
319449	**FU**	P	*FC*	BF	77435	62963	71868	77434
319450	**FU**	P	*FC*	BF	77437	62964	71869	77436
319451	**FU**	P	*FC*	BF	77439	62965	71870	77438
319452	**FU**	P	*FC*	BF	77441	62966	71871	77440
319453	**FU**	P	*FC*	BF	77443	62967	71872	77442
319454	**FU**	P	*FC*	BF	77445	62968	71873	77444
319455	**FU**	P	*FC*	BF	77447	62969	71874	77446
319456	**FU**	P	*FC*	BF	77449	62970	71875	77448
319457	**FU**	P	*FC*	BF	77451	62971	71876	77450
319458	**FU**	P	*FC*	BF	77453	62972	71877	77452
319459	**FU**	P	*FC*	BF	77455	62973	71878	77454
319460	**FU**	P	*FC*	BF	77457	62974	71879	77456

Names (carried on TSO):

319425 Transforming Travel
319435 Adrian Jackson-Robbins Chairman 1987–2007 Association of Public Transport Users
319446 St Pancras International
319448 Elstree Studios The Home of British Film and Television production
319449 King's Cross Thameslink

CLASS 320 BREL YORK

Suburban units.

Formation: DTSO–MSO–DTSO.
Construction: Steel
Traction Motors: Four Brush TM2141B of 268 kW.
Wheel Arrangement: 2-2 + Bo-Bo + 2-2.
Braking: Disc.
Dimensions: 19.95 x 2.82 m.
Bogies: P7-4 (MSO), T3-7 (others).
Couplers: Tightlock.
Gangways: Within unit.
Control System: Thyristor.
Doors: Sliding.
Maximum Speed: 90 mph.
Seating Layout: 3+2 facing.
Multiple Working: Within class & with Classes 317, 318, 319, 321, 322 and 323.

DTSO (A). Lot No. 31060 1990. –/76 1W (* –/51(4) 1TD 2W). 29.1 t (* 41.0 t).
MSO. Lot No. 31062 1990. –/76 1W (* –/78). 52.1 t.
DTSO (B). Lot No. 31061 1990. –/75 (* –/77). 31.7 t.

Note: Units marked * have been fitted with a toilet in the DTSO (A) vehicle.

320301		**SC**	E	*SR*	GW	77899	63021	77921
320302	*	**SR**	E	*SR*	GW	77900	63022	77922
320303		**SC**	E	*SR*	GW	77901	63023	77923
320304	*	**SR**	E	*SR*	GW	77902	63024	77924
320305		**SC**	E	*SR*	GW	77903	63025	77925
320306	*	**SR**	E	*SR*	GW	77904	63026	77926

320 307		**SC**	E	*SR*	GW	77905	63027	77927
320 308		**SC**	E	*SR*	GW	77906	63028	77928
320 309		**SC**	E	*SR*	GW	77907	63029	77929
320 310		**SC**	E	*SR*	GW	77908	63030	77930
320 311		**SC**	E	*SR*	GW	77909	63031	77931
320 312		**SC**	E	*SR*	GW	77910	63032	77932
320 313		**SC**	E	*SR*	GW	77911	63033	77933
320 314	*	**SR**	E	*SR*	GW	77912	63034	77934
320 315	*	**SR**	E	*SR*	GW	77913	63035	77935
320 316		**SC**	E	*SR*	GW	77914	63036	77936
320 317		**SC**	E	*SR*	GW	77915	63037	77937
320 318	*	**SR**	E	*SR*	GW	77916	63038	77938
320 319		**SC**	E	*SR*	GW	77917	63039	77939
320 320		**SC**	E	*SR*	GW	77918	63040	77940
320 321		**SC**	E	*SR*	GW	77919	63041	77941
320 322		**SC**	E	*SR*	GW	77920	63042	77942

Names (carried on MSO, all to be removed on repainting):

320 305 GLASGOW SCHOOL OF ART 1845 150 1995
320 308 High Road 20th Anniversary 2000
320 309 Radio Clyde 25th Anniversary
320 311 Royal College of Physicians and Surgeons of Glasgow
320 312 Sir William A Smith Founder of the Boys' Brigade
320 321 The Rt. Hon. John Smith, QC, MP
320 322 Festive Glasgow Orchid

CLASS 321 BREL YORK

Outer suburban units.

Formation: DTCO (DTSO on Class 321/9)–MSO–TSO–DTSO.
Construction: Steel.
Traction Motors: Four Brush TM2141C (268 kW).
Wheel Arrangement: 2-2 + Bo-Bo + 2-2 + 2-2.
Braking: Disc.
Dimensions: 19.95 x 2.82 m.
Bogies: P7-4 (MSO), T3-7 (others).
Couplers: Tightlock.
Gangways: Within unit.
Control System: Thyristor.
Doors: Sliding.
Maximum Speed: 100 mph.
Seating Layout: 1: 2+2 facing, 2: 3+2 facing.
Multiple Working: Within class & with Classes 317, 318, 319, 320, 322 and 323.

Class 321/3.

DTCO. Lot No. 31053 1988–90. 16/57. 29.7 t.
MSO. Lot No. 31054 1988–90. –/82. 51.5 t.
TSO. Lot No. 31055 1988–90. –/75 2T. 29.1 t.
DTSO. Lot No. 31056 1988–90. –/78. 29.7 t.

321 301	**NX**	E	*EA*	IL	78049	62975	71880	77853
321 302	**NX**	E	*EA*	IL	78050	62976	71881	77854
321 303	**NX**	E	*EA*	IL	78051	62977	71882	77855
321 304	**NX**	E	*EA*	IL	78052	62978	71883	77856
321 305	**NX**	E	*EA*	IL	78053	62979	71884	77857

321 306	**NX**	E	*EA*	IL	78054	62980	71885	77858
321 307	**NX**	E	*EA*	IL	78055	62981	71886	77859
321 308	**NX**	E	*EA*	IL	78056	62982	71887	77860
321 309	**NX**	E	*EA*	IL	78057	62983	71888	77861
321 310	**NX**	E	*EA*	IL	78058	62984	71889	77862
321 311	**NX**	E	*EA*	IL	78059	62985	71890	77863
321 312	**NX**	E	*EA*	IL	78060	62986	71891	77864
321 313	**NX**	E	*EA*	IL	78061	62987	71892	77865
321 314	**NX**	E	*EA*	IL	78062	62988	71893	77866
321 315	**NX**	E	*EA*	IL	78063	62989	71894	77867
321 316	**NX**	E	*EA*	IL	78064	62990	71895	77868
321 317	**NX**	E	*EA*	IL	78065	62991	71896	77869
321 318	**NX**	E	*EA*	IL	78066	62992	71897	77870
321 319	**NX**	E	*EA*	IL	78067	62993	71898	77871
321 320	**NX**	E	*EA*	IL	78068	62994	71899	77872
321 321	**NX**	E	*EA*	IL	78069	62995	71900	77873
321 322	**NX**	E	*EA*	IL	78070	62996	71901	77874
321 323	**NX**	E	*EA*	IL	78071	62997	71902	77875
321 324	**NX**	E	*EA*	IL	78072	62998	71903	77876
321 325	**NX**	E	*EA*	IL	78073	62999	71904	77877
321 326	**NX**	E	*EA*	IL	78074	63000	71905	77878
321 327	**NC**	E	*EA*	IL	78075	63001	71906	77879
321 328	**NX**	E	*EA*	IL	78076	63002	71907	77880
321 329	**NX**	E	*EA*	IL	78077	63003	71908	77881
321 330	**NC**	E	*EA*	IL	78078	63004	71909	77882
321 331	**NC**	E	*EA*	IL	78079	63005	71910	77883
321 332	**NC**	E	*EA*	IL	78080	63006	71911	77884
321 333	**NC**	E	*EA*	IL	78081	63007	71912	77885
321 334	**NC**	E	*EA*	IL	78082	63008	71913	77886
321 335	**NC**	E	*EA*	IL	78083	63009	71914	77887
321 336	**NC**	E	*EA*	IL	78084	63010	71915	77888
321 337	**NC**	E	*EA*	IL	78085	63011	71916	77889
321 338	**NC**	E	*EA*	IL	78086	63012	71917	77890
321 339	**NC**	E	*EA*	IL	78087	63013	71918	77891
321 340	**NC**	E	*EA*	IL	78088	63014	71919	77892
321 341	**NC**	E	*EA*	IL	78089	63015	71920	77893
321 342	**NC**	E	*EA*	IL	78090	63016	71921	77894
321 343	**NC**	E	*EA*	IL	78091	63017	71922	77895
321 344	**NC**	E	*EA*	IL	78092	63018	71923	77896
321 345	**NC**	E	*EA*	IL	78093	63019	71924	77897
321 346	**NC**	E	*EA*	IL	78094	63020	71925	77898
321 347	**NC**	E	*EA*	IL	78131	63105	71991	78280
321 348	**NC**	E	*EA*	IL	78132	63106	71992	78281
321 349	**NC**	E	*EA*	IL	78133	63107	71993	78282
321 350	**NC**	E	*EA*	IL	78134	63108	71994	78283
321 351	**NC**	E	*EA*	IL	78135	63109	71995	78284
321 352	**NC**	E	*EA*	IL	78136	63110	71996	78285
321 353	**NC**	E	*EA*	IL	78137	63111	71997	78286
321 354	**NC**	E	*EA*	IL	78138	63112	71998	78287
321 355	**NC**	E	*EA*	IL	78139	63113	71999	78288
321 356	**NC**	E	*EA*	IL	78140	63114	72000	78289

321357	**NC**	E	*EA*	IL	78141	63115	72001	78290
321358	**GE**	E	*EA*	IL	78142	63116	72002	78291
321359	**GE**	E	*EA*	IL	78143	63117	72003	78292
321360	**NC**	E	*EA*	IL	78144	63118	72004	78293
321361	**GE**	E	*EA*	IL	78145	63119	72005	78294
321362	**GE**	E	*EA*	IL	78146	63120	72006	78295
321363	**GE**	E	*EA*	IL	78147	63121	72007	78296
321364	**GE**	E	*EA*	IL	78148	63122	72008	78297
321365	**GE**	E	*EA*	IL	78149	63123	72009	78298
321366	**GE**	E	*EA*	IL	78150	63124	72010	78299

Names (carried on TSO):

321312 Southend-on-Sea
321313 University of Essex
321321 NSPCC ESSEX FULL STOP
321334 Amsterdam
321336 GEOFFREY FREEMAN ALLEN
321342 R. Barnes
321343 RSA RAILWAY STUDY ASSOCIATION
321351 London Southend Airport
321361 Phoenix

Class 321/4.

DTCO. Lot No. 31067 1989–90. 28/40. 29.8 t.
MSO. Lot No. 31068 1989–90. –/79. 51.6 t.
TSO. Lot No. 31069 1989–90. –/74 2T. 29.2 t.
DTSO. Lot No. 31070 1989–90. –/78. 29.8 t.

Notes: The original vehicles 71966 and 77960 from 321418 and 78114 and 63082 from 321420 were written off after the Watford Junction accident in 1996. The undamaged vehicles were formed together as 321418 whilst four new vehices were built in 1997, taking the same numbers as the scrapped vehicles, and these became the second 321420.

The DTCOs of 321438–448 have had 12 First Class seats declassified.

321401	**FU**	E	*FC*	HE	78095	63063	71949	77943
321402	**FU**	E	*FC*	HE	78096	63064	71950	77944
321403	**FU**	E	*FC*	HE	78097	63065	71951	77945
321404	**FU**	E	*FC*	HE	78098	63066	71952	77946
321405	**FU**	E	*FC*	HE	78099	63067	71953	77947
321406	**FU**	E	*FC*	HE	78100	63068	71954	77948
321407	**FU**	E	*FC*	HE	78101	63069	71955	77949
321408	**FU**	E	*FC*	HE	78102	63070	71956	77950
321409	**FU**	E	*FC*	HE	78103	63071	71957	77951
321410	**FU**	E	*FC*	HE	78104	63072	71958	77952
321411	**LM**	E	*LM*	NN	78105	63073	71959	77953
321412	**LM**	E	*LM*	NN	78106	63074	71960	77954
321413	**LM**	E	*LM*	NN	78107	63075	71961	77955
321414	**LM**	E	*LM*	NN	78108	63076	71962	77956
321415	**LM**	E	*LM*	NN	78109	63077	71963	77957
321416	**LM**	E	*LM*	NN	78110	63078	71964	77958

321417	**LM**	E	*LM*	NN	78111	63079	71965	77959
321418	**FU**	E	*FC*	HE	78112	63080	71968	77962
321419	**FU**	E	*FC*	HE	78113	63081	71967	77961
321420	**FU**	E	*FC*	HE	78114	63082	71966	77960
321421	**NC**	E	*EA*	IL	78115	63083	71969	77963
321422	**NC**	E	*EA*	IL	78116	63084	71970	77964
321423	**NC**	E	*EA*	IL	78117	63085	71971	77965
321424	**NX**	E	*EA*	IL	78118	63086	71972	77966
321425	**SL**	E	*EA*	IL	78119	63087	71973	77967
321426	**NX**	E	*EA*	IL	78120	63088	71974	77968
321427	**NX**	E	*EA*	IL	78121	63089	71975	77969
321428	**NX**	E	*EA*	IL	78122	63090	71976	77970
321429	**NX**	E	*EA*	IL	78123	63091	71977	77971
321430	**NX**	E	*EA*	IL	78124	63092	71978	77972
321431	**NX**	E	*EA*	IL	78151	63125	72011	78300
321432	**NC**	E	*EA*	IL	78152	63126	72012	78301
321433	**NC**	E	*EA*	IL	78153	63127	72013	78302
321434	**NC**	E	*EA*	IL	78154	63128	72014	78303
321435	**NC**	E	*EA*	IL	78155	63129	72015	78304
321436	**NC**	E	*EA*	IL	78156	63130	72016	78305
321437	**NC**	E	*EA*	IL	78157	63131	72017	78306
321438	**GE**	E	*EA*	IL	78158	63132	72018	78307
321439	**GE**	E	*EA*	IL	78159	63133	72019	78308
321440	**GE**	E	*EA*	IL	78160	63134	72020	78309
321441	**GE**	E	*EA*	IL	78161	63135	72021	78310
321442	**GE**	E	*EA*	IL	78162	63136	72022	78311
321443	**GE**	E	*EA*	IL	78125	63099	71985	78274
321444	**GE**	E	*EA*	IL	78126	63100	71986	78275
321445	**GE**	E	*EA*	IL	78127	63101	71987	78276
321446	**1**	E	*EA*	IL	78128	63102	71988	78277
321447	**GE**	E	*EA*	IL	78129	63103	71989	78278
321448	**GE**	E	*EA*	IL	78130	63104	71990	78279

Names (carried on TSO):

321403 Stewart Fleming Signalman King's Cross
321428 The Essex Commuter
321444 Essex Lifeboats
321446 George Mullings

Class 321/9. DTSO(A)–MSO–TSO–DTSO(B).

DTSO(A). Lot No. 31108 1991. –/70(8). 29.2 t.
MSO. Lot No. 31109 1991. –/79. 51.1 t.
TSO. Lot No. 31110 1991. –/74 2T. 29.0 t.
DTSO(B). Lot No. 31111 1991. –/70(7) 1W. 29.2 t.

321901	**YR**	E	*NO*	NL	77990	63153	72128	77993
321902	**YR**	E	*NO*	NL	77991	63154	72129	77994
321903	**YR**	E	*NO*	NL	77992	63155	72130	77995

CLASS 322 BREL YORK

Units built for use on Stansted Airport services, used for a number of years with ScotRail before transfer to Northern.

Formation: DTSO–MSO–TSO–DTSO.
Construction: Steel.
Traction Motors: Four Brush TM2141C (268 kW).
Wheel Arrangement: 2-2 + Bo-Bo + 2-2 + 2-2.
Braking: Disc.
Dimensions: 19.95/19.92 x 2.82 m.
Bogies: P7-4 (MSO), T3-7 (others).
Couplers: Tightlock.
Gangways: Within unit.
Control System: Thyristor.
Doors: Sliding.
Maximum Speed: 100 mph.
Seating Layout: 3+2 facing.
Multiple Working: Within class & with Classes 317, 318, 319, 320, 321 and 323.

DTSO(A). Lot No. 31094 1990. –/58. 29.3 t.
MSO. Lot No. 31092 1990. –/83. 51.5 t.
TSO. Lot No. 31093 1990. –/76 2T. 28.8 t.
DTSO(B). Lot No. 31091 1990. –/89(3) 1W. 29.1 t.

322481	**FB**	E	*NO*	NL	78163	63137	72023	77985
322482	**FB**	E	*NO*	NL	78164	63138	72024	77986
322483	**FB**	E	*NO*	NL	78165	63139	72025	77987
322484	**FB**	E	*NO*	NL	78166	63140	72026	77988
322485	**FB**	E	*NO*	NL	78167	63141	72027	77989

CLASS 323 HUNSLET TRANSPORTATION PROJECTS

Suburban units.

Formation: DMSO–PTSO–DMSO.
Construction: Welded aluminium alloy.
Traction Motors: Four Holec DMKT 52/24 asynchronous of 146 kW.
Wheel Arrangement: Bo-Bo + 2-2 + Bo-Bo.
Braking: Disc.
Dimensions: 23.37/23.44 x 2.80 m.
Bogies: SRP BP62 (DMSO), BT52 (PTSO).
Couplers: Tightlock.
Gangways: Within unit.
Control System: GTO Inverter.
Doors: Sliding plug.
Maximum Speed: 90 mph.
Seating Layout: 3+2 facing/unidirectional.
Multiple Working: Within class & with Classes 317, 318, 319, 320, 321 and 322.

DMSO(A). Lot No. 31112 Hunslet 1992–93. –/98 (* –/82). 41.0 t.
TSO. Lot No. 31113 Hunslet 1992–93. –/88(5) 1T 2W. (* –/80 1T 2W). 39.4t.
DMSO(B). Lot No. 31114 Hunslet 1992–93. –/98 (* –/82). 41.0 t.

323201	**LM**	P	*LM*	SO	64001	72201	65001
323202	**LM**	P	*LM*	SO	64002	72202	65002
323203	**LM**	P	*LM*	SO	64003	72203	65003
323204	**LM**	P	*LM*	SO	64004	72204	65004
323205	**LM**	P	*LM*	SO	64005	72205	65005
323206	**LM**	P	*LM*	SO	64006	72206	65006
323207	**LM**	P	*LM*	SO	64007	72207	65007

323 208	**LM**	P	*LM*	SO	64008	72208	65008
323 209	**LM**	P	*LM*	SO	64009	72209	65009
323 210	**LM**	P	*LM*	SO	64010	72210	65010
323 211	**LM**	P	*LM*	SO	64011	72211	65011
323 212	**LM**	P	*LM*	SO	64012	72212	65012
323 213	**LM**	P	*LM*	SO	64013	72213	65013
323 214	**LM**	P	*LM*	SO	64014	72214	65014
323 215	**LM**	P	*LM*	SO	64015	72215	65015
323 216	**LM**	P	*LM*	SO	64016	72216	65016
323 217	**LM**	P	*LM*	SO	64017	72217	65017
323 218	**LM**	P	*LM*	SO	64018	72218	65018
323 219	**LM**	P	*LM*	SO	64019	72219	65019
323 220	**LM**	P	*LM*	SO	64020	72220	65020
323 221	**LM**	P	*LM*	SO	64021	72221	65021
323 222	**LM**	P	*LM*	SO	64022	72222	65022
323 223 *	**NO**	P	*NO*	LG	64023	72223	65023
323 224 *	**NO**	P	*NO*	LG	64024	72224	65024
323 225 *	**NO**	P	*NO*	LG	64025	72225	65025
323 226	**NO**	P	*NO*	LG	64026	72226	65026
323 227	**NO**	P	*NO*	LG	64027	72227	65027
323 228	**NO**	P	*NO*	LG	64028	72228	65028
323 229	**NO**	P	*NO*	LG	64029	72229	65029
323 230	**NO**	P	*NO*	LG	64030	72230	65030
323 231	**NO**	P	*NO*	LG	64031	72231	65031
323 232	**NO**	P	*NO*	LG	64032	72232	65032
323 233	**NO**	P	*NO*	LG	64033	72233	65033
323 234	**NO**	P	*NO*	LG	64034	72234	65034
323 235	**NO**	P	*NO*	LG	64035	72235	65035
323 236	**NO**	P	*NO*	LG	64036	72236	65036
323 237	**NO**	P	*NO*	LG	64037	72237	65037
323 238	**NO**	P	*NO*	LG	64038	72238	65038
323 239	**NO**	P	*NO*	LG	64039	72239	65039
323 240	**LM**	P	*LM*	SO	64040	72340	65040
323 241	**LM**	P	*LM*	SO	64041	72341	65041
323 242	**LM**	P	*LM*	SO	64042	72342	65042
323 243	**LM**	P	*LM*	SO	64043	72343	65043

CLASS 325 ABB DERBY

Postal units based on Class 319s. Compatible with diesel or electric locomotive haulage.

Formation: DTPMV–MPMV–TPMV–DTPMV.
System: 25 kV AC overhead/750 V DC third rail.
Construction: Steel.
Traction Motors: Four GEC G315BZ of 268 kW.
Wheel Arrangement: 2-2 + Bo-Bo + 2-2 + 2-2.
Braking: Disc.
Bogies: P7-4 (MSO), T3-7 (others).
Gangways: None.
Doors: Roller shutter.
Dimensions: 19.33 x 2.82 m.
Couplers: Drop-head buckeye.
Control System: GTO Chopper.
Maximum Speed: 100 mph.

Multiple Working: Within class.

DTPMV. Lot No. 31144 1995. 29.1 t.
MPMV. Lot No. 31145 1995. 49.5 t.
TPMV. Lot No. 31146 1995. 30.7 t.

325 001	**RM**	RM	*DB*	CE	68300	68340	68360	68301
325 002	**RM**	RM	*DB*	CE	68302	68341	68361	68303
325 003	**RM**	RM	*DB*	CE	68304	68342	68362	68305
325 004	**RM**	RM	*DB*	CE	68306	68343	68363	68307
325 005	**RM**	RM	*DB*	CE	68308	68344	68364	68309
325 006	**RM**	RM	*DB*	CE	68310	68345	68365	68311
325 007	**RM**	RM	*DB*	CE	68312	68346	68366	68313
325 008	**RM**	RM	*DB*	CE	68314	68347	68367	68315
325 009	**RM**	RM	*DB*	CE	68316	68349	68368	68317
325 010	**RM**	RM		DR	68318	68348	68369	68319
325 011	**RM**	RM	*DB*	CE	68320	68350	68370	68321
325 012	**RM**	RM	*DB*	CE	68322	68351	68371	68323
325 013	**RM**	RM	*DB*	CE	68324	68352	68372	68325
325 014	**RM**	RM	*DB*	CE	68326	68353	68373	68327
325 015	**RM**	RM	*DB*	CE	68328	68354	68374	68329
325 016	**RM**	RM	*DB*	CE	68330	68355	68375	68331

Names (carried on one side of each DTPMV):

325 002 Royal Mail North Wales & North West
325 006 John Grierson
325 008 Peter Howarth CBE

CLASS 332 HEATHROW EXPRESS SIEMENS

Dedicated Heathrow Express units. Five units were increased from 4-car to 5-car in 2002. Usually operate in coupled pairs.

Formations: Various.
Construction: Steel.
Traction Motors: Two Siemens monomotors asynchronous of 350 kW.
Wheel Arrangement: B-B + 2-2 + 2-2 (+ 2-2) + B-B.
Braking: Disc.
Dimensions: 23.63/23.35 x 2.75 m.
Bogies: CAF.
Couplers: Scharfenberg 10L.
Gangways: Within unit.
Control System: IGBT Inverter.
Doors: Sliding plug.
Maximum Speed: 100 mph.
Heating & ventilation: Air conditioning.
Seating Layout: 1: 2+1 facing, 2: 2+2 mainly unidirectional.
Multiple Working: Within class.

332 001–007. DMFO–TSO–PTSO–(TSO)–DMSO.

DMFO. CAF 1997–98. 26/–. 48.8 t.
72400–413. TSO. CAF 1997–98. –/56 35.8 t.
72414–418. TSO. CAF 2002. –/56 35.8 t.
PTSO. CAF 1997–98. –/44 1TD 1W. 45.6 t.
DMSO. CAF 1997–1998. –/48. 48.8 t.
DMLFO. CAF 1997–1998. 14/– 1W. 48.8 t.

Advertising livery: Vehicles 78401, 78402, 78405, 78406, 78408, 78410, 78412 Vodafone (red).

332001	**HE**	HE	*HE*	OH	78400	72412	63400	78401	
332002	**HE**	HE	*HE*	OH	78402	72409	63401	78403	
332003	**HE**	HE	*HE*	OH	78404	72407	63402	78405	
332004	**HE**	HE	*HE*	OH	78406	72405	63403	78407	
332005	**HE**	HE	*HE*	OH	78408	72411	63404	72417	78409
332006	**HE**	HE	*HE*	OH	78410	72410	63405	72415	78411
332007	**HE**	HE	*HE*	OH	78412	72401	63406	72414	78413

332008–014. DMSO–TSO–PTSO–(TSO)–DMLFO.

Advertising livery: Vehicles 78414, 78416, 78419, 78421, 78423, 78425, 78427 Vodafone (red).

332008	**HE**	HE	*HE*	OH	78414	72413	63407	72418	78415
332009	**HE**	HE	*HE*	OH	78416	72400	63408	72416	78417
332010	**HE**	HE	*HE*	OH	78418	72402	63409		78419
332011	**HE**	HE	*HE*	OH	78420	72403	63410		78421
332012	**HE**	HE	*HE*	OH	78422	72404	63411		78423
332013	**HE**	HE	*HE*	OH	78424	72408	63412		78425
332014	**HE**	HE	*HE*	OH	78426	72406	63413		78427

CLASS 333 SIEMENS

West Yorkshire area suburban units.

Formation: DMSO–PTSO–TSO–DMSO.
Construction: Steel.
Traction Motors: Two Siemens monomotors asynchronous of 350 kW.
Wheel Arrangement: B-B + 2-2 + 2-2 + B-B.
Braking: Disc.
Dimensions: 23.74 (outer ends)/23.35 (TSO) x 2.75 m.
Bogies: CAF.
Couplers: Dellner 10L.
Gangways: Within unit.
Control System: IGBT Inverter.
Doors: Sliding plug.
Maximum Speed: 100 mph.
Heating & ventilation: Air conditioning.
Seating Layout: 3+2 facing/unidirectional.
Multiple Working: Within class.

DMSO(A). (Odd Nos.) CAF 2001. –/90. 50.6 t.
PTSO. CAF 2001. –/73(6) 1TD 2W. 46.0 t.
TSO. CAF 2002–03. –/100. 38.5 t.
DMSO(B). (Even Nos.) CAF 2001. –/90. 50.0 t.

Notes: 333001–008 were made up to 4-car units from 3-car units in 2002.

333009–016 were made up to 4-car units from 3-car units in 2003.

333001	**YR**	A	*NO*	NL	78451	74461	74477	78452
333002	**YR**	A	*NO*	NL	78453	74462	74478	78454
333003	**YR**	A	*NO*	NL	78455	74463	74479	78456
333004	**YR**	A	*NO*	NL	78457	74464	74480	78458
333005	**YR**	A	*NO*	NL	78459	74465	74481	78460

333 006	**YR**	A	*NO*	NL	78461	74466	74482	78462
333 007	**YR**	A	*NO*	NL	78463	74467	74483	78464
333 008	**YR**	A	*NO*	NL	78465	74468	74484	78466
333 009	**YR**	A	*NO*	NL	78467	74469	74485	78468
333 010	**YR**	A	*NO*	NL	78469	74470	74486	78470
333 011	**YR**	A	*NO*	NL	78471	74471	74487	78472
333 012	**YR**	A	*NO*	NL	78473	74472	74488	78474
333 013	**YR**	A	*NO*	NL	78475	74473	74489	78476
333 014	**YR**	A	*NO*	NL	78477	74474	74490	78478
333 015	**YR**	A	*NO*	NL	78479	74475	74491	78480
333 016	**YR**	A	*NO*	NL	78481	74476	74492	78482

Name (carried on end cars):

333 007 Alderman J Arthur Godwin First Lord Mayor of Bradford 1907

CLASS 334 JUNIPER ALSTOM BIRMINGHAM

Outer suburban units.

Formation: DMSO–PTSO–DMSO.
Construction: Steel.
Traction Motors: Two Alstom ONIX 800 asynchronous of 270 kW.
Wheel Arrangement: 2-Bo + 2-2 + Bo-2.
Braking: Disc.
Dimensions: 21.01/19.94 x 2.80 m.
Bogies: Alstom LTB3/TBP3.
Couplers: Tightlock.
Gangways: Within unit.
Control System: IGBT Inverter.
Doors: Sliding plug.
Maximum Speed: 90 mph.
Heating & ventilation: Pressure heating and ventilation.
Seating Layout: 2+2 facing/unidirectional (3+2 in PTSO).
Multiple Working: Within class.

DMSO(A). Alstom Birmingham 1999–2001. –/64. 42.6 t.
PTSO. Alstom Birmingham 1999–2001. –/55 1TD 1W. 39.4 t.
DMSO(B). Alstom Birmingham 1999–2001. –/64. 42.6 t.

334 001	**SP**	E	*SR*	GW	64101	74301	65101	Donald Dewar
334 002	**SP**	E	*SR*	GW	64102	74302	65102	
334 003	**SP**	E	*SR*	GW	64103	74303	65103	
334 004	**SP**	E	*SR*	GW	64104	74304	65104	
334 005	**SP**	E	*SR*	GW	64105	74305	65105	
334 006	**SR**	E	*SR*	GW	64106	74306	65106	
334 007	**SP**	E	*SR*	GW	64107	74307	65107	
334 008	**SP**	E	*SR*	GW	64108	74308	65108	
334 009	**SP**	E	*SR*	GW	64109	74309	65109	
334 010	**SP**	E	*SR*	GW	64110	74310	65110	
334 011	**SP**	E	*SR*	GW	64111	74311	65111	
334 012	**SR**	E	*SR*	GW	64112	74312	65112	
334 013	**SP**	E	*SR*	GW	64113	74313	65113	
334 014	**SP**	E	*SR*	GW	64114	74314	65114	
334 015	**SP**	E	*SR*	GW	64115	74315	65115	
334 016	**SP**	E	*SR*	GW	64116	74316	65116	
334 017	**SP**	E	*SR*	GW	64117	74317	65117	

334 018	**SP**	E	*SR*	GW	64118	74318	65118	
334 019	**SP**	E	*SR*	GW	64119	74319	65119	
334 020	**SP**	E	*SR*	GW	64120	74320	65120	
334 021	**SP**	E	*SR*	GW	64121	74321	65121	Larkhall
334 022	**SP**	E	*SR*	GW	64122	74322	65122	
334 023	**SP**	E	*SR*	GW	64123	74323	65123	
334 024	**SP**	E	*SR*	GW	64124	74324	65124	
334 025	**SP**	E	*SR*	GW	64125	74325	65125	
334 026	**SP**	E	*SR*	GW	64126	74326	65126	
334 027	**SP**	E	*SR*	GW	64127	74327	65127	
334 028	**SP**	E	*SR*	GW	64128	74328	65128	
334 029	**SP**	E	*SR*	GW	64129	74329	65129	
334 030	**SP**	E	*SR*	GW	64130	74330	65130	
334 031	**SP**	E	*SR*	GW	64131	74331	65131	
334 032	**SP**	E	*SR*	GW	64132	74332	65132	
334 033	**SP**	E	*SR*	GW	64133	74333	65133	
334 034	**SP**	E	*SR*	GW	64134	74334	65134	
334 035	**SP**	E	*SR*	GW	64135	74335	65135	
334 036	**SP**	E	*SR*	GW	64136	74336	65136	
334 037	**SP**	E	*SR*	GW	64137	74337	65137	
334 038	**SP**	E	*SR*	GW	64138	74338	65138	
334 039	**SP**	E	*SR*	GW	64139	74339	65139	
334 040	**SP**	E	*SR*	GW	64140	74340	65140	

CLASS 350 DESIRO UK SIEMENS

Outer suburban and long distance units.

Formation: DMCO–TCO–PTSO–DMCO.
Systems: 25 kV AC overhead (350/1s built with 750 V DC).
Construction: Welded aluminium.
Traction Motors: 4 Siemens 1TB2016-0GB02 asynchronous of 250 kW.
Wheel Arrangement: Bo-Bo + 2-2 + 2-2 + Bo-Bo.
Braking: Disc & regenerative.
Dimensions: 20.34 x 2.79 m.
Bogies: SGP SF5000.
Couplers: Dellner 12.
Gangways: Throughout.
Control System: IGBT Inverter.
Doors: Sliding plug.
Maximum Speed: 100 mph.
Heating & ventilation: Air conditioning.
Seating Layout: 1: 2+2 facing, 2: 2+2 facing/unidirectional (3+2 in 350/2s).
Multiple Working: Within class.

Class 350/1. Original build units owned by Angel Trains. Formerly part of an aborted South West Trains 5-car Class 450/2 order. 2+2 seating.

DMSO(A). Siemens Krefeld 2004–05. –/60. 48.7 t.
TCO. Siemens Krefeld/Prague 2004–05. 24/32 1T. 36.2 t.
PTSO. Siemens Krefeld/Prague 2004–05. –/50(9) 1TD 2W. 45.2 t.
DMSO(B). Siemens Krefeld 2004–05. –/60. 49.2 t.

350 101	**LM**	A	*LM*	NN	63761	66811	66861	63711
350 102	**LM**	A	*LM*	NN	63762	66812	66862	63712
350 103	**LM**	A	*LM*	NN	63765	66813	66863	63713
350 104	**LM**	A	*LM*	NN	63764	66814	66864	63714

350 105	**LM**	A	*LM*	NN	63763	66815	66868	63715
350 106	**LM**	A	*LM*	NN	63766	66816	66866	63716
350 107	**LM**	A	*LM*	NN	63767	66817	66867	63717
350 108	**LM**	A	*LM*	NN	63768	66818	66865	63718
350 109	**LM**	A	*LM*	NN	63769	66819	66869	63719
350 110	**LM**	A	*LM*	NN	63770	66820	66870	63720
350 111	**LM**	A	*LM*	NN	63771	66821	66871	63721
350 112	**LM**	A	*LM*	NN	63772	66822	66872	63722
350 113	**LM**	A	*LM*	NN	63773	66823	66873	63723
350 114	**LM**	A	*LM*	NN	63774	66824	66874	63724
350 115	**LM**	A	*LM*	NN	63775	66825	66875	63725
350 116	**LM**	A	*LM*	NN	63776	66826	66876	63726
350 117	**LM**	A	*LM*	NN	63777	66827	66877	63727
350 118	**LM**	A	*LM*	NN	63778	66828	66878	63728
350 119	**LM**	A	*LM*	NN	63779	66829	66879	63729
350 120	**LM**	A	*LM*	NN	63780	66830	66880	63730
350 121	**LM**	A	*LM*	NN	63781	66831	66881	63731
350 122	**LM**	A	*LM*	NN	63782	66832	66882	63732
350 123	**LM**	A	*LM*	NN	63783	66833	66883	63733
350 124	**LM**	A	*LM*	NN	63784	66834	66884	63734
350 125	**LM**	A	*LM*	NN	63785	66835	66885	63735
350 126	**LM**	A	*LM*	NN	63786	66836	66886	63736
350 127	**LM**	A	*LM*	NN	63787	66837	66887	63737
350 128	**LM**	A	*LM*	NN	63788	66838	66888	63738
350 129	**LM**	A	*LM*	NN	63789	66839	66889	63739
350 130	**LM**	A	*LM*	NN	63790	66840	66890	63740

Class 350/2. Owned by Porterbrook Leasing. 3+2 seating.

DMSO(A). Siemens Krefeld 2008–09. –/70. 43.7 t.
TCO. Siemens Prague 2008–09. 24/42 1T. 35.3 t.
PTSO. Siemens Prague 2008–09. –/61(9) 1TD 2W. 42.9 t.
DMSO(B). Siemens Krefeld 2008–09. –/70. 44.2 t.

350 231	**LM**	P	*LM*	NN	61431	65231	67531	61531
350 232	**LM**	P	*LM*	NN	61432	65232	67532	61532
350 233	**LM**	P	*LM*	NN	61433	65233	67533	61533
350 234	**LM**	P	*LM*	NN	61434	65234	67534	61534
350 235	**LM**	P	*LM*	NN	61435	65235	67535	61535
350 236	**LM**	P	*LM*	NN	61436	65236	67536	61536
350 237	**LM**	P	*LM*	NN	61437	65237	67537	61537
350 238	**LM**	P	*LM*	NN	61438	65238	67538	61538
350 239	**LM**	P	*LM*	NN	61439	65239	67539	61539
350 240	**LM**	P	*LM*	NN	61440	65240	67540	61540
350 241	**LM**	P	*LM*	NN	61441	65241	67541	61541
350 242	**LM**	P	*LM*	NN	61442	65242	67542	61542
350 243	**LM**	P	*LM*	NN	61443	65243	67543	61543
350 244	**LM**	P	*LM*	NN	61444	65244	67544	61544
350 245	**LM**	P	*LM*	NN	61445	65245	67545	61545
350 246	**LM**	P	*LM*	NN	61446	65246	67546	61546
350 247	**LM**	P	*LM*	NN	61447	65247	67547	61547
350 248	**LM**	P	*LM*	NN	61448	65248	67548	61548

350 249	**LM**	P	*LM*	NN	61449	65249	67549	61549
350 250	**LM**	P	*LM*	NN	61450	65250	67550	61550
350 251	**LM**	P	*LM*	NN	61451	65251	67551	61551
350 252	**LM**	P	*LM*	NN	61452	65252	67552	61552
350 253	**LM**	P	*LM*	NN	61453	65253	67553	61553
350 254	**LM**	P	*LM*	NN	61454	65254	67554	61554
350 255	**LM**	P	*LM*	NN	61455	65255	67555	61555
350 256	**LM**	P	*LM*	NN	61456	65256	67556	61556
350 257	**LM**	P	*LM*	NN	61457	65257	67557	61557
350 258	**LM**	P	*LM*	NN	61458	65258	67558	61558
350 259	**LM**	P	*LM*	NN	61459	65259	67559	61559
350 260	**LM**	P	*LM*	NN	61460	65260	67560	61560
350 261	**LM**	P	*LM*	NN	61461	65261	67561	61561
350 262	**LM**	P	*LM*	NN	61462	65262	67562	61562
350 263	**LM**	P	*LM*	NN	61463	65263	67563	61563
350 264	**LM**	P	*LM*	NN	61464	65264	67564	61564
350 265	**LM**	P	*LM*	NN	61465	65265	67565	61565
350 266	**LM**	P	*LM*	NN	61466	65266	67566	61566
350 267	**LM**	P	*LM*	NN	61467	65267	67567	61567

CLASS 357 ELECTROSTAR
ADTRANZ/BOMBARDIER DERBY

Provision for 750 V DC supply if required.

Formation: DMSO–MSO–PTSO–DMSO.
Construction: Welded aluminium alloy underframe, sides and roof with steel ends. All sections bolted together.
Traction Motors: Two Adtranz asynchronous of 250 kW.
Wheel Arrangement: 2-Bo + 2-Bo + 2-2 + Bo-2.
Braking: Disc & regenerative.
Bogies: Adtranz P3-25/T3-25.
Gangways: Within unit.
Doors: Sliding plug.
Dimensions: 20.40/19.99 x 2.80 m.
Couplers: Tightlock.
Control System: IGBT Inverter.
Maximum Speed: 100 mph.
Heating & ventilation: Air conditioning.
Seating Layout: 3+2 facing/unidirectional.
Multiple Working: Within class.

Class 357/0. Owned by Porterbrook Leasing.

DMSO(A). Adtranz Derby 1999–2001. –/71. 40.7 t.
MSO. Adtranz Derby 1999–2001. –/78. 36.7 t.
PTSO. Adtranz Derby 1999–2001. –/58(4) 1TD 2W. 39.5 t.
DMSO(B). Adtranz Derby 1999–2001. –/71. 40.7 t.

357 001	**NC**	P	*C2*	EM	67651	74151	74051	67751
357 002	**NC**	P	*C2*	EM	67652	74152	74052	67752
357 003	**NC**	P	*C2*	EM	67653	74153	74053	67753
357 004	**NC**	P	*C2*	EM	67654	74154	74054	67754
357 005	**NC**	P	*C2*	EM	67655	74155	74055	67755
357 006	**NC**	P	*C2*	EM	67656	74156	74056	67756

357 007	**NC**	P	*C2*	EM	67657	74157	74057	67757
357 008	**NC**	P	*C2*	EM	67658	74158	74058	67758
357 009	**NC**	P	*C2*	EM	67659	74159	74059	67759
357 010	**NC**	P	*C2*	EM	67660	74160	74060	67760
357 011	**NC**	P	*C2*	EM	67661	74161	74061	67761
357 012	**NC**	P	*C2*	EM	67662	74162	74062	67762
357 013	**NC**	P	*C2*	EM	67663	74163	74063	67763
357 014	**NC**	P	*C2*	EM	67664	74164	74064	67764
357 015	**NC**	P	*C2*	EM	67665	74165	74065	67765
357 016	**NC**	P	*C2*	EM	67666	74166	74066	67766
357 017	**NC**	P	*C2*	EM	67667	74167	74067	67767
357 018	**NC**	P	*C2*	EM	67668	74168	74068	67768
357 019	**NC**	P	*C2*	EM	67669	74169	74069	67769
357 020	**NC**	P	*C2*	EM	67670	74170	74070	67770
357 021	**NC**	P	*C2*	EM	67671	74171	74071	67771
357 022	**NC**	P	*C2*	EM	67672	74172	74072	67772
357 023	**NC**	P	*C2*	EM	67673	74173	74073	67773
357 024	**NC**	P	*C2*	EM	67674	74174	74074	67774
357 025	**NC**	P	*C2*	EM	67675	74175	74075	67775
357 026	**NC**	P	*C2*	EM	67676	74176	74076	67776
357 027	**NC**	P	*C2*	EM	67677	74177	74077	67777
357 028	**NC**	P	*C2*	EM	67678	74178	74078	67778
357 029	**NC**	P	*C2*	EM	67679	74179	74079	67779
357 030	**NC**	P	*C2*	EM	67680	74180	74080	67780
357 031	**NC**	P	*C2*	EM	67681	74181	74081	67781
357 032	**NC**	P	*C2*	EM	67682	74182	74082	67782
357 033	**NC**	P	*C2*	EM	67683	74183	74083	67783
357 034	**NC**	P	*C2*	EM	67684	74184	74084	67784
357 035	**NC**	P	*C2*	EM	67685	74185	74085	67785
357 036	**NC**	P	*C2*	EM	67686	74186	74086	67786
357 037	**NC**	P	*C2*	EM	67687	74187	74087	67787
357 038	**NC**	P	*C2*	EM	67688	74188	74088	67788
357 039	**NC**	P	*C2*	EM	67689	74189	74089	67789
357 040	**NC**	P	*C2*	EM	67690	74190	74090	67790
357 041	**NC**	P	*C2*	EM	67691	74191	74091	67791
357 042	**NC**	P	*C2*	EM	67692	74192	74092	67792
357 043	**NC**	P	*C2*	EM	67693	74193	74093	67793
357 044	**NC**	P	*C2*	EM	67694	74194	74094	67794
357 045	**NC**	P	*C2*	EM	67695	74195	74095	67795
357 046	**NC**	P	*C2*	EM	67696	74196	74096	67796

Names (carried on DMSO(A) and DMSO(B) (one plate on each)):

357 001 BARRY FLAXMAN
357 002 ARTHUR LEWIS STRIDE 1841–1922
357 003 SOUTHEND city.on.sea
357 004 TONY AMOS
357 011 JOHN LOWING
357 028 London, Tilbury & Southend Railway 1854–2004
357 029 THOMAS WHITELEGG 1840–1922
357 030 ROBERT HARBEN WHITELEGG 1871–1957

Class 357/2. Owned by Angel Trains.

DMSO(A). Bombardier Derby 2001–02. –/71. 40.7 t.
MSO. Bombardier Derby 2001–02. –/78. 36.7 t.
PTSO. Bombardier Derby 2001–02. –/58(4) 1TD 2W. 39.5 t.
DMSO(B). Bombardier Derby 2001–02. –/71. 40.7 t.

357 201	**NC**	A	*C2*	EM	68601	74701	74601	68701
357 202	**NC**	A	*C2*	EM	68602	74702	74602	68702
357 203	**NC**	A	*C2*	EM	68603	74703	74603	68703
357 204	**NC**	A	*C2*	EM	68604	74704	74604	68704
357 205	**NC**	A	*C2*	EM	68605	74705	74605	68705
357 206	**NC**	A	*C2*	EM	68606	74706	74606	68706
357 207	**NC**	A	*C2*	EM	68607	74707	74607	68707
357 208	**NC**	A	*C2*	EM	68608	74708	74608	68708
357 209	**NC**	A	*C2*	EM	68609	74709	74609	68709
357 210	**NC**	A	*C2*	EM	68610	74710	74610	68710
357 211	**NC**	A	*C2*	EM	68611	74711	74611	68711
357 212	**NC**	A	*C2*	EM	68612	74712	74612	68712
357 213	**NC**	A	*C2*	EM	68613	74713	74613	68713
357 214	**NC**	A	*C2*	EM	68614	74714	74614	68714
357 215	**NC**	A	*C2*	EM	68615	74715	74615	68715
357 216	**NC**	A	*C2*	EM	68616	74716	74616	68716
357 217	**NC**	A	*C2*	EM	68617	74717	74617	68717
357 218	**NC**	A	*C2*	EM	68618	74718	74618	68718
357 219	**NC**	A	*C2*	EM	68619	74719	74619	68719
357 220	**NC**	A	*C2*	EM	68620	74720	74620	68720
357 221	**NC**	A	*C2*	EM	68621	74721	74621	68721
357 222	**NC**	A	*C2*	EM	68622	74722	74622	68722
357 223	**NC**	A	*C2*	EM	68623	74723	74623	68723
357 224	**NC**	A	*C2*	EM	68624	74724	74624	68724
357 225	**NC**	A	*C2*	EM	68625	74725	74625	68725
357 226	**NC**	A	*C2*	EM	68626	74726	74626	68726
357 227	**NC**	A	*C2*	EM	68627	74727	74627	68727
357 228	**NC**	A	*C2*	EM	68628	74728	74628	68728

Names (carried on DMSO(A) and DMSO(B) (one plate on each)):

357 201 KEN BIRD
357 202 KENNY MITCHELL
357 203 HENRY PUMFRETT
357 204 DEREK FOWERS
357 205 JOHN D'SILVA
357 206 MARTIN AUNGIER
357 207 JOHN PAGE
357 208 DAVE DAVIS
357 209 JAMES SNELLING
357 213 UPMINSTER I.E.C.C.
357 217 ALLAN BURNELL

CLASS 360/0 DESIRO UK SIEMENS

Outer suburban/express units.

Formation: DMCO–PTSO–TSO–DMCO.
Construction: Welded aluminium.
Traction Motors: 4 Siemens 1TB2016-0GB02 asynchronous of 250 kW.
Wheel Arrangement: Bo-Bo + 2-2 + 2-2 + Bo-Bo.

Braking: Disc & regenerative.
Bogies: SGP SF5000.
Gangways: Within unit.
Doors: Sliding plug.
Dimensions: 20.34 x 2.80 m.
Couplers: Dellner 12.
Control System: IGBT Inverter.
Maximum Speed: 100 mph.
Heating & ventilation: Air conditioning.
Seating Layout: 1: 2+2 facing, 2: 3+2 facing/unidirectional.
Multiple Working: Within class.

DMCO(A). Siemens Krefeld 2002–03. 8/59. 45.0 t.
PTSO. Siemens Vienna 2002–03. –/60(9) 1TD 2W. 43.0 t.
TSO. Siemens Vienna 2002–03. –/78. 35.0 t.
DMCO(B). Siemens Krefeld 2002–03. 8/59. 45.0 t.

360 101	**FB**	A	*EA*	IL	65551	72551	74551	68551
360 102	**FB**	A	*EA*	IL	65552	72552	74552	68552
360 103	**FB**	A	*EA*	IL	65553	72553	74553	68553
360 104	**FB**	A	*EA*	IL	65554	72554	74554	68554
360 105	**FB**	A	*EA*	IL	65555	72555	74555	68555
360 106	**FB**	A	*EA*	IL	65556	72556	74556	68556
360 107	**FB**	A	*EA*	IL	65557	72557	74557	68557
360 108	**FB**	A	*EA*	IL	65558	72558	74558	68558
360 109	**FB**	A	*EA*	IL	65559	72559	74559	68559
360 110	**FB**	A	*EA*	IL	65560	72560	74560	68560
360 111	**FB**	A	*EA*	IL	65561	72561	74561	68561
360 112	**FB**	A	*EA*	IL	65562	72562	74562	68562
360 113	**FB**	A	*EA*	IL	65563	72563	74563	68563
360 114	**FB**	A	*EA*	IL	65564	72564	74564	68564
360 115	**NX**	A	*EA*	IL	65565	72565	74565	68565
360 116	**FB**	A	*EA*	IL	65566	72566	74566	68566
360 117	**FB**	A	*EA*	IL	65567	72567	74567	68567
360 118	**FB**	A	*EA*	IL	65568	72568	74568	68568
360 119	**FB**	A	*EA*	IL	65569	72569	74569	68569
360 120	**FB**	A	*EA*	IL	65570	72570	74570	68570
360 121	**FB**	A	*EA*	IL	65571	72571	74571	68571

CLASS 360/2 DESIRO UK SIEMENS

4-car Class 350 testbed units rebuilt for use by Heathrow Express on Paddington–Heathrow Airport stopping services ("Heathrow Connect").

Original 4-car sets 360 201–204 were made up to 5-cars during 2007 using additional TSOs. A fifth unit (360 205) was delivered in late 2005 as a 5-car set. This set is now dedicated to Terminals 1&3–Terminal 4 shuttle services.

Formation: DMSO–PTSO–TSO–TSO–DMSO.
Construction: Welded aluminium.
Traction Motors: 4 Siemens 1TB2016-0GB02 asynchronous of 250 kW.
Wheel Arrangement: Bo-Bo + 2-2 + 2-2 + 2-2 + Bo-Bo.
Braking: Disc & regenerative.
Bogies: SGP SF5000.
Gangways: Within unit.
Doors: Sliding plug.
Dimensions: 20.34 x 2.80 m.
Couplers: Dellner 12.
Control System: IGBT Inverter.
Maximum Speed: 100 mph.

Heating & ventilation: Air conditioning.
Seating Layout: 3+2 (* 2+2) facing/unidirectional.
Multiple Working: Within class.

DMSO(A). Siemens Krefeld 2002–06. –/63 (* –/54). 44.8 t.
PTSO. Siemens Krefeld 2002–06. –/57(9) 1TD 2W (* –/48(9) 2W). 44.2 t.
TSO. Siemens Krefeld 2005–06. –/74 (* –/62). 35.3 t.
TSO. Siemens Krefeld 2002–06. –/74 (* –/62). 34.1 t.
DMSO(B). Siemens Krefeld 2002–06. –/63 (* –/54). 44.4 t.

360 201		**HC**	HE	*HC*	OH	78431	63421	72431	72421	78441
360 202		**HC**	HE	*HC*	OH	78432	63422	72432	72422	78442
360 203		**HC**	HE	*HC*	OH	78433	63423	72433	72423	78443
360 204		**HC**	HE	*HC*	OH	78434	63424	72434	72424	78444
360 205	*	**HE**	HE	*HE*	OH	78435	63425	72435	72425	78445

CLASS 365 NETWORKER EXPRESS ABB YORK

Outer suburban units.

Formations: DMCO–TSO–PTSO–DMCO.
Systems: 25 kV AC overhead but with 750 V DC third rail capability (units marked * were formerly used on DC lines in the South-East).
Construction: Welded aluminium alloy.
Traction Motors: Four GEC-Alsthom G354CX asynchronous of 157 kW.
Wheel Arrangement: Bo-Bo + 2-2 + 2-2 + Bo-Bo.
Braking: Disc & rheostatic.
Dimensions: 20.89/20.06 x 2.81 m.
Bogies: ABB P3-16/T3-16.
Couplers: Tightlock.
Gangways: Within unit.
Control System: GTO Inverter.
Doors: Sliding plug.
Maximum Speed: 100 mph.
Seating Layout: 1: 2+2 facing, 2: 2+2 facing.
Multiple Working: Within class only.

DMCO(A). Lot No. 31133 1994–95. 12/56. 41.7 t.
TSO. Lot No. 31134 1994–95. –/65 1TD (* –/64 1TD) 32.9 t.
PTSO. Lot No. 31135 1994–95. –/68 1T. 34.6 t.
DMCO(B). Lot No. 31136 1994–95. 12/56. 41.7 t.

Advertising liveries:

365 510 Cambridge & Ely; Cathedral cities (blue & white with various images).
365 519 Peterborough; environment capital (blue & white with various images).
365 531 Nelson's County; Norfolk (blue & white with various images).
365 540 Garden cities of Hertfordshire (blue & white with various images).

365 501	*	**FU**	E	*FC*	HE	65894	72241	72240	65935
365 502	*	**FU**	E	*FC*	HE	65895	72243	72242	65936
365 503	*	**FU**	E	*FC*	HE	65896	72245	72244	65937
365 504	*	**FU**	E	*FC*	HE	65897	72247	72246	65938
365 505	*	**FU**	E	*FC*	HE	65898	72249	72248	65939
365 506	*	**FU**	E	*FC*	HE	65899	72251	72250	65940
365 507	*	**FU**	E	*FC*	HE	65900	72253	72252	65941
365 508	*	**FU**	E	*FC*	HE	65901	72255	72254	65942

365 509	*	**FU**	E	*FC*	HE	65902	72257	72256	65943
365 510	*	**AL**	E	*FC*	HE	65903	72259	72258	65944
365 511	*	**FU**	E	*FC*	HE	65904	72261	72260	65945
365 512	*	**FU**	E	*FC*	HE	65905	72263	72262	65946
365 513	*	**FU**	E	*FC*	HE	65906	72265	72264	65947
365 514	*	**FU**	E	*FC*	HE	65907	72267	72266	65948
365 515	*	**FU**	E	*FC*	HE	65908	72269	72268	65949
365 516	*	**FU**	E	*FC*	HE	65909	72271	72270	65950
365 517		**FU**	E	*FC*	HE	65910	72273	72272	65951
365 518		**FU**	E	*FC*	HE	65911	72275	72274	65952
365 519		**AL**	E	*FC*	HE	65912	72277	72276	65953
365 520		**FU**	E	*FC*	HE	65913	72279	72278	65954
365 521		**FU**	E	*FC*	HE	65914	72281	72280	65955
365 522		**FU**	E	*FC*	HE	65915	72283	72282	65956
365 523		**FU**	E	*FC*	HE	65916	72285	72284	65957
365 524		**FU**	E	*FC*	HE	65917	72287	72286	65958
365 525		**FU**	E	*FC*	HE	65918	72289	72288	65959
365 526		**N**	E		ZN	65919	72291	72290	65960
365 527		**FU**	E	*FC*	HE	65920	72293	72292	65961
365 528		**FU**	E	*FC*	HE	65921	72295	72294	65962
365 529		**FU**	E	*FC*	HE	65922	72297	72296	65963
365 530		**FU**	E	*FC*	HE	65923	72299	72298	65964
365 531		**AL**	E	*FC*	HE	65924	72301	72300	65965
365 532		**FU**	E	*FC*	HE	65925	72303	72302	65966
365 533		**FU**	E	*FC*	HE	65926	72305	72304	65967
365 534		**FU**	E	*FC*	HE	65927	72307	72306	65968
365 535		**FU**	E	*FC*	HE	65928	72309	72308	65969
365 536		**FU**	E	*FC*	HE	65929	72311	72310	65970
365 537		**FU**	E	*FC*	HE	65930	72313	72312	65971
365 538		**FU**	E	*FC*	HE	65931	72315	72314	65972
365 539		**FU**	E	*FC*	HE	65932	72317	72316	65973
365 540		**AL**	E	*FC*	HE	65933	72319	72318	65974
365 541		**FU**	E	*FC*	HE	65934	72321	72320	65975

Names (carried on each DMCO):

365 506 The Royston Express
365 513 Hornsey Depot
365 514 Captain George Vancouver
365 518 The Fenman
365 527 Robert Stripe Passengers' Champion
365 530 The Intalink Partnership promoting integrated transport in Hertfordshire since 1999
365 536 Rufus Barnes Chief Executive of London TravelWatch for 25 years
365 537 Daniel Edwards (1974–2010) Cambridge Driver

CLASS 375 ELECTROSTAR
ADTRANZ/BOMBARDIER DERBY

Express and outer suburban units.

Formations: Various.
Systems: 25 kV AC overhead/750 V DC third rail (some third rail only with provision for retro-fitting of AC equipment).
Construction: Welded aluminium alloy underframe, sides and roof with steel ends. All sections bolted together.
Traction Motors: Two Adtranz asynchronous of 250 kW.
Wheel Arrangement: 2-Bo (+ 2-Bo) + 2-2 + Bo-2.
Braking: Disc & regenerative.
Dimensions: 20.40/19.99 x 2.80 m.
Bogies: Adtranz P3-25/T3-25.
Couplers: Dellner 12.
Gangways: Throughout.
Control System: IGBT Inverter.
Doors: Sliding plug.
Maximum Speed: 100 mph.
Heating & ventilation: Air conditioning.
Seating Layout: 1: 2+2 facing/unidirectional (seats behind drivers cab in each DMCO). 2: 2+2 facing/unidirectional (except 375/9 – 3+2 facing/unidirectional).
Multiple Working: Within class and with Classes 376, 377, 378 and 379.

Class 375/3. Express units. 750 V DC only. DMCO–TSO–DMCO.

DMCO(A). Bombardier Derby 2001–02. 12/48. 43.8 t.
TSO. Bombardier Derby 2001–02. –/56 1TD 2W. 35.5 t.
DMCO(B). Bombardier Derby 2001–02. 12/48. 43.8 t.

375 301	**CN**	E	*SE*	RM	67921	74351	67931
375 302	**CN**	E	*SE*	RM	67922	74352	67932
375 303	**CN**	E	*SE*	RM	67923	74353	67933
375 304	**CN**	E	*SE*	RM	67924	74354	67934
375 305	**CN**	E	*SE*	RM	67925	74355	67935
375 306	**CN**	E	*SE*	RM	67926	74356	67936
375 307	**CN**	E	*SE*	RM	67927	74357	67937
375 308	**SE**	E	*SE*	RM	67928	74358	67938
375 309	**CN**	E	*SE*	RM	67929	74359	67939
375 310	**CN**	E	*SE*	RM	67930	74360	67940

Name (carried on TSO):

375 304 Medway Valley Line 1856–2006

Class 375/6. Express units. 25 kV AC/750 V DC. DMCO–MSO–PTSO–DMCO.

DMCO(A). Adtranz Derby 1999–2001. 12/48. 46.2 t.
MSO. Adtranz Derby 1999–2001. –/66 1T. 40.5 t.
PTSO. Adtranz Derby 1999–2001. –/56 1TD 2W. 40.7 t.
DMCO(B). Adtranz Derby 1999–2001. 12/48. 46.2 t.

375 601	**CN**	E	*SE*	RM	67801	74251	74201	67851
375 602	**CN**	E	*SE*	RM	67802	74252	74202	67852
375 603	**CN**	E	*SE*	RM	67803	74253	74203	67853
375 604	**CN**	E	*SE*	RM	67804	74254	74204	67854
375 605	**CN**	E	*SE*	RM	67805	74255	74205	67855

375606	**CN**	E	*SE*	RM	67806	74256	74206	67856
375607	**CN**	E	*SE*	RM	67807	74257	74207	67857
375608	**CN**	E	*SE*	RM	67808	74258	74208	67858
375609	**CN**	E	*SE*	RM	67809	74259	74209	67859
375610	**CN**	E	*SE*	RM	67810	74260	74210	67860
375611	**CN**	E	*SE*	RM	67811	74261	74211	67861
375612	**CN**	E	*SE*	RM	67812	74262	74212	67862
375613	**CN**	E	*SE*	RM	67813	74263	74213	67863
375614	**CN**	E	*SE*	RM	67814	74264	74214	67864
375615	**CN**	E	*SE*	RM	67815	74265	74215	67865
375616	**CN**	E	*SE*	RM	67816	74266	74216	67866
375617	**CN**	E	*SE*	RM	67817	74267	74217	67867
375618	**CN**	E	*SE*	RM	67818	74268	74218	67868
375619	**CN**	E	*SE*	RM	67819	74269	74219	67869
375620	**CN**	E	*SE*	RM	67820	74270	74220	67870
375621	**CN**	E	*SE*	RM	67821	74271	74221	67871
375622	**CN**	E	*SE*	RM	67822	74272	74222	67872
375623	**CN**	E	*SE*	RM	67823	74273	74223	67873
375624	**SE**	E	*SE*	RM	67824	74274	74224	67874
375625	**CN**	E	*SE*	RM	67825	74275	74225	67875
375626	**CN**	E	*SE*	RM	67826	74276	74226	67876
375627	**CN**	E	*SE*	RM	67827	74277	74227	67877
375628	**CN**	E	*SE*	RM	67828	74278	74228	67878
375629	**CN**	E	*SE*	RM	67829	74279	74229	67879
375630	**CN**	E	*SE*	RM	67830	74280	74230	67880

Names (carried on one side of each MSO or PTSO):

375608 Bromley Travelwise
375610 Royal Tunbridge Wells
375611 Dr. William Harvey
375619 Driver John Neve
375623 Hospice in the Weald

Class 375/7. Express units. 750 V DC only. DMCO–MSO–TSO–DMCO.

DMCO(A). Bombardier Derby 2001–02. 12/48. 43.8 t.
MSO. Bombardier Derby 2001–02. –/66 1T. 36.4 t.
TSO. Bombardier Derby 2001–02. –/56 1TD 2W. 34.1 t.
DMCO(B). Bombardier Derby 2001–02. 12/48. 43.8 t.

375701	**CN**	E	*SE*	RM	67831	74281	74231	67881
375702	**CN**	E	*SE*	RM	67832	74282	74232	67882
375703	**CN**	E	*SE*	RM	67833	74283	74233	67883
375704	**CN**	E	*SE*	RM	67834	74284	74234	67884
375705	**SE**	E	*SE*	RM	67835	74285	74235	67885
375706	**CN**	E	*SE*	RM	67836	74286	74236	67886
375707	**CN**	E	*SE*	RM	67837	74287	74237	67887
375708	**CN**	E	*SE*	RM	67838	74288	74238	67888
375709	**CN**	E	*SE*	RM	67839	74289	74239	67889
375710	**CN**	E	*SE*	RM	67840	74290	74240	67890
375711	**CN**	E	*SE*	RM	67841	74291	74241	67891
375712	**CN**	E	*SE*	RM	67842	74292	74242	67892
375713	**CN**	E	*SE*	RM	67843	74293	74243	67893
375714	**CN**	E	*SE*	RM	67844	74294	74244	67894

375715	**CN**	E	*SE*	RM	67845	74295	74245	67895

Name (carried on one side of each MSO or TSO):

375701 Kent Air Ambulance Explorer

Class 375/8. Express units. 750 V DC only. DMCO–MSO–TSO–DMCO.

DMCO(A). Bombardier Derby 2004. 12/48. 43.3 t.
MSO. Bombardier Derby 2004. –/66 1T. 39.8 t.
TSO. Bombardier Derby 2004. –/52 1TD 2W. 35.9 t.
DMCO(B). Bombardier Derby 2004. 12/52. 43.3 t.

Note: 375 801–820 are fitted with de-icing equipment. TSO weighs 36.5 t.

375801	**CN**	E	*SE*	RM	73301	79001	78201	73701
375802	**CN**	E	*SE*	RM	73302	79002	78202	73702
375803	**CN**	E	*SE*	RM	73303	79003	78203	73703
375804	**CN**	E	*SE*	RM	73304	79004	78204	73704
375805	**CN**	E	*SE*	RM	73305	79005	78205	73705
375806	**CN**	E	*SE*	RM	73306	79006	78206	73706
375807	**CN**	E	*SE*	RM	73307	79007	78207	73707
375808	**CN**	E	*SE*	RM	73308	79008	78208	73708
375809	**CN**	E	*SE*	RM	73309	79009	78209	73709
375810	**CN**	E	*SE*	RM	73310	79010	78210	73710
375811	**CN**	E	*SE*	RM	73311	79011	78211	73711
375812	**CN**	E	*SE*	RM	73312	79012	78212	73712
375813	**CN**	E	*SE*	RM	73313	79013	78213	73713
375814	**CN**	E	*SE*	RM	73314	79014	78214	73714
375815	**CN**	E	*SE*	RM	73315	79015	78215	73715
375816	**CN**	E	*SE*	RM	73316	79016	78216	73716
375817	**CN**	E	*SE*	RM	73317	79017	78217	73717
375818	**CN**	E	*SE*	RM	73318	79018	78218	73718
375819	**CN**	E	*SE*	RM	73319	79019	78219	73719
375820	**CN**	E	*SE*	RM	73320	79020	78220	73720
375821	**CN**	E	*SE*	RM	73321	79021	78221	73721
375822	**CN**	E	*SE*	RM	73322	79022	78222	73722
375823	**CN**	E	*SE*	RM	73323	79023	78223	73723
375824	**CN**	E	*SE*	RM	73324	79024	78224	73724
375825	**CN**	E	*SE*	RM	73325	79025	78225	73725
375826	**CN**	E	*SE*	RM	73326	79026	78226	73726
375827	**CN**	E	*SE*	RM	73327	79027	78227	73727
375828	**CN**	E	*SE*	RM	73328	79028	78228	73728
375829	**CN**	E	*SE*	RM	73329	79029	78229	73729
375830	**CN**	E	*SE*	RM	73330	79030	78230	73730

Name (carried on one side of each MSO or TSO):

375830 City of London

Class 375/9. Outer suburban units. 750 V DC only. DMCO–MSO–TSO–DMCO.

DMCO(A). Bombardier Derby 2003–04. 12/59. 43.4 t.
MSO. Bombardier Derby 2003–04. –/73 1T. 39.3 t.
TSO. Bombardier Derby 2003–04. –/59 1TD 2W. 35.6 t.
DMCO(B). Bombardier Derby 2003–04. 12/59. 43.4 t.

375901	**CN**	E	*SE*	RM	73331	79031	79061	73731
375902	**CN**	E	*SE*	RM	73332	79032	79062	73732
375903	**CN**	E	*SE*	RM	73333	79033	79063	73733
375904	**CN**	E	*SE*	RM	73334	79034	79064	73734
375905	**CN**	E	*SE*	RM	73335	79035	79065	73735
375906	**CN**	E	*SE*	RM	73336	79036	79066	73736
375907	**CN**	E	*SE*	RM	73337	79037	79067	73737
375908	**CN**	E	*SE*	RM	73338	79038	79068	73738
375909	**CN**	E	*SE*	RM	73339	79039	79069	73739
375910	**CN**	E	*SE*	RM	73340	79040	79070	73740
375911	**CN**	E	*SE*	RM	73341	79041	79071	73741
375912	**CN**	E	*SE*	RM	73342	79042	79072	73742
375913	**CN**	E	*SE*	RM	73343	79043	79073	73743
375914	**CN**	E	*SE*	RM	73344	79044	79074	73744
375915	**CN**	E	*SE*	RM	73345	79045	79075	73745
375916	**CN**	E	*SE*	RM	73346	79046	79076	73746
375917	**CN**	E	*SE*	RM	73347	79047	79077	73747
375918	**CN**	E	*SE*	RM	73348	79048	79078	73748
375919	**CN**	E	*SE*	RM	73349	79049	79079	73749
375920	**CN**	E	*SE*	RM	73350	79050	79080	73750
375921	**CN**	E	*SE*	RM	73351	79051	79081	73751
375922	**CN**	E	*SE*	RM	73352	79052	79082	73752
375923	**CN**	E	*SE*	RM	73353	79053	79083	73753
375924	**CN**	E	*SE*	RM	73354	79054	79084	73754
375925	**CN**	E	*SE*	RM	73355	79055	79085	73755
375926	**CN**	E	*SE*	RM	73356	79056	79086	73756
375927	**CN**	E	*SE*	RM	73357	79057	79087	73757

CLASS 376 ELECTROSTAR BOMBARDIER DERBY

Inner suburban units.

Formation: DMSO–MSO–TSO–MSO–DMSO.
System: 750 V DC third rail.
Construction: Welded aluminium alloy underframe, sides and roof with steel ends. All sections bolted together.
Traction Motors: Two Bombardier asynchronous of 250 kW.
Wheel Arrangement: 2-Bo + 2-Bo + 2-2 + Bo-2 + Bo-2.
Braking: Disc & regenerative.
Bogies: Bombardier P3-25/T3-25.
Gangways: Within unit.
Doors: Sliding.
Dimensions: 20.40/19.99 x 2.80 m.
Couplers: Dellner 12.
Control System: IGBT Inverter.
Maximum Speed: 75 mph.
Heating & ventilation: Pressure heating and ventilation.
Seating Layout: 2+2 low density facing.
Multiple Working: Within class and with Classes 375, 377, 378 and 379.

DMSO(A). Bombardier Derby 2004–05. –/36(6) 1W. 42.1 t.
MSO. Bombardier Derby 2004–05. –/48. 36.2 t.
TSO. Bombardier Derby 2004–05. –/48. 36.3 t.
DMSO(B). Bombardier Derby 2004–05. –/36(6) 1W. 42.1 t.

376 001	**CN**	E	*SE*	SG	61101	63301	64301	63501	61601
376 002	**CN**	E	*SE*	SG	61102	63302	64302	63502	61602
376 003	**CN**	E	*SE*	SG	61103	63303	64303	63503	61603
376 004	**CN**	E	*SE*	SG	61104	63304	64304	63504	61604
376 005	**CN**	E	*SE*	SG	61105	63305	64305	63505	61605
376 006	**CN**	E	*SE*	SG	61106	63306	64306	63506	61606
376 007	**CN**	E	*SE*	SG	61107	63307	64307	63507	61607
376 008	**CN**	E	*SE*	SG	61108	63308	64308	63508	61608
376 009	**CN**	E	*SE*	SG	61109	63309	64309	63509	61609
376 010	**CN**	E	*SE*	SG	61110	63310	64310	63510	61610
376 011	**CN**	E	*SE*	SG	61111	63311	64311	63511	61611
376 012	**CN**	E	*SE*	SG	61112	63312	64312	63512	61612
376 013	**CN**	E	*SE*	SG	61113	63313	64313	63513	61613
376 014	**CN**	E	*SE*	SG	61114	63314	64314	63514	61614
376 015	**CN**	E	*SE*	SG	61115	63315	64315	63515	61615
376 016	**CN**	E	*SE*	SG	61116	63316	64316	63516	61616
376 017	**CN**	E	*SE*	SG	61117	63317	64317	63517	61617
376 018	**CN**	E	*SE*	SG	61118	63318	64318	63518	61618
376 019	**CN**	E	*SE*	SG	61119	63319	64319	63519	61619
376 020	**CN**	E	*SE*	SG	61120	63320	64320	63520	61620
376 021	**CN**	E	*SE*	SG	61121	63321	64321	63521	61621
376 022	**CN**	E	*SE*	SG	61122	63322	64322	63522	61622
376 023	**CN**	E	*SE*	SG	61123	63323	64323	63523	61623
376 024	**CN**	E	*SE*	SG	61124	63324	64324	63524	61624
376 025	**CN**	E	*SE*	SG	61125	63325	64325	63525	61625
376 026	**CN**	E	*SE*	SG	61126	63326	64326	63526	61626
376 027	**CN**	E	*SE*	SG	61127	63327	64327	63527	61627
376 028	**CN**	E	*SE*	SG	61128	63328	64328	63528	61628
376 029	**CN**	E	*SE*	SG	61129	63329	64329	63529	61629
376 030	**CN**	E	*SE*	SG	61130	63330	64330	63530	61630
376 031	**CN**	E	*SE*	SG	61131	63331	64331	63531	61631
376 032	**CN**	E	*SE*	SG	61132	63332	64332	63532	61632
376 033	**CN**	E	*SE*	SG	61133	63333	64333	63533	61633
376 034	**CN**	E	*SE*	SG	61134	63334	64334	63534	61634
376 035	**CN**	E	*SE*	SG	61135	63335	64335	63535	61635
376 036	**CN**	E	*SE*	SG	61136	63336	64336	63536	61636

CLASS 377 ELECTROSTAR BOMBARDIER DERBY

Express and outer suburban units.

Formations: Various.
Systems: 25 kV AC overhead/750 V DC third rail or third rail only with provision for retro-fitting of AC equipment.
Construction: Welded aluminium alloy underframe, sides and roof with steel ends. All sections bolted together.
Traction Motors: Two Bombardier asynchronous of 250 kW.
Wheel Arrangement: 2-Bo (+ 2-Bo) + 2-2 + Bo-2.
Braking: Disc & regenerative.
Dimensions: 20.39/19.99 x 2.80 m.
Bogies: Bombardier P3-25/T3-25.
Couplers: Dellner 12.
Gangways: Throughout.
Control System: IGBT Inverter.
Doors: Sliding plug.
Maximum Speed: 100 mph.
Heating & ventilation: Air conditioning.
Seating Layout: Various.
Multiple Working: Within class and with Classes 375, 376, 378 and 379.

Class 377/1. 750 V DC only. DMCO–MSO–TSO–DMCO.
Seating layout: 1: 2+2 facing/unidirectional, 2: 2+2 facing/unidirectional (377 101–119), 3+2 and 2+2 facing/unidirectional (377 120–164) (3+2 seating in middle cars only 377 140–164).

DMCO(A). Bombardier Derby 2002–03. 12/48 (s 12/56). 44.8 t.
MSO. Bombardier Derby 2002–03. –/62 (s –/70, t –/69). 1T. 39.0 t.
TSO. Bombardier Derby 2002–03. –/52 (s –/60, t –/57). 1TD 2W. 35.4 t.
DMCO(B). Bombardier Derby 2002–03. 12/48 (s 12/56). 43.4 t.

377 101		**SN**	P	*SN*	BI	78501	77101	78901	78701
377 102		**SN**	P	*SN*	BI	78502	77102	78902	78702
377 103		**SN**	P	*SN*	BI	78503	77103	78903	78703
377 104		**SN**	P	*SN*	BI	78504	77104	78904	78704
377 105		**SN**	P	*SN*	BI	78505	77105	78905	78705
377 106		**SN**	P	*SN*	BI	78506	77106	78906	78706
377 107		**SN**	P	*SN*	BI	78507	77107	78907	78707
377 108		**SN**	P	*SN*	BI	78508	77108	78908	78708
377 109		**SN**	P	*SN*	BI	78509	77109	78909	78709
377 110		**SN**	P	*SN*	BI	78510	77110	78910	78710
377 111		**SN**	P	*SN*	BI	78511	77111	78911	78711
377 112		**SN**	P	*SN*	BI	78512	77112	78912	78712
377 113		**SN**	P	*SN*	BI	78513	77113	78913	78713
377 114		**SN**	P	*SN*	BI	78514	77114	78914	78714
377 115		**SN**	P	*SN*	BI	78515	77115	78915	78715
377 116		**SN**	P	*SN*	BI	78516	77116	78916	78716
377 117		**SN**	P	*SN*	BI	78517	77117	78917	78717
377 118		**SN**	P	*SN*	BI	78518	77118	78918	78718
377 119		**SN**	P	*SN*	BI	78519	77119	78919	78719
377 120	s	**SN**	P	*SN*	BI	78520	77120	78920	78720
377 121	s	**SN**	P	*SN*	BI	78521	77121	78921	78721
377 122	s	**SN**	P	*SN*	BI	78522	77122	78922	78722
377 123	s	**SN**	P	*SN*	BI	78523	77123	78923	78723

377 124	s	**SN**	P	*SN*	BI	78524	77124	78924	78724
377 125	s	**SN**	P	*SN*	BI	78525	77125	78925	78725
377 126	s	**SN**	P	*SN*	BI	78526	77126	78926	78726
377 127	s	**SN**	P	*SN*	BI	78527	77127	78927	78727
377 128	s	**SN**	P	*SN*	BI	78528	77128	78928	78728
377 129	s	**SN**	P	*SN*	BI	78529	77129	78929	78729
377 130	s	**SN**	P	*SN*	BI	78530	77130	78930	78730
377 131	s	**SN**	P	*SN*	BI	78531	77131	78931	78731
377 132	s	**SN**	P	*SN*	BI	78532	77132	78932	78732
377 133	s	**SN**	P	*SN*	BI	78533	77133	78933	78733
377 134	s	**SN**	P	*SN*	BI	78534	77134	78934	78734
377 135	s	**SN**	P	*SN*	BI	78535	77135	78935	78735
377 136	s	**SN**	P	*SN*	BI	78536	77136	78936	78736
377 137	s	**SN**	P	*SN*	BI	78537	77137	78937	78737
377 138	s	**SN**	P	*SN*	BI	78538	77138	78938	78738
377 139	s	**SN**	P	*SN*	BI	78539	77139	78939	78739
377 140	t	**SN**	P	*SN*	BI	78540	77140	78940	78740
377 141	t	**SN**	P	*SN*	BI	78541	77141	78941	78741
377 142	t	**SN**	P	*SN*	BI	78542	77142	78942	78742
377 143	t	**SN**	P	*SN*	BI	78543	77143	78943	78743
377 144	t	**SN**	P	*SN*	BI	78544	77144	78944	78744
377 145	t	**SN**	P	*SN*	BI	78545	77145	78945	78745
377 146	t	**SN**	P	*SN*	BI	78546	77146	78946	78746
377 147	t	**SN**	P	*SN*	BI	78547	77147	78947	78747
377 148	t	**SN**	P	*SN*	BI	78548	77148	78948	78748
377 149	t	**SN**	P	*SN*	BI	78549	77149	78949	78749
377 150	t	**SN**	P	*SN*	BI	78550	77150	78950	78750
377 151	t	**SN**	P	*SN*	BI	78551	77151	78951	78751
377 152	t	**SN**	P	*SN*	BI	78552	77152	78952	78752
377 153	t	**SN**	P	*SN*	BI	78553	77153	78953	78753
377 154	t	**SN**	P	*SN*	BI	78554	77154	78954	78754
377 155	t	**SN**	P	*SN*	BI	78555	77155	78955	78755
377 156	t	**SN**	P	*SN*	BI	78556	77156	78956	78756
377 157	t	**SN**	P	*SN*	BI	78557	77157	78957	78757
377 158	t	**SN**	P	*SN*	BI	78558	77158	78958	78758
377 159	t	**SN**	P	*SN*	BI	78559	77159	78959	78759
377 160	t	**SN**	P	*SN*	BI	78560	77160	78960	78760
377 161	t	**SN**	P	*SN*	BI	78561	77161	78961	78761
377 162	t	**SN**	P	*SN*	BI	78562	77162	78962	78762
377 163	t	**SN**	P	*SN*	BI	78563	77163	78963	78763
377 164	t	**SN**	P	*SN*	BI	78564	77164	78964	78764

Class 377/2. 25 kV AC/750 V DC. DMCO–MSO–PTSO–DMCO. These dual-voltage units are used on the South Croydon–Milton Keynes cross-London service. Three units transferred to First Capital Connect in 2011.
Seating layout: 1: 2+2 facing/unidirectional, 2: 2+2 and 3+2 facing/unidirectional (3+2 seating in middle cars only).

DMCO(A). Bombardier Derby 2003–04. 12/48. 44.2 t.
MSO. Bombardier Derby 2003–04. –/69 1T. 39.8 t.
PTSO. Bombardier Derby 2003–04. –/57 1TD 2W. 40.1 t.
DMCO(B). Bombardier Derby 2003–04. 12/48. 44.2 t.

377 201	**SN**	P	*SN*	SU	78571	77171	78971	78771
377 202	**SN**	P	*SN*	SU	78572	77172	78972	78772
377 203	**SN**	P	*SN*	SU	78573	77173	78973	78773
377 204	**SN**	P	*SN*	SU	78574	77174	78974	78774
377 205	**SN**	P	*SN*	SU	78575	77175	78975	78775
377 206	**SN**	P	*SN*	SU	78576	77176	78976	78776
377 207	**FU**	P	*FC*	BF	78577	77177	78977	78777
377 208	**SN**	P	*SN*	SU	78578	77178	78978	78778
377 209	**SN**	P	*SN*	SU	78579	77179	78979	78779
377 210	**SN**	P	*SN*	SU	78580	77180	78980	78780
377 211	**FU**	P	*FC*	BF	78581	77181	78981	78781
377 212	**FU**	P	*FC*	BF	78582	77182	78982	78782
377 213	**SN**	P	*SN*	SU	78583	77183	78983	78783
377 214	**SN**	P	*SN*	SU	78584	77184	78984	78784
377 215	**SN**	P	*SN*	SU	78585	77185	78985	78785

Class 377/3. 750 V DC only. DMCO–TSO–DMCO.
Seating Layout: 1: 2+2 facing/unidirectional, 2: 2+2 facing/unidirectional.

Note: Units built as Class 375, but renumbered in the Class 377/3 range when fitted with Dellner couplers.

DMCO(A). Bombardier Derby 2001–02. 12/48. 43.5 t.
TSO. Bombardier Derby 2001–02. –/56 1TD 2W. 35.4 t.
DMCO(B). Bombardier Derby 2001–02. 12/48. 43.5 t.

377 301	(375 311)	**SN**	P	*SN*	SU	68201	74801	68401
377 302	(375 312)	**SN**	P	*SN*	SU	68202	74802	68402
377 303	(375 313)	**SN**	P	*SN*	SU	68203	74803	68403
377 304	(375 314)	**SN**	P	*SN*	SU	68204	74804	68404
377 305	(375 315)	**SN**	P	*SN*	SU	68205	74805	68405
377 306	(375 316)	**SN**	P	*SN*	SU	68206	74806	68406
377 307	(375 317)	**SN**	P	*SN*	SU	68207	74807	68407
377 308	(375 318)	**SN**	P	*SN*	SU	68208	74808	68408
377 309	(375 319)	**SN**	P	*SN*	SU	68209	74809	68409
377 310	(375 320)	**SN**	P	*SN*	SU	68210	74810	68410
377 311	(375 321)	**SN**	P	*SN*	SU	68211	74811	68411
377 312	(375 322)	**SN**	P	*SN*	SU	68212	74812	68412
377 313	(375 323)	**SN**	P	*SN*	SU	68213	74813	68413
377 314	(375 324)	**SN**	P	*SN*	SU	68214	74814	68414
377 315	(375 325)	**SN**	P	*SN*	SU	68215	74815	68415
377 316	(375 326)	**SN**	P	*SN*	SU	68216	74816	68416
377 317	(375 327)	**SN**	P	*SN*	SU	68217	74817	68417
377 318	(375 328)	**SN**	P	*SN*	SU	68218	74818	68418
377 319	(375 329)	**SN**	P	*SN*	SU	68219	74819	68419
377 320	(375 330)	**SN**	P	*SN*	SU	68220	74820	68420
377 321	(375 331)	**SN**	P	*SN*	SU	68221	74821	68421
377 322	(375 332)	**SN**	P	*SN*	SU	68222	74822	68422
377 323	(375 333)	**SN**	P	*SN*	SU	68223	74823	68423
377 324	(375 334)	**SN**	P	*SN*	SU	68224	74824	68424
377 325	(375 335)	**SN**	P	*SN*	SU	68225	74825	68425
377 326	(375 336)	**SN**	P	*SN*	SU	68226	74826	68426
377 327	(375 337)	**SN**	P	*SN*	SU	68227	74827	68427

377 328	(375 338)	**SN**	P	*SN*	SU	68228	74828	68428

Class 377/4. 750 V DC only. DMCO–MSO–TSO–DMCO.
Seating Layout: 1: 2+2 facing/two seats longitudinal, 2: 2+2 and 3+2 facing/unidirectional (3+2 seating in middle cars only).

DMCO(A). Bombardier Derby 2004–05. 10/48. 43.1 t.
MSO. Bombardier Derby 2004–05. –/69 1T. 39.3 t.
TSO. Bombardier Derby 2004–05. –/56 1TD 2W. 35.3 t.
DMCO(B). Bombardier Derby 2004–05. 10/48. 43.2 t.

377 401	**SN**	P	*SN*	BI	73401	78801	78601	73801
377 402	**SN**	P	*SN*	BI	73402	78802	78602	73802
377 403	**SN**	P	*SN*	BI	73403	78803	78603	73803
377 404	**SN**	P	*SN*	BI	73404	78804	78604	73804
377 405	**SN**	P	*SN*	BI	73405	78805	78605	73805
377 406	**SN**	P	*SN*	BI	73406	78806	78606	73806
377 407	**SN**	P	*SN*	BI	73407	78807	78607	73807
377 408	**SN**	P	*SN*	BI	73408	78808	78608	73808
377 409	**SN**	P	*SN*	BI	73409	78809	78609	73809
377 410	**SN**	P	*SN*	BI	73410	78810	78610	73810
377 411	**SN**	P	*SN*	BI	73411	78811	78611	73811
377 412	**SN**	P	*SN*	BI	73412	78812	78612	73812
377 413	**SN**	P	*SN*	BI	73413	78813	78613	73813
377 414	**SN**	P	*SN*	BI	73414	78814	78614	73814
377 415	**SN**	P	*SN*	BI	73415	78815	78615	73815
377 416	**SN**	P	*SN*	BI	73416	78816	78616	73816
377 417	**SN**	P	*SN*	BI	73417	78817	78617	73817
377 418	**SN**	P	*SN*	BI	73418	78818	78618	73818
377 419	**SN**	P	*SN*	BI	73419	78819	78619	73819
377 420	**SN**	P	*SN*	BI	73420	78820	78620	73820
377 421	**SN**	P	*SN*	BI	73421	78821	78621	73821
377 422	**SN**	P	*SN*	BI	73422	78822	78622	73822
377 423	**SN**	P	*SN*	BI	73423	78823	78623	73823
377 424	**SN**	P	*SN*	BI	73424	78824	78624	73824
377 425	**SN**	P	*SN*	BI	73425	78825	78625	73825
377 426	**SN**	P	*SN*	BI	73426	78826	78626	73826
377 427	**SN**	P	*SN*	BI	73427	78827	78627	73827
377 428	**SN**	P	*SN*	BI	73428	78828	78628	73828
377 429	**SN**	P	*SN*	BI	73429	78829	78629	73829
377 430	**SN**	P	*SN*	BI	73430	78830	78630	73830
377 431	**SN**	P	*SN*	BI	73431	78831	78631	73831
377 432	**SN**	P	*SN*	BI	73432	78832	78632	73832
377 433	**SN**	P	*SN*	BI	73433	78833	78633	73833
377 434	**SN**	P	*SN*	BI	73434	78834	78634	73834
377 435	**SN**	P	*SN*	BI	73435	78835	78635	73835
377 436	**SN**	P	*SN*	BI	73436	78836	78636	73836
377 437	**SN**	P	*SN*	BI	73437	78837	78637	73837
377 438	**SN**	P	*SN*	BI	73438	78838	78638	73838
377 439	**SN**	P	*SN*	BI	73439	78839	78639	73839
377 440	**SN**	P	*SN*	BI	73440	78840	78640	73840
377 441	**SN**	P	*SN*	BI	73441	78841	78641	73841

377 442	**SN**	P	*SN*	BI	73442	78842	78642	73842
377 443	**SN**	P	*SN*	BI	73443	78843	78643	73843
377 444	**SN**	P	*SN*	BI	73444	78844	78644	73844
377 445	**SN**	P	*SN*	BI	73445	78845	78645	73845
377 446	**SN**	P	*SN*	BI	73446	78846	78646	73846
377 447	**SN**	P	*SN*	BI	73447	78847	78647	73847
377 448	**SN**	P	*SN*	BI	73448	78848	78648	73848
377 449	**SN**	P	*SN*	BI	73449	78849	78649	73849
377 450	**SN**	P	*SN*	BI	73450	78850	78650	73850
377 451	**SN**	P	*SN*	BI	73451	78851	78651	73851
377 452	**SN**	P	*SN*	BI	73452	78852	78652	73852
377 453	**SN**	P	*SN*	BI	73453	78853	78653	73853
377 454	**SN**	P	*SN*	BI	73454	78854	78654	73854
377 455	**SN**	P	*SN*	BI	73455	78855	78655	73855
377 456	**SN**	P	*SN*	BI	73456	78856	78656	73856
377 457	**SN**	P	*SN*	BI	73457	78857	78657	73857
377 458	**SN**	P	*SN*	BI	73458	78858	78658	73858
377 459	**SN**	P	*SN*	BI	73459	78859	78659	73859
377 460	**SN**	P	*SN*	BI	73460	78860	78660	73860
377 461	**SN**	P	*SN*	BI	73461	78861	78661	73861
377 462	**SN**	P	*SN*	BI	73462	78862	78662	73862
377 463	**SN**	P	*SN*	BI	73463	78863	78663	73863
377 464	**SN**	P	*SN*	BI	73464	78864	78664	73864
377 465	**SN**	P	*SN*	BI	73465	78865	78665	73865
377 466	**SN**	P	*SN*	BI	73466	78866	78666	73866
377 467	**SN**	P	*SN*	BI	73467	78867	78667	73867
377 468	**SN**	P	*SN*	BI	73468	78868	78668	73868
377 469	**SN**	P	*SN*	BI	73469	78869	78669	73869
377 470	**SN**	P	*SN*	BI	73470	78870	78670	73870
377 471	**SN**	P	*SN*	BI	73471	78871	78671	73871
377 472	**SN**	P	*SN*	BI	73472	78872	78672	73872
377 473	**SN**	P	*SN*	BI	73473	78873	78673	73873
377 474	**SN**	P	*SN*	BI	73474	78874	78674	73874
377 475	**SN**	P	*SN*	BI	73475	78875	78675	73875

Class 377/5. 25 kV AC/750 V DC. DMCO–MSO–PTSO–DMCO. Dual voltage First Capital Connect units (sub-leased from Southern). Details as Class 377/2 unless stated.

DMCO(A). Bombardier Derby 2008–09. 10/48. 43.1 t.
MSO. Bombardier Derby 2008–09. –/69 1T. 40.3 t.
PTSO. Bombardier Derby 2008–09. –/56 1TD 2W. 40.6 t.
DMCO(B). Bombardier Derby 2008–09. 10/48. 43.1 t.

377 501	**FU**	P	*FC*	BF	73501	75901	74901	73601
377 502	**FU**	P	*FC*	BF	73502	75902	74902	73602
377 503	**FU**	P	*FC*	BF	73503	75903	74903	73603
377 504	**FU**	P	*FC*	BF	73504	75904	74904	73604
377 505	**FU**	P	*FC*	BF	73505	75905	74905	73605
377 506	**FU**	P	*FC*	BF	73506	75906	74906	73606
377 507	**FU**	P	*FC*	BF	73507	75907	74907	73607
377 508	**FU**	P	*FC*	BF	73508	75908	74908	73608

377509	**FU**	P	*FC*	BF	73509	75909	74909	73609
377510	**FU**	P	*FC*	BF	73510	75910	74910	73610
377511	**FU**	P	*FC*	BF	73511	75911	74911	73611
377512	**FU**	P	*FC*	BF	73512	75912	74912	73612
377513	**FU**	P	*FC*	BF	73513	75913	74913	73613
377514	**FU**	P	*FC*	BF	73514	75914	74914	73614
377515	**FU**	P	*FC*	BF	73515	75915	74915	73615
377516	**FU**	P	*FC*	BF	73516	75916	74916	73616
377517	**FU**	P	*FC*	BF	73517	75917	74917	73617
377518	**FU**	P	*FC*	BF	73518	75918	74918	73618
377519	**FU**	P	*FC*	BF	73519	75919	74919	73619
377520	**FU**	P	*FC*	BF	73520	75920	74920	73620
377521	**FU**	P	*FC*	BF	73521	75921	74921	73621
377522	**FU**	P	*FC*	BF	73522	75922	74922	73622
377523	**FU**	P	*FC*	BF	73523	75923	74923	73623

CLASS 378 CAPITALSTAR BOMBARDIER DERBY

57 new Class 378 suburban Electrostars (designated Capitalstars by TfL) used by London Overground.

Formation: DMSO–MSO–TSO–DMSO or DMSO–MSO–PTSO–DMSO.
System: Class 378/1 750 V DC third rail only. Class 378/2 25 kV AC overhead and 750 V DC third rail.
Construction: Welded aluminium alloy underframe, sides and roof with steel ends. All sections bolted together.
Traction Motors: Two Bombardier asynchronous of 250 kW.
Wheel Arrangement: 2-Bo + 2-Bo + 2-2 + Bo-2.
Braking: Disc & regenerative.
Dimensions: 20.46/20.14 x 2.80 m.
Bogies: Bombardier P3-25/T3-25.
Couplers: Dellner 12.
Gangways: Within unit + end doors.
Control System: IGBT Inverter.
Doors: Sliding.
Maximum Speed: 75 mph.
Heating & ventilation: Air conditioning.
Seating Layout: Longitudinal ("tube style") low density.
Multiple Working: Within class and with Classes 375, 376, 377 and 379.

Class 378/1. 750 V DC. DMSO–MSO–TSO–DMSO. Third rail only units used on East London Line services. Provision for retro-fitting as dual voltage.

DMSO(A). Bombardier Derby 2009–10. –/36. 43.5 t.
MSO. Bombardier Derby 2009–10. –/40. 39.4 t.
TSO. Bombardier Derby 2009–10. –/34(6) 2W. 34.3t.
DMSO(B). Bombardier Derby 2009–10. –/36. 43.1 t.

Note: 378 150–154 are fitted with de-icing equipment. TSO weighs 34.8t.

378135	**LO**	QW	*LO*	NG	38035	38235	38335	38135
378136	**LO**	QW	*LO*	NG	38036	38236	38336	38136
378137	**LO**	QW	*LO*	NG	38037	38237	38337	38137
378138	**LO**	QW	*LO*	NG	38038	38238	38338	38138
378139	**LO**	QW	*LO*	NG	38039	38239	38339	38139
378140	**LO**	QW	*LO*	NG	38040	38240	38340	38140
378141	**LO**	QW	*LO*	NG	38041	38241	38341	38141

378142	**LO**	QW	*LO*	NG	38042	38242	38342	38142
378143	**LO**	QW	*LO*	NG	38043	38243	38343	38143
378144	**LO**	QW	*LO*	NG	38044	38244	38344	38144
378145	**LO**	QW	*LO*	NG	38045	38245	38345	38145
378146	**LO**	QW	*LO*	NG	38046	38246	38346	38146
378147	**LO**	QW	*LO*	NG	38047	38247	38347	38147
378148	**LO**	QW	*LO*	NG	38048	38248	38348	38148
378149	**LO**	QW	*LO*	NG	38049	38249	38349	38149
378150	**LO**	QW	*LO*	NG	38050	38250	38350	38150
378151	**LO**	QW	*LO*	NG	38051	38251	38351	38151
378152	**LO**	QW	*LO*	NG	38052	38252	38352	38152
378153	**LO**	QW	*LO*	NG	38053	38253	38353	38153
378154	**LO**	QW	*LO*	NG	38054	38254	38354	38154

Class 378/2. 25kV AC/750V DC. DMSO–MSO–PTSO–DMSO. Dual voltage units mainly used on North London Railway services. 378201–224 built as 378001–024 (3-car units) and extended to 4-car units in 2010.

DMSO(A). Bombardier Derby 2008–11. –/36. 43.2 t.
MSO. Bombardier Derby 2008–11. –/40. 39.8 t.
PTSO. Bombardier Derby 2008–11. –/34(6) 2W. 39.0t.
DMSO(B). Bombardier Derby 2008–11. –/36. 42.8 t.

Note: 378216–220 are fitted with de-icing equipment.

378201	**LO**	QW	*LO*	NG	38001	38201	38301	38101
378202	**LO**	QW	*LO*	NG	38002	38202	38302	38102
378203	**LO**	QW	*LO*	NG	38003	38203	38303	38103
378204	**LO**	QW	*LO*	NG	38004	38204	38304	38104
378205	**LO**	QW	*LO*	NG	38005	38205	38305	38105
378206	**LO**	QW	*LO*	NG	38006	38206	38306	38106
378207	**LO**	QW	*LO*	NG	38007	38207	38307	38107
378208	**LO**	QW	*LO*	NG	38008	38208	38308	38108
378209	**LO**	QW	*LO*	NG	38009	38209	38309	38109
378210	**LO**	QW	*LO*	NG	38010	38210	38310	38110
378211	**LO**	QW	*LO*	NG	38011	38211	38311	38111
378212	**LO**	QW	*LO*	NG	38012	38212	38312	38112
378213	**LO**	QW	*LO*	NG	38013	38213	38313	38113
378214	**LO**	QW	*LO*	NG	38014	38214	38314	38114
378215	**LO**	QW	*LO*	NG	38015	38215	38315	38115
378216	**LO**	QW	*LO*	NG	38016	38216	38316	38116
378217	**LO**	QW	*LO*	NG	38017	38217	38317	38117
378218	**LO**	QW	*LO*	NG	38018	38218	38318	38118
378219	**LO**	QW	*LO*	NG	38019	38219	38319	38119
378220	**LO**	QW	*LO*	NG	38020	38220	38320	38120
378221	**LO**	QW	*LO*	NG	38021	38221	38321	38121
378222	**LO**	QW	*LO*	NG	38022	38222	38322	38122
378223	**LO**	QW	*LO*	NG	38023	38223	38323	38123
378224	**LO**	QW	*LO*	NG	38024	38224	38324	38124
378225	**LO**	QW	*LO*	NG	38025	38225	38325	38125
378226	**LO**	QW	*LO*	NG	38026	38226	38326	38126
378227	**LO**	QW	*LO*	NG	38027	38227	38327	38127
378228	**LO**	QW	*LO*	NG	38028	38228	38328	38128

378 229	**LO**	QW	*LO*	NG	38029	38229	38329	38129
378 230	**LO**	QW	*LO*	NG	38030	38230	38330	38130
378 231	**LO**	QW	*LO*	NG	38031	38231	38331	38131
378 232	**LO**	QW	*LO*	NG	38032	38232	38332	38132
378 233	**LO**	QW	*LO*	NG	38033	38233	38333	38133
378 234	**LO**	QW	*LO*	NG	38034	38234	38334	38134
378 255	**LO**	QW	*LO*	NG	38055	38255	38355	38155
378 256	**LO**	QW	*LO*	NG	38056	38256	38356	38156
378 257	**LO**	QW	*LO*	NG	38057	38257	38357	38157

Name (carried on 38033):

378 233 Ian Brown CBE

CLASS 379 ELECTROSTAR BOMBARDIER DERBY

New EMUs principally used on Liverpool Street–Stansted Airport services and Liverpool Street–Cambridge services.

Formation: DMSO–MSO–PTSO–DMCO.
System: 25 kV AC overhead.
Construction: Welded aluminium alloy underframe, sides and roof with steel ends. All sections bolted together.
Traction Motors: Two Bombardier asynchronous of 250 kW.
Wheel Arrangement: 2-Bo + 2-Bo + 2-2 + Bo-2.
Braking: Disc & regenerative.
Bogies: Bombardier P3-25/T3-25.
Gangways: Throughout.
Doors: Sliding plug.
Dimensions: 20.0 x 2.80 m.
Couplers: Dellner 12.
Control System: IGBT Inverter.
Maximum Speed: 100 mph.
Heating & ventilation: Air conditioning.
Seating Layout: 1: 2+1 facing. 2: 2+2 facing/unidirectional.
Multiple Working: Within class and with Classes 375, 376, 377 and 378.

DMSO. Bombardier Derby 2010–11. –/60. 42.1 t.
MSO. Bombardier Derby 2010–11. –/62 1T. 38.6 t.
PTSO. Bombardier Derby 2010–11. –/43(2) 1TD 2W. 40.9 t.
DMCO. Bombardier Derby 2010–11. 20/24. 42.3 t.

379 001	**NC**	LY	*EA*	IL	61201	61701	61901	62101
379 002	**NC**	LY	*EA*	IL	61202	61702	61902	62102
379 003	**NC**	LY	*EA*	IL	61203	61703	61903	62103
379 004	**NC**	LY	*EA*	IL	61204	61704	61904	62104
379 005	**NC**	LY	*EA*	IL	61205	61705	61905	62105
379 006	**NC**	LY	*EA*	IL	61206	61706	61906	62106
379 007	**NC**	LY	*EA*	IL	61207	61707	61907	62107
379 008	**NC**	LY	*EA*	IL	61208	61708	61908	62108
379 009	**NC**	LY	*EA*	IL	61209	61709	61909	62109
379 010	**NC**	LY	*EA*	IL	61210	61710	61910	62110
379 011	**NC**	LY	*EA*	IL	61211	61711	61911	62111
379 012	**NC**	LY	*EA*	IL	61212	61712	61912	62112
379 013	**NC**	LY	*EA*	IL	61213	61713	61913	62113
379 014	**NC**	LY	*EA*	IL	61214	61714	61914	62114
379 015	**NC**	LY	*EA*	IL	61215	61715	61915	62115

379016	**NC**	LY	*EA*	IL	61216	61716	61916	62116
379017	**NC**	LY	*EA*	IL	61217	61717	61917	62117
379018	**NC**	LY	*EA*	IL	61218	61718	61918	62118
379019	**NC**	LY	*EA*	IL	61219	61719	61919	62119
379020	**NC**	LY	*EA*	IL	61220	61720	61920	62120
379021	**NC**	LY	*EA*	IL	61221	61721	61921	62121
379022	**NC**	LY	*EA*	IL	61222	61722	61922	62122
379023	**NC**	LY	*EA*	IL	61223	61723	61923	62123
379024	**NC**	LY	*EA*	IL	61224	61724	61924	62124
379025	**NC**	LY	*EA*	IL	61225	61725	61925	62125
379026	**NC**	LY	*EA*	IL	61226	61726	61926	62126
379027	**NC**	LY	*EA*	IL	61227	61727	61927	62127
379028	**NC**	LY	*EA*	IL	61228	61728	61928	62128
379029	**NC**	LY	*EA*	IL	61229	61729	61929	62129
379030	**NC**	LY	*EA*	IL	61230	61730	61930	62130

Names (carried on end cars):

379005 Stansted Express
379011 Ely Cathedral
379012 The West Anglian
379015 City of Cambridge
379025 Go Discover

CLASS 380 DESIRO UK SIEMENS

New EMUs mainly used on Strathclyde area services from Glasgow Central as well as Edinburgh–North Berwick trains.

Formation: DMSO–PTSO–DMSO or DMSO–PTSO–TSO–DMSO.
System: 25 kV AC overhead.
Construction: Welded aluminium with steel ends.
Traction Motors: Four Siemens ITB2016-0GB02 asynchronous of 250 kW.
Wheel Arrangement: Bo-Bo + 2-2 (+2-2) + Bo-Bo
Braking: Disc & regenerative.
Dimensions: 23.78/23.57 x 2.80 m.
Bogies: SGP SF5000.
Couplers: Voith.
Gangways: Throughout.
Control System: IGBT Inverter.
Doors: Sliding plug.
Maximum Speed: 100 mph.
Heating & ventilation: Air conditioning.
Seating Layout: 2+2 facing/unidirectional.
Multiple Working: Within class.

DMSO(A). Siemens Krefeld 2009–10. –/70. 45.0 t.
PTSO. Siemens Krefeld 2009–10. –/57(12) 1TD 2W. 42.7 t.
TSO. Siemens Krefeld 2009–10. –/74 1T. 34.8 t.
DMSO(B). Siemens Krefeld 2009–10. –/64(5). 44.9 t.

Class 380/0. 3-car units.

380001	**SR**	E	*SR*	GW	38501	38601		38701
380002	**SR**	E	*SR*	GW	38502	38602		38702
380003	**SR**	E	*SR*	GW	38503	38603		38703
380004	**SR**	E	*SR*	GW	38504	38604		38704
380005	**SR**	E	*SR*	GW	38505	38605		38705
380006	**SR**	E	*SR*	GW	38506	38606		38706

380007	**SR**	E	*SR*	GW	38507	38607		38707
380008	**SR**	E	*SR*	GW	38508	38608		38708
380009	**SR**	E	*SR*	GW	38509	38609		38709
380010	**SR**	E	*SR*	GW	38510	38610		38710
380011	**SR**	E	*SR*	GW	38511	38611		38711
380012	**SR**	E	*SR*	GW	38512	38612		38712
380013	**SR**	E	*SR*	GW	38513	38613		38713
380014	**SR**	E	*SR*	GW	38514	38614		38714
380015	**SR**	E	*SR*	GW	38515	38615		38715
380016	**SR**	E	*SR*	GW	38516	38616		38716
380017	**SR**	E	*SR*	GW	38517	38617		38717
380018	**SR**	E	*SR*	GW	38518	38618		38718
380019	**SR**	E	*SR*	GW	38519	38619		38719
380020	**SR**	E	*SR*	GW	38520	38620		38720
380021	**SR**	E	*SR*	GW	38521	38621		38721
380022	**SR**	E	*SR*	GW	38522	38622		38722

Class 380/1. 4-car units.

Note: 380101–108 are fitted with NRN radios for working North Berwick services.

380101	**SR**	E	*SR*	GW	38551	38651	38851	38751
380102	**SR**	E	*SR*	GW	38552	38652	38852	38752
380103	**SR**	E	*SR*	GW	38553	38653	38853	38753
380104	**SR**	E	*SR*	GW	38554	38654	38854	38754
380105	**SR**	E	*SR*	GW	38555	38655	38855	38755
380106	**SR**	E	*SR*	GW	38556	38656	38856	38756
380107	**SR**	E	*SR*	GW	38557	38657	38857	38757
380108	**SR**	E	*SR*	GW	38558	38658	38858	38758
380109	**SR**	E	*SR*	GW	38559	38659	38859	38759
380110	**SR**	E	*SR*	GW	38560	38660	38860	38760
380111	**SR**	E	*SR*	GW	38561	38661	38861	38761
380112	**SR**	E	*SR*	GW	38562	38662	38862	38762
380113	**SR**	E	*SR*	GW	38563	38663	38863	38763
380114	**SR**	E	*SR*	GW	38564	38664	38864	38764
380115	**SR**	E	*SR*	GW	38565	38665	38865	38765
380116	**SR**	E	*SR*	GW	38566	38666	38866	38766

CLASS 390 PENDOLINO ALSTOM

Tilting West Coast Main Line units.

Formation: DMRFO–MFO–PTFO–MFO–(TSO)–(MSO)–TSO–MSO–PTSRMB–MSO–DMSO.
Construction: Welded aluminium alloy.
Traction Motors: Two Alstom ONIX 800 of 425 kW.
Wheel Arrangement: 1A-A1 + 1A-A1 + 2-2 + 1A-A1 (+ 2-2 + 1A-A1) + 2-2 + 1A-A1 + 2-2 + 1A-A1 + 1A-A1.
Braking: Disc, rheostatic & regenerative.
Dimensions: 24.80/23.90 x 2.73 m.
Couplers: Dellner 12.
Bogies: Fiat-SIG.
Control System: IGBT Inverter.
Gangways: Within unit.
Maximum Speed: 125 mph.
Doors: Sliding plug.
Heating & ventilation: Air conditioning.
Seating Layout: 1: 2+1 facing/unidirectional, 2: 2+2 facing/unidirectional.
Multiple Working: Within class. Can also be controlled from Class 57/3 locos.

DMRFO: Alstom Birmingham 2001–05. 18/–. 55.6 t.
MFO(A): Alstom Birmingham 2001–05. 37/–(2) 1TD 1W. 52.0 t.
PTFO: Alstom Birmingham 2001–05. 44/– 1T. 50.1 t.
MFO(B): Alstom Birmingham 2001–05. 46/– 1T. 51.8 t.
(**TSO:** Alstom Savigliano 2010–12. –/74 1T. 49.2 t.)
(**MSO:** Alstom Savigliano 2010–12. –/76 1T. 52.2 t.)
TSO: Alstom Birmingham 2001–05. –/76 1T. 45.5 t.
MSO(A): Alstom Birmingham 2001–05. –/62(4) 1TD 1W. 50.0 t.
PTSRMB: Alstom Birmingham 2001–05. –/48. 52.0 t.
MSO(B): Alstom Birmingham 2001–05. –/62(2) 1TD 1W. 51.7 t.
DMSO: Alstom Birmingham 2001–05. –/46 1T. 51.0 t.

Advertising livery: 390004 – Black Alstom vinyls on Virgin silver livery.

Notes: Units up to 390034 were delivered as 8-car sets, without the TSO (688xx). During 2004–05 these units had their 9th cars added.

62 extra vehicles are under construction to lengthen 31 sets to 11-cars, but it has not yet been finalised which sets these extra vehicles will be added to. Four new complete 11-car units (390054–057) are also being delivered. 390 054/055 initially entered service as a 9-car sets.

390033 was written off following accident damage in the Lambrigg accident of February 2007.

390001	**VT**	A	*VW*	MA	69101 69401 69501 69601 68801 69701 69801 69901 69201
390002	**VT**	A	*VW*	MA	69102 69402 69502 69602 68802 69702 69802 69902 69202
390003	**VT**	A	*VW*	MA	69103 69403 69503 69603 68803 69703 69803 69903 69203
390004	**AL**	A	*VW*	MA	69104 69404 69504 69604 68804 69704 69804 69904 69204
390005	**VT**	A	*VW*	MA	69105 69405 69505 69605 68805 69705 69805 69905 69205
390006	**VT**	A	*VW*	MA	69106 69406 69506 69606 68806 69706 69806 69906 69206

390 007	**VT**	A	*VW*	MA	69107 69407 69507 69607 68807 69707 69807 69907 69207
390 008	**VT**	A	*VW*	MA	69108 69408 69508 69608 68808 69708 69808 69908 69208
390 009	**VT**	A	*VW*	MA	69109 69409 69509 69609 68809 69709 69809 69909 69209
390 010	**VT**	A	*VW*	MA	69110 69410 69510 69610 68810 69710 69810 69910 69210
390 011	**VT**	A	*VW*	MA	69111 69411 69511 69611 68811 69711 69811 69911 69211
390 012	**VT**	A	*VW*	MA	69112 69412 69512 69612 68812 69712 69812 69912 69212
390 013	**VT**	A	*VW*	MA	69113 69413 69513 69613 68813 69713 69813 69913 69213
390 014	**VT**	A	*VW*	MA	69114 69414 69514 69614 68814 69714 69814 69914 69214
390 015	**VT**	A	*VW*	MA	69115 69415 69515 69615 68815 69715 69815 69915 69215
390 016	**VT**	A	*VW*	MA	69116 69416 69516 69616 68816 69716 69816 69916 69216
390 017	**VT**	A	*VW*	MA	69117 69417 69517 69617 68817 69717 69817 69917 69217
390 018	**VT**	A	*VW*	MA	69118 69418 69518 69618 68818 69718 69818 69918 69218
390 019	**VT**	A	*VW*	MA	69119 69419 69519 69619 68819 69719 69819 69919 69219
390 020	**VT**	A	*VW*	MA	69120 69420 69520 69620 68820 69720 69820 69920 69220
390 021	**VT**	A	*VW*	MA	69121 69421 69521 69621 68821 69721 69821 69921 69221
390 022	**VT**	A	*VW*	MA	69122 69422 69522 69622 68822 69722 69822 69922 69222
390 023	**VT**	A	*VW*	MA	69123 69423 69523 69623 68823 69723 69823 69923 69223
390 024	**VT**	A	*VW*	MA	69124 69424 69524 69624 68824 69724 69824 69924 69224
390 025	**VT**	A	*VW*	MA	69125 69425 69525 69625 68825 69725 69825 69925 69225
390 026	**VT**	A	*VW*	MA	69126 69426 69526 69626 68826 69726 69826 69926 69226
390 027	**VT**	A	*VW*	MA	69127 69427 69527 69627 68827 69727 69827 69927 69227
390 028	**VT**	A	*VW*	MA	69128 69428 69528 69628 68828 69728 69828 69928 69228
390 029	**VT**	A	*VW*	MA	69129 69429 69529 69629 68829 69729 69829 69929 69229
390 030	**VT**	A	*VW*	MA	69130 69430 69530 69630 68830 69730 69830 69930 69230
390 031	**VT**	A	*VW*	MA	69131 69431 69531 69631 68831 69731 69831 69931 69231

390 032	**VT**	A	*VW*	MA	69132 69432 69532 69632 68832 69732 69832 69932 69232
390 034	**VT**	A	*VW*	MA	69134 69434 69534 69634 68834 69734 69834 69934 69234
390 035	**VT**	A	*VW*	MA	69135 69435 69535 69635 68835 69735 69835 69935 69235
390 036	**VT**	A	*VW*	MA	69136 69436 69536 69636 68836 69736 69836 69936 69236
390 037	**VT**	A	*VW*	MA	69137 69437 69537 69637 68837 69737 69837 69937 69237
390 038	**VT**	A	*VW*	MA	69138 69438 69538 69638 68838 69738 69838 69938 69238
390 039	**VT**	A	*VW*	MA	69139 69439 69539 69639 68839 69739 69839 69939 69239
390 040	**VT**	A	*VW*	MA	69140 69440 69540 69640 68840 69740 69840 69940 69240
390 041	**VT**	A	*VW*	MA	69141 69441 69541 69641 68841 69741 69841 69941 69241
390 042	**VT**	A	*VW*	MA	69142 69442 69542 69642 68842 69742 69842 69942 69242
390 043	**VT**	A	*VW*	MA	69143 69443 69543 69643 68843 69743 69843 69943 69243
390 044	**VT**	A	*VW*	MA	69144 69444 69544 69644 68844 69744 69844 69944 69244
390 045	**VT**	A	*VW*	MA	69145 69445 69545 69645 68845 69745 69845 69945 69245
390 046	**VT**	A	*VW*	MA	69146 69446 69546 69646 68846 69746 69846 69946 69246
390 047	**VT**	A	*VW*	MA	69147 69447 69547 69647 68847 69747 69847 69947 69247
390 048	**VT**	A	*VW*	MA	69148 69448 69548 69648 68848 69748 69848 69948 69248
390 049	**VT**	A	*VW*	MA	69149 69449 69549 69649 68849 69749 69849 69949 69249
390 050	**VT**	A	*VW*	MA	69150 69450 69550 69650 68850 69750 69850 69950 69250
390 051	**VT**	A	*VW*	MA	69151 69451 69551 69651 68851 69751 69851 69951 69251
390 052	**VT**	A	*VW*	MA	69152 69452 69552 69652 68852 69752 69852 69952 69252
390 053	**VT**	A	*VW*	MA	69153 69453 69553 69653 68853 69753 69853 69953 69253
390 054	**VT**	A	*VW*	MA	69154 69454 69554 69654 *65354 68954* 68854 69754 69854 69954 69254
390 055	**VT**	A	*VW*	MA	69155 69455 69555 69655 *65355 68955* 68855 69755 69855 69955 69255
390 056	**VT**	A			69156 69456 69556 69656 65356 68956 68856 69756 69856 69956 69256
390 057	**VT**	A			69157 69457 69557 69657 65357 68957 68857 69757 69857 69957 69257

Names (carried on MFO No. 696xx):

390 001 Virgin Pioneer
390 002 Virgin Angel
390 003 Virgin Hero
390 004 Alstom Pendolino
390 005 City of Wolverhampton
390 006 Tate Liverpool
390 007 Virgin Lady
390 008 Virgin King
390 009 Treaty of Union
390 010 A Decade of Progress
390 011 City of Lichfield
390 012 Virgin Star
390 013 Virgin Spirit
390 014 City of Manchester
390 015 Virgin Crusader
390 016 Virgin Champion
390 017 Virgin Prince
390 018 Virgin Princess
390 019 Virgin Warrior
390 020 Virgin Cavalier
390 021 Virgin Dream
390 022 Penny the Pendolino
390 023 Virgin Glory
390 024 Virgin Venturer
390 025 Virgin Stagecoach
390 026 Virgin Enterprise
390 027 Virgin Buccaneer
390 028 City of Preston
390 029 City of Stoke-on-Trent
390 030 City of Edinburgh
390 031 City of Liverpool
390 032 City of Birmingham
390 034 City of Carlisle
390 035 City of Lancaster
390 036 City of Coventry
390 037 Virgin Difference
390 038 City of London
390 039 Virgin Quest
390 040 Virgin Pathfinder
390 041 City of Chester
390 042 City of Bangor/Dinas Bangor
390 043 Virgin Explorer
390 044 Virgin Lionheart
390 045 101 Squadron
390 046 Virgin Soldiers
390 047 CLIC Sargent
390 048 Virgin Harrier
390 049 Virgin Express
390 050 Virgin Invader
390 051 Virgin Ambassador
390 052 Virgin Knight
390 053 Mission Accomplished

CLASS 395 HS1 DOMESTIC SETS HITACHI JAPAN

New 6-car dual-voltage units for Southeastern domestic services from St Pancras International to Ashford/Dover/Margate via Ramsgate and Faversham.

Formation: PDTSO–MSO–MSO–MSO–MSO–PDTSO.
Systems: 25 kV AC overhead/750 V DC third rail.
Construction: Aluminium.
Traction Motors: Hitachi asynchronous of 210 kW.
Wheel Arrangement: 2-2 + Bo-Bo + Bo-Bo + Bo-Bo + Bo-Bo + 2-2.
Braking: Disc, rheostatic & regenerative braking.
Dimensions: 20.88/20.0 x 2.81 m.
Couplers: Scharfenberg.
Bogies: Hitachi.
Control System: IGBT Inverter.
Gangways: Within unit.
Maximum Speed: 140 mph.
Doors: Single-leaf sliding.
Multiple Working: Within class only.
Heating & ventilation: Air conditioning.
Seating Layout: 2+2 facing/unidirectional (mainly unidirectional).

PDTSO(A): Hitachi Kasado, Japan 2006–09. –/28(12) 1TD 2W. 46.7 t.
MSO: Hitachi Kasado, Japan 2006–09. –/66. 45.0 t–45.7 t.
PDTSO(B): Hitachi Kasado, Japan 2006–09. –/48 1T. 46.7 t.

395 001	**SB**	E	*SE*	AD	39011	39012	39013	39014	39015	39016
395 002	**SB**	E	*SE*	AD	39021	39022	39023	39024	39025	39026
395 003	**SB**	E	*SE*	AD	39031	39032	39033	39034	39035	39036
395 004	**SB**	E	*SE*	AD	39041	39042	39043	39044	39045	39046
395 005	**SB**	E	*SE*	AD	39051	39052	39053	39054	39055	39056
395 006	**SB**	E	*SE*	AD	39061	39062	39063	39064	39065	39066
395 007	**SB**	E	*SE*	AD	39071	39072	39073	39074	39075	39076
395 008	**SB**	E	*SE*	AD	39081	39082	39083	39084	39085	39086
395 009	**SB**	E	*SE*	AD	39091	39092	39093	39094	39095	39096
395 010	**SB**	E	*SE*	AD	39101	39102	39103	39104	39105	39106
395 011	**SB**	E	*SE*	AD	39111	39112	39113	39114	39115	39116
395 012	**SB**	E	*SE*	AD	39121	39122	39123	39124	39125	39126
395 013	**SB**	E	*SE*	AD	39131	39132	39133	39134	39135	39136
395 014	**SB**	E	*SE*	AD	39141	39142	39143	39144	39145	39146
395 015	**SB**	E	*SE*	AD	39151	39152	39153	39154	39155	39156
395 016	**SB**	E	*SE*	AD	39161	39162	39163	39164	39165	39166
395 017	**SB**	E	*SE*	AD	39171	39172	39173	39174	39175	39176
395 018	**SB**	E	*SE*	AD	39181	39182	39183	39184	39185	39186
395 019	**SB**	E	*SE*	AD	39191	39192	39193	39194	39195	39196
395 020	**SB**	E	*SE*	AD	39201	39202	39203	39204	39205	39206
395 021	**SB**	E	*SE*	AD	39211	39212	39213	39214	39215	39216
395 022	**SB**	E	*SE*	AD	39221	39222	39223	39224	39225	39226
395 023	**SB**	E	*SE*	AD	39231	39232	39233	39234	39235	39236
395 024	**SB**	E	*SE*	AD	39241	39242	39243	39244	39245	39246
395 025	**SB**	E	*SE*	AD	39251	39252	39253	39254	39255	39256
395 026	**SB**	E	*SE*	AD	39261	39262	39263	39264	39265	39266
395 027	**SB**	E	*SE*	AD	39271	39272	39273	39274	39275	39276
395 028	**SB**	E	*SE*	AD	39281	39282	39283	39284	39285	39286
395 029	**SB**	E	*SE*	AD	39291	39292	39293	39294	39295	39296

Names (carried on end cars):

395 001 Dame Kelly Holmes
395 002 Sebastian Coe
395 003 Sir Steve Redgrave
395 004 Sir Chris Hoy
395 005 Dame Tanni Grey-Thompson
395 006 Daley Thompson
395 007 Steve Backley
395 008 Ben Ainslie
395 009 Rebecca Adlington
395 016 Jamie Staff

4.2. 750 V DC THIRD RAIL EMUs

These classes use the third rail system at 750 V DC (unless stated). Outer couplers are buckeyes on units built before 1982 with bar couplers within the units. Newer units generally have Dellner outer couplers.

CLASS 442 WESSEX EXPRESS BREL DERBY

Stock built for Waterloo–Bournemouth–Weymouth services. Previously used by South West Trains, all units now used by Southern, principally on Victoria–Gatwick Airport–Brighton services.

Formation: DTSO(A)–TSO–MBC–TSO(W)–DTSO(B).
Construction: Steel.
Traction Motors: Four EE546 of 300 kW recovered from Class 432s.
Wheel Arrangement: 2-2 + 2-2 + Bo-Bo + 2-2 + 2-2.
Braking: Disc.
Dimensions: 23.15/23.00 x 2.74 m.
Bogies: Two BREL P7 motor bogies (MBSO). T4 bogies (trailer cars).
Couplers: Buckeye.
Control System: 1986-type.
Gangways: Throughout.
Maximum Speed: 100 mph.
Doors: Sliding plug.
Heating & Ventilation: Air conditioning.
Seating Layout: 1: 2+1 facing, 2: 2+2 mainly unidirectional.
Multiple Working: Within class and Class 33/1 & 73 locos in an emergency.

DTSO(A). Lot No. 31030 Derby 1988–89. –/74. 38.5 t.
TSO. Lot No. 31032 Derby 1988–89. –/76 2T. 37.5 t.
MBC. Lot No. 31034 Derby 1988–89. 24/28. 55.0 t.
TSO(W). Lot No. 31033 Derby 1988–89. –/66(4) 1TD 1T 2W. 37.8 t.
DTSO(B). Lot No. 31031 Derby 1988–89. –/74. 37.3 t.

442401	**GV**	A	*SN*	SL	77382	71818	62937	71842	77406
442402	**GV**	A	*SN*	SL	77383	71819	62938	71843	77407
442403	**GV**	A	*SN*	SL	77384	71820	62941	71844	77408
442404	**GV**	A	*SN*	SL	77385	71821	62939	71845	77409
442405	**GV**	A	*SN*	SL	77386	71822	62944	71846	77410
442406	**GV**	A	*SN*	SL	77389	71823	62942	71847	77411
442407	**GV**	A	*SN*	SL	77388	71824	62943	71848	77412
442408	**GV**	A	*SN*	SL	77387	71825	62945	71849	77413
442409	**GV**	A	*SN*	SL	77390	71826	62946	71850	77414
442410	**GV**	A	*SN*	SL	77391	71827	62948	71851	77415
442411	**GV**	A	*SN*	SL	77392	71828	62940	71858	77422
442412	**GV**	A	*SN*	SL	77393	71829	62947	71853	77417
442413	**GV**	A	*SN*	SL	77394	71830	62949	71854	77418
442414	**GV**	A	*SN*	SL	77395	71831	62950	71855	77419
442415	**GV**	A	*SN*	SL	77396	71832	62951	71856	77420
442416	**GV**	A	*SN*	SL	77397	71833	62952	71857	77421
442417	**GV**	A	*SN*	SL	77398	71834	62953	71852	77416
442418	**GV**	A	*SN*	SL	77399	71835	62954	71859	77423
442419	**GV**	A	*SN*	SL	77400	71836	62955	71860	77424
442420	**GV**	A	*SN*	SL	77401	71837	62956	71861	77425
442421	**GV**	A	*SN*	SL	77402	71838	62957	71862	77426

442 422	**GV**	A	*SN*	SL	77403	71839	62958	71863	77427
442 423	**GV**	A	*SN*	SL	77404	71840	62959	71864	77428
442 424	**GV**	A	*SN*	SL	77405	71841	62960	71865	77429

CLASS 444 DESIRO UK SIEMENS

Express units.

Formation: DMCO–TSO–TSO–TSORMB–DMSO.
Construction: Aluminium.
Traction Motors: 4 Siemens 1TB2016-0GB02 asynchronous of 250 kW.
Wheel Arrangement: Bo-Bo + 2-2 + 2-2 + 2-2 + Bo-Bo.
Braking: Disc, rheostatic & regenerative.
Dimensions: 23.57 x 2.80 m.
Bogies: SGP SF5000.
Couplers: Dellner 12.
Gangways: Throughout.
Control System: IGBT Inverter.
Doors: Single-leaf sliding plug.
Maximum Speed: 100 mph.
Heating & Ventilation: Air conditioning.
Seating Layout: 1: 2+1 facing/unidirectional, 2: 2+2 facing/unidirectional.
Multiple Working: Within class and with Class 450.

DMSO. Siemens Vienna/Krefeld 2003–04. –/76. 51.3t.
TSO 67101–145. Siemens Vienna/Krefeld 2003–04. –/76 1T. 40.3t.
TSO 67151–195. Siemens Vienna/Krefeld 2003–04. –/76 1T. 36.8t.
TSORMB. Siemens Vienna/Krefeld 2003–04. –/47 1T 1TD 2W. 42.1t.
DMCO. Siemens Vienna/Krefeld 2003–04. 35/24. 51.3t.

444 001	**ST**	A	*SW*	NT	63801	67101	67151	67201	63851
444 002	**ST**	A	*SW*	NT	63802	67102	67152	67202	63852
444 003	**ST**	A	*SW*	NT	63803	67103	67153	67203	63853
444 004	**ST**	A	*SW*	NT	63804	67104	67154	67204	63854
444 005	**ST**	A	*SW*	NT	63805	67105	67155	67205	63855
444 006	**ST**	A	*SW*	NT	63806	67106	67156	67206	63856
444 007	**ST**	A	*SW*	NT	63807	67107	67157	67207	63857
444 008	**ST**	A	*SW*	NT	63808	67108	67158	67208	63858
444 009	**ST**	A	*SW*	NT	63809	67109	67159	67209	63859
444 010	**ST**	A	*SW*	NT	63810	67110	67160	67210	63860
444 011	**ST**	A	*SW*	NT	63811	67111	67161	67211	63861
444 012	**ST**	A	*SW*	NT	63812	67112	67162	67212	63862
444 013	**ST**	A	*SW*	NT	63813	67113	67163	67213	63863
444 014	**ST**	A	*SW*	NT	63814	67114	67164	67214	63864
444 015	**ST**	A	*SW*	NT	63815	67115	67165	67215	63865
444 016	**ST**	A	*SW*	NT	63816	67116	67166	67216	63866
444 017	**ST**	A	*SW*	NT	63817	67117	67167	67217	63867
444 018	**ST**	A	*SW*	NT	63818	67118	67168	67218	63868
444 019	**ST**	A	*SW*	NT	63819	67119	67169	67219	63869
444 020	**ST**	A	*SW*	NT	63820	67120	67170	67220	63870
444 021	**ST**	A	*SW*	NT	63821	67121	67171	67221	63871
444 022	**ST**	A	*SW*	NT	63822	67122	67172	67222	63872
444 023	**ST**	A	*SW*	NT	63823	67123	67173	67223	63873
444 024	**ST**	A	*SW*	NT	63824	67124	67174	67224	63874

444 025	**ST**	A	*SW*	NT	63825	67125	67175	67225	63875
444 026	**ST**	A	*SW*	NT	63826	67126	67176	67226	63876
444 027	**ST**	A	*SW*	NT	63827	67127	67177	67227	63877
444 028	**ST**	A	*SW*	NT	63828	67128	67178	67228	63878
444 029	**ST**	A	*SW*	NT	63829	67129	67179	67229	63879
444 030	**ST**	A	*SW*	NT	63830	67130	67180	67230	63880
444 031	**ST**	A	*SW*	NT	63831	67131	67181	67231	63881
444 032	**ST**	A	*SW*	NT	63832	67132	67182	67232	63882
444 033	**ST**	A	*SW*	NT	63833	67133	67183	67233	63883
444 034	**ST**	A	*SW*	NT	63834	67134	67184	67234	63884
444 035	**ST**	A	*SW*	NT	63835	67135	67185	67235	63885
444 036	**ST**	A	*SW*	NT	63836	67136	67186	67236	63886
444 037	**ST**	A	*SW*	NT	63837	67137	67187	67237	63887
444 038	**ST**	A	*SW*	NT	63838	67138	67188	67238	63888
444 039	**ST**	A	*SW*	NT	63839	67139	67189	67239	63889
444 040	**ST**	A	*SW*	NT	63840	67140	67190	67240	63890
444 041	**ST**	A	*SW*	NT	63841	67141	67191	67241	63891
444 042	**ST**	A	*SW*	NT	63842	67142	67192	67242	63892
444 043	**ST**	A	*SW*	NT	63843	67143	67193	67243	63893
444 044	**ST**	A	*SW*	NT	63844	67144	67194	67244	63894
444 045	**ST**	A	*SW*	NT	63845	67145	67195	67245	63895

Names (carried on TSORMB):

444 001 NAOMI HOUSE
444 012 DESTINATION WEYMOUTH
444 018 THE FAB 444

▲ Southern uses 19 Class 313s transferred from the London area on Coastway services. With its pantograph removed, 313 214 leaves Lancing with the 09.09 West Worthing–Brighton on 12/04/11. **Alex Dasi-Sutton**

▼ Carrying the new blue ScotRail "Saltire" livery, 314 212 approaches Cathcart with the 16.23 Glasgow Central–Neilston on 01/05/11. **Robin Ralston**

▲ "One"-liveried 315 854/852 pass Pudding Mill Lane DLR station with the 09.40 London Liverpool Street–Shenfield on 14/05/11. **Alex Dasi-Sutton**

▼ First Capital Connect-liveried 317 346 passes Harringay with the 09.55 Cambridge–London King's Cross on 23/05/11. **Robert Pritchard**

▲ First Capital Connect-liveried 319 375 passes Selhurst depot, near Norwood Junction with the 08.02 Brighton–Bedford on 27/04/10. **Alex Dasi-Sutton**

▼ ScotRail Saltire-liveried 320 314 pauses at Coatbridge Sunnyside whilst working the 13.10 Balloch–Airdrie with 320 304 on 29/07/11. **Ian Lothian**

▲ In the joint West Yorkshire PTE/Northern livery, 321 903 passes Millhouse, near South Elmsall, with the 12.19 Leeds–Doncaster stopping service on 30/04/11.
Robert Pritchard

▼ Northern-liveried 323 225 arrives at Burnage with the 18.14 Manchester Piccadilly–Manchester Airport on 03/05/10. **Robert Pritchard**

▲ 333 001 arrives at Ilkley with the 13.02 from Leeds on 22/04/11.
Robert Pritchard

▼ Most of the Class 334s are still in SPT Carmine & Cream colours. On 03/09/10 334 033 arrives at Partick with the 11.23 Dalmuir–Lanark. **Robert Pritchard**

▲ London Midland-liveried 350 108 pauses at Rugby with the 13.46 London Euston–Crewe via Northampton on 04/03/11. **Robert Pritchard**

▼ National Express white-liveried 357 011 "JOHN LOWING" and 357 212 arrive at Rainham with the 16.39 Grays–London Fenchurch Street on 23/03/11. **Robert Pritchard**

▲ In First Group blue with a white National Express stripe, 360 109 arrives at Witham with the 10.50 Clacton-on-Sea–London Liverpool Street on 11/08/10.
Robert Pritchard

▼ First Capital Connect "Urban Lights"-liveried 365 521 arrives at Welwyn North with the 14.55 Cambridge–London King's Cross on 23/05/10. **Robert Pritchard**

▲ In the Connex-inspired white livery with yellow doors, Southeastern's 375 830 passes Wandsworth Road bound for London Victoria on 22/08/11. **Robert Pritchard**

▼ Southern-liveried 377 429 is seen between Southease and Newhaven with the 14.10 Brighton–Seaford on 30/10/10. **Alex Dasi-Sutton**

▲ London Overground-liveried 378 209 is seen near Headstone Lane with the 13.41 Watford Junction–London Euston "DC line" service on 06/04/11. **Brian Denton**

▼ National Express white-liveried 379 012/011 pass Hackney Downs with the 14.00 Stansted Airport–London Liverpool Street on 11/06/11. **Alex Dasi-Sutton**

▲ ScotRail Saltire-liveried 380 104 is seen on the approaches to Ayr with the 15.30 Glasgow Central–Ayr on 16/03/11. **Stuart Fowler**

▼ Virgin Trains-liveried 390 049 "Virgin Express" is seen near Lichfield Trent Valley with the 14.07 London Euston–Liverpool on 03/06/11. **Dave Gommersall**

▲ Southeastern blue-liveried 395 009 at Gravesend with the 09.55 London St Pancras International–Faversham on 21/05/11. **Alex Dasi-Sutton**

▼ Gatwick Express-liveried 442 402/412 are seen near Earlswood with the 15.06 London Victoria–Brighton on 02/05/11. **Alex Dasi-Sutton**

▲ South West Trains white-liveried 444 042/026 pass Vauxhall shortly after departure with the 09.35 London Waterloo–Weymouth on 02/0511.

Alex Dasi-Sutton

▼ South West Trains blue-liveried 450 094 is seen on the approaches to Brockenhurst with the 09.20 Weymouth–London Waterloo on 22/05/10. Most Weymouth services are in the hands of Class 444s. **Robert Pritchard**

▲ South West Trains red-liveried 5909 leads the 07.11 Shepperton–Waterloo into the London terminus on 12/04/11. **Brian Denton**

▼ Southern-liveried 456 002 leads a 6-car formation on the 14.13 London Victoria–Caterham at South Croydon on 06/04/11. **Alex Dasi-Sutton**

▲ South West Trains-liveried 8005 and 8013 are seen near Twickenham with the 07.24 Reading–London Waterloo on 31/05/11. **Alex Dasi-Sutton**

▼ In Southeastern livery of white with blue doors (but without the dark blue lower bodyside stripe as on some units), 466 039 leads a Class 465 at Shortlands with the 07.40 London Victoria–Orpington on 15/07/11. **Alisdair Anderson**

▲ Merseyrail-liveried 507 006 is seen at Spital with the 13.31 Chester–Liverpool Central–Chester Wirral Line service on 03/05/11. **Mark Bearton**

▼ Eurostar set 3106/05 heads towards London St Pancras with the 15.13 from Paris Nord on 23/03/11, seen at Rainham on High Speed 1. **Robert Pritchard**

▲ The first of the new Bombardier Flexity 2 trams for Blackpool was launched at the resort on 08/09/11. Here car 001 leaves the new Starr Gate depot with a press run to Pleasure Beach. These cars were due to enter traffic at Easter 2012.

Ian McLoughlin

▼ London Tramlink 2540 leaves the East Croydon stop with a service for Beckenham Junction on 12/04/11. **Brian Denton**

CLASS 450 DESIRO UK SIEMENS

Outer suburban units.

Formation: DMSO–TCO–TSO–DMSO (DMSO–TSO–TCO–DMSO 450 111–127).
Construction: Aluminium.
Traction Motors: 4 Siemens 1TB2016-0GB02 asynchronous of 250 kW.
Wheel Arrangement: Bo-Bo + 2-2 + 2-2 + Bo-Bo.
Braking: Disc, rheostatic & regenerative.
Dimensions: 20.34 x 2.79 m.
Bogies: SGP SF5000.
Couplers: Dellner 12.
Gangways: Throughout.
Control System: IGBT Inverter.
Doors: Sliding plug.
Maximum Speed: 100 mph.
Heating & Ventilation: Air conditioning.
Seating Layout: 1: 2+2 facing/unidirectional, 2: 3+2 facing/unidirectional.
Multiple Working: Within class and with Class 444.

Class 450/0. Standard units.

DMSO(A). Siemens Krefeld/Vienna 2002–06. –/70. 48.0 t.
TCO. Siemens Krefeld/Vienna 2002–06. 24/32(4) 1T. 35.8 t.
TSO. Siemens Krefeld/Vienna 2002–06. –/61(9) 1TD 2W. 39.8 t.
DMSO(B). Siemens Krefeld/Vienna 2002–06. –/70. 48.6 t.

450 001	**SD**	A	*SW*	NT	63201	64201	68101	63601
450 002	**SD**	A	*SW*	NT	63202	64202	68102	63602
450 003	**SD**	A	*SW*	NT	63203	64203	68103	63603
450 004	**SD**	A	*SW*	NT	63204	64204	68104	63604
450 005	**SD**	A	*SW*	NT	63205	64205	68105	63605
450 006	**SD**	A	*SW*	NT	63206	64206	68106	63606
450 007	**SD**	A	*SW*	NT	63207	64207	68107	63607
450 008	**SD**	A	*SW*	NT	63208	64208	68108	63608
450 009	**SD**	A	*SW*	NT	63209	64209	68109	63609
450 010	**SD**	A	*SW*	NT	63210	64210	68110	63610
450 011	**SD**	A	*SW*	NT	63211	64211	68111	63611
450 012	**SD**	A	*SW*	NT	63212	64212	68112	63612
450 013	**SD**	A	*SW*	NT	63213	64213	68113	63613
450 014	**SD**	A	*SW*	NT	63214	64214	68114	63614
450 015	**SD**	A	*SW*	NT	63215	64215	68115	63615
450 016	**SD**	A	*SW*	NT	63216	64216	68116	63616
450 017	**SD**	A	*SW*	NT	63217	64217	68117	63617
450 018	**SD**	A	*SW*	NT	63218	64218	68118	63618
450 019	**SD**	A	*SW*	NT	63219	64219	68119	63619
450 020	**SD**	A	*SW*	NT	63220	64220	68120	63620
450 021	**SD**	A	*SW*	NT	63221	64221	68121	63621
450 022	**SD**	A	*SW*	NT	63222	64222	68122	63622
450 023	**SD**	A	*SW*	NT	63223	64223	68123	63623
450 024	**SD**	A	*SW*	NT	63224	64224	68124	63624
450 025	**SD**	A	*SW*	NT	63225	64225	68125	63625
450 026	**SD**	A	*SW*	NT	63226	64226	68126	63626
450 027	**SD**	A	*SW*	NT	63227	64227	68127	63627
450 028	**SD**	A	*SW*	NT	63228	64228	68128	63628
450 029	**SD**	A	*SW*	NT	63229	64229	68129	63629

450 030	**SD**	A	*SW*	NT	63230	64230	68130	63630
450 031	**SD**	A	*SW*	NT	63231	64231	68131	63631
450 032	**SD**	A	*SW*	NT	63232	64232	68132	63632
450 033	**SD**	A	*SW*	NT	63233	64233	68133	63633
450 034	**SD**	A	*SW*	NT	63234	64234	68134	63634
450 035	**SD**	A	*SW*	NT	63235	64235	68135	63635
450 036	**SD**	A	*SW*	NT	63236	64236	68136	63636
450 037	**SD**	A	*SW*	NT	63237	64237	68137	63637
450 038	**SD**	A	*SW*	NT	63238	64238	68138	63638
450 039	**SD**	A	*SW*	NT	63239	64239	68139	63639
450 040	**SD**	A	*SW*	NT	63240	64240	68140	63640
450 041	**SD**	A	*SW*	NT	63241	64241	68141	63641
450 042	**SD**	A	*SW*	NT	63242	64242	68142	63642
450 071	**SD**	A	*SW*	NT	63271	64271	68171	63671
450 072	**SD**	A	*SW*	NT	63272	64272	68172	63672
450 073	**SD**	A	*SW*	NT	63273	64273	68173	63673
450 074	**SD**	A	*SW*	NT	63274	64274	68174	63674
450 075	**SD**	A	*SW*	NT	63275	64275	68175	63675
450 076	**SD**	A	*SW*	NT	63276	64276	68176	63676
450 077	**SD**	A	*SW*	NT	63277	64277	68177	63677
450 078	**SD**	A	*SW*	NT	63278	64278	68178	63678
450 079	**SD**	A	*SW*	NT	63279	64279	68179	63679
450 080	**SD**	A	*SW*	NT	63280	64280	68180	63680
450 081	**SD**	A	*SW*	NT	63281	64281	68181	63681
450 082	**SD**	A	*SW*	NT	63282	64282	68182	63682
450 083	**SD**	A	*SW*	NT	63283	64283	68183	63683
450 084	**SD**	A	*SW*	NT	63284	64284	68184	63684
450 085	**SD**	A	*SW*	NT	63285	64285	68185	63685
450 086	**SD**	A	*SW*	NT	63286	64286	68186	63686
450 087	**SD**	A	*SW*	NT	63287	64287	68187	63687
450 088	**SD**	A	*SW*	NT	63288	64288	68188	63688
450 089	**SD**	A	*SW*	NT	63289	64289	68189	63689
450 090	**SD**	A	*SW*	NT	63290	64290	68190	63690
450 091	**SD**	A	*SW*	NT	63291	64291	68191	63691
450 092	**SD**	A	*SW*	NT	63292	64292	68192	63692
450 093	**SD**	A	*SW*	NT	63293	64293	68193	63693
450 094	**SD**	A	*SW*	NT	63294	64294	68194	63694
450 095	**SD**	A	*SW*	NT	63295	64295	68195	63695
450 096	**SD**	A	*SW*	NT	63296	64296	68196	63696
450 097	**SD**	A	*SW*	NT	63297	64297	68197	63697
450 098	**SD**	A	*SW*	NT	63298	64298	68198	63698
450 099	**SD**	A	*SW*	NT	63299	64299	68199	63699
450 100	**SD**	A	*SW*	NT	63300	64300	68200	63700
450 101	**SD**	A	*SW*	NT	63701	66851	66801	63751
450 102	**SD**	A	*SW*	NT	63702	66852	66802	63752
450 103	**SD**	A	*SW*	NT	63703	66853	66803	63753
450 104	**SD**	A	*SW*	NT	63704	66854	66804	63754
450 105	**SD**	A	*SW*	NT	63705	66855	66805	63755
450 106	**SD**	A	*SW*	NT	63706	66856	66806	63756
450 107	**SD**	A	*SW*	NT	63707	66857	66807	63757
450 108	**SD**	A	*SW*	NT	63708	66858	66808	63758

450 109	**SD**	A	*SW*	NT	63709	66859	66809	63759
450 110	**SD**	A	*SW*	NT	63710	66860	66810	63760
450 111	**SD**	A	*SW*	NT	63901	66921	66901	63921
450 112	**SD**	A	*SW*	NT	63902	66922	66902	63922
450 113	**SD**	A	*SW*	NT	63903	66923	66903	63923
450 114	**SD**	A	*SW*	NT	63904	66924	66904	63924
450 115	**SD**	A	*SW*	NT	63905	66925	66905	63925
450 116	**SD**	A	*SW*	NT	63906	66926	66906	63926
450 117	**SD**	A	*SW*	NT	63907	66927	66907	63927
450 118	**SD**	A	*SW*	NT	63908	66928	66908	63928
450 119	**SD**	A	*SW*	NT	63909	66929	66909	63929
450 120	**SD**	A	*SW*	NT	63910	66930	66910	63930
450 121	**SD**	A	*SW*	NT	63911	66931	66911	63931
450 122	**SD**	A	*SW*	NT	63912	66932	66912	63932
450 123	**SD**	A	*SW*	NT	63913	66933	66913	63933
450 124	**SD**	A	*SW*	NT	63914	66934	66914	63934
450 125	**SD**	A	*SW*	NT	63915	66935	66915	63935
450 126	**SD**	A	*SW*	NT	63916	66936	66916	63936
450 127	**SD**	A	*SW*	NT	63917	66937	66917	63937

Names (carried on DMSO(B)):

450 015 DESIRO
450 042 TRELOAR COLLEGE
450 114 FAIRBRIDGE investing in the future

Class 450/5. "High density" units. 28 units converted at Bournemouth for Waterloo–Windsor/Weybridge/Hounslow services. First Class removed and modified seating layout with more standing room. Details as Class 450/0 except:

Formation: DMSO–TSO–TSO–DMSO.

DMSO(A). Siemens Krefeld/Vienna 2002–04. –/64. 48.0 t.
TSO(A). Siemens Krefeld/Vienna 2002–04. –/56(4) 1T. 35.5 t.
TSO(B). Siemens Krefeld/Vienna 2002–04. –/56(9) 1TD 2W. 39.8 t.
DMSO(B). Siemens Krefeld/Vienna 2002–04. –/64. 48.6 t.

450 543	(450 043)	**SD**	A	*SW*	NT	63243	64243	68143	63643
450 544	(450 044)	**SD**	A	*SW*	NT	63244	64244	68144	63644
450 545	(450 045)	**SD**	A	*SW*	NT	63245	64245	68145	63645
450 546	(450 046)	**SD**	A	*SW*	NT	63246	64246	68146	63646
450 547	(450 047)	**SD**	A	*SW*	NT	63247	64247	68147	63647
450 548	(450 048)	**SD**	A	*SW*	NT	63248	64248	68148	63648
450 549	(450 049)	**SD**	A	*SW*	NT	63249	64249	68149	63649
450 550	(450 050)	**SD**	A	*SW*	NT	63250	64250	68150	63650
450 551	(450 051)	**SD**	A	*SW*	NT	63251	64251	68151	63651
450 552	(450 052)	**SD**	A	*SW*	NT	63252	64252	68152	63652
450 553	(450 053)	**SD**	A	*SW*	NT	63253	64253	68153	63653
450 554	(450 054)	**SD**	A	*SW*	NT	63254	64254	68154	63654
450 555	(450 055)	**SD**	A	*SW*	NT	63255	64255	68155	63655
450 556	(450 056)	**SD**	A	*SW*	NT	63256	64256	68156	63656
450 557	(450 057)	**SD**	A	*SW*	NT	63257	64257	68157	63657
450 558	(450 058)	**SD**	A	*SW*	NT	63258	64258	68158	63658
450 559	(450 059)	**SD**	A	*SW*	NT	63259	64259	68159	63659

450560	(450060)	**SD**	A	*SW*	NT	63260	64260	68160	63660
450561	(450061)	**SD**	A	*SW*	NT	63261	64261	68161	63661
450562	(450062)	**SD**	A	*SW*	NT	63262	64262	68162	63662
450563	(450063)	**SD**	A	*SW*	NT	63263	64263	68163	63663
450564	(450064)	**SD**	A	*SW*	NT	63264	64264	68164	63664
450565	(450065)	**SD**	A	*SW*	NT	63265	64265	68165	63665
450566	(450066)	**SD**	A	*SW*	NT	63266	64266	68166	63666
450567	(450067)	**SD**	A	*SW*	NT	63267	64267	68167	63667
450568	(450068)	**SD**	A	*SW*	NT	63268	64268	68168	63668
450569	(450069)	**SD**	A	*SW*	NT	63269	64269	68169	63669
450570	(450070)	**SD**	A	*SW*	NT	63270	64270	68170	63670

CLASS 455 BREL YORK

Inner suburban units.

Formation: DTSO–MSO–TSO–DTSO.
Construction: Steel. Class 455/7 TSO have a steel underframe and an aluminium alloy body & roof.
Traction Motors: Four GEC507-20J of 185 kW, some recovered from Class 405s.
Wheel Arrangement: 2-2 + Bo-Bo + 2-2 + 2-2.
Braking: Disc. **Dimensions:** 19.92/19.83 x 2.82 m.
Bogies: P7 (motor) and T3 (455/8 & 455/9) BX1 (455/7) trailer.
Gangways: Within unit + end doors (sealed on Southern units).
Couplers: Tightlock. **Control System:** 1982-type, camshaft.
Doors: Sliding. **Maximum Speed:** 75 mph.
Heating & Ventilation: Various.
Seating Layout: All units refurbished. SWT units: 2+2 high-back unidirectional/facing seating. Southern units: 3+2 high back mainly facing seating.
Multiple Working: Within class and with Class 456.

Class 455/7. South West Trains units. Second series with TSOs originally in Class 508s. Pressure heating & ventilation.

DTSO. Lot No. 30976 1984–85. –/50(4) 1W. 30.8t.
MSO. Lot No. 30975 1984–85. –/68. 45.7t.
TSO. Lot No. 30944 1979–80. –/68. 26.1t.

5701	**SS**	P	*SW*	WD	77727	62783	71545	77728
5702	**SS**	P	*SW*	WD	77729	62784	71547	77730
5703	**SS**	P	*SW*	WD	77731	62785	71540	77732
5704	**SS**	P	*SW*	WD	77733	62786	71548	77734
5705	**SS**	P	*SW*	WD	77735	62787	71565	77736
5706	**SS**	P	*SW*	WD	77737	62788	71534	77738
5707	**SS**	P	*SW*	WD	77739	62789	71536	77740
5708	**SS**	P	*SW*	WD	77741	62790	71560	77742
5709	**SS**	P	*SW*	WD	77743	62791	71532	77744
5710	**SS**	P	*SW*	WD	77745	62792	71566	77746
5711	**SS**	P	*SW*	WD	77747	62793	71542	77748
5712	**SS**	P	*SW*	WD	77749	62794	71546	77750
5713	**SS**	P	*SW*	WD	77751	62795	71567	77752
5714	**SS**	P	*SW*	WD	77753	62796	71539	77754
5715	**SS**	P	*SW*	WD	77755	62797	71535	77756

5716	**SS**	P	*SW*	WD	77757	62798	71564	77758
5717	**SS**	P	*SW*	WD	77759	62799	71528	77760
5718	**SS**	P	*SW*	WD	77761	62800	71557	77762
5719	**SS**	P	*SW*	WD	77763	62801	71558	77764
5720	**SS**	P	*SW*	WD	77765	62802	71568	77766
5721	**SS**	P	*SW*	WD	77767	62803	71553	77768
5722	**SS**	P	*SW*	WD	77769	62804	71533	77770
5723	**SS**	P	*SW*	WD	77771	62805	71526	77772
5724	**SS**	P	*SW*	WD	77773	62806	71561	77774
5725	**SS**	P	*SW*	WD	77775	62807	71541	77776
5726	**SS**	P	*SW*	WD	77777	62808	71556	77778
5727	**SS**	P	*SW*	WD	77779	62809	71562	77780
5728	**SS**	P	*SW*	WD	77781	62810	71527	77782
5729	**SS**	P	*SW*	WD	77783	62811	71550	77784
5730	**SS**	P	*SW*	WD	77785	62812	71551	77786
5731	**SS**	P	*SW*	WD	77787	62813	71555	77788
5732	**SS**	P	*SW*	WD	77789	62814	71552	77790
5733	**SS**	P	*SW*	WD	77791	62815	71549	77792
5734	**SS**	P	*SW*	WD	77793	62816	71531	77794
5735	**SS**	P	*SW*	WD	77795	62817	71563	77796
5736	**SS**	P	*SW*	WD	77797	62818	71554	77798
5737	**SS**	P	*SW*	WD	77799	62819	71544	77800
5738	**SS**	P	*SW*	WD	77801	62820	71529	77802
5739	**SS**	P	*SW*	WD	77803	62821	71537	77804
5740	**SS**	P	*SW*	WD	77805	62822	71530	77806
5741	**SS**	P	*SW*	WD	77807	62823	71559	77808
5742	**SS**	P	*SW*	WD	77809	62824	71543	77810
5750	**SS**	P	*SW*	WD	77811	62825	71538	77812

Class 455/8. Southern units. First series. Pressure heating & ventilation. Fitted with in-cab air conditioning systems meaning that the end door has been sealed.

DTSO. Lot No. 30972 York 1982–84. –/74. 33.6 t.
MSO. Lot No. 30973 York 1982–84. –/84. 37.9 t.
TSO. Lot No. 30974 York 1982–84. –/75(3) 2W. 34.0 t.

455801	**SN**	E	*SN*	SU	77627	62709	71657	77580
455802	**SN**	E	*SN*	SU	77581	62710	71664	77582
455803	**SN**	E	*SN*	SU	77583	62711	71639	77584
455804	**SN**	E	*SN*	SU	77585	62712	71640	77586
455805	**SN**	E	*SN*	SU	77587	62713	71641	77588
455806	**SN**	E	*SN*	SU	77589	62714	71642	77590
455807	**SN**	E	*SN*	SU	77591	62715	71643	77592
455808	**SN**	E	*SN*	SU	77637	62716	71644	77594
455809	**SN**	E	*SN*	SU	77623	62717	71648	77602
455810	**SN**	E	*SN*	SU	77597	62718	71646	77598
455811	**SN**	E	*SN*	SU	77599	62719	71647	77600
455812	**SN**	E	*SN*	SU	77595	62720	71645	77626
455813	**SN**	E	*SN*	SU	77603	62721	71649	77604
455814	**SN**	E	*SN*	SU	77605	62722	71650	77606
455815	**SN**	E	*SN*	SU	77607	62723	71651	77608
455816	**SN**	E	*SN*	SU	77609	62724	71652	77633

455817	**SN**	E	*SN*	SU	77611	62725	71653	77612
455818	**SN**	E	*SN*	SU	77613	62726	71654	77632
455819	**SN**	E	*SN*	SU	77615	62727	71637	77616
455820	**SN**	E	*SN*	SU	77617	62728	71656	77618
455821	**SN**	E	*SN*	SU	77619	62729	71655	77620
455822	**SN**	E	*SN*	SU	77621	62730	71658	77622
455823	**SN**	E	*SN*	SU	77601	62731	71659	77596
455824	**SN**	E	*SN*	SU	77593	62732	71660	77624
455825	**SN**	E	*SN*	SU	77579	62733	71661	77628
455826	**SN**	E	*SN*	SU	77630	62734	71662	77629
455827	**SN**	E	*SN*	SU	77610	62735	71663	77614
455828	**SN**	E	*SN*	SU	77631	62736	71638	77634
455829	**SN**	E	*SN*	SU	77635	62737	71665	77636
455830	**SN**	E	*SN*	SU	77625	62743	71666	77638
455831	**SN**	E	*SN*	SU	77639	62739	71667	77640
455832	**SN**	E	*SN*	SU	77641	62740	71668	77642
455833	**SN**	E	*SN*	SU	77643	62741	71669	77644
455834	**SN**	E	*SN*	SU	77645	62742	71670	77646
455835	**SN**	E	*SN*	SU	77647	62738	71671	77648
455836	**SN**	E	*SN*	SU	77649	62744	71672	77650
455837	**SN**	E	*SN*	SU	77651	62745	71673	77652
455838	**SN**	E	*SN*	SU	77653	62746	71674	77654
455839	**SN**	E	*SN*	SU	77655	62747	71675	77656
455840	**SN**	E	*SN*	SU	77657	62748	71676	77658
455841	**SN**	E	*SN*	SU	77659	62749	71677	77660
455842	**SN**	E	*SN*	SU	77661	62750	71678	77662
455843	**SN**	E	*SN*	SU	77663	62751	71679	77664
455844	**SN**	E	*SN*	SU	77665	62752	71680	77666
455845	**SN**	E	*SN*	SU	77667	62753	71681	77668
455846	**SN**	E	*SN*	SU	77669	62754	71682	77670

Class 455/8. South West Trains units. First series. Pressure heating & ventilation.

DTSO. Lot No. 30972 York 1982–84. –50(4) 1W. 29.5 t.
MSO. Lot No. 30973 York 1982–84. –/84 –/68. 45.6 t.
TSO. Lot No. 30974 York 1982–84. –/84 –/68. 27.1 t.

5847	**SS**	P	*SW*	WD	77671	62755	71683	77672
5848	**SS**	P	*SW*	WD	77673	62756	71684	77674
5849	**SS**	P	*SW*	WD	77675	62757	71685	77676
5850	**SS**	P	*SW*	WD	77677	62758	71686	77678
5851	**SS**	P	*SW*	WD	77679	62759	71687	77680
5852	**SS**	P	*SW*	WD	77681	62760	71688	77682
5853	**SS**	P	*SW*	WD	77683	62761	71689	77684
5854	**SS**	P	*SW*	WD	77685	62762	71690	77686
5855	**SS**	P	*SW*	WD	77687	62763	71691	77688
5856	**SS**	P	*SW*	WD	77689	62764	71692	77690
5857	**SS**	P	*SW*	WD	77691	62765	71693	77692
5858	**SS**	P	*SW*	WD	77693	62766	71694	77694
5859	**SS**	P	*SW*	WD	77695	62767	71695	77696
5860	**SS**	P	*SW*	WD	77697	62768	71696	77698
5861	**SS**	P	*SW*	WD	77699	62769	71697	77700

5862		**SS**	P	*SW*	WD	77701	62770	71698	77702
5863		**SS**	P	*SW*	WD	77703	62771	71699	77704
5864		**SS**	P	*SW*	WD	77705	62772	71700	77706
5865		**SS**	P	*SW*	WD	77707	62773	71701	77708
5866		**SS**	P	*SW*	WD	77709	62774	71702	77710
5867		**SS**	P	*SW*	WD	77711	62775	71703	77712
5868		**SS**	P	*SW*	WD	77713	62776	71704	77714
5869		**SS**	P	*SW*	WD	77715	62777	71705	77716
5870		**SS**	P	*SW*	WD	77717	62778	71706	77718
5871		**SS**	P	*SW*	WD	77719	62779	71707	77720
5872		**SS**	P	*SW*	WD	77721	62780	71708	77722
5873		**SS**	P	*SW*	WD	77723	62781	71709	77724
5874		**SS**	P	*SW*	WD	77725	62782	71710	77726

Class 455/9. South West Trains units. Third series. Convection heating.
Dimensions: 19.96/20.18 x 2.82 m.

DTSO. Lot No. 30991 York 1985. –/50(4) 1W. 30.7 t.
MSO. Lot No. 30992 York 1985. –/68. 46.3 t.
TSO. Lot No. 30993 York 1985. –/68. 28.3 t.
TSO†. Lot No. 30932 Derby 1981. –/68. 26.5 t.

Note: † Prototype vehicle 67400 converted from a Class 210 DEMU.

5901		**SS**	P	*SW*	WD	77813	62826	71714	77814
5902		**SS**	P	*SW*	WD	77815	62827	71715	77816
5903		**SS**	P	*SW*	WD	77817	62828	71716	77818
5904		**SS**	P	*SW*	WD	77819	62829	71717	77820
5905		**SS**	P	*SW*	WD	77821	62830	71725	77822
5906		**SS**	P	*SW*	WD	77823	62831	71719	77824
5907		**SS**	P	*SW*	WD	77825	62832	71720	77826
5908		**SS**	P	*SW*	WD	77827	62833	71721	77828
5909		**SS**	P	*SW*	WD	77829	62834	71722	77830
5910		**SS**	P	*SW*	WD	77831	62835	71723	77832
5911		**SS**	P	*SW*	WD	77833	62836	71724	77834
5912	†	**SS**	P	*SW*	WD	77835	62837	67400	77836
5913		**SS**	P		ZN	77837	62838	71726	77838
5914		**SS**	P	*SW*	WD	77839	62839	71727	77840
5915		**SS**	P	*SW*	WD	77841	62840	71728	77842
5916		**SS**	P	*SW*	WD	77843	62841	71729	77844
5917		**SS**	P	*SW*	WD	77845	62842	71730	77846
5918		**SS**	P	*SW*	WD	77847	62843	71732	77848
5919		**SS**	P	*SW*	WD	77849	62844	71718	77850
5920		**SS**	P	*SW*	WD	77851	62845	71733	77852

CLASS 456 BREL YORK

Inner suburban units.

Formation: DMSO–DTSO.
Construction: Steel underframe, aluminium alloy body & roof.
Traction Motors: Two GEC507-20J of 185 kW, some recovered from Class 405s.
Wheel Arrangement: 2-Bo + 2-2. **Dimensions:** 20.61 x 2.82 m.

Braking: Disc.
Bogies: P7 (motor) and T3 (trailer).
Gangways: Within unit.
Doors: Sliding.
Couplers: Tightlock.
Control System: GTO Chopper.
Maximum Speed: 75 mph.
Seating Layout: 3+2 facing.
Heating & Ventilation: Convection heating.
Multiple Working: Within class and with Class 455.

DMSO. Lot No. 31073 1990–91. –/79. 41.1t.
DTSO. Lot No. 31074 1990–91. –/73. 31.4t.

Advertising livery: 456006 TfL/City of London (blue & green with various images).

456001	**SN**	P	*SN*	SU	64735	78250	
456002	**SN**	P	*SN*	SU	64736	78251	
456003	**SN**	P	*SN*	SU	64737	78252	
456004	**SN**	P	*SN*	SU	64738	78253	
456005	**SN**	P	*SN*	SU	64739	78254	
456006	**AL**	P	*SN*	SU	64740	78255	
456007	**SN**	P	*SN*	SU	64741	78256	
456008	**SN**	P	*SN*	SU	64742	78257	
456009	**SN**	P	*SN*	SU	64743	78258	
456010	**SN**	P	*SN*	SU	64744	78259	
456011	**SN**	P	*SN*	SU	64745	78260	
456012	**SN**	P	*SN*	SU	64746	78261	
456013	**SN**	P	*SN*	SU	64747	78262	
456014	**SN**	P	*SN*	SU	64748	78263	
456015	**SN**	P	*SN*	SU	64749	78264	
456016	**SN**	P	*SN*	SU	64750	78265	
456017	**SN**	P	*SN*	SU	64751	78266	
456018	**SN**	P	*SN*	SU	64752	78267	
456019	**SN**	P	*SN*	SU	64753	78268	
456020	**SN**	P	*SN*	SU	64754	78269	
456021	**SN**	P	*SN*	SU	64755	78270	
456022	**SN**	P	*SN*	SU	64756	78271	
456023	**SN**	P	*SN*	SU	64757	78272	
456024	**SN**	P	*SN*	SU	64758	78273	Sir Cosmo Bonsor

CLASS 458 JUNIPER ALSTOM BIRMINGHAM

Outer suburban units.

Formation: DMCO–TSO–MSO–DMCO.
Construction: Steel.
Traction Motors: Two Alstom ONIX 800 asynchronous of 270kW.
Wheel Arrangement: 2-Bo + 2-2 + Bo-2 + Bo-2.
Braking: Disc & regenerative.
Bogies: ACR.
Gangways: Throughout (not in use).
Doors: Sliding plug.
Heating & Ventilation: Air conditioning.
Dimensions: 21.16/19.94 x 2.80 m.
Couplers: Scharfenberg AAR.
Control System: IGBT Inverter.
Maximum Speed: 100 mph.
Multiple Working: Within class.
Seating Layout: 1: 2+2 facing, 2: 3+2 facing/unidirectional.

DMCO(A). Alstom 1998–2000. 12/63. 46.4 t.
TSO. Alstom 1998–2000. –/54(6) 1TD 2W. 34.6 t.
MSO. Alstom 1998–2000. –/75 1T. 42.1 t.
DMCO(B). Alstom 1998–2000. 12/63. 46.4 t.

8001	**ST**	P	*SW*	WD	67601	74001	74101	67701
8002	**ST**	P	*SW*	WD	67602	74002	74102	67702
8003	**ST**	P	*SW*	WD	67603	74003	74103	67703
8004	**ST**	P	*SW*	WD	67604	74004	74104	67704
8005	**ST**	P	*SW*	WD	67605	74005	74105	67705
8006	**ST**	P	*SW*	WD	67606	74006	74106	67706
8007	**ST**	P	*SW*	WD	67607	74007	74107	67707
8008	**ST**	P	*SW*	WD	67608	74008	74108	67708
8009	**ST**	P	*SW*	WD	67609	74009	74109	67709
8010	**ST**	P	*SW*	WD	67610	74010	74110	67710
8011	**ST**	P	*SW*	WD	67611	74011	74111	67711
8012	**ST**	P	*SW*	WD	67612	74012	74112	67712
8013	**ST**	P	*SW*	WD	67613	74013	74113	67713
8014	**ST**	P	*SW*	WD	67614	74014	74114	67714
8015	**ST**	P	*SW*	WD	67615	74015	74115	67715
8016	**ST**	P	*SW*	WD	67616	74016	74116	67716
8017	**ST**	P	*SW*	WD	67617	74017	74117	67717
8018	**ST**	P	*SW*	WD	67618	74018	74118	67718
8019	**ST**	P	*SW*	WD	67619	74019	74119	67719
8020	**ST**	P	*SW*	WD	67620	74020	74120	67720
8021	**ST**	P	*SW*	WD	67621	74021	74121	67721
8022	**ST**	P	*SW*	WD	67622	74022	74122	67722
8023	**ST**	P	*SW*	WD	67623	74023	74123	67723
8024	**ST**	P	*SW*	WD	67624	74024	74124	67724
8025	**ST**	P	*SW*	WD	67625	74025	74125	67725
8026	**ST**	P	*SW*	WD	67626	74026	74126	67726
8027	**ST**	P	*SW*	WD	67627	74027	74127	67727
8028	**ST**	P	*SW*	WD	67628	74028	74128	67728
8029	**ST**	P	*SW*	WD	67629	74029	74129	67729
8030	**ST**	P	*SW*	WD	67630	74030	74130	67730

CLASS 460 JUNIPER GEC-ALSTHOM

Only the last two digits of the unit number are carried on the front ends of these units. Most units have been stood down from Gatwick Express services, having been replaced by Class 442s.

Formation: DMLFO–TFO–TCO–MSO–MSO–TSO–MSO–DMSO.
Construction: Steel.
Traction Motors: Two Alstom ONIX 800 asynchronous of 270 kW.
Wheel Arrangement: 2-Bo + 2-2 + 2-2 + Bo-2 + 2-Bo + 2-2 + Bo-2 + Bo-2.
Braking: Disc & regenerative. **Dimensions**: 21.01/19.94 x 2.80 m.
Bogies: ACR.
Couplers: Scharfenberg 330 at outer ends and between cars 4 and 5.
Gangways: Within unit. **Control System**: IGBT Inverter.
Doors: Sliding plug. **Maximum Speed**: 100 mph.

Heating & Ventilation: Air conditioning.
Seating Layout: 1: 2+1 facing, 2: 2+2 facing/unidirectional.
Multiple Working: Within class.

DMLFO. Alstom 1998–99. 10/– 42.7 t.
TFO. Alstom 1998–99. 25/– 1TD 1W. 34.5 t.
TCO. Alstom 1998–99. 8/38 1T. 35.6 t.
MSO(A). Alstom 1998–99. –/58. 42.8 t.
MSO(B). Alstom 1998–99. –/58. 42.5 t.
TSO. Alstom 1998–99. –/33 1TD 1T 1W. 35.2 t.
MSO(C). Alstom 1998–99. –/58. 40.5 t.
DMSO. Alstom 1998–99. –/54. 45.4 t.

460001	**GV**	P	*SN*	SL	67901	74401	74411	74421
					74431	74441	74451	67911
460002	**GV**	P	*SN*	SL	67902	74402	74412	74422
					74432	74442	74452	67912
460003	**GV**	P		BM	67903	74403	74413	74423
					74433	74443	74453	67913
460004	**GV**	P		BM	67904	74404	74414	74424
					74434	74444	74454	67914
460005	**GV**	P		SL	67905	74405	74415	74425
					74435	74445	74455	67915
460006	**GV**	P		BM	67906	74406	74416	74426
					74436	74446	74456	67916
460007	**GV**	P		SL	67907	74407	74417	74427
					74437	74447	74457	67917
460008	**GV**	P		BM	67908	74408	74418	74428
					74438	74448	74458	67918

CLASS 465 NETWORKER

Inner/outer suburban units.

Formation: DMSO–TSO–TSO–DMSO.
Construction: Welded aluminium alloy.
Traction Motors: Hitachi asynchronous of 280 kW (Classes 465/0 and 465/1) or GEC-Alsthom G352BY (Classes 465/2 and 465/9).
Wheel Arrangement: Bo-Bo + 2-2 + 2-2 + Bo-Bo.
Braking: Disc & rheostatic and regenerative (Classes 465/0 and 465/1 only).
Bogies: BREL P3/T3 (465/0 and 465/1), SRP BP62/BT52 (465/2 and 465/9).
Dimensions: 20.89/20.06 x 2.81 m.
Control System: IGBT Inverter (465/0 and 465/1) or 1992-type GTO Inverter.
Gangways: Within unit. **Couplers:** Tightlock.
Doors: Sliding plug. **Maximum Speed:** 75 mph.
Seating Layout: 3+2 facing/unidirectional.
Multiple Working: Within class and with Class 466.

64759–808. DMSO(A). Lot No. 31100 BREL York 1991–93. –/86. 39.2t.
64809–858. DMSO(B). Lot No. 31100 BREL York 1991–93. –/86. 39.2t.
65734–749. DMSO(A). Lot No. 31103 Metro-Cammell 1991–93. –/86. 39.2t.
65784–799. DMSO(B). Lot No. 31103 Metro-Cammell 1991–93. –/86. 39.2t.

65800–846. DMSO(A). Lot No. 31130 ABB York 1993–94. –/86. 39.2t.
65847–893. DMSO(B). Lot No. 31130 ABB York 1993–94. –/86. 39.2t.
72028–126 (even nos.) TSO. Lot No. 31102 BREL York 1991–93. –/90. 27.2t.
72029–127 (odd nos.) TSO. Lot No. 31101 BREL York 1991–93. –/86 1T. 28.0t.
72787–817 (odd nos.) TSO. Lot No. 31104 Metro-Cammell 1991–92. –/86 1T. 28.0t.
72788–818 (even nos.) TSO. Lot No. 31105 Metro-Cammell 1991–92. –/90. 27.2t.
72900–992 (even nos.) TSO. Lot No. 31102 ABB York 1993–94. –/90. 27.2t.
72901–993 (odd nos.) TSO. Lot No. 31101 ABB York 1993–94. –/86 1T. 28.0t.

Class 465/0. Built by BREL/ABB.

465001	**SE**	E	*SE*	SG	64759	72028	72029	64809
465002	**SE**	E	*SE*	SG	64760	72030	72031	64810
465003	**SE**	E	*SE*	SG	64761	72032	72033	64811
465004	**SE**	E	*SE*	SG	64762	72034	72035	64812
465005	**SE**	E	*SE*	SG	64763	72036	72037	64813
465006	**SE**	E	*SE*	SG	64764	72038	72039	64814
465007	**SE**	E	*SE*	SG	64765	72040	72041	64815
465008	**SE**	E	*SE*	SG	64766	72042	72043	64816
465009	**SE**	E	*SE*	SG	64767	72044	72045	64817
465010	**SE**	E	*SE*	SG	64768	72046	72047	64818
465011	**SE**	E	*SE*	SG	64769	72048	72049	64819
465012	**SE**	E	*SE*	SG	64770	72050	72051	64820
465013	**SE**	E	*SE*	SG	64771	72052	72053	64821
465014	**CN**	E	*SE*	SG	64772	72054	72055	64822
465015	**SE**	E	*SE*	SG	64773	72056	72057	64823
465016	**SE**	E	*SE*	SG	64774	72058	72059	64824
465017	**SE**	E	*SE*	SG	64775	72060	72061	64825
465018	**SE**	E	*SE*	SG	64776	72062	72063	64826
465019	**SE**	E	*SE*	SG	64777	72064	72065	64827
465020	**SE**	E	*SE*	SG	64778	72066	72067	64828
465021	**CN**	E	*SE*	SG	64779	72068	72069	64829
465022	**SE**	E	*SE*	SG	64780	72070	72071	64830
465023	**CN**	E	*SE*	SG	64781	72072	72073	64831
465024	**SE**	E	*SE*	SG	64782	72074	72075	64832
465025	**SE**	E	*SE*	SG	64783	72076	72077	64833
465026	**SE**	E	*SE*	SG	64784	72078	72079	64834
465027	**SE**	E	*SE*	SG	64785	72080	72081	64835
465028	**SE**	E	*SE*	SG	64786	72082	72083	64836
465029	**CN**	E	*SE*	SG	64787	72084	72085	64837
465030	**SE**	E	*SE*	SG	64788	72086	72087	64838
465031	**SE**	E	*SE*	SG	64789	72088	72089	64839
465032	**SE**	E	*SE*	SG	64790	72090	72091	64840
465033	**SE**	E	*SE*	SG	64791	72092	72093	64841
465034	**SE**	E	*SE*	SG	64792	72094	72095	64842
465035	**SE**	E	*SE*	SG	64793	72096	72097	64843
465036	**SE**	E	*SE*	SG	64794	72098	72099	64844
465037	**SE**	E	*SE*	SG	64795	72100	72101	64845
465038	**SE**	E	*SE*	SG	64796	72102	72103	64846
465039	**SE**	E	*SE*	SG	64797	72104	72105	64847
465040	**SE**	E	*SE*	SG	64798	72106	72107	64848
465041	**SE**	E	*SE*	SG	64799	72108	72109	64849

465 042	**SE**	E	*SE*	SG	64800	72110	72111	64850
465 043	**SE**	E	*SE*	SG	64801	72112	72113	64851
465 044	**SE**	E	*SE*	SG	64802	72114	72115	64852
465 045	**SE**	E	*SE*	SG	64803	72116	72117	64853
465 046	**SE**	E	*SE*	SG	64804	72118	72119	64854
465 047	**SE**	E	*SE*	SG	64805	72120	72121	64855
465 048	**SE**	E	*SE*	SG	64806	72122	72123	64856
465 049	**SE**	E	*SE*	SG	64807	72124	72125	64857
465 050	**SE**	E	*SE*	SG	64808	72126	72127	64858

Class 465/1. Built by BREL/ABB. Similar to Class 465/0 but with detail differences.

465 151	**SE**	E	*SE*	SG	65800	72900	72901	65847
465 152	**SE**	E	*SE*	SG	65801	72902	72903	65848
465 153	**SE**	E	*SE*	SG	65802	72904	72905	65849
465 154	**SE**	E	*SE*	SG	65803	72906	72907	65850
465 155	**SE**	E	*SE*	SG	65804	72908	72909	65851
465 156	**SE**	E	*SE*	SG	65805	72910	72911	65852
465 157	**SE**	E	*SE*	SG	65806	72912	72913	65853
465 158	**SE**	E	*SE*	SG	65807	72914	72915	65854
465 159	**SE**	E	*SE*	SG	65808	72916	72917	65855
465 160	**CN**	E	*SE*	SG	65809	72918	72919	65856
465 161	**SE**	E	*SE*	SG	65810	72920	72921	65857
465 162	**SE**	E	*SE*	SG	65811	72922	72923	65858
465 163	**SE**	E	*SE*	SG	65812	72924	72925	65859
465 164	**SE**	E	*SE*	SG	65813	72926	72927	65860
465 165	**SE**	E	*SE*	SG	65814	72928	72929	65861
465 166	**CN**	E	*SE*	SG	65815	72930	72931	65862
465 167	**SE**	E	*SE*	SG	65816	72932	72933	65863
465 168	**SE**	E	*SE*	SG	65817	72934	72935	65864
465 169	**CN**	E	*SE*	SG	65818	72936	72937	65865
465 170	**SE**	E	*SE*	SG	65819	72938	72939	65866
465 171	**SE**	E	*SE*	SG	65820	72940	72941	65867
465 172	**SE**	E	*SE*	SG	65821	72942	72943	65868
465 173	**CN**	E	*SE*	SG	65822	72944	72945	65869
465 174	**SE**	E	*SE*	SG	65823	72946	72947	65870
465 175	**CN**	E	*SE*	SG	65824	72948	72949	65871
465 176	**CN**	E	*SE*	SG	65825	72950	72951	65872
465 177	**SE**	E	*SE*	SG	65826	72952	72953	65873
465 178	**SE**	E	*SE*	SG	65827	72954	72955	65874
465 179	**CN**	E	*SE*	SG	65828	72956	72957	65875
465 180	**SE**	E	*SE*	SG	65829	72958	72959	65876
465 181	**CN**	E	*SE*	SG	65830	72960	72961	65877
465 182	**SE**	E	*SE*	SG	65831	72962	72963	65878
465 183	**SE**	E	*SE*	SG	65832	72964	72965	65879
465 184	**CN**	E	*SE*	SG	65833	72966	72967	65880
465 185	**SE**	E	*SE*	SG	65834	72968	72969	65881
465 186	**CN**	E	*SE*	SG	65835	72970	72971	65882
465 187	**SE**	E	*SE*	SG	65836	72972	72973	65883
465 188	**SE**	E	*SE*	SG	65837	72974	72975	65884
465 189	**CN**	E	*SE*	SG	65838	72976	72977	65885
465 190	**SE**	E	*SE*	SG	65839	72978	72979	65886

465191	**SE**	E	*SE*	SG	65840	72980	72981	65887
465192	**CN**	E	*SE*	SG	65841	72982	72983	65888
465193	**SE**	E	*SE*	SG	65842	72984	72985	65889
465194	**SE**	E	*SE*	SG	65843	72986	72987	65890
465195	**SE**	E	*SE*	SG	65844	72988	72989	65891
465196	**SE**	E	*SE*	SG	65845	72990	72991	65892
465197	**SE**	E	*SE*	SG	65846	72992	72993	65893

Class 465/2. Built by Metro-Cammell.
Dimensions: 20.80/20.15 x 2.81 m.

465235	**SE**	A	*SE*	SG	65734	72787	72788	65784
465236	**CN**	A	*SE*	SG	65735	72789	72790	65785
465237	**SE**	A	*SE*	SG	65736	72791	72792	65786
465238	**CN**	A	*SE*	SG	65737	72793	72794	65787
465239	**CN**	A	*SE*	SG	65738	72795	72796	65788
465240	**SE**	A	*SE*	SG	65739	72797	72798	65789
465241	**SE**	A	*SE*	SG	65740	72799	72800	65790
465242	**CN**	A	*SE*	SG	65741	72801	72802	65791
465243	**SE**	A	*SE*	SG	65742	72803	72804	65792
465244	**CN**	A	*SE*	SG	65743	72805	72806	65793
465245	**CN**	A	*SE*	SG	65744	72807	72808	65794
465246	**CN**	A	*SE*	SG	65745	72809	72810	65795
465247	**CN**	A	*SE*	SG	65746	72811	72812	65796
465248	**CN**	A	*SE*	SG	65747	72813	72814	65797
465249	**CN**	A	*SE*	SG	65748	72815	72816	65798
465250	**CN**	A	*SE*	SG	65749	72817	72818	65799

Class 465/9. Built by Metro-Cammell. Refurbished 2005 for longer distance services, with the addition of First Class seats. Details as Class 465/0 unless stated.
Formation: DMCO–TSO(A)–TSO(B)–DMCO.
Seating Layout: 1: 2+2 facing/unidirectional, 2: 3+2 facing/unidirectional.

65700–733. DMCO(A). Lot No. 31103 Metro-Cammell 1991–93. 12/68. 39.2t.
72719–785 (odd nos.) TSO(A). Lot No. 31104 Metro-Cammell 1991–92. –/76 1T 2W. 30.3t.
72720–786 (even nos.) TSO(B). Lot No. 31105 Metro-Cammell 1991–92. –/90. 29.5t.
65750–783. DMCO(B). Lot No. 31103 Metro-Cammell 1991–93. 12/68. 39.2t.

465901	(465201)	**CN**	A	*SE*	SG	65700	72719	72720	65750
465902	(465202)	**CN**	A	*SE*	SG	65701	72721	72722	65751
465903	(465203)	**CN**	A	*SE*	SG	65702	72723	72724	65752
465904	(465204)	**CN**	A	*SE*	SG	65703	72725	72726	65753
465905	(465205)	**CN**	A	*SE*	SG	65704	72727	72728	65754
465906	(465206)	**CN**	A	*SE*	SG	65705	72729	72730	65755
465907	(465207)	**SE**	A	*SE*	SG	65706	72731	72732	65756
465908	(465208)	**CN**	A	*SE*	SG	65707	72733	72734	65757
465909	(465209)	**CN**	A	*SE*	SG	65708	72735	72736	65758
465910	(465210)	**SE**	A	*SE*	SG	65709	72737	72738	65759
465911	(465211)	**CN**	A	*SE*	SG	65710	72739	72740	65760
465912	(465212)	**CN**	A	*SE*	SG	65711	72741	72742	65761
465913	(465213)	**SE**	A	*SE*	SG	65712	72743	72744	65762
465914	(465214)	**CN**	A	*SE*	SG	65713	72745	72746	65763
465915	(465215)	**CN**	A	*SE*	SG	65714	72747	72748	65764

465916	(465216)	**SE**	A	*SE*	SG	65715	72749	72750	65765
465917	(465217)	**CN**	A	*SE*	SG	65716	72751	72752	65766
465918	(465218)	**CN**	A	*SE*	SG	65717	72753	72754	65767
465919	(465219)	**CN**	A	*SE*	SG	65718	72755	72756	65768
465920	(465220)	**CN**	A	*SE*	SG	65719	72757	72758	65769
465921	(465221)	**SE**	A	*SE*	SG	65720	72759	72760	65770
465922	(465222)	**CN**	A	*SE*	SG	65721	72761	72762	65771
465923	(465223)	**SE**	A	*SE*	SG	65722	72763	72764	65772
465924	(465224)	**SE**	A	*SE*	SG	65723	72765	72766	65773
465925	(465225)	**CN**	A	*SE*	SG	65724	72767	72768	65774
465926	(465226)	**CN**	A	*SE*	SG	65725	72769	72770	65775
465927	(465227)	**CN**	A	*SE*	SG	65726	72771	72772	65776
465928	(465228)	**CN**	A	*SE*	SG	65727	72773	72774	65777
465929	(465229)	**CN**	A	*SE*	SG	65728	72775	72776	65778
465930	(465230)	**CN**	A	*SE*	SG	65729	72777	72778	65779
465931	(465231)	**CN**	A	*SE*	SG	65730	72779	72780	65780
465932	(465232)	**CN**	A	*SE*	SG	65731	72781	72782	65781
465933	(465233)	**SE**	A	*SE*	SG	65732	72783	72784	65782
465934	(465234)	**CN**	A	*SE*	SG	65733	72785	72786	65783

Name: 465903 Remembrance

CLASS 466 NETWORKER GEC-ALSTHOM

Inner/outer suburban units.

Formation: DMSO–DTSO.
Construction: Welded aluminium alloy.
Traction Motors: Two GEC-Alsthom G352AY asynchronous of 280 kW.
Wheel Arrangement: Bo-Bo + 2-2.
Couplers: Tightlock.
Braking: Disc, rheostatic & regen.
Control System: 1992-type GTO Inverter.
Dimensions: 20.80 x 2.80 m.
Maximum Speed: 75 mph.
Bogies: BREL P3/T3.
Doors: Sliding plug.
Gangways: Within unit.
Seating Layout: 3+2 facing/unidirectional.
Multiple Working: Within class and with Class 465.

DMSO. Lot No. 31128 Birmingham 1993–94. –/86. 40.6t.
DTSO. Lot No. 31129 Birmingham 1993–94. –/82 1T. 31.4t.

466001	**CN**	A	*SE*	SG	64860	78312
466002	**CN**	A	*SE*	SG	64861	78313
466003	**SE**	A	*SE*	SG	64862	78314
466004	**CN**	A	*SE*	SG	64863	78315
466005	**SE**	A	*SE*	SG	64864	78316
466006	**SE**	A	*SE*	SG	64865	78317
466007	**CN**	A	*SE*	SG	64866	78318
466008	**SE**	A	*SE*	SG	64867	78319
466009	**CN**	A	*SE*	SG	64868	78320
466010	**CN**	A	*SE*	SG	64869	78321
466011	**SE**	A	*SE*	SG	64870	78322
466012	**CN**	A	*SE*	SG	64871	78323
466013	**SE**	A	*SE*	SG	64872	78324

466014	**CN**	A	*SE*	SG	64873	78325
466015	**CN**	A	*SE*	SG	64874	78326
466016	**CN**	A	*SE*	SG	64875	78327
466017	**CN**	A	*SE*	SG	64876	78328
466018	**CN**	A	*SE*	SG	64877	78329
466019	**SE**	A	*SE*	SG	64878	78330
466020	**CN**	A	*SE*	SG	64879	78331
466021	**SE**	A	*SE*	SG	64880	78332
466022	**SE**	A	*SE*	SG	64881	78333
466023	**SE**	A	*SE*	SG	64882	78334
466024	**CN**	A	*SE*	SG	64883	78335
466025	**CN**	A	*SE*	SG	64884	78336
466026	**SE**	A	*SE*	SG	64885	78337
466027	**SE**	A	*SE*	SG	64886	78338
466028	**CN**	A	*SE*	SG	64887	78339
466029	**CN**	A	*SE*	SG	64888	78340
466030	**CN**	A	*SE*	SG	64889	78341
466031	**CN**	A	*SE*	SG	64890	78342
466032	**SE**	A	*SE*	SG	64891	78343
466033	**CN**	A	*SE*	SG	64892	78344
466034	**SE**	A	*SE*	SG	64893	78345
466035	**SE**	A	*SE*	SG	64894	78346
466036	**CN**	A	*SE*	SG	64895	78347
466037	**CN**	A	*SE*	SG	64896	78348
466038	**SE**	A	*SE*	SG	64897	78349
466039	**SE**	A	*SE*	SG	64898	78350
466040	**SE**	A	*SE*	SG	64899	78351
466041	**CN**	A	*SE*	SG	64900	78352
466042	**SE**	A	*SE*	SG	64901	78353
466043	**CN**	A	*SE*	SG	64902	78354

CLASS 483 METRO-CAMMELL

Built 1938 onwards for LTE. Converted 1989–1990 for the Isle of Wight Line.

Formation: DMSO–DMSO.
System: 660 V DC third rail.
Construction: Steel.
Traction Motors: Two Crompton Parkinson/GEC/BTH LT100 of 125 kW.
Braking: Tread. **Dimensions:** 16.15 x 2.69 m.
Bogies: LT design. **Couplers:** Wedglock.
Gangways: None. End doors.
Control System: Pneumatic Camshaft Motor (PCM).
Doors: Sliding. **Maximum Speed:** 45 mph.
Seating Layout: Longitudinal or 2+2 facing/unidirectional.
Multiple Working: Within class.
Notes: The last three numbers of the unit number only are carried.

Former London Underground numbers are shown in parentheses.

DMSO (A). Lot No. 31071. –/40. 27.4 t.
DMSO (B). Lot No. 31072. –/42. 27.4 t.

483 002	**LT**	SW		RY	122	(10221)	225	(11142)	RAPTOR
483 004	**LT**	SW	*SW*	RY	124	(10205)	224	(11205)	
483 006	**LT**	SW	*SW*	RY	126	(10297)	226	(11297)	
483 007	**LT**	SW	*SW*	RY	127	(10291)	227	(11291)	
483 008	**LT**	SW	*SW*	RY	128	(10255)	228	(11255)	
483 009	**LT**	SW	*SW*	RY	129	(10289)	229	(11229)	

CLASS 507 BREL YORK

Suburban units.

Formation: BDMSO–TSO–DMSO.
Construction: Steel underframe, aluminium alloy body and roof.
Traction Motors: Four GEC G310AZ of 82.125 kW.
Wheel Arrangement: Bo-Bo + 2-2 + Bo-Bo.
Braking: Disc & rheostatic.
Dimensions: 20.18 x 2.82 m.
Bogies: BX1.
Couplers: Tightlock.
Gangways: Within unit + end doors.
Control System: Camshaft.
Doors: Sliding.
Maximum Speed: 75 mph.
Seating Layout: All refurbished with 2+2 high-back facing seating.
Multiple Working: Within class and with Class 508.

BDMSO. Lot No. 30906 1978–80. –/56(3) 1W. 37.0 t.
TSO. Lot No. 30907 1978–80. –/74. 25.5 t.
DMSO. Lot No. 30908 1978–80. –/56(3) 1W. 35.5 t.

507 001	**ME**	A	*ME*	BD	64367	71342	64405	
507 002	**ME**	A	*ME*	BD	64368	71343	64406	
507 003	**ME**	A	*ME*	BD	64369	71344	64407	
507 004	**ME**	A	*ME*	BD	64388	71345	64408	Bob Paisley
507 005	**ME**	A	*ME*	BD	64371	71346	64409	
507 006	**ME**	A	*ME*	BD	64372	71347	64410	
507 007	**ME**	A	*ME*	BD	64373	71348	64411	
507 008	**ME**	A	*ME*	BD	64374	71349	64412	
507 009	**ME**	A	*ME*	BD	64375	71350	64413	Dixie Dean
507 010	**ME**	A	*ME*	BD	64376	71351	64414	
507 011	**ME**	A	*ME*	BD	64377	71352	64415	
507 012	**ME**	A	*ME*	BD	64378	71353	64416	
507 013	**ME**	A	*ME*	BD	64379	71354	64417	
507 014	**ME**	A	*ME*	BD	64380	71355	64418	
507 015	**ME**	A	*ME*	BD	64381	71356	64419	
507 016	**ME**	A	*ME*	BD	64382	71357	64420	
507 017	**ME**	A	*ME*	BD	64383	71358	64421	
507 018	**ME**	A	*ME*	BD	64384	71359	64422	
507 019	**ME**	A	*ME*	BD	64385	71360	64423	
507 020	**ME**	A	*ME*	BD	64386	71361	64424	John Peel
507 021	**ME**	A	*ME*	BD	64387	71362	64425	Red Rum
507 023	**ME**	A	*ME*	BD	64389	71364	64427	
507 024	**ME**	A	*ME*	BD	64390	71365	64428	

507025	**ME**	A	*ME*	BD	64391	71366	64429	
507026	**ME**	A	*ME*	BD	64392	71367	64430	
507027	**ME**	A	*ME*	BD	64393	71368	64431	
507028	**ME**	A	*ME*	BD	64394	71369	64432	
507029	**ME**	A	*ME*	BD	64395	71370	64433	
507030	**ME**	A	*ME*	BD	64396	71371	64434	
507031	**ME**	A	*ME*	BD	64397	71372	64435	
507032	**ME**	A	*ME*	BD	64398	71373	64436	
507033	**ME**	A	*ME*	BD	64399	71374	64437	Councillor Jack Spriggs

CLASS 508 BREL YORK

Suburban units.

Formation: DMSO–TSO–BDMSO.
Construction: Steel underframe, aluminium alloy body and roof.
Traction Motors: Four GEC G310AZ of 82.125 kW.
Wheel Arrangement: Bo-Bo + 2-2 + Bo-Bo.
Braking: Disc & rheostatic. **Dimensions:** 20.18 x 2.82 m.
Bogies: BX1. **Couplers:** Tightlock.
Gangways: Within unit + end doors. **Control System:** Camshaft.
Doors: Sliding. **Maximum Speed:** 75 mph.
Seating Layout: All Merseyrail units refurbished with 2+2 high-back facing seating. 508/2 and 508/3 units have 3+2 low-back facing seating.
Multiple Working: Within class and with Class 507.

DMSO. Lot No. 30979 1979–80. –/56(3) 1W. 36.0 t.
TSO. Lot No. 30980 1979–80. –/74. 26.5 t.
BDMSO. Lot No. 30981 1979–80. –/56(3) 1W. 36.5 t.

Advertising livery: 508 111 Beatles Story (blue).

Class 508/1. Merseyrail units.

508 103	**ME**	A	*ME*	BD	64651	71485	64694
508 104	**ME**	A	*ME*	BD	64652	71486	64695
508 108	**ME**	A	*ME*	BD	64656	71490	64699
508 110	**ME**	A	*ME*	BD	64658	71492	64701
508 111	**AL**	A	*ME*	BD	64659	71493	64702
508 112	**ME**	A	*ME*	BD	64660	71494	64703
508 114	**ME**	A	*ME*	BD	64662	71496	64705
508 115	**ME**	A	*ME*	BD	64663	71497	64706
508 117	**ME**	A	*ME*	BD	64665	71499	64708
508 120	**ME**	A	*ME*	BD	64668	71502	64711
508 122	**ME**	A	*ME*	BD	64670	71504	64713
508 123	**ME**	A	*ME*	BD	64671	71505	64714
508 124	**ME**	A	*ME*	BD	64672	71506	64715
508 125	**ME**	A	*ME*	BD	64673	71507	64716
508 126	**ME**	A	*ME*	BD	64674	71508	64717
508 127	**ME**	A	*ME*	BD	64675	71509	64718
508 128	**ME**	A	*ME*	BD	64676	71510	64719

508 130	**ME**	A	*ME*	BD	64678	71512	64721
508 131	**ME**	A	*ME*	BD	64679	71513	64722
508 134	**ME**	A	*ME*	BD	64682	71516	64725
508 136	**ME**	A	*ME*	BD	64684	71518	64727
508 137	**ME**	A	*ME*	BD	64685	71519	64728
508 138	**ME**	A	*ME*	BD	64686	71520	64729
508 139	**ME**	A	*ME*	BD	64687	71521	64730
508 140	**ME**	A	*ME*	BD	64688	71522	64731
508 141	**ME**	A	*ME*	BD	64689	71523	64732
508 143	**ME**	A	*ME*	BD	64691	71525	64734

Class 508/2. Units facelifted for the South Eastern lines by Wessex Traincare/Alstom, Eastleigh 1998–99.

DMSO. Lot No. 30979 1979–80. –/66. 36.0 t.
TSO. Lot No. 30980 1979–80. –/79 1W. 26.5 t.
BDMSO. Lot No. 30981 1979–80. –/74. 36.5 t.

508 201	(508 101)	**CX**	A	ZG	64649	71483	64692
508 202	(508 105)	**CX**	A	ZG	64653	71487	64696
508 203	(508 106)	**CN**	A	ZG	64654	71488	64697
508 204	(508 107)	**CX**	A	ZG	64655	71489	64698
508 205	(508 109)	**CN**	A	ZG	64657	71491	64700
508 206	(508 113)	**CX**	A	ZG	64661	71495	64704
508 207	(508 116)	**CN**	A	ZG	64664	71498	64707
508 208	(508 119)	**CN**	A	ZG	64667	71501	64710
508 209	(508 121)	**CX**	A	ZG	64669	71503	64712
508 210	(508 129)	**CN**	A	ZG	64677	71515	64720
508 211	(508 132)	**CN**	A	ZG	64680	71514	64723
508 212	(508 133)	**CX**	A	ZG	64681	71511	64724

Class 508/3. Units facelifted units for use on Euston–Watford Junction services by Alstom, Eastleigh 2002–03.

DMSO. Lot No. 30979 1979–80. –/68 1W. 36.0 t.
TSO. Lot No. 30980 1979–80. –/86. 26.5 t.
BDMSO. Lot No. 30981 1979–80. –/68 1W. 36.5 t.

508 301	(508 102)	**SL**	A	ZG	64650	71484	64693
508 302	(508 135)	**SL**	A	ZG	64683	71517	64726
508 303	(508 142)	**SL**	A	ZG	64690	71524	64733

PLATFORM 5 MAIL ORDER

PRESERVED LOCOMOTIVES OF BRITISH RAILWAYS

14th edition

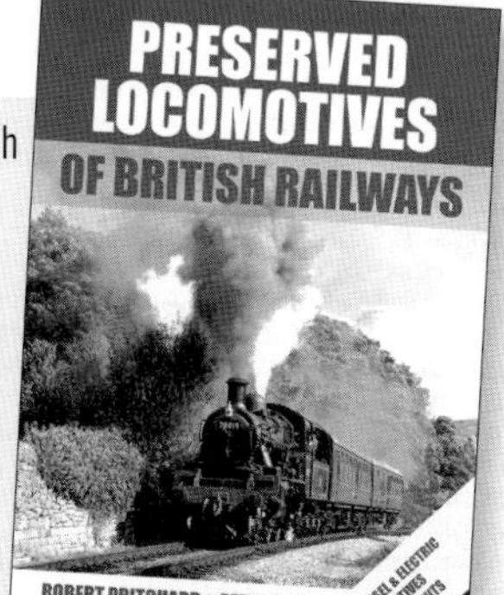

The complete guide to all ex-British Railways and constituent companies' steam, diesel & electric locomotives and diesel & electric multiple units that are still in existence. Contains details of numbers carried, names and locations for every locomotive, plus a full list of preservation sites and operating heritage railways. Also includes technical details for each class of vehicle including builder, year of manufacture, wheel arrangement and tractive effort. Fully revised and updated to spring 2011. 160 pages including over 100 colour photographs. **£14.95 plus P&P.**

Please add postage: 10% UK, 20% Europe, 30% Rest of World.

Telephone, fax or send your order to the Platform 5 Mail Order Department. **See page 384 of this book for details.**

4.3. EUROSTAR UNITS (CLASS 373)

Eurostar units were built for and are normally used on services between Britain and continental Europe via the Channel Tunnel. SNCF-owned units 3203/04, 3225/26 and 3227/28 have been removed from the Eurostar pool and only operate SNCF internal services between Paris and Lille. As they are not now permitted through the Channel Tunnel they are not listed here.

Each train consists of two 10-car units coupled, with a motor car at each driving end. All units are articulated with an extra motor bogie on the coach adjacent to the motor car.

All sets can be used between London St Pancras and Paris, Brussels and Disneyland Paris. Certain sets (shown *) are equipped for 1500 V DC operation and are used for the winter service to Bourg Saint Maurice and the summer service to Avignon.

Seven 8-car sets were built for Regional Eurostar services, but all except one power car (3308) and one half set are on long-term hire to SNCF for use on French internal services so are not listed here. The spare half set (from 3308/07) is stored at Temple Mills depot.

Formation: DM–MSO–4TSO–RB–2TFO–TBFO. Gangwayed within pair of units. Air conditioned.
Construction: Steel.
Supply Systems: 25 kV AC 50 Hz overhead or 3000 V DC overhead
(* also equipped for 1500 V DC overhead operation).
Control System: GTO–GTO Inverter on UK 750V DC and 25kVAC, GTO Chopper on SNCB 3000VDC.
Wheel Arrangement: Bo–Bo + Bo–2–2–2–2–2–2–2–2–2.
Length: 22.15 m (DM), 21.85 m (MS & TBF), 18.70 m (other cars).
Couplers: Schaku 10S at outer ends, Schaku 10L at inner end of each DM and outer ends of each sub set.
Maximum Speed: 186mph (300km/h)
Built: 1992–93 by GEC-Alsthom/Brush/ANF/De Dietrich/BN Construction/ACEC.
Note: DM vehicles carry the set numbers indicated below.

Class 373/0. 10-car sets. Built for services starting from/terminating in London Waterloo (now St Pancras). Individual vehicles in each set are allocated numbers 373xxx0 + 373xxx1 + 373xxx2 + 373xxx3 + 373xxx4 + 373xxx5 + 373xxx6 + 373xxx7 + 373xxx8 + 373xxx9, where 3xxx denotes the set number.

373xxx0 series. DM. Lot No. 31118 1992–95. 68.5 t.
373xxx1 series. MSO. Lot No. 31119 1992–95. –/48 2T. 44.6 t.
373xxx2 series. TSO. Lot No. 31120 1992–95. –/56 1T. 28.1 t.
373xxx3 series. TSO. Lot No. 31121 1992–95. –/56 2T. 29.7 t.
373xxx4 series. TSO. Lot No. 31122 1992–95. –/56 1T. 28.3 t.
373xxx5 series. TSO. Lot No. 31123 1992–95. –/56 2T. 29.2 t.
373xxx6 series. RB. Lot No.31124 1992–95. 31.1 t.
373xxx7 series. TFO. Lot No. 31125 1992–95. 39/– 1T. 29.6 t.
373xxx8 series. TFO. Lot No. 31126 1992–95. 39/– 1T. 32.2 t.
373xxx9 series. TBFO. Lot No. 31127 1992–95. 25/– 1TD. 39.4 t.

3001	**EU**	EU	*EU*	TI
3002	**EU**	EU	*EU*	TI
3003	**EU**	EU	*EU*	TI
3004	**EU**	EU	*EU*	TI
3005	**EU**	EU	*EU*	TI
3006	**EU**	EU	*EU*	TI
3007	**EU**	EU	*EU*	TI
3008	**EU**	EU	*EU*	TI
3009	**EU**	EU	*EU*	TI
3010	**EU**	EU	*EU*	TI
3011	**EU**	EU	*EU*	TI
3012	**EU**	EU	*EU*	TI
3013	**EU**	EU	*EU*	TI
3014	**EU**	EU	*EU*	TI
3015	**EU**	EU	*EU*	TI
3016	**EU**	EU	*EU*	TI
3017	**EU**	EU	*EU*	TI
3018	**EU**	EU	*EU*	TI
3019	**EU**	EU	*EU*	TI
3020	**EU**	EU	*EU*	TI
3021	**EU**	EU	*EU*	TI
3022	**EU**	EU	*EU*	TI
3101	**EU**	SB		TI
3102	**EU**	SB		TI
3103	**EU**	SB	*EU*	FF
3104	**EU**	SB	*EU*	FF
3105	**EU**	SB	*EU*	FF
3106	**EU**	SB	*EU*	FF
3107	**EU**	SB	*EU*	FF
3108	**EU**	SB	*EU*	FF
3201 *	**EU**	SF	*EU*	LY
3202 *	**EU**	SF	*EU*	LY
3205	**EU**	SF	*EU*	LY
3206	**EU**	SF	*EU*	LY
3207 *	**EU**	SF	*EU*	LY
3208 *	**EU**	SF	*EU*	LY
3209 *	**EU**	SF	*EU*	LY
3210 *	**EU**	SF	*EU*	LY
3211	**EU**	SF	*EU*	LY
3212	**EU**	SF	*EU*	LY
3213 *	**EU**	SF	*EU*	LY
3214 *	**EU**	SF	*EU*	LY
3215 *	**EU**	SF	*EU*	LY
3216 *	**EU**	SF	*EU*	LY
3217	**EU**	SF	*EU*	LY
3218	**EU**	SF	*EU*	LY
3219	**EU**	SF	*EU*	LY
3220	**EU**	SF	*EU*	LY
3221	**EU**	SF	*EU*	LY
3222	**EU**	SF	*EU*	LY
3223 *	**EU**	SF	*EU*	LY
3224 *	**EU**	SF	*EU*	LY
3229 *	**EU**	SF	*EU*	LY
3230 *	**EU**	SF	*EU*	LY
3231	**EU**	SF	*EU*	LY
3232	**EU**	SF	*EU*	LY

Spare Regional Eurostar DM:

3308	**EU**	EU		LB

Spare DM:

3999	**EU**	EU	*EU*	TI

Names:

3001/02	Tread Lightly/Voyage Vert
3003/04	Tri-City-Athlon 2010
3007/08	Waterloo Sunset
3009/10	REMEMBERING FROMELLES
3013/14	LONDON 2012
3207/08	MICHEL HOLLARD
3209/10	THE DA VINCI CODE

4.4. INTERNAL USE EMUS

The following two vehicles are used for staff training at Virgin's training centre in Crewe. They are from Pendolino 390 033 which was damaged in the Lambrigg accident of February 2007.

(390 033)	**VT**	VI	Crewe	69133	69833

4.5. EMUS AWAITING DISPOSAL

The list below comprises vehicles awaiting disposal which are stored on the national railway network.

25 kV AC 50 Hz OVERHEAD UNITS:

(390 033)	**VT**	VI	LM	69433	69533

Spare car:

Cl. 309	**RR**	WC	CS	71758

750 V DC THIRD RAIL UNITS:

3905	**CX**	BT	AF	76398	62266	70904	76397
3918	**CX**	BT	AF	76528	62321	70950	76527
930 010	**B/RK**	EM	DY	975600	(10988)	975601	(10843)

Spare cars:

Non-standard liveries:
76112 – Silver (prototype Class 424 "Networker Classic" conversion).

Cl. 210	**N**	E	ZN	67301*
Cl. 421	**G**	NR	ZA	62384
Cl. 424	**0**	BT	ZD	76112

* Former Class 210 DEMU vehicle being assessed for use as a replacement for one of the damaged vehicles of Class 455 5913.

5. ON-TRACK MACHINES

These machines are used for maintaining, renewing and enhancing the infrastructure of the national railway network. With the exception of snowploughs all can be self-propelled. They are permitted to operate either under their own power or in train formations throughout the network both within and outside engineering possessions. Machines only permitted to be used within engineering possessions, referred to as On-Track Plant, are not included. For each machine its Network Rail registered number, owner/responsible custodian and type is given, plus its name if carried. In addition, for snow clearance equipment, the berthing location is also given. Actual operation of each machine is undertaken by either the owner/responsible custodian or a contracted responsible custodian.

(S) after the registered number designates a machine that is currently stored (the storage location of each is given at the end of this section).

DYNAMIC TRACK STABILISERS

DR 72201 (S)	FA	Plasser & Theurer DGS 62-N
DR 72203 (S)	FA	Plasser & Theurer DGS 62-N
DR 72208 (S)	FA	Plasser & Theurer DGS 62-N
DR 72211	BB	Plasser & Theurer DGS 62-N
DR 72213	BB	Plasser & Theurer DGS 62-N

TAMPERS

DR 73103	CS	Plasser & Theurer 09-32 CSM	
DR 73105 (S)	CS	Plasser & Theurer 09-32 CSM	
DR 73106 (S)	FA	Plasser & Theurer 09-32 CSM	
DR 73108	AY	Plasser & Theurer 09-32-RT	Tiger
DR 73109	SK	Plasser & Theurer 09-3X-RT	
DR 73110	SK	Plasser & Theurer 09-3X-RT	Peter White
DR 73111	NR	Plasser & Theurer 09-3X-Dynamic	Reading Panel 1965–2005
DR 73113	NR	Plasser & Theurer 09-3X-Dynamic	
DR 73114	NR	Plasser & Theurer 09-3X-Dynamic	Ron Henderson
DR 73115	NR	Plasser & Theurer 09-3X-Dynamic	
DR 73116	NR	Plasser & Theurer 09-3X Dynamic	
DR 73117	NR	Plasser & Theurer 09-3X Dynamic	
DR 73118	NR	Plasser & Theurer 09-3X Dynamic	
DR 73246 (S)	BB	Plasser & Theurer 07-16 Universal	
DR 73251 (S)	BB	Plasser & Theurer 07-16 Universal	
DR 73257 (S)	BB	Plasser & Theurer 07-16 Universal	
DR 73261	BB	Plasser & Theurer 07-16 Universal	
DR 73263 (S)	BB	Plasser & Theurer 07-16 Universal	
DR 73266 (S)	BB	Plasser & Theurer 07-16 Universal	
DR 73276 (S)	BB	Plasser & Theurer 07-16 Universal	
DR 73278 (S)	BB	Plasser & Theurer 07-16 Universal	
DR 73404 (S)	FA	Plasser & Theurer 07-32 Duomatic	
DR 73413 (S)	FA	Plasser & Theurer 07-32 Duomatic	

DR 73423 (S)	FA	Plasser & Theurer 07-32 Duomatic	
DR 73424 (S)	BB	Plasser & Theurer 07-32 Duomatic	
DR 73428 (S)	GL	Plasser & Theurer 07-32 Duomatic	
DR 73431 (S)	FA	Plasser & Theurer 07-32 Duomatic	
DR 73434 (S)	BB	Plasser & Theurer 07-32 Duomatic	
DR 73435 (S)	FA	Plasser & Theurer 07-32 Duomatic	
DR 73502	BB	Plasser & Theurer 08-16/90 ZW	
DR 73503	BB	Plasser & Theurer 08-16/90 ZW	
DR 73803	SK	Plasser & Theurer 08-32U-RT	Alexander Graham Bell
DR 73804	SK	Plasser & Theurer 08-32U-RT	James Watt
DR 73805	CS	Plasser & Theurer 08-16/32U-RT	
DR 73806	CS	Plasser & Theurer 08-16/32U-RT	Karine
DR 73902 (S)	FA	Plasser & Theurer 08-275 Switch & Crossing	
DR 73903 (S)	FA	Plasser & Theurer 08-275 Switch & Crossing	George Mullineux
DR 73904	SK	Plasser & Theurer 08-4x4/4S-RT	Thomas Telford
DR 73905	AY	Plasser & Theurer 08-4x4/4S-RT	Eddie King
DR 73906	AY	Plasser & Theurer 08-4x4/4S-RT	Panther
DR 73907	CS	Plasser & Theurer 08-4x4/4S-RT	
DR 73908	CS	Plasser & Theurer 08-4x4/4S-RT	
DR 73909	CS	Plasser & Theurer 08-4x4/4S-RT	Saturn
DR 73910	CS	Plasser & Theurer 08-4x4/4S-RT	Jupiter
DR 73911 (S)	AY	Plasser & Theurer 08-16/4x4C-RT	Puma
DR 73912 (S)	AY	Plasser & Theurer 08-16/4x4C-RT	Lynx
DR 73913	CS	Plasser & Theurer 08-12/4x4C-RT	
DR 73914	SK	Plasser & Theurer 08-4x4/4S-RT	Robert McAlpine
DR 73915	SK	Plasser & Theurer 08-16/4x4C-RT	William Arrol
DR 73916	SK	Plasser & Theurer 08-16/4x4C-RT	First Engineering
DR 73917	BB	Plasser & Theurer 08-4x4/4S-RT	
DR 73918	BB	Plasser & Theurer 08-4x4/4S-RT	
DR 73919	CS	Plasser & Theurer 08-16/4x4C100-RT	
DR 73920	AY	Plasser & Theurer 08-16/4x4C80-RT	
DR 73921	AY	Plasser & Theurer 08-16/4x4C80-RT	
DR 73922	AY	Plasser & Theurer 08-16/4x4C80-RT	John Snowdon
DR 73923	CS	Plasser & Theurer 08-4x4/4S-RT	Mercury
DR 73924	CS	Plasser & Theurer 08-16/4x4C100-RT	Atlas
DR 73925	CS	Plasser & Theurer 08-16/4x4C100-RT	Europa
DR 73926	BB	Plasser & Theurer 08-16/4x4C100-RT	Stephen Keith Blanchard
DR 73927	BB	Plasser & Theurer 08-16/4x4C100-RT	
DR 73928	BB	Plasser & Theurer 08-16/4x4C100-RT	
DR 73929	CS	Plasser & Theurer 08-4x4/4S-RT	
DR 73930	CS	Plasser & Theurer 08-4x4/4S-RT	
DR 73931	CS	Plasser & Theurer 08-16/4x4C100-RT	
DR 73932	SK	Plasser & Theurer 08-4x4/4S-RT	
DR 73933	SK	Plasser & Theurer 08-16/4x4/C100-RT	
DR 73934	SK	Plasser & Theurer 08-16/4x4/C100-RT	
DR 73935	CS	Plasser & Theurer 08-4x4/4S-RT	
DR 73936	CS	Plasser & Theurer 08-4x4/4S-RT	
DR 73937	BB	Plasser & Theurer 08-16/4x4C100-RT	
DR 73938	BB	Plasser & Theurer 08-16/4x4C100-RT	
DR 73939	BB	Plasser & Theurer 08-16/4x4C100-RT	

DR 73940	SK	Plasser & Theurer 08-4x4/4S-RT
DR 73941	SK	Plasser & Theurer 08-4x4/4S-RT
DR 73942	CS	Plasser & Theurer 08-4x4/4S-RT
DR 73943	BB	Plasser & Theurer 08-16/4x4C100-RT
DR 73944	BB	Plasser & Theurer 08-16/4x4C100-RT
DR 73945	BB	Plasser & Theurer 08-16/4x4C100-RT
DR 73946	VO	Plasser & Theurer Euromat 08-4x4/4S
DR 73947	CS	Plasser & Theurer 08-4x4/4S-RT
DR 73948	CS	Plasser & Theurer 08-4x4/4S-RT
DR 75201	BB	Plasser & Theurer 08-275 Switch & Crossing
DR 75202	BB	Plasser & Theurer 08-275 Switch & Crossing
DR 75301	VO	Matisa B 45 UE
DR 75302	VO	Matisa B 45 UE
DR 75303	VO	Matisa B 45 UE
DR 75401	VO	Matisa B 41 UE
DR 75402	VO	Matisa B 41 UE
DR 75403	VO	Matisa B 41 UE
DR 75404	VO	Matisa B 41 UE
DR 75405	VO	Matisa B 41 UE
DR 75406	CS	Matisa B 41 UE
DR 75407	CS	Matisa B 41 UE
DR 75408	BB	Matisa B 41 UE
DR 75409	BB	Matisa B 41 UE
DR 75410	BB	Matisa B 41 UE
DR 75411	BB	Matisa B 41 UE
DR 75501	BB	Matisa B 66 UC
DR 75502	BB	Matisa B 66 UC

BALLAST CLEANERS

DR 76323	NR	Plasser & Theurer RM95-RT	
DR 76324	NR	Plasser & Theurer RM95-RT	
DR 76501	NR	Plasser & Theurer RM-900-RT	*(works with DR 76703)*
DR 76502	NR	Plasser & Theurer RM-900-RT	*(works with DR 76702)*
DR 76503	NR	Plasser & Theurer RM-900-RT	*(works with DR 76701/DR 76801)*
DR 76601	CS	Plasser & Theurer RM90-NR	Olwen

BALLAST CLEANING VACUUM PREPARATION MACHINES

DR 76701	NR	Plasser & Theurer VM80-NR	*(works with DR 76503/DR 76801)*
DR 76702	NR	Plasser & Theurer VM80-NR	*(works with DR 76502)*
DR 76703	NR	Plasser & Theurer VM80-NR	*(works with DR 76501)*
DR 76710	NR	Plasser & Theurer VM80-TRS	*(works with DR 76750/DR 78802/ DR 78812/DR 78822/DR 78832)*
DR 76711	NR	Plasser & Theurer VM80-TRS	*(works with DR 76751/DR 78801/ DR 78811/DR 78821/DR 78831)*

TRACK LOWERING MACHINES

DR 76750	NR	Matisa D75	*(works with DR 76710/DR 78802/DR 78812/DR 78822/DR 78832)*
DR 76751	NR	Matisa D75	*(works with DR 76711/DR 78801/DR 78811/DR 78821/DR 78831)*

CONSOLIDATION MACHINE

DR 76801	NR	Plasser & Theurer 09-CM-NR	*(works with DR 76503/DR 76701)*

FINISHING MACHINES & REGULATORS

DR 77001		SK	Plasser & Theurer AFM 2000-RT Finishing Machine	
DR 77002		SK	Plasser & Theurer AFM 2000-RT Finishing Machine	
DR 77315	(S)	BB	Plasser & Theurer USP 5000C Regulator	
DR 77316	(S)	BB	Plasser & Theurer USP 5000C Regulator	
DR 77319		CS	Plasser & Theurer USP 5000C Regulator	
DR 77322		BB	Plasser & Theurer USP 5000C Regulator	
DR 77327		CS	Plasser & Theurer USP 5000C Regulator	
DR 77335	(S)	CS	Plasser & Theurer USP 5000C Regulator	
DR 77336		BB	Plasser & Theurer USP 5000C Regulator	
DR 77801		VO	Matisa R 24 S Regulator	
DR 77802		VO	Matisa R 24 S Regulator	
DR 77901		CS	Plasser & Theurer USP 5000-RT Regulator	
DR 77903		NR	Plasser & Theurer USP 5000-RT Regulator	Frank Jones
DR 77904		NR	Plasser & Theurer USP 5000-RT Regulator	
DR 77905		NR	Plasser & Theurer USP 5000-RT Regulator	
DR 77906		NR	Plasser & Theurer USP 5000-RT Regulator	
DR 77907		NR	Plasser & Theurer USP 5000-RT Regulator	
DR 77908		SK	Plasser & Theurer USP 5000-RT Regulator	

TWIN JIB TRACK RELAYERS

DRP 78211	(S)	NR	Plasser & Theurer Self-Propelled Heavy Duty
DRP 78212	(S)	NR	Plasser & Theurer Self-Propelled Heavy Duty
DRP 78213		VO	Plasser & Theurer Self-Propelled Heavy Duty
DRP 78215		SK	Plasser & Theurer Self-Propelled Heavy Duty
DRP 78216		BB	Plasser & Theurer Self-Propelled Heavy Duty
DRP 78217	(S)	SK	Plasser & Theurer Self-Propelled Heavy Duty
DRP 78218	(S)	BB	Plasser & Theurer Self-Propelled Heavy Duty
DRP 78219		SK	Plasser & Theurer Self-Propelled Heavy Duty
DRP 78221		BB	Plasser & Theurer Self-Propelled Heavy Duty
DRP 78222		BB	Plasser & Theurer Self-Propelled Heavy Duty
DRP 78223	(S)	BB	Plasser & Theurer Self-Propelled Heavy Duty
DRP 78224	(S)	BB	Plasser & Theurer Self-Propelled Heavy Duty
DRC 78226		CS	Cowans Sheldon Self-Propelled Heavy Duty

DRC 78229 (S) NR Cowans Sheldon Self-Propelled Heavy Duty
DRC 78231 (S) GL Cowans Sheldon Self-Propelled Heavy Duty
DRC 78234 (S) GL Cowans Sheldon Self-Propelled Heavy Duty
DRC 78235 CS Cowans Sheldon Self-Propelled Heavy Duty
DRC 78237 (S) GL Cowans Sheldon Self-Propelled Heavy Duty

TRACK RENEWAL MACHINES

Matisa P95 Track Renewals Trains
DR 78801+DR 78811+DR 78821+DR 78831 NR *(works with DR 76711/DR 76751)*
DR 78802+DR 78812+DR 78822+DR 78832 NR *(works with DR 76710/DR 76750)*

RAIL GRINDING TRAINS

Loram SPML 15
DR 79200A + DR 79200B + DR 79200C LO

Loram SPML 17
DR 79201A + DR 79201B LO

Speno RPS-32
DR 79221 + DR 79222 + DR 79223 + DR 79224 + DR 79225 + DR 79226 SI

Loram C21
DR 79231 + DR 79232 + DR 79233 + DR 79234 + DR 79235 + DR 79236 + DR 79237 LO
DR 79241 + DR 79242 + DR 79243 + DR 79244 + DR 79245 + DR 79246 + DR 79247 NR
DR 79251 + DR 79252 + DR 79253 + DR 79254 + DR 79255 + DR 79256 + DR 79257 NR

Name: DR 79247 Roger South

Harsco Track Technologies RGH20C
DR 79261 + DR 79271 NR
DR 79262 + DR 79272 NR
DR 79263 + DR 79273 NR
DR 79264 + DR 79274 NR
DR 79265 (S) NR *spare vehicle*
DR 79266 + DR 79276 HT

STONE BLOWERS

DR 80200 (S) NR Pandrol Jackson Plain Line
DR 80201 (S) NR Pandrol Jackson Plain Line
DR 80202 (S) NR Pandrol Jackson Plain Line
DR 80203 (S) NR Pandrol Jackson Plain Line
DR 80204 (S) NR Pandrol Jackson Plain Line
DR 80205 NR Pandrol Jackson Plain Line
DR 80206 NR Pandrol Jackson Plain Line
DR 80207 (S) NR Pandrol Jackson Plain Line
DR 80208 NR Pandrol Jackson Plain Line
DR 80209 NR Pandrol Jackson Plain Line

DR 80210 (S)	NR	Pandrol Jackson Plain Line	
DR 80211	NR	Pandrol Jackson Plain Line	
DR 80212	NR	Pandrol Jackson Plain Line	
DR 80213	NR	Harsco Track Technologies Plain Line	
DR 80214	NR	Harsco Track Technologies Plain Line	
DR 80215	NR	Harsco Track Technologies Plain Line	
DR 80216	NR	Harsco Track Technologies Plain Line	
DR 80217	NR	Harsco Track Technologies Plain Line	
DR 80301	NR	Harsco Track Technologies Multi-purpose	Stephen Cornish
DR 80302	NR	Harsco Track Technologies Multi-purpose	
DR 80303	NR	Harsco Track Technologies Multi-purpose	

CRANES

DRP 81505	BB	Plasser & Theurer 12 tonne Heavy Duty Diesel Hydraulic
DRP 81507 (S)	BB	Plasser & Theurer 12 tonne Heavy Duty Diesel Hydraulic
DRP 81508	BB	Plasser & Theurer 12 tonne Heavy Duty Diesel Hydraulic
DRP 81511 (S)	BB	Plasser & Theurer 12 tonne Heavy Duty Diesel Hydraulic
DRP 81513	BB	Plasser & Theurer 12 tonne Heavy Duty Diesel Hydraulic
DRP 81517	BB	Plasser & Theurer 12 tonne Heavy Duty Diesel Hydraulic
DRP 81519 (S)	BB	Plasser & Theurer 12 tonne Heavy Duty Diesel Hydraulic
DRP 81522	BB	Plasser & Theurer 12 tonne Heavy Duty Diesel Hydraulic
DRP 81525	BB	Plasser & Theurer 12 tonne Heavy Duty Diesel Hydraulic
DRP 81532	BB	Plasser & Theurer 12 tonne Heavy Duty Diesel Hydraulic
DRK 81601	VO	Kirow KRC810UK 100 tonne Heavy Duty Diesel Hydraulic
DRK 81602	BB	Kirow KRC810UK 100 tonne Heavy Duty Diesel Hydraulic
DRK 81611	BB	Kirow KRC1200UK 125 tonne Heavy Duty Diesel Hydraulic
DRK 81612	CS	Kirow KRC1200UK 125 tonne Heavy Duty Diesel Hydraulic
DRK 81613	VO	Kirow KRC1200UK 125 tonne Heavy Duty Diesel Hydraulic
DRK 81621	VO	Kirow KRC250UK 25 tonne Diesel Hydraulic
DRK 81622	VO	Kirow KRC250UK 25 tonne Diesel Hydraulic
DRK 81623	SK	Kirow KRC250UK 25 tonne Diesel Hydraulic
DRK 81624	SK	Kirow KRC250UK 25 tonne Diesel Hydraulic
DRK 81625	SK	Kirow KRC250UK 25 tonne Diesel Hydraulic
ADRC 96710	NR	Cowans Sheldon 75 tonne Diesel Hydraulic (telescopic) Breakdown
ADRC 96713	NR	Cowans Sheldon 75 tonne Diesel Hydraulic (telescopic) Breakdown
ADRC 96714	NR	Cowans Sheldon 75 tonne Diesel Hydraulic (telescopic) Breakdown
ADRC 96715	NR	Cowans Sheldon 75 tonne Diesel Hydraulic (telescopic) Breakdown

Names:

DRK 81601	Nigel Chester	DRK 81611	Malcolm L. Pearce

GENERAL PURPOSE MAINTENANCE VEHICLES

DR 97001	H1	Eiv de Brieve DU94BA TRAMM with Crane	
DR 97011	H1	Windhoff MPV Master	
DR 97012	H1	Windhoff MPV Master	Geoff Bell
DR 97013	H1	Windhoff MPV Master	
DR 97014	H1	Windhoff MPV Master	
DR 98001 (S)	NR	Windhoff MPV Master with Piling Equipment	

DR 98002 (S)	NR	Windhoff MPV Master with Piling Equipment
DR 98003	NR	Windhoff MPV Master with Overhead Line Renewal Equipment
DR 98004	NR	Windhoff MPV Master with Overhead Line Renewal Equipment
DR 98005 (S)	NR	Windhoff MPV Master with Piling Equipment
DR 98006 (S)	NR	Windhoff MPV Master with Piling Equipment
DR 98007 (S)	NR	Windhoff MPV Master with Piling Equipment
DR 98008	NR	Windhoff MPV Twin-cab Master with test equipment
DR 98009	NR	Windhoff MPV Master with Overhead Line Renewal Equipment
DR 98010	NR	Windhoff MPV Master with Overhead Line Renewal Equipment
DR 98011 (S)	NR	Windhoff MPV Master with Overhead Line Renewal Equipment
DR 98012 (S)	NR	Windhoff MPV Master with Overhead Line Renewal Equipment
DR 98013 (S)	NR	Windhoff MPV Master with Overhead Line Renewal Equipment
DR 98014 (S)	NR	Windhoff MPV Master with Overhead Line Renewal Equipment

DR 98210A + DR 98210B (S)	AY	Plasser & Theurer GP-TRAMM with Trailer
DR 98215A + DR 98215B	BB	Plasser & Theurer GP-TRAMM with Trailer
DR 98216A + DR 98216B	BB	Plasser & Theurer GP-TRAMM with Trailer
DR 98217A + DR 98217B	BB	Plasser & Theurer GP-TRAMM with Trailer
DR 98218A + DR 98218B	BB	Plasser & Theurer GP-TRAMM with Trailer
DR 98219A + DR 98219B	BB	Plasser & Theurer GP-TRAMM with Trailer
DR 98220A + DR 98220B	BB	Plasser & Theurer GP-TRAMM with Trailer

DR 98305 (S)	NR	Geismar GP-TRAMM VMT 860 PL/UM
DR 98306 (S)	NR	Geismar GP-TRAMM VMT 860 PL/UM

DR 98307A + DR 98307B	CS	Geismar GP-TRAMM VMT 860 PL/UM with Trailer
DR 98308A + DR 98308B	CS	Geismar GP-TRAMM VMT 860 PL/UM with Trailer

DR 98901 + DR 98951	NR	Windhoff MPV Master & Slave
DR 98902 + DR 98952	NR	Windhoff MPV Master & Slave
DR 98903 + DR 98953	NR	Windhoff MPV Master & Slave
DR 98904 + DR 98954	NR	Windhoff MPV Master & Slave
DR 98905 + DR 98955	NR	Windhoff MPV Master & Slave
DR 98906 + DR 98956	NR	Windhoff MPV Master & Slave
DR 98907 + DR 98957	NR	Windhoff MPV Master & Slave
DR 98908 + DR 98958	NR	Windhoff MPV Master & Slave
DR 98909 + DR 98959	NR	Windhoff MPV Master & Slave
DR 98910 + DR 98960	NR	Windhoff MPV Master & Slave
DR 98911 + DR 98961	NR	Windhoff MPV Master & Slave
DR 98912 + DR 98962	NR	Windhoff MPV Master & Slave
DR 98913 + DR 98963	NR	Windhoff MPV Master & Slave
DR 98914 + DR 98964	NR	Windhoff MPV Master & Slave
DR 98915 + DR 98965	NR	Windhoff MPV Master & Slave
DR 98916 + DR 98966	NR	Windhoff MPV Master & Slave
DR 98917 + DR 98967	NR	Windhoff MPV Master & Slave
DR 98918 + DR 98968	NR	Windhoff MPV Master & Slave
DR 98919 + DR 98969	NR	Windhoff MPV Master & Slave
DR 98920 + DR 98970	NR	Windhoff MPV Master & Slave
DR 98921 + DR 98971	NR	Windhoff MPV Master & Slave
DR 98922 + DR 98972	NR	Windhoff MPV Master & Slave
DR 98923 + DR 98973	NR	Windhoff MPV Master & Slave
DR 98924 + DR 98974	NR	Windhoff MPV Master & Slave

DR 98925 + DR 98975	NR	Windhoff MPV Master & Slave
DR 98926 + DR 98976	NR	Windhoff MPV Master & Powered Slave
DR 98927 + DR 98977	NR	Windhoff MPV Master & Powered Slave
DR 98928 + DR 98978	NR	Windhoff MPV Master & Powered Slave
DR 98929 + DR 98979	NR	Windhoff MPV Master & Powered Slave
DR 98930 + DR 98980	NR	Windhoff MPV Master & Powered Slave
DR 98931 + DR 98981	NR	Windhoff MPV Master & Powered Slave
DR 98932 + DR 98982	NR	Windhoff MPV Master & Powered Slave

SNOWPLOUGHS

ADB 965203	NR	Independent Drift Plough	Tees Yard
ADB 965206	NR	Independent Drift Plough	Doncaster Carr Depot
ADB 965208	NR	Independent Drift Plough	Inverness Millburn Yard
ADB 965209	NR	Independent Drift Plough	Bristol Barton Hill Depot
ADB 965210	NR	Independent Drift Plough	Tonbridge West Yard
ADB 965211	NR	Independent Drift Plough	Peterborough
ADB 965217	NR	Independent Drift Plough	Edinburgh Slateford Yard
ADB 965219	NR	Independent Drift Plough	Mossend Yard
ADB 965223	NR	Independent Drift Plough	Margam Knuckle Yard
ADB 965224	NR	Independent Drift Plough	Carlisle Kingmoor Yard
ADB 965230	NR	Independent Drift Plough	Carlisle Kingmoor Yard
ADB 965231	NR	Independent Drift Plough	Bristol Barton Hill Depot
ADB 965232	NR	Independent Drift Plough	Peterborough Station
ADB 965233	NR	Independent Drift Plough	Peterborough Station
ADB 965234	NR	Independent Drift Plough	Mossend Yard
ADB 965235	NR	Independent Drift Plough	Margam Knuckle Yard
ADB 965236	NR	Independent Drift Plough	Tonbridge West Yard
ADB 965237	NR	Independent Drift Plough	Peterborough
ADB 965240	NR	Independent Drift Plough	Inverness Millburn Yard
ADB 965241	NR	Independent Drift Plough	Doncaster Carr Depot
ADB 965242	NR	Independent Drift Plough	Tees Yard
ADB 965243	NR	Independent Drift Plough	Edinburgh Slateford Yard
ADB 965576	NR	Beilhack Type PB600 Plough	Toton Depot
ADB 965577	NR	Beilhack Type PB600 Plough	Toton Depot
ADB 965578	NR	Beilhack Type PB600 Plough	Carlisle Kingmoor Yard
ADB 965579	NR	Beilhack Type PB600 Plough	Carlisle Kingmoor Yard
ADB 965580	NR	Beilhack Type PB600 Plough	Wigan Springs Branch
ADB 965581	NR	Beilhack Type PB600 Plough	Wigan Springs Branch
ADB 966098	NR	Beilhack Type PB600 Plough	Doncaster Carr Depot
ADB 966099	NR	Beilhack Type PB600 Plough	Doncaster Carr Depot

SNOWBLOWERS

ADB 968500	NR	Beilhack Self Propelled Rotary	Rutherglen Depot
ADB 968501	NR	Beilhack Self Propelled Rotary	Rutherglen Depot

INFRASTRUCTURE MONITORING VEHICLES

999800	NR	Plasser & Theurer EM-SAT 100/RT Track Survey Car
999801	NR	Plasser & Theurer EM-SAT 100/RT Track Survey Car

Name: 999800 Richard Spoors

ON-TRACK MACHINES AWAITING DISPOSAL

Tampers

DR 73311	Plasser & Theurer 07-275 Switch & Crossing	Ashford
DR 73314	Plasser & Theurer 07-275 Switch & Crossing	Frodingham
DR 86101	Plasser & Theurer 08-16 Universal	Hither Green

Ballast Cleaners

DR 76304	Plasser & Theurer RM74	Plasser UK, West Ealing
DR 76318	Plasser & Theurer RM74	Plasser UK, West Ealing

Twin Jib track relayer

DRB 78123	British Hoist & Crane Non-Self-Propelled	Polmadie DHS

LOCATIONS OF STORED ON-TRACK MACHINES

The locations of machines shown above as stored (S) are shown here.

DR 72201	Hitchin
DR 72203	Hitchin
DR 72208	Hitchin
DR 73105	Rugby
DR 73106	Hitchin
DR 73246	Ashford
DR 73251	Hither Green
DR 73257	Ashford
DR 73263	Ashford
DR 73266	Ashford
DR 73276	Ashford
DR 73278	Colchester
DR 73404	Hitchin
DR 73413	Hitchin
DR 73423	Hitchin
DR 73424	Ashford
DR 73428	Russell Storage, Hillington
DR 73431	Hitchin
DR 73434	Ashford
DR 73435	Hitchin
DR 73902	Hitchin
DR 73903	Hitchin
DR 73911	Plasser UK, West Ealing
DR 73912	Plasser UK, West Ealing
DR 77315	Ashford
DR 77316	Ashford
DR 77335	Rugby
DRP 78211	Doncaster Marshgate
DRP 78212	Doncaster Marshgate
DRP 78217	Glasgow Rutherglen
DRP 78218	Ashford
DRP 78223	Ashford
DRP 78224	Hither Green
DRC 78229	Doncaster Marshgate
DRC 78231	Long Marston
DRC 78234	Long Marston
DRC 78237	Long Marston
DR 79265	Eastleigh Works
DR 80200	East Dereham
DR 80201	Eastleigh Works
DR 80202	Eastleigh Works
DR 80203	Eastleigh Works
DR 80204	East Dereham
DR 80207	Eastleigh Works
DR 80210	Ashford
DRP 81507	Ashford
DRP 81511	Sandiacre
DRP 81519	Woking
DR 98001	York Holgate
DR 98002	York Holgate
DR 98005	York Holgate
DR 98006	York Holgate
DR 98007	York Holgate
DR 98011	York Holgate
DR 98012	York Holgate
DR 98013	York Holgate
DR 98014	York Holgate
DR 98210A	+
DR 98210B	Plasser UK, West Ealing
DR 98305	Eastleigh Works
DR 98306	Eastleigh Works

PLATFORM 5 MAIL ORDER

FREIGHTMASTER

Freightmaster Publishing

Freightmaster is the Great Britain National Railfreight Timetable. It contains full timetable listings for over 70 key locations around the country, including dates of operation, train type and booked motive power for every train. Most locations feature 0700-2300 listings, with full 24 hour timetables for busy locations. Also includes a separate analysis of national freight flows. Well illustrated by a series of detailed maps.160 pages. **£14.95**

Note: Freightmaster is published 4 times a year in January, April, July and September. Customers ordering this title will be supplied with the latest edition available unless requested otherwise.

RAILWAY TRACK DIAGRAMS

Trackmaps

Each volume of the Quail reference work contains detailed track diagrams for the former British Rail Regions, plus private railways, preservation sites and industrial layouts. Includes extensive notation, list of abbreviations, engineers' line references and an index to stations, lines and selected other places. All volumes have been digitally redrawn and now feature full colour printing to denote electrification type and voltage. Used extensively throughout the railway industry.

Railway Track Diagrams 1: Scotland **£11.95**
Railway Track Diagrams 2: Eastern **£14.95**
Railway Track Diagrams 3: Western **£11.95**
Railway Track Diagrams 5: Southern & TfL **£14.95**

Please add postage: 10% UK, 20% Europe, 30% Rest of World.

Telephone, fax or send your order to the Platform 5 Mail Order Department. **See page 384 of this book for details.**

6. UK LIGHT RAIL & METRO SYSTEMS

This section lists the rolling stock of the various light rail and metro systems in the UK. Passenger carrying vehicles only are covered (not works vehicles). This listing does not cover the London Underground network.

6.1. BLACKPOOL & FLEETWOOD TRAMWAY

Until the opening of Manchester Metrolink, the Blackpool tramway was the only urban/inter-urban tramway system left in Britain. The infrastructure is owned by Blackpool Corporation, and the tramway is operated by Blackpool Transport Services Ltd. The 11½ miles from Fleetwood to Starr Gate is due to reopen at Easter 2012 as a modern light rail system with a new fleet of 16 Bombardier "Flexity 2" trams. A number of modified "Balloon" double deckers will also be used on the system, most of the other trams listed here are awaiting disposal.

System: 600 V DC overhead.
Depot & Workshops: Starr Gate and Rigby Road (heritage fleet).
Standard livery: Flexity 2s: White, black & purple. Heritage trams: cream & green.

All cars are single-deck unless stated otherwise. For advertising liveries predominating colours are given. (S) = Stored out of service.

FLEXITY 2 — 5-SECTION TRAMS

16 new articulated Supertrams currently being delivered.

Built: 2011–12 by Bombardier Transportation, Bautzen, Germany.
Wheel arrangement: Bo-2-Bo.
Traction Motors: Four Bombardier 3-phase asynchronous of 120 kW.
Dimensions: 32.2 x 2.65 m. **Seats**: 70 (4).
Doors: Sliding plug. **Couplers**:
Weight: 40.9 t. **Maximum Speed**: 43 mph.
Braking: Regenerative, disc and magnetic track.

001	005	009	013
002	006	010	014
003	007	011	015
004	008	012	016

OPEN BOAT CARS — A1-1A

Built: 1934 by English Electric. 12 built. **Seats**: 56 (* 52).
Traction Motors: Two EE327 of 30 kW.

600	604 *(S)	607 (S) **Yellow & Green**
602 *(S) **Yellow & Black**	605 *(S) **Green & Cream**	

Named: 600 "THE DUCHESS OF CORNWALL".

BRUSH CARS A1-1A

Built: 1937 by Brush, Loughborough. 20 built.
Traction Motors: Two EE305 of 40 kW. **Seats**: 48.
Advertising liveries:

631 – Walls ice cream (red)
637 – Blackpool Zoo (green & white)

631	**AL**	632	637 (S)	**AL**

CENTENARY CLASS A1-1A

Built: 1984–87. Body by East Lancs. Coachbuilders, Blackburn. Driver Only Operated.
Traction Motors: Two EE305 of 40 kW. **Seats**: 53.
† Rebuilt from GEC car 651.
Advertising liveries:

646 – Paul Gaunt Furniture (blue)
647 – B&M Bargain Stores (black, blue & yellow)
648 – Houndshill Shopping Centre (purple & white)

642	**Yellow**	646	**AL**	647	**AL**	648†	**AL**
645	**Red**						

PROGRESS TWIN CARS A1-1A + 2-2

Built: Motor cars (672–676) rebuilt 1958–60 from English Electric Railcoaches by Blackpool Corporation Transport. Driving trailers (682–686) built 1960 by Metro-Cammell.
Traction Motors: Two EE305 of 40 kW. **Seats**: 53 + 61.

672+682	**Orange/yellow**	674+684 (S)	**Blue/yellow**	676+686	(S)
673+683 (S)	**Turquoise/yellow**	675+685	**Red/yellow**		

ENGLISH ELECTRIC RAILCOACHES A1-1A

Built: Rebuilt 1960 from EE Railcoach. Originally ran with trailer.
Traction Motors: Two EE305 of 40 kW. **Seats**: 48.

680 (S)

"BALLOON" DOUBLE DECKERS A1-1A

A number of these cars are being retained for use after the Flexity 2 trams enter service.

Built: 1934–35 by English Electric. 700–712 were originally built with open tops and 706 has now reverted to open top.
Traction Motors: Two EE305 of 40 kW. **Seats**: 94 (*† 92, ‡ 90).

Notes: 717 is named "PHILLIP R THORPE" and 719 is "DONNA'S DREAM HOUSE"
* Rebuilt with a new flat front end design and air-conditioned cabs. Known as "Millennium Class".

o 706 – Rebuilt as an open-topped double-decker seating 92. Named "PRINCESS ALICE". Also carries original number 243.
d Rebuilt with new wider doors for continued operation.

Advertising liveries:

704 – Eclipse at the Globe, Pleasure Beach (black & orange)
707 – Coral Island – The Jewel on the Mile (black)
709 – Blackpool Sealife Centre (blue)
711 – Blackpool Zoo (various)
713 – Houndshill Shopping Centre (purple & white)
718 – Madame Tassaud's (purple & red)
719 and 721 – Pleasure Beach Resort (black/gold)
720 – Walls ice cream (red)
723 – Sands Venue nightclub (black)
724 – Lyndene Hotel (blue)

700 d	**White**	711 †	**AL**	719	**AL**
701 ‡	**Yellow**	713 d	**AL**	720 d	**AL**
704 (S)	**AL**	715		721 (S)	**AL**
706 o		717		723 †	**AL**
707 *d	**AL**	718 *d	**AL**	724 *d	**AL**
709 *d	**AL**				

ILLUMINATED CARS

732 (S)	The Rocket	Rebuilt: 1961	Seats: 47
733	Western Train loco & tender	Rebuilt: 1962	Seats: 35
734	Western Train coach	Rebuilt: 1962	Seats: 60
736	"Warship" HMS Blackpool	Rebuilt: 1965	Seats: 71
737	Illuminated Trawler – "Fisherman's Friend"	Rebuilt: 2001	Seats: 48

VINTAGE CARS

These trams are used for special services as well as for occasional normal services, particularly during the Illuminations.

Blackpool 8	BCT One Man Car	Rebuilt: 1974
Blackpool & Fleetwood 40	Single deck "box car"	Built: 1914
Bolton 66	Bogie double-decker	Built: 1901
Blackpool 143	Open balcony standard double-decker	Built: 1924
Blackpool 147 MICHAEL AIREY	Standard double-decker	Built: 1924
Blackpool 304	Coronation Class single-decker	Built: 1952
Blackpool 660	Coronation Class single-decker	Built: 1953

6.2. DOCKLANDS LIGHT RAILWAY

This system runs for a total of approximately 23 route miles from termini at Bank and Tower Gateway in central London to Lewisham, Stratford, Beckton and Woolwich Arsenal. A new line from Canning Town to Stratford International also opened in 2011. The first part of the network opened in 1987 from Tower Gateway to Island Gardens. Originally owned by London Transport, it is now part of the London Rail division of Transport for London and operated by Serco Docklands. Cars are normally "driven" automatically using the Alcatel "Seltrack" moving block signalling system.
Notes: Original P86 and P89 Class vehicles 01–21 were withdrawn from service in 1991 (01–11) and 1995 (12–21) and sold for use in Essen, Germany.

55 new cars from Bombardier in Germany entered traffic between 2008 and 2010. Along with platform extensions, these new vehicles have enabled 3-unit trains to start operating on all routes.

System: 750 V DC third rail (bottom contact). High-floor.
Depots: Beckton (main depot) and Poplar.
Livery: Red with a curving blue stripe to represent the River Thames.

CLASS B90 — 2-SECTION UNITS

Built: 1991–92 by BN Construction, Bruges, Belgium. Chopper control.
Wheel Arrangement: B-2-B. **Traction Motors:** Two Brush of 140 kW.
Seats: 52 (4). **Weight:** 37t.
Dimensions: 28.80 x 2.65 m. **Braking:** Rheostatic.
Couplers: Scharfenberg. **Maximum Speed:** 50 mph.
Doors: Sliding. End doors for staff use.

22	26	30	34	38	42
23	27	31	35	39	43
24	28	32	36	40	44
25	29	33	37	41	

CLASS B92 — 2-SECTION UNITS

Built: 1992–95 by BN Construction, Bruges, Belgium. Chopper control.
Wheel Arrangement: B-2-B. **Traction Motors:** Two Brush of 140 kW.
Seats: 52 (4). **Weight:** 37t.
Dimensions: 28.80 x 2.65 m. **Braking:** Rheostatic.
Couplers: Scharfenberg. **Maximum Speed:** 50 mph.
Doors: Sliding. End doors for staff use.

45	53	61	69	77	85
46	54	62	70	78	86
47	55	63	71	79	87
48	56	64	72	80	88
49	57	65	73	81	89
50	58	66	74	82	90
51	59	67	75	83	91
52	60	68	76	84	

CLASS B2K 2-SECTION UNITS

Built: 2002–03 by Bombardier Transportation, Bruges, Belgium.
Wheel Arrangement: B-2-B. **Traction Motors:** Two Brush of 140 kW.
Seats: 52 (4). **Weight:** 37 t.
Dimensions: 28.80 x 2.65 m. **Braking:** Rheostatic.
Couplers: Scharfenberg. **Maximum Speed:** 50 mph.
Doors: Sliding. End doors for staff use.

92	96	01	05	09	13
93	97	02	06	10	14
94	98	03	07	11	15
95	99	04	08	12	16

CLASS B07 2-SECTION UNITS

Built: 2007–10 by Bombardier Transportation, Bautzen, Germany.
Wheel Arrangement: B-2-B. **Traction Motors:** Two Brush of 140 kW.
Seats: 52 (4). **Weight:** 37 t.
Dimensions: **Braking:** Rheostatic.
Couplers: Scharfenberg. **Maximum Speed:** 50 mph.
Doors: Sliding. End doors for staff use.

101	111	120	129	138	147
102	112	121	130	139	148
103	113	122	131	140	149
104	114	123	132	141	150
105	115	124	133	142	151
106	116	125	134	143	152
107	117	126	135	144	153
108	118	127	136	145	154
109	119	128	137	146	155
110					

6.3. EDINBURGH TRAMWAY

A new tramway is under construction in Edinburgh, however the scheme has been dogged by construction problems, with the originally planned terminus of Newhaven in the north of the city cut back to St Andrew Square in the city centre. In the west side of the city trams will run to Edinburgh Airport. At the time of writing the tramway is due to open in 2014, although it is likely that not all of the 27 trams on order will be required for the reduced system. The trams will be the longest to operate in the UK.

System: 750 V DC overhead.
Platform Height: 350 mm.
Depot & Workshops: Gogar.
Livery: White, red & black.

CAF 7-SECTION TRAMS

Built: 2009–11 by CAF, Irun, Spain.
Wheel Arrangement: Bo-Bo-2-Bo.
Seats: 78.
Dimensions: 42.8 x 2.65 m.
Couplers:
Doors: Sliding plug.
Traction Motors: 12 CAF of 80 kW.
Weight:
Braking:
Maximum Speed: 50 mph.

251	257	263	268	273
252	258	264	269	274
253	259	265	270	275
254	260	266	271	276
255	261	267	272	277
256	262			

6.4. GLASGOW SUBWAY

This circular 4 ft gauge underground line is the smallest metro system in the UK, running for just over six miles. Operated by Strathclyde PTE the system has 15 stations. The entire passenger railway is underground, contained in twin tunnels, allowing for clockwise operation on the "outer" circle and anti-clockwise operation on the "inner" circle.

Trains are formed of 3-cars – either three power cars or two power cars sandwiching one of the newer trailer cars.

System: 600 V DC third rail.
Depot & Workshops: Broomloan.
Liveries: Strathclyde PTE carmine & cream unless stated.
S: New Subway livery (orange & grey).

SINGLE POWER CARS

Built: 1977–79 by Metro-Cammell, Birmingham. Refurbished 1993–95 by ABB Derby.
Wheel Arrangement: Bo-Bo.
Traction Motors: Four GEC G312AZ of 35.6 kW each.
Seats: 36.
Couplers: Wedglock.
Weight: 19.6 t.
Dimensions: 12.81 m x 2.34 m.
Doors: Sliding.
Maximum Speed: 33.5 mph.

101	108	115	122	128
102	109	116	123	129
103 S	110	117	124	130
104 S	111	118	125	131
105	112	119	126	132
106 S	113	120	127	133
107	114	121		

INTERMEDIATE BOGIE TRAILERS

Built: 1992 by Hunslet Barclay, Kilmarnock.
Seats: 40.
Couplers: Wedglock.
Weight: 17.2t.
Dimensions: 12.70m x 2.34m.
Doors: Sliding.
Maximum Speed: 33.5mph.
Advertising/Special liveries:

203 – Capital FM (blue).
204 – SPT Zonecard ticket (blue).
205 – Robert Burns (different images of the famous poet).

201	**S**	203	**AL**	205	**AL**	207	208
202		204	**AL**	206			

6.5. GREATER MANCHESTER METROLINK

Metrolink was the first modern tramway system in the UK, combining street running with longer distance running over former BR lines. The system opened in 1992 from Bury to Altrincham with a street section through the centre of Manchester and a spur to Piccadilly station. A second line opened in 2000 from Cornbrook to Eccles. A short spur off the Eccles line to MediaCityUK opened in September 2010 whilst the first part of the South Manchester Line to Chorlton and St Werburgh's Road opened in July 2011, extending the total route mileage to approximately 25 miles.
Further extensions are under construction as follows:

- Rochdale station via Oldham to (involving converting the former National Rail line to light rail use) by summer 2012.
- The East Manchester Line to Droylsden (summer 2012) and Ashton-under-Lyne (winter 2013–14).
- The South Manchester Line from St Werburgh's Road to East Didsbury (summer 2013) and Manchester Airport (2016).

Further extensions will see trams running into Oldham and Rochdale town centres (2014) and a second city crossing in Manchester (by 2021).

Operator: RATP Dev.
System: 750 V DC overhead. High floor.
Depot & Workshops: Queens Road and Trafford.

1000 SERIES 2-SECTION TRAMS

Built: 1991–92 by Firema, Italy. Chopper control.
Wheel Arrangement: Bo-2-Bo.
Traction Motors: Four GEC of 130 kW.
Dimensions: 29.0 x 2.65 m.
Seats: 82 (4).
Doors: Sliding.
Couplers: Scharfenberg.
Weight: 45t.
Maximum Speed: 50mph.
Braking: Regenerative, disc and emergency track.

Liveries: White, dark grey & blue with light blue doors.
M: New Manchester Metrolink silver & yellow.

1001	*		1014	*	Vans. The original since 1966
1002	*		1015	*	
1003	**M***		1016		
1004	*	Vans. The original since 1966	1017		BURY HOSPICE
1005	*		1018		
1006	*	Vans. The original since 1966	1019		
1007	*	EAST LANCASHIRE RAILWAY	1020		LANCASHIRE FUSILIER
1008	*		1021	*	
1009	*		1022	*	POPPY APPEAL
1010	*		1023	*	
1011	*	Vans. The original since 1966	1024	*	
1012	*		1025	*	
1013	*		1026	*	

* Fitted with front-end valances, retractable couplers and controllable magnetic track brakes for on-street running mixed with private vehicles.

2000 SERIES 2-SECTION TRAMS

Built: 1999 by Ansaldo, Italy. Chopper control. Fitted with front-end valances, retractable couplers and controllable magnetic track brakes for on-street running mixed with private vehicles.
Wheel Arrangement: Bo-2-Bo. **Traction Motors**: Four GEC of 130 kW.
Dimensions: 29.0 x 2.65 m. **Seats**: 82 (4).
Doors: Sliding. **Couplers**: Scharfenberg.
Weight: 45t. **Maximum Speed**: 50 mph.
Braking: Regenerative, disc and magnetic track.

Livery: White, dark grey & blue with light blue doors.

2001	2004
2002	2005
2003	2006

3000 SERIES FLEXITY SWIFT 2-SECTION TRAMS

A total of 74 new Bombardier M5000 "Flexity Swift" are being delivered to strengthen services on existing routes and for the extensions listed above. Further options exist for more M5000 trams.
Built: 2009–12 by Bombardier, Vienna, Austria.
Wheel Arrangement: Bo-2-Bo.
Traction Motors: Four Bombardier 3-phase asynchronous of 120 kW.
Dimensions: 28.4 x 2.65 m. **Seats**: 52.
Doors: Sliding. **Couplers**: Scharfenberg.
Weight: 39.7t. **Maximum Speed**: 50 mph.
Braking: Regenerative, disc and magnetic track.

Livery: New Manchester Metrolink silver & yellow.

3001	3016	3031	3046	3061
3002	3017	3032	3047	3062
3003	3018	3033	3048	3063
3004	3019	3034	3049	3064
3005	3020	3035	3050	3065
3006	3021	3036	3051	3066
3007	3022	3037	3052	3067
3008	3023	3038	3053	3068
3009	3024	3039	3054	3069
3010	3025	3040	3055	3070
3011	3026	3041	3056	3071
3012	3027	3042	3057	3072
3013	3028	3043	3058	3073
3014	3029	3044	3059	3074
3015	3030	3045	3060	

6.6. LONDON TRAMLINK

This system runs through central Croydon via a one-way loop, with lines radiating out to Wimbledon, New Addington and Beckenham Junction/ Elmers End, the total route mileage being 18½ miles. It opened in 2000 and is now operated by Transport for London. Six new Stadler trams should be in traffic by spring 2012.

System: 750 V DC overhead. **Platform Height**: 350 mm.
Depot & Workshops: Therapia Lane, Croydon.
Livery: Light grey & lime green with a blue solebar.

BOMBARDIER 3-SECTION TRAMS

Built: 1998–99 by Bombardier, Vienna, Austria.
Wheel Arrangement: Bo-2-Bo. **Traction Motors**: Four of 120 kW each.
Dimensions: 30.1 x 2.65 m. **Seats**: 70.
Doors: Sliding plug. **Couplers**: Scharfenberg.
Weight: 36.3t. **Maximum Speed**: 50 mph.
Braking: Disc, regenerative and magnetic track.

2530	2534	2538	2542	2546	2550
2531	2535	2539	2543	2547	2551
2532	2536	2540	2544	2548	2552
2533	2537	2541	2545	2549	2553

Name: 2535 STEPHEN PARASCANDOLO 1980–2007

STADLER 5-SECTION TRAMS

Six new Variobahn trams currently being delivered to help ease overcrowding on the existing Croydon network. There is an option for eight further vehicles. Full details awaited.

Built: 2011–12 by Stadler, Berlin, Germany.
Wheel Arrangement:
Dimensions: 32.4 x 2.65 m.
Doors: Sliding plug.
Weight: 41.8 t.
Braking:
Traction Motors: 8 of 45 kW.
Seats: 72.
Couplers:
Maximum Speed: 50 mph.

2554	2555	2556	2557	2558	2559

6.7. NOTTINGHAM EXPRESS TRANSIT

This was the last light rail system in the UK, opened in 2004. Line 1 runs for 8¾ miles from Station Street, Nottingham (alongside Nottingham station) to Hucknall, including a short spur to Phoenix Park. There is around three miles of street running through Nottingham. Extensions are planned to open in 2014 to Clifton (Line 2) to the south of Nottingham, and Chilwell via Beeston to the west (Line 3). 22 Alstom Citadis trams are on order for these extensions.

The system is operated by the Tramlink Nottingham consortium (formed of Taylor Woodrow, Alstom, Keolis, Wellglade, Meridiam Infrastructure and Infravia Fund).

System: 750 V DC overhead.
Platform Height: 350 mm.
Depot & Workshops: Wilkinson Street.

BOMBARDIER INCENTRO 5-SECTION TRAMS

Built: 2002–03 by Bombardier, Derby Litchurch Lane Works.
Wheel Arrangement: Bo-2-Bo.
Dimensions: 33.0 x 2.4 m
Doors: Sliding plug.
Weight: 36.7 t.
Traction Motors: 8 x 45 kW wheelmotors.
Seats: 54 (4).
Couplers: Not equipped.
Maximum Speed: 50 mph.
Braking: Disc, regenerative and magnetic track for emergency use.
Standard livery: Black, silver & green unless stated.
Advertising liveries:

201 – Nottinghamcontemporary.org (yellow/light blue & white).
211 – NET "Tram It" (various).

201	AL	Torvill and Dean
202		DH Lawrence
203		Bendigo Thompson
204		Erica Beardsmore
205		Lord Byron
206		Angela Alcock
207		Mavis Worthington
208		Dinah Minton
209		Sid Standard
210		Sir Jesse Boot
211	AL	Robin Hood
212		William Booth
213		Mary Potter
214		Dennis McCarthy
215		Brian Clough

6.8. MIDLAND METRO

This system opened in 1999 and has one 12½mile line from Birmingham Snow Hill to Wolverhampton along the former GWR line to Wolverhampton Low Level. On the approach to Wolverhampton it leaves the former railway alignment to run on-street to the St George's terminus. It is operated by Travel West Midlands Ltd. An extension is under construction from Birmingham Snow Hill into the city centre (to terminate near New Street station) and a city centre loop in Wolverhampton is also planned. Midland Metro is to order 19 new trams to serve the expanded system.

System: 750 V DC overhead. **Platform Height**: 350 mm.
Depot & Workshops: Wednesbury.

ANSALDO 2-SECTION TRAMS

Built: 1998–99 by Ansaldo Transporti, Italy.
Wheel Arrangement: Bo-2-Bo. **Traction Motors**: Four of 105 kW each.
Dimensions: 24.00 x 2.65 m. **Seats**: 52.
Doors: Sliding plug. **Couplers**: Not equipped.
Weight: 35.6 t. **Maximum Speed**: 43 mph.
Braking: Regenerative, disc and magnetic track.

Standard livery: Dark blue & light grey with green stripe, yellow doors & red front end.

MW: New Network West Midlands tram livery (silver & pink).
Note: 01 and 02 have been withdrawn and are stored at Wednesbury depot.

01	(S)	
02	(S)	
03		RAY LEWIS
04		SIR FRANK WHITTLE
05	**MW**	SISTER DORA
06		ALAN GARNER
07	**MW**	BILLY WRIGHT
08		JOSEPH CHAMBERLAIN
09	**MW**	JEFF ASTLE
10	**MW**	JOHN STANLEY WEBB
11		THERESA STEWART
12		
13		ANTHONY NOLAN
14		JIM EAMES
15		AGENORIA
16		GERWYN JOHN

6.9. SHEFFIELD SUPERTRAM

This system opened in 1994 and has three lines radiating from Sheffield City Centre. These run to Halfway in the south-east, with a spur from Gleadless Townend to Herdings Park, to Middlewood in the north with a spur from Hillsborough to Malin Bridge and to Meadowhall Interchange in the north east, adjacent to the large shopping complex. The total route mileage is 18 miles. The system is a mixture of on-street and segregated running.

The cars are owned by South Yorkshire Light Rail Ltd., a subsidiary of South Yorkshire PTE. The operating company, South Yorkshire Supertram Ltd. is leased to Stagecoach who operate the system as Stagecoach Supertram.

Because of severe gradients in Sheffield (up to 1 in 10) all axles are powered on the vehicles, which have low-floor outer sections.

System: 750 V DC overhead. **Platform Height**: 450 mm.
Depot & Workshops: Nunnery.
Standard livery: Stagecoach (All over blue with red & orange ends).

Non-standard/Advertising liveries: 111 – East Midlands Trains (blue).
120 – Original Sheffield Corporation tram livery (cream & blue).

SIEMENS 3-SECTION TRAMS

Built: 1993–94 by Siemens, Krefeld, Germany.
Wheel Arrangement: B-B-B-B.
Traction Motors: Four monomotor drives of 250 kW.
Dimensions: 34.75 x 2.65 m. **Seats**: 80 (6).
Doors: Sliding plug. **Couplers**: Not equipped.
Weight: 52 t. **Maximum Speed**: 50 mph.
Braking: Regenerative, disc and emergency track.

101	106	110	114	118	122
102	107	111 **AL**	115	119	123
103	108	112	116	120 **0**	124
104	109	113	117	121	125
105					

6.10. TYNE & WEAR METRO

The Tyne & Wear Metro system covers 48 route miles and can be described as the UK's first modern light rail system.

The initial network opened between 1980 and 1984 consisting of a line from South Shields via Gateshead and Newcastle Central station to Bank Foot (later extended to Newcastle Airport in 1991) and the North Tyneside loop (over former BR lines) serving North Shields, Tynemouth and Whitley Bay with a terminus at St. James in Newcastle city centre. A more recent extension came from Pelaw to Sunderland and South Hylton in 2002, making use of existing heavy rail infrastructure between Heworth and Sunderland.

The system is owned by Nexus (the Tyne & Wear PTE) and operated by DB Regio.

System: 1500 V DC overhead. **Depot & Workshops**: South Gosforth.

METRO-CAMMELL 2-SECTION UNITS

Built: 1978–81 by Metropolitan Cammell, Birmingham (Prototype cars 4001 and 4002 were built by Metropolitan Cammell in 1975 and rebuilt 1984–87 by Hunslet TPL, Leeds).
Wheel Arrangement: B-2-B.
Traction Motors: Two Siemens of 187 kW each.
Dimensions: 27.80 x 2.65 m. **Seats:** 68.
Doors: Sliding plug. **Couplers:** BSI.
Weight: 39.0 t. **Maximum Speed:** 50 mph.

Standard livery: Red & yellow unless otherwise indicated.
B Blue & yellow. **G** Green & yellow.
0 (4001) Original 1975 Tyne & Wear Metro livery of yellow & cream.
0 (4027) Original North Eastern Railway style (red & white).
TW New Tyne & Wear Metro (grey, black & yellow). All cars will be refurbished and repainted in this new livery at Wabtec, Doncaster by 2015. Full details awaited.

Advertising liveries:

4002 – Tyne & Wear Metro (orange & black).
4020 – Modern Apprenticeships (white, red & blue).
4038 – Talktofrank.com (white).
4040 – Cut your CO_2 day (blue & white).
4045 – Newcastle International Airport – 75 years (purple).
4049 – Kidd & Spoor Harper Solicitors (blue).
4055 – European Regional Development Fund (blue & yellow).
4067 – Artist Alexander Millar (white & blue).
4075 – Tyne & Wear Public Services (purple & white).
4080 – South Shields market (white).
4084 – Pop smartcard (various).

4001	**0**	4016	**B**	4031	**B**	4046	**TW**	4061	**TW**	4076	**B**
4002	**AL**	4017		4032		4047	**B**	4062	**G**	4077	
4003		4018	**G**	4033		4048		4063		4078	
4004	**G**	4019		4034		4049	**AL**	4064		4079	
4005		4020	**AL**	4035	**B**	4050		4065		4080	**AL**
4006		4021		4036	**G**	4051	**G**	4066	**B**	4081	**B**
4007		4022		4037		4052		4067	**AL**	4082	**TW**
4008		4023	**G**	4038	**AL**	4053	**B**	4068		4083	**B**
4009		4024	**B**	4039	**B**	4054	**B**	4069		4084	**AL**
4010		4025		4040	**AL**	4055	**AL**	4070		4085	
4011		4026		4041	**TW**	4056		4071		4086	
4012		4027	**0**	4042	**TW**	4057		4072	**TW**	4087	
4013		4028		4043		4058	**B**	4073		4088	
4014		4029	**B**	4044		4059		4074		4089	
4015		4030		4045	**AL**	4060		4075	**AL**	4090	

Names:

4026	George Stephenson	4065	DAME Catherine Cookson
4041	HARRY COWANS	4073	Danny Marshall
4060	Thomas Bewick	4077	Robert Stephenson
4064	Michael Campbell	4078	Ellen Wilkinson

7. CODES

7.1. LIVERY CODES

Livery codes are used to denote the various liveries carried. It is impossible to list every livery variation which currently exists. In particular items ignored for this publication include:

- Minor colour variations.
- Omission of logos.
- All numbering, lettering and brandings.

Descriptions quoted are thus a general guide only. Logos as appropriate for each livery are normally deemed to be carried.

The colour of the lower half of the bodyside is stated first. Minor variations to these liveries are ignored.

Code Description

1 "One" (metallic grey with a broad black bodyside stripe. White National Express interim stripe as branding).
AB Arriva Trains Wales "executive" dark & light blue.
AG Arlington Fleet Services (green).
AI Aggregate Industries (green, light grey & blue).
AL Advertising/promotional livery (see class heading for details).
AN Anglia Railways Class 170s (white & turquoise with blue vignette).
AR Anglia Railways (turquoise blue with a white stripe).
AV Arriva Trains (turquoise blue with white doors & a cream "swish").
AZ Advenza Freight (deep blue with green Advenza brandings).
B BR blue.
BG BR blue & grey lined out in white.
BL BR Revised blue with yellow cabs, grey roof, large numbers & logo.
CC BR Carmine & Cream.
CD Cotswold Rail (silver with blue & red logo).
CE BR Civil Engineers (yellow & grey with black cab doors & window surrounds).
CH BR Western Region/GWR (chocolate & cream lined out in gold).
CI Centro (light green with a broad blue lower bodyside band & blue cab end sections).
CN Connex/Southeastern (white with black window surrounds & grey lower band).
CR Chiltern Railways (blue & white with a red stripe).
CS Colas Rail (yellow, orange & black).
CT Central Trains (two-tone green with yellow doors. Blue flash & red stripe at vehicle ends).
CU Corus (silver with red logos).
CX Connex (white with yellow lower body & blue solebar).
DB DB Schenker (Deutsche Bahn red with grey roof & solebar).
DC Devon & Cornwall Railway (dark green).
DG BR Departmental (dark grey with black cab doors & window surrounds).
DR Direct Rail Services (dark blue with light blue or dark grey roof).
DS Revised Direct Rail Services (dark blue, light blue & green. "Compass" logo).

E English Welsh & Scottish Railway (maroon bodyside & roof with a broad gold bodyside band).
EB Eurotunnel (two-tone grey with a broad blue stripe).
EC East Coast (silver or grey with a purple stripe).
ECR Euro Cargo Rail (light grey).
EG "EWS grey" (as **F** but with large yellow & red EWS logo).
EL Electric Traction Limited (silver & red).
EP European Passenger Services (two-tone grey with dark blue roof).
EM East Midlands Trains {Connect} (blue with red & orange swish at unit ends).
EU Eurostar (white with dark blue & yellow stripes).
EX Europhoenix (silver, blue & red).
F BR Trainload Freight (two-tone grey with black cab doors & window surrounds. Various logos).
FA Fastline Freight (grey & black with white & orange stripes).
FB First Group dark blue.
FD First Great Western & First Hull Trains "Dynamic Lines" (dark blue with thin multi-coloured lines on the lower bodyside).
FE Railfreight Distribution International (two tone-grey with black cab doors & dark blue roof).
FER Fertis (light grey with a dark grey roof & solebar).
FF Freightliner grey (two-tone grey with black cab doors & window surrounds. Freightliner logo).
FG First Group InterCity (indigo blue with a white roof & gold, pink & white stripes).
FH Revised Freightliner {PowerHaul} (dark green with yellow cab ends & grey stripe/buffer beam).
FI First Great Western "Local Lines" DMU (varying blue with local visitor attractions applied to the lower bodyside).
FL Freightliner (dark green with yellow cabs).
FP Old First Great Western (green & ivory with thin green & broad gold stripes).
FO BR Railfreight (grey bodysides, yellow cabs & red lower bodyside stipe, large BR logo).
FR Fragonset Railways (black with silver roof & a red bodyside band lined out in white).
FS First Group (indigo blue with pink & white stripes).
FT First TransPennine Express "Dynamic Lines" (varying blue with thin multi-coloured lines on the lower bodyside).
FU First Group "Urban Lights" (varying blue with pink, white and blue markings on the lower bodyside).
FY Foster Yeoman (blue & silver. Cast numberplates).
G[1] BR Green (plain green, with white stripe on main line locomotives).
G[2] BR Southern Region/SR or BR DMU green.
GB GB Railfreight (blue with orange cantrail & solebar stripes, orange cabs).
GC Grand Central (all over black with an orange stripe).
GE First Great Eastern (grey, green, blue & white).
GG BR two-tone green.
GL First Great Western locos (green with a gold stripe).
GN Great North Eastern Railway {modified} (dark blue with a white stripe).
GS Royal Scotsman maroon.

GV Gatwick Express EMU (red, white & indigo blue with mauve & blue doors).
GW Great Western Railway (green, lined out in black & orange).
GX Gatwick Express InterCity (dark grey/white/burgundy/white).
GY Eurotunnel (grey & yellow).
HA Hanson Quarry Products (dark blue/silver with oxide red roof).
HB HSBC Rail (Oxford blue & white).
HC Heathrow Connect (grey with a broad deep blue bodyside band & orange doors).
HE Heathrow Express (grey & indigo blue with black window surrounds).
IC BR InterCity (dark grey/white/red/white).
K Black.
LH BR Loadhaul (black with orange cabsides).
LM London Midland (white/grey & green with broad black stripe around the windows).
LN LNER Tourist (green & cream).
LO London Overground (all over white with a blue solebar & black window surrounds).
LT London Transport maroon & cream.
M BR maroon (maroon lined out in straw & black).
ME Merseyrail (metallic silver with yellow doors).
ML BR Mainline Freight (aircraft blue with a silver stripe).
MN Midland Mainline (thin tangerine stripe on the lower bodyside, ocean blue, grey & white).
MT GB Railfreight Metronet (blue with orange cabsides).
N BR Network SouthEast (white & blue with red lower bodyside stripe, grey solebar & cab ends).
NC National Express white (white with blue doors).
NO Northern (deep blue, purple & white). Some units have area-specific promotional vinyls (see class headings for details).
NR Network Rail (blue with a red stripe).
NX National Express (white with grey ends).
0 Non-standard (see class heading for details).
P Porterbrook Leasing Company (white or grey & purple).
PB Porterbrook Leasing Company blue.
PC Pullman Car Company (umber & cream with gold lettering lined out in gold).
RG BR Parcels (dark grey & red).
RK Railtrack (green & blue).
RM Royal Mail (red with yellow stripes above solebar).
RP Royal Train (claret, lined out in red & black).
RR Regional Railways (dark blue & grey with light blue & white stripes, three narrow dark blue stripes at vehicle ends).
RV Riviera Trains (Oxford blue & cream lined out in gold {blue only for locos}).
RX Rail Express Systems (dark grey & red with or without blue markings).
RZ Royal Train revised (plain claret, no lining).
SB Southeastern High Speed (all over blue with black window surrounds).
SC Strathclyde PTE (carmine & cream lined out in black & gold).
SD South West Trains outer suburban {Class 450 style} (deep blue with red doors & orange & red cab sides).
SE Southeastern (all over white with black window surrounds, light blue doors and (on some units) dark blue lower bodyside stripe).
SL Silverlink (indigo blue with white stripe, green lower body & yellow doors).

SP Strathclyde PTE {revised} (carmine & cream, with a turquoise stripe).
SN Southern (white & dark green with light green semi-circles at one end of each vehicle. Light grey band at solebar level).
SR ScotRail – Scotland's Railways (dark blue with Scottish Saltire flag & white/light blue flashes).
SS South West Trains inner suburban {Class 455 style} (red with blue & orange flashes at unit ends).
ST Stagecoach {long-distance stock} (white & dark blue with dark blue window surrounds and red & orange swishes at unit ends).
TT Transmart Trains (all over green).
U White or grey undercoat.
V Virgin Trains (red with black doors extending into bodysides, three white lower bodysides stripes).
VP Virgin Trains shunters (black with a large black & white chequered flag on the bodyside).
VN Northern Belle (crimson lake & cream lined out in gold).
VT Virgin Trains silver (silver, with black window surrounds, white cantrail stripe & red roof. Red swept down at unit ends).
WA Wabtec Rail (black).
WB Wales & Borders Alphaline (metallic silver with blue doors).
WC West Coast Railway Company maroon (57601 carries a black bodyside stripe).
WM Network West Midlands (light blue with green lower bodyside stripe and white stripe at cantrail level).
WS Wrexham & Shropshire (two-tone grey & silver).
XC CrossCountry (two-tone silver with deep crimson ends & pink doors).
Y Network Rail yellow.
YR West Yorkshire PTE/Northern EMUs (red, lilac & grey).

7.2. OWNER CODES

The following codes are used to define the ownership details of the locomotives or rolling stock listed in this book. Codes shown indicate either the legal owner or "responsible custodian" of each vehicle.

20 Class 20189
24 6024 Preservation Society
40 Class Forty Preservation Society
47 Stratford 47 Group
50 Class 50 Alliance
53 5305 Locomotive Association
56 Class 56 Locomotives
62 The Princess Royal Class Locomotive Trust
70 7029 Clun Castle
71 71A Locomotives
92 City of Wells Supporters Association
2L Class Twenty Locomotives
A Angel Trains
A4 The A4 Locomotive Society
AI Aggregate Industries
AM Alstom

AY	Amey Infrastructure Services
AV	Arriva UK Trains
B1	Thompson B1 Locomotive
BA	British American Railway Services
BB	Balfour Beatty Rail Infrastructure Services
BK	The Scottish Railway Preservation Society
BN	Beacon Rail Leasing
BS	Royal Scot Locomotive and General Trust
BT	Bombardier Transportation UK
CG	Cargo-D (*in administration*)
CR	The Chiltern Railway Company
CS	Colas Rail
DB	DB Schenker Rail (UK)
DG	Duke of Gloucester Steam Locomotive Trust
DM	Dartmoor Railway
DR	Direct Rail Services
DT	The Diesel Traction Group
E	Eversholt Rail (UK)
ED	Edward Stevenson
EL	Electric Traction Limited
EM	East Midlands Trains
EP	Europhoenix
ET	Eurotunnel
EU	Eurostar (UK)
FA	Fastline (*in administration*)
FG	First Group
FL	Freightliner
FW	First Great Western (assets of the Greater Western franchise)
GB	GB Railfreight
GL	GE Capital
H1	High Speed One (HS1)
HA	Hanson Group
HD	Hastings Diesels
HE	British Airports Authority
HN	Harry Needle Railroad Company
HR	Heritage Rail Traction
HT	Harsco Track Technologies
HU	Hunslet Engine Company
IR	Riley & Son (Railways)
JC	John Cameron
JH	Jeremy Hosking Locomotive Services
JU	The Jubilee Locomotive Company
LM	London Midland
LO	Loram
LY	Lloyds Banking Group
MG	Mid Glamorgan County Council
MN	Merchant Navy Locomotive Preservation Society
MW	Beaver Sports (Yorkshire)
NE	North Eastern Locomotive Preservation Group
NM	National Museum of Science & Industry
NR	Network Rail

NS	Nemesis Rail
NY	North Yorkshire Moors Railway Enterprises
OE	Orient Express Hotels
P	Porterbrook Leasing Company
PO	Other owner
PP	Peter Pan Locomotive Company
QW	QW Rail Leasing
RA	Railfilms
RE	Railway Vehicle Engineering
RL	Rail Management Services (trading as RMS Locotec)
RM	Royal Mail
RV	Riviera Trains
SB	SNCB/NMBS (Société Nationale des Chemins de fer Belges/ Nationale Maatschappij der Belgische Spoorwegen)
SF	SNCF (Société Nationale des Chemins de fer Français)
SG	South Glamorgan County Council
SI	Speno International
SK	Swietelsky Babcock Rail
SM	Siemens Transportation
SN	Southern
SW	South West Trains
TT	Transmart Trains
VI	Virgin Trains
VL	Voyager Leasing (Lloyds Banking Group/Angel Trains)
VO	VolkerRail
VT	Vintage Trains
WA	Wabtec Rail
WC	West Coast Railway Company
X	Sold for scrap/further use and awaiting collection

7.3. LOCOMOTIVE POOL CODES

Locomotives are split into operational groups ("pools") for diagramming and maintenance purposes. The official codes used to denote these pools are shown in this publication.

Code	*Pool*
ACAC	Electric Traction Limited locomotives
ACXX	Electric Traction Limited locomotives for static depot use.
ATLO	Alstom Class 08.
ATZZ	Alstom stored locomotives.
CFOL	Class 50 Operations locomotives.
COLO	Colas Rail locomotives.
DFEP	Freightliner locos for export to Poland.
DFGC	Freightliner Intermodal Class 86/5.
DFGH	Freightliner Heavy Haul Class 70.
DFGI	Freightliner Intermodal Class 70.
DFGM	Freightliner Intermodal Class 66.
DFHG	Freightliner Heavy Haul modified Class 66.
DFHH	Freightliner Heavy Haul Class 66.

DFIM Freightliner Intermodal modified Class 66.
DFIN Freightliner Intermodal Class 66 (low emission).
DFLC Freightliner Intermodal Class 90.
DFLH Freightliner Heavy Haul Class 47.
DFLS Freightliner Class 08.
DFNC Freightliner Intermodal Class 86/6.
DFRT Freightliner Heavy Haul Class 66. Infrastructure services.
DFTZ Freightliner locomotives (holding pool).
DHLT Freightliner locomotives awaiting maintenance/repair/disposal.
EFOO First Great Western Class 57.
EFPC First Great Western Class 43.
EFSH First Great Western Class 08.
EHPC CrossCountry Class 43.
EJLO London Midland Class 08.
ELRD East Lancashire Railway-based main line registered locomotives.
EMPC East Midlands Trains Class 43.
EMSL East Midlands Trains Class 08.
EPXS Europhoenix locomotives (stored).
EPXX Europhoenix Class 86.
ETLO Electric Traction Limited Class 86/7.
GBCM GB Railfreight Class 66. General.
GBED GB Railfreight Class 73.
GBEE GB Railfreight Class 20. On hire from DRS.
GBET GB Railfreight Class 92.
GBFM GB Railfreight Class 66. RETB fitted.
GBHL GB Railfreight. Class 66. Hire locos.
GBRT GB Railfreight Class 66. Network Rail duties.
GBSD GB Railfreight Class 66.
GBWM GB Railfreight Class 08/09.
GBZZ GB Railfreight. Stored locomotives.
GCHP Grand Central Class 43.
GPSS Eurostar (UK) Class 08.
HBSH Wabtec hire shunting locomotives.
HNRL Harry Needle Railroad Company hire locomotives.
HNRS Harry Needle Railroad Company stored locomotives.
HTLX British American Railway Services locomotives.
HWSU Southern Class 09.
HYWD South West Trains Class 73.
IANA National Express East Anglia Class 90.
IECA East Coast Class 91.
IECP East Coast Class 43.
IVGA Southern Class 73 (standby use).
IWCA Virgin Trains Class 57.
MBDL Non TOC-owned diesel locomotives.
MBED Non TOC-owned electro-diesel locomotives.
MBEL Non TOC-owned electric locomotives.
MOLO Privately-owned Class 20s.
MRSO RMS Locotec Class 08.
NRLO Nemesis Rail locomotives.
PTXX GB Railfreight Class 92 (stored).
QACL Network Rail Class 86.

QADD	Network Rail diesel locomotives.
QCAR	Network Rail New Measurement Train Class 43.
QETS	Network Rail Class 37.
RFSH	Wabtec Rail locomotives.
RTLO	Riviera Trains Class 47.
RVLO	Rail Vehicle Engineering locomotives.
SAXL	Eversholt Rail (UK) off-lease locomotives.
SBXL	Porterbrook Leasing Company off-lease locomotives.
WAAN	DB Schenker Class 67.
WABN	DB Schenker Class 67. RETB fitted.
WATN	DB Schenker Class 67 for hire to Arriva Trains Wales.
WAWN	DB Schenker Class 67 for hire to Chiltern Railways.
WBAI	DB Schenker Industrial Class 66.
WBAL	DB Schenker Logistics Class 66.
WBAK	DB Schenker Construction Class 66.
WBBI	DB Schenker Industrial Class 66. RETB fitted.
WBBL	DB Schenker Logistics Class 66. RETB fitted.
WBBK	DB Schenker Construction Class 66. RETB fitted.
WBEI	DB Schenker Industrial Class 66. Restricted use.
WBES	DB Schenker Class 66 (Sandite work). Restricted use.
WBLI	DB Schenker Industrial Class 66. Dedicated locomotives for Lickey Incline banking duties.
WCAI	DB Schenker Industrial Class 60.
WCAK	DB Schenker Construction Class 60.
WCBI	DB Schenker Industrial Class 60. Extended-range fuel tanks.
WCBK	DB Schenker Construction Class 60. Extended-range fuel tanks.
WDAI	DB Schenker Industrial Class 59.
WDAK	DB Schenker Construction Class 59.
WEFE	DB Schenker Class 90.
WEGE	DB Schenker Class 90 for hire to National Express East Anglia.
WFMU	DB Schenker Fleet Management Unit locomotives.
WNSO	DB Schenker locomotives sold awaiting collection.
WNTR	DB Schenker locomotives – short-term maintenance/tactical reserve.
WNTS	DB Schenker locomotives – tactical stored unserviceable.
WNWX	DB Schenker locomotives – stored locomotives on heavy repair or for heavy repair.
WNYX	DB Schenker Class 08/09 tactical reserve.
WSSI	DB Schenker Industrial operational Shunters.
WSSK	DB Schenker Construction operational Shunters.
WSXX	DB Schenker shunting locomotives – internal/depot use.
WTAE	DB Schenker Class 92.
WTHE	DB Schenker Class 92 with commissioned TVM430 cab signalling equipment for use on High Speed 1.
XHAC	Direct Rail Services Class 37/4 and 47.
XHCK	Direct Rail Services Class 57.
XHHP	Direct Rail Services locomotives – holding pool.
XHIM	Direct Rail Services locomotives – Intermodal traffic.
XHNC	Direct Rail Services locomotives – nuclear traffic/general.
XHSS	Direct Rail Services stored locomotives.
XYPA	Mendip Rail Class 59/1.
XYPO	Mendip Rail Class 59/0.

7.4. OPERATOR CODES

Operator codes are used to denote the organisation that facilitates the use of that vehicle, and may not be the actual Train Operating Company which runs the train. Where no operator code is shown, vehicles are currently not in use.

62	The Princess Royal Class Locomotive Trust
AW	Arriva Trains Wales
BK	The Scottish Railway Preservation Society
BP	British Pullman (Orient Express Hotels)
C2	c2c
CR	Chiltern Railways
DB	DB Schenker
DR	Direct Rail Services
EA	National Express East Anglia
EC	East Coast
EM	East Midlands Trains
EU	Eurostar (UK)
FC	First Capital Connect
GB	GB Railfreight
GC	Grand Central
GW	First Great Western
HC	Heathrow Connect
HD	Hastings Diesels
HE	Heathrow Express
HT	First Hull Trains
LO	London Overground
LM	London Midland
ME	Merseyrail
NB	Northern Belle (Orient Express Hotels)
NO	Northern
NY	North Yorkshire Moors Railway
RP	Royal Train
RS	The Royal Scotsman (Orient Express Hotels)
RV	Riviera Trains
SE	Southeastern
SN	Southern
SR	ScotRail
ST	Statesman Rail
SW	South West Trains
TP	TransPennine Express
VT	Vintage Trains
VW	Virgin Trains
WC	West Coast Railway Company
XC	CrossCountry

7.5. ALLOCATION & LOCATION CODES

Allocation codes are used in this publication to denote the normal maintenance base ("depots") of each operational locomotive, multiple unit or coach. However, maintenance may be carried out at other locations and may also be carried out by mobile maintenance teams.

Location codes are used to denote common storage locations whilst the full place name is used for other locations. The designation (S) denotes stored.

Code	*Depot*	*Operator*
AD	Ashford	Hitachi
AF	Ashford Chart Leacon Works	Bombardier Transportation
AK	Ardwick (Manchester)	Siemens
AL	Aylesbury	Chiltern Railways
AN	Allerton (Liverpool)	Northern
AP*	Ashford Rail Plant (Kent)	Balfour Beatty Rail Infrastructure Services
BA	Basford Hall Yard (Crewe)	*Storage location only*
BD	Birkenhead North	Merseyrail
BF	Bedford Cauldwell Walk	First Capital Connect
BH	Barrow Hill (Chesterfield)	Barrow Hill Engine Shed Society
BI	Brighton Lovers Walk	Southern
BM	Bournemouth	South West Trains
BN	Bounds Green (London)	East Coast
BO	Burton-upon-Trent	Nemesis Rail
BQ	Bury (Greater Manchester)	East Lancashire Rly/Riley & Son (Railways)
BS	Bescot (Walsall)	DB Schenker Rail (UK)
BT	Bo'ness (West Lothian)	The Bo'ness & Kinneil Railway
BY	Bletchley	London Midland
CD	Crewe Diesel	DB Schenker Rail (UK)
CE	Crewe International	DB Schenker Rail (UK)
CF	Cardiff Canton	Arriva Trains Wales/Pullman Rail
CH	Chester	Alstom
CK	Corkerhill (Glasgow)	ScotRail
CO	Coquelles (France)	Eurotunnel
CP	Crewe Carriage	LNWR (part of Arriva)
CQ	Crewe Heritage Centre	LNWR Heritage Company
CR	Crewe Gresty Bridge	Direct Rail Services
CS	Carnforth	West Coast Railway Company
CZ	Central Rivers (Barton-under-Needwood)	Bombardier Transportation
DR	Doncaster	DB Schenker Rail (UK)
DY	Derby Etches Park	East Midlands Trains
EC	Edinburgh Craigentinny	East Coast
EH	Eastleigh	LNWR
EM	East Ham (London)	c2c
EX	Exeter	First Great Western
FA	Fawley (Hampshire)	*Storage location only*
FF	Forest (Brussels)	SNCB/NMBS
GW	Glasgow Shields Road	ScotRail
HA	Haymarket (Edinburgh)	ScotRail
HE	Hornsey (London)	First Capital Connect

HM	Healey Mills (Wakefield)	*Storage location only*
HQ	Headquarters	Network Rail
HT	Heaton (Newcastle)	Northern
IL	Ilford (London)	National Express East Anglia
IS	Inverness	ScotRail
KM	Carlisle Kingmoor	Direct Rail Services
KT	MoD Kineton (Warwickshire)	Ministry of Defence
KY	Knottingley	DB Schenker Rail (UK)
LA	Laira (Plymouth)	First Great Western
LB	Loughborough Works	Wabtec Rail
LD	Leeds Midland Road	Freightliner Engineering
LE	Landore (Swansea)	First Great Western
LG	Longsight (Manchester)	Northern
LM	Long Marston (Warwickshire)	Motorail Logistics
LU*	MoD Ludgershall	Ministry of Defence
LY	Le Landy (Paris)	SNCF
MA	Manchester Longsight	Alstom
MD	Merehead	Mendip Rail
ME	Mossend Yard	DB Schenker Rail (UK)
MG	Margam (Port Talbot)	DB Schenker Rail (UK)
MI*	Minehead	West Somerset Railway
MH	Millerhill (Edinburgh)	DB Schenker Rail (UK)
MN	Machynlleth	Arriva Trains Wales
MQ*	Meldon Quarry (Okehampton)	*Storage location only*
NC	Norwich Crown Point	National Express East Anglia
NG	New Cross Gate (London)	London Overground
NH	Newton Heath (Manchester)	Northern
NL	Neville Hill (Leeds)	East Midlands Trains/Northern
NM	Nottingham Eastcroft	East Midlands Trains
NN	Northampton King's Heath	Siemens
NT	Northam (Southampton)	Siemens
NY	Grosmont (North Yorkshire)	North Yorkshire Moors Railway
OH	Old Oak Common Heathrow	Heathrow Express
OO	Old Oak Common HST	First Great Western
PG	Peterborough	GB Railfreight
PM	St Philip's Marsh (Bristol)	First Great Western
PZ	Penzance Long Rock	First Great Western
RG	Reading	First Great Western
RM	Ramsgate	Southeastern
RU	Rugby Rail Plant	Colas Rail
RY	Ryde (Isle of Wight)	South West Trains
SA	Salisbury	South West Trains
SE	St Leonards (Hastings)	St Leonards Railway Engineering
SG	Slade Green (London)	Southeastern
SH	Southall (Greater London)	Jeremy Hosking Locomotive Services
SJ*	Stourbridge Junction	Parry People Movers
SK	Swanwick Junction (Derbyshire)	Midland Railway-Butterley
SL	Stewarts Lane (London)	Southern/Orient Express Hotels
SN*	MoD Shoeburyness	Ministry of Defence
SO	Soho (Birmingham)	London Midland
SU	Selhurst (Croydon)	Southern

TI	Temple Mills (London)	Eurostar (UK)
TJ	Tavistock Junction (Plymouth)	*Storage location only*
TM	Tyseley Locomotive Works	Birmingham Railway Museum
TN	Thornton (Fife)	John Cameron
TO	Toton (Nottinghamshire)	DB Schenker Rail (UK)
TS	Tyseley (Birmingham)	London Midland
TW*	Tonbridge West Yard	GB Railfreight
TY	Tyne Yard (Newcastle)	DB Schenker Rail (UK)
WB	Wembley (London)	Alstom
WD	Wimbledon (London)	South West Trains
WE	Willesden Brent sidings	*Storage location only*
WF	Wansford (Cambridgeshire)	Nene Valley Railway
WH*	Washwood Heath (Birmingham)	Boden Rail Engineering
WN	Willesden (London)	London Overground
WO*	Wolsingham, Weardale Railway	British American Railway Services
WR*	Willesden Railnet PRDC	Royal Mail
WT	Warrington	DB Schenker Rail (UK)
XW	Crofton (Wakefield)	Bombardier Transportation
YK	National Railway Museum (York)	National Museum of Science & Industry
YJ	Yeovil Junction Railway Centre	South West Main Line Steam Company
ZA	RTC Business Park (Derby)	Railway Vehicle Engineering
ZB	Doncaster Works	Wabtec Rail
ZC	Crewe Works	Bombardier Transportation
ZD	Derby Works	Bombardier Transportation
ZG	Eastleigh Works	Knights Rail Services
ZH	Springburn Depot (Glasgow)	Railcare
ZI	Ilford Works	Bombardier Transportation
ZJ	Stoke Works	Axiom Rail
ZK	Kilmarnock Works	Wabtec Rail
ZN	Wolverton Works	Railcare
ZR	York (Holgate Works)	Network Rail

* unofficial code.

SUBSCRIPTION ORDER FORM

To subscribe, please complete the form below (or a copy) and return it with your remittance to:

Today's Railways UK (Dept. LCS),
3 Wyvern House, Sark Road, SHEFFIELD, S2 4HG, ENGLAND.

BLOCK CAPITALS PLEASE

(All prices include postage and packing.)

Today's Railways UK: Subscription (12 issues)

☐ **UK £45.00 (post free);** ☐ **Overseas Airmail £54.60.**

JAN FEB MAR APR MAY JUN JUL AUG SEP OCT NOV DEC

Please circle start issue required

Name: ....

Address: ....

....

.... **Postcode:** ....

Daytime Tel. No: ....

E-mail: ....

I enclose my cheque/UK postal order for £ ....

made payable to 'PLATFORM 5 PUBLISHING LTD.'

Please debit my Visa/Mastercard/Maestro

Card No: .... **Expiry Date:** ....

Card Issue No./Date (Maestro only): .... **Security No.:** ....

for £ .... **Date:** ....

Signature: ....

or if ordering by debit/credit card, telephone our subscription department on the numbers opposite.

Special note: Subscriptions may begin with the current issue or the next to be published. Subscriptions cannot be backdated.

7.6. ABBREVIATIONS

The following general abbreviations are used in this book:

AC	Alternating Current (ie Overhead supply)
AFD	Air Force Department
BAA	British Airports Authority
BR	British Railways
BSI	Bergische Stahl Industrie
CRDC	Component Recovery & Disposal Centre
C&W	Carriage & Wagon
DC	Direct Current (ie Third Rail)
DEMU	Diesel Electric Multiple Unit
DERA	Defence Evaluation & Research Agency
DfT	Department for Transport
Dia	Diagram number
DMU	Diesel Multiple Unit (general term)
DSDC	Defence Storage & Distribution Centre
DRS	Direct Rail Services
EMU	Electric Multiple Unit (general term)
GWR	Great Western Railway
FLT	Freightliner Terminal
H-B	Hunslet-Barclay
hp	Horse power
HNRC	Harry Needle Railroad Company
Hz	Hertz
kN	Kilonewtons
km/h	Kilometres per hour
kW	Kilowatts
lbf	Pounds force
LT	London Transport
LUL	London Underground Limited
m	Metres
mm	Millimetres
mph	Miles per hour
NPCCS	Non Passenger Carrying Coaching Stock
PTE	Passenger Transport Executive
RCH	Railway Clearing House
rpm	Revolutions per minute
RR	Rolls Royce
RSL	Rolling Stock Library
SR	BR Southern Region and Southern Railway
t	Tonnes
T	Toilet
TD	Toilet suitable for disabled passengers
TDM	Time Division Multiplex
TOPS	Total Operations Processing System
V	Volts
W	Wheelchair space

7.7 BUILDERS

These are shown in class headings. The workshops of British Railways and the pre-nationalisation and pre-grouping companies were first transferred to a wholly-owned subsidiary called "British Rail Engineering Ltd.", abbreviated to BREL. These workshops were later privatised, BREL then becoming "BREL Ltd.". Some of the works were then taken over by ABB, which was later merged with Daimler-Benz Transportation to become "Adtranz". This company has now been taken over by Bombardier Transportation, which had taken over Procor at Horbury previously. Bombardier also builds vehicles for the British market in Brugge, Belgium.

Other workshops were the subject of separate sales, Springburn, Glasgow and Wolverton becoming "Railcare" and Eastleigh becoming "Wessex Traincare". All three were sold to GEC-Alsthom (now Alstom) but Eastleigh Works closed in 2006, although the site is now used as a storage and refurbishment location.

Part of Doncaster works was sold to RFS Engineering, which became insolvent and was bought out and renamed RFS Industries. This is now Wabtec.

The builder details in the class headings show the owner at the time of vehicle construction followed by the works as follows:

Ashford	Ashford Works (now Ashford Rail Plant depot). Note that this is not the same as the current Bombardier Ashford depot which is at Chart Leacon.
Birmingham	The former Metro-Cammell works at Saltley, Birmingham.
Cowlairs	Cowlairs Works, Glasgow.
Derby	Derby Carriage Works (also known as Litchurch Lane).
Doncaster	Doncaster Works.
Eastleigh	Eastleigh Works
Swindon	Swindon Works.
Wolverton	Wolverton Works.
York	York Carriage Works.

Other builders are:

Alexander	Walter Alexander, Falkirk.
Barclay	Andrew Barclay, Caledonia Works, Kilmarnock (now Hunslet-Barclay).
BRCW	Birmingham Railway Carriage & Wagon, Smethwick.
CAF	Construcciones y Auxiliar de Ferrocarriles, Zaragosa, Spain.
Cravens	Cravens, Sheffield.
Gloucester	Gloucester Railway Carriage & Wagon, Gloucester.
Hunslet-Barclay	Hunslet-Barclay, Caledonia Works, Kilmarnock.
Hunslet TPL	Hunslet Transportation Projects, Leeds.
Lancing	SR, Lancing Works.
Leyland Bus	Leyland Bus, Workington.
Metro-Cammell	Metropolitan-Cammell, Saltley, Birmingham
Pressed Steel	Pressed Steel, Linwood.
Charles Roberts	Charles Roberts, Horbury Junction, Wakefield.
SGP	Simmering-Graz-Pauker, Austria (now owned by Siemens).
Siemens	Siemens Transportation Systems (works in Germany (Krefeld), Austria (Vienna) and the Czech Republic (Prague).
SRP	Specialist Rail Products Ltd (A subsidiary of RFS).

PLATFORM 5 MAIL ORDER

The Platform 5 Publishing Mail Order Catalogues contain a wide range of high quality transport books from many leading and smaller publishers. Topics covered include:

- **British Railways.**
- **Overseas Railways.**
- **Light Rail Transit & Metros.**
- **Preservation.**
- **Nostalgia.**
- **Maps & Track Diagrams.**
- **CD-ROMs.**
- **Road Transport.**
- **Clearance Titles.**

64 pages in full colour throughout plus regular updates including the very latest publications.

For your **FREE** copy, please phone, fax or write to:

Mail Order Department (LCS),
Platform 5 Publishing Ltd.,
3 Wyvern House, Sark Road,
SHEFFIELD, S2 4HG, ENGLAND.
☎: (+44) 0114 255 8000 Fax: (+44) 0114 255 2471